Contemporary Plays by
African American Women

Contemporary Plays by African American Women

Ten Complete Works

EDITED BY SANDRA ADELL

UNIVERSITY OF ILLINOIS PRESS

Urbana, Chicago, and Springfield

Compilation and introduction © 2015 by
the Board of Trustees of the University of Illinois
All rights reserved
Manufactured in the United States of America
1 2 3 4 5 C P 5 4 3 2 1
♾ This book is printed on acid-free paper.

Library of Congress Control Number: 2015954294
ISBN 978-0-252-03971-3 (hardcover)
ISBN 978-0-252-08119-4 (paperback)
ISBN 978-0-252-09781-2 (e-book)

These are works of fiction. Characters, places, and events are the product
of the authors' imagination or are used fictitiously and do not represent
actual people, places, or events.

For the Makers of Theatre Magic

Contents

Acknowledgments

I thank the University of Wisconsin–Madison for granting me a Vilas Associate Award, which enabled me to attend performances of new plays by African American women playwrights in regional theaters throughout the country. The award also provided me with much-needed funding to participate in two Black Theatre Network conferences and, in 2011, the National Black Theatre Festival in Winston-Salem, North Carolina. I thank the members of the Black Theatre Network, whose collective knowledge about all things concerning black theater is a living archive. Special thanks are due Kathy Perkins, who unselfishly offered advice and guidance based on her many years of working in theater as this country's premier African American lighting designer. I also thank Sandra G. Shannon and Sandra L. Richards, whose work on black theater and performance studies has helped establish black theater history and research as a solid academic area of inquiry. Thank you to the women who graciously contributed their plays to this anthology and to the editors at the University of Illinois Press. Finally, I thank Lisa B. Thompson, who suggested to me several years ago that it was time for a new anthology of plays by African American women, and Dawn Durante and Derek Zasky, who taught me important lessons about the business of publishing.

Sandra Adell
University of Wisconsin–Madison

Introduction

One hopes that the decades that are focused on the
literature of African American women will provide success
for the playwrights as it has for the novelists.

—Darwin T. Turner

In the introduction to the 1994 expanded and revised edition of *Black Drama in America*, the literary scholar Darwin Turner lamented the fact that although African American women novelists had finally begun to receive the recognition they deserve from the literary mainstream, their playwriting counterparts were barely visible in the world of professional theater. As Turner showed in his historical overview of black drama, with the exception of Alice Childress, whose play *Trouble in Mind* was produced Off-Broadway in 1955, and Lorraine Hansberry and Ntozake Shange, who had Broadway successes with *A Raisin in the Sun* in 1959 and *for colored girls who have considered suicide/when the rainbow is enuf* in 1976, most African American women playwrights by the early 1990s had yet to break through the racial and gender barriers that kept their work off the stages of professional regional theater companies. Tracing the development of African American theater from the early 1900s through the beginning of the last decade of the twentieth century, Turner noted that by 1990 only three black playwrights had won the coveted Pulitzer Prize for drama.[1] He also mentioned that since 1950, when Gwendolyn Brooks became the first African American to win a Pulitzer Prize in any genre, "several African American writers have earned Pulitzer Prizes for poetry and fiction. But no African American woman has ever won a Pulitzer Prize for drama."[2]

Turner didn't live long enough to see the publication of his revised anthology or witness the accomplishments of African American women playwrights in the first two decades of the twenty-first century. He died in 1991. By that time, a few were beginning to attract some of the attention their sister novelists and poets have been enjoying since the black feminist movement of the 1970s helped launch them onto the stages of national and world literature. In 2002, Suzan-Lori Parks won a Pulitzer Prize for drama for her play *Topdog/Underdog*, making her the first African American woman to be so honored. Lynn Nottage received the award in 2009 for her play *Ruined*, making her the fifth African American playwright and the second African American woman to receive a Pulitzer for drama.

An even more stunning achievement was the 2011–2012 theater season, when the works of three African American women playwrights were produced on Broadway: Lydia R. Diamond's *Stick Fly*, Katori Hall's *The Mountaintop,* and Suzan-Lori Parks's adaptation of *Porgy and Bess*. In the December 2011 issue of *Black Enterprise* magazine, whose cover hailed the season as "The New Look of Broadway," senior editor Carolyn M. Brown attributed this "new look" to the people behind the scenes—an elite group of African American investors, producers, and directors, including the singer-songwriter Alicia Keys, who are helping "pav[e] the way for a greater diversity of faces, voices, and stories onstage."[3] A year later, during the 2012–2013 Broadway season, the faces, voices, and stories of black women playwrights had all but faded away. Not one of the dramas produced that season was by an African American. During the 2013–2014 season only one African American playwright made it to Broadway—Lorraine Hansberry in a revival of *A Raisin in the Sun*, with Denzel Washington playing the role of Walter Lee Younger and LaTonya Richardson Jackson as Lena (Mama) Younger.[4] There were no works by blacks on Broadway during the 2014–15 season. The 2011–2012 Broadway season might have helped raise the visibility of a few African American women playwrights, but for the most part they continue to struggle to have their work produced on any of the country's stages.

A major obstacle to recognition of black women playwrights as participants in the construction of a truly American theater is that, with the exception of the few women who've won awards, most of them have yet to see their work published. Unlike black women novelists who benefited greatly from the institutionalizing of African American literature, black studies, and gender and women's studies in colleges and universities across the country, black women playwrights have yet to find a comparable and consistent audience of readers among college students. Their work also has not generated the kind of critiques and scholarly studies that developed along with black women's literature as an academic discipline. As much as writers, painters, and others who make their living making art are leery of scholars and critics, their work cannot survive without them. Critics, even those who write negative reviews, help create theater history. The same is true for scholars. The work of theater scholars and critics ensures that the archive, the historical record, is preserved and that the artists' legacies are passed on to future generations.

This anthology is a step toward creating the archive for the twenty-first century. It also is my effort as a literary scholar to make new plays by African American women available to artistic directors, educators, and students who have little or no knowledge about this group of writers for the theater. I feel strongly that those of us who are in a position to help steer their work to an interested public—that is, those of us who are scholars and critics—are in some ways perpetuating what is happening with artistic directors in regional theater. We keep writing about the same small group of playwrights—those who have won prestigious drama awards—while the work of equally gifted black women playwrights languishes on their computer hard drives or sits unread on the desks of busy artistic directors. As Harry Elam remarks in the introduction to *The Fire This Time*, an anthology of plays he edited with Robert Alexander, "Too often the production of a single work by a playwright of color represents a regional theater's one and only excursion that season into the realm of diversity. Whiteness stays at the center of aesthetic standards and artistic control as artists of color can only fight amongst themselves for the limited 'diversity' slots that are open to them."[5] They also must fight or, rather, compete with white playwrights writing plays about black people for the coveted "diversity" slot. As Darwin Turner showed in the introduction to *Black Drama in America*, African American playwrights have been trying to overcome this obstacle since 1917, when Ridgely Torrence tried (unsuccessfully) to create meaningful characters in his folk plays for black actors that did not perpetuate popular negative stereotypes.[6]

One way to bring their plays to a broader audience, especially in colleges and universities, is to publish them in anthologies. The first anthology of plays by African American women, *9 Plays by Black Women*,[7] was published in 1986 by Margaret B. Wilkerson. In addition to scenes from Lorraine Hansberry's unfinished play *Toussaint* and Ntozake Shange's *Spell #7*, Wilkerson included plays by those who might not otherwise have been recognized as playwrights, including the writer Alexis DeVeaux, Kathleen Collins, who was more widely recognized as a filmmaker, and the late legendary actress Beah Richards.

The 1990s saw the publication of two important anthologies of plays by African American women: Elizabeth Brown-Guillory's *Wines in the Wilderness*[8] and Sydné Mahone's *Moon Marked and Touched by Sun*.[9] Another important anthology from this period is Kathy A. Perkins and Roberta Uno's *Contemporary Plays for Women of Color*.[10] Perkins and Uno broke new ground with this collaborative project, which includes plays by five African American women, by showing the diversity of theater-making women who define themselves as *women of color*. Together these collections establish a tradition of playwriting by black women and the basis for critical examinations of the contributions they've made to American theater throughout the twentieth and the early twenty-first centuries. These anthologies, and the 2013 collection compiled and edited by E. Patrick Johnson and Ramón H. Rivera-Servera in *solo/black/woman*,[11] are the building blocks for a body of work that can be codified under the rubrics African American Women's Dramatic Literature and Black Women's theater history.

Contemporary Plays by African American Women is another block in the building of this history. This collection of ten complete plays is but a sampling of the ways in which African American women playwrights in the twenty-first century are engaging with history, delving into and shaking up issues of gender and class, creating compelling stories of African American existence in urban and rural landscapes, and disrupting traditional modes of theatrical representation. Thanks to the ground-breaking work of their predecessors, these playwrights represent a new generation of black women whose experiments with form, style, and language engage with the present while still paying homage to the past.

In Tanya Barfield's two-actor play *Blue Door*, Lewis spends his nights haunted by the ghost of his brother, who reminds him of their family's history. Barfield brings to American theater something unique: a play about a black man who inhabits the rarefied world of theoretical mathematics. But somewhere along his way to success Lewis lost his sense of self. He has become un-rooted, no longer connected to his cultural heritage. He questions his identity as a black man. The voices that speak to him through his brother Rex's recounting of their family's genealogy and history during a long and sleepless night summon Lewis back to a true and more authentic sense of his self. Although he struggles against that history—there are things he doesn't want to remember but that are too hard to forget—Lewis finally accepts that what his brother shares with him is what makes him black.

Memory in S. M. Shephard-Massat's *Levee James* has as much to do with language as it does the legacy of a family whose hard work and loving care built the family farm that Wesley Slaton is determined to keep at all costs. Shephard-Massat writes in dialect in an effort to re-create, in writing, not only her own voice but also the way she remembers her mother and other members of her family speaking. Set in 1923 in Senoia, Georgia, a small farming community just south of Atlanta, this three-character play looks at the lives, struggles, and hopes of people who did not join the Great Migration north. Lily Grace Hoterfield got as far north as Atlanta. She's been gone for four years and has returned to Senoia to convince her widowed brother-in-law, Wesley Slaton, to marry Mamie Jane Brown, a successful businesswoman, so that her two nieces will have the benefit of a woman helping to raise them. Lily also tries to talk Wesley and their friend Fitzhugh into leaving Senoia. She knows that a group of racist white men think that both Fitzhugh and Wesley have grown too prosperous for their own good. Wesley refuses to be run off the land his father-in-law helped him turn into a farm after he married Lily's sister Clareesa. Since her death Wesley has turned the couple's "shotgun shack into a sacred sight to behold," as Lily remarks to Wesley. Another sacred sight to behold is an old kitchen table Wesley kept that has inscribed into its wood the names of all the family members who have passed on. Memories of the deceased permeate the house, but Wesley assures Lily that there are no *haints* in the family house. The voices Lily claims to hear are memories that reaffirm Wesley's determination to keep his farm and to claim his identity as a man.

Katori Hall's *Hoodoo Love* is also set in the South, in a neighborhood near the famed Beale Street in Memphis. The characters in *Hoodoo Love* are blues people, believers in *haints* and hoodoo and the power of one's mojo to keep a lover from leaving and a brother from staying way too long. Each of the characters, Toulou, Candylady, Ace of Spades, and Jib, sings the blues. Ace makes his living singing the blues. Toulou sings to keep Ace from wandering too far from her shack. The conjure woman Candylady's blues are connected to her conjuring rituals. Jib sings the blues when he drinks too much liquor and forgets that he's been saved and sanctified. Candylady is the repository for memory. She keeps her memories in her mojo bag. She communicates with the spirits of the ancestors by listening to the river, and she practices rituals intended to "fix" a wandering man but which sometimes go badly awry.

Like the other playwrights with works in this collection, Katori Hall delves deep into the lives of her characters and their relationships with each other. What she reveals is bound to make audiences uncomfortable. There is much humor and joy in *Hoodoo Love* as Hall's characters sing to each other and to the audience. But this play with music also deals with abuse. Both Candylady and Toulou have endured abusive relationships for most of their lives. Yet they are determined to survive, each in her own way: Candylady by working her roots and Toulou by setting out on her own, guitar in hand, to make a name for herself singing the blues.

While the blues resounds throughout *Hoodoo Love*, it's the rhythms and beats of rap and hip hop that provide the soundscape for Nikkole Salter's *Carnaval*. Salter shares with Suzan-Lori Parks an uncanny ability to explore the psyches of young black men who are caught up in dangerous activities that ultimately lead to disaster. This gritty play about three young black men who decide to take a vacation to Brazil is written in a language and style that will take many of us out of our comfort zones. But the issues that Salter raises—for example, the exploitation of Brazilian women and girls—are intended to make us think about how we explain away all kinds of industries that exploit poor people in the interest of the free market and capitalism. *Carnaval* is set in New York and Brazil. The time shifts from 1996, when the three friends go to Brazil, to 2010, when one of them, Raheem, who made his fortune arranging Brazilian sex tours for young black men, celebrates the opening of his new night club, which he named Club Carnaval. It has been more than a decade since the former best friends have been together, and the meeting is not a happy one. One of them, Demetrius, lost too much during the trip to Brazil. Now, in 2010, there is no possibility for celebration or reconciliation, but there is still love. The videotaped message that Demetrius leaves for Raheem during Club Carnaval's opening celebration is all about loss and love and the consequences of making very bad choices in one's life.

Lisa B. Thompson's *Single Black Female* looks into the lives of two unnamed "thirty-something" black women as they reflect on the possibilities of finding true love. Single Black Female One (SBF 1) is a literature professor; Single Black

Female 2 (SBF 2) is an attorney. Both are financially independent and have the material goods to prove it: nice homes, fine wardrobes, and money to support an active social life. In this dialogue-driven play, the women invite us into their space as they discuss, among other things, the "crisis" within the black community of women who are unable to find that special someone who will love them.

In the play's prologue SBF 2 asks, "What happens to the black family if we don't find love? What will happen to the African American legacy?" Before they launch into discussions about everything from images of black womanhood, Oprah, the absence of black women on popular television shows such as *The Bachelorette*, shopping, and, of course, men, SBF 1 informs us, "This ain't sex in the inner city! That's another show. Let's be more specific, welcome to the lives of single middle-class black women." What they reveal through their dialogues and vignettes are the real lives of black women living in the twenty-first century who ultimately accept that in terms of marriage, the game has changed. Unlike the loving couple SBF 2 recalls meeting in a local Starbucks who told her they had been married for fifty-five years, SBF 1 and SBF 2 accept that, at this point in their lives, marriage is a steadily fleeting possibility. They share a great deal of laughter but also moments of sadness as they talk about their loneliness and their desire for someone to come along and make them feel like "chocolate magic sunshine." But they are resourceful and resilient. In the end, they agree that although they each want to find that ideal mate, in the new millennium they are changing the rules of the game. They are making their own history just by being themselves.

In Lynn Nottage's comedy *Fabulation, Or the Re-Education of Undine*, the life of another middle-class black woman, Undine, comes apart as she tries to do business in her plush New York office. Undine is busy lining up talent for a high-profile fundraising event when her accountant arrives to inform her that her young and handsome Argentinian husband, Hervé, has taken all of the money from their joint bank accounts and is nowhere to be found. An agent from the FBI also arrives in the office bearing bad news: she's being investigated for possible identity fraud. To make matters worse, her pregnancy test comes back positive.

After losing everything, Undine has nowhere to go except back to where she was raised, to Brooklyn and the Walt Whitman projects. It's there, amid her tight-knit and unconventional family that her re-education begins. Undine must relearn how to survive in an urban environment she wanted so desperately to escape that she denied that she even had a family. Nottage is at her comic best as she portrays Undine's family as hard-working security officers who get by as best they know how. She also acknowledges the influence of hip hop on urban culture through Undine's brother Flow, who at one point recites part of his unfinished hip hop epic poem about Brer Rabbit. Although they don't believe her lies about why she has returned after fourteen years, Undine's relatives forgive her for rejecting them and join together to help coax her into breathing new life into the world.

Christina Anderson's *BlackTop Sky* is also set in public housing. The setting is simple: a blacktop courtyard, street lamps, a couple of benches, and a soundscape that suggests the bustling activity of an overcrowded and dangerous space that two of the play's three characters, Ida and Klass, call home. It is through sound that the David L. Hynn Housing Project is revealed as a place of containment where the inhabitants see everything that's going on in the courtyard while seeing nothing at all. The action revolves around a confrontation over a lost set of keys that brings Ida and her boyfriend Wynn together with Klass, who lives with the crates of junk that he has accumulated on a bench in the center of the blacktop courtyard. Klass spends most of his time sitting on the bench he has claimed as his own, polishing one piece of junk after another and trying to forget about the events that brought him there. They know that Klass has Ida's keys but do not want to confront him. They think he's crazy. Wynn wants to call the police, but Ida reminds him about what happened to another homeless man when the police came to take him away.

One night, as Klass struggles with the invisible demons that plague his sleep, someone calls the police to complain about the disturbance. They come and try to coax Klass into going to a shelter for the homeless. They use a taser on him when he resists. In the closing scene, the benches are gone and so is Klass. After having cleared away someone whom he perceived as a rival, Wynn enters and crosses the now-empty courtyard to gather up Ida and her things.

The plays by Lydia Diamond, J. Nicole Brooks, and Keli Garrett depart from the realism of the other plays. In *Voyeurs de Venus*, Sara is a successful academic, a cultural anthropologist who is haunted by the subject of her latest book project, a South African woman named Saartjie Baartman, who in the nineteenth and early part of the twentieth century was popularly known as the Hottentot Venus. The action of the play moves from the present to the past and back, from Sara's bedroom in Chicago to London, England, where in 1810 Saartjie was introduced to the public as one of several displays of human abnormality. Sara's dilemma is discovering how to represent Saartjie, who died in 1815, in a book about her without further exploiting her. Lydia Diamond grounds her play in the historical facts concerning Saartjie, who even after her death was an object of public display. But *Voyeurs de Venus* is not a history lesson. As Sara struggles with her conscience, the action of the play shifts from Sara and the men in her life to Saartjie and the men who profited from her black body.

The real and the imaginary are intertwined as Saartjie appears to Sara, haunting her space and challenging her to think hard about how much she's willing to compromise, and also what she's willing to lose in order to gain fame. The dream sequences, the ghoulish scenes of George Cuvier at work in his examination room and the ever-increasing African music that threatens to drown out Sara's voice at the end of the play as she acknowledges the people who supported her and her work suggest that Saartjie Baartman is speaking from her grave. Perhaps the

African music is Saartjie's way of conveying her dissatisfaction with having been disturbed once again and put on display.

Fedra by J. Nicole Brooks is adapted from Jean Racine's *Phedre* and is set Haiti. But this is not the earthquake-ravaged and impoverished Haiti of the first half of the twenty-first century. The futuristic Haiti over which Fedra presides as queen is the most powerful country on the planet. Familiar characters from the Greek tale are present in this newly envisioned Haiti. The play simmers with intrigue as the Queen struggles to contain her lust for her stepson Hippolytus and her addictions. Fedra drinks too much, takes too many pills, and has a nasty habit of cutting herself.

The play opens with Fedra standing in her boudoir wearing a hospital gown. Her wrists are bandaged owing to her most recent suicide attempt. She is listening to a radio report about the plane crash in which, it is believed, her husband, King Theseus, has died. Much of the intrigue revolves around the question of succession. Who will now rule the most powerful country on earth? Clearly Fedra is not capable. She is in great need of help to deal with her addictions and her lust for Hippolytus, the king's successor. Hippolytus is in love with Aricia Toussaint, the imprisoned daughter of the overthrown King Pallas Toussaint. The goddess Afrodite saw to that. When Fedra finds out, she has her revenge, only to have it turn on her. But she is unable to reverse the treachery she unleashed on Hippolytus. In the final scene Theseus, who survived the plane crash, must deal with the aftermath.

There's quite a bit of drinking in Keli Garrett's comedy *Uppa Creek: A Modern Anachronistic Parody in the Minstrel Tradition*, especially at tea time. Garrett draws her inspiration for this play, which takes place on the Friendly Confines Plantation, from the visual artist Kara Walker's silhouette etching titled *The Means to an End: A Shadow Drama in Five Acts*. Like Walker's silhouette cutouts, Garrett's play parodies the master-slave relationship and the sexual dynamics of plantation life. Familiar stereotypes inhabit this plantation, but the structures of power are subverted and chaos erupts when the Young Negress, Hepthesput, serves mid-day tea to Ms. Anne and her daughter Li'l Annie in keeping with the illusion that the ladies are high society. The play shares with novelist Ishmael Reed's *Flight to Canada* a demand that we suspend our disbelief. The world of the Friendly Confines Plantation is absurd, with both master and slave sending and receiving messages via cell phones and fax machines, the Young Negress using a microwave to prepare her poisonous concoctions over the objections of her mentor, Ol' Negress, and Li'l Annie bursting out in a lively rap after the afternoon cup of poisoned tea she drank with her mother drives them both crazy.

This play is written in dialect, but Garrett makes it clear that language in this play is at the service of parody. For example, when Ol' Negress complains about Young Negress's not performing her "conjugal duties" with Li'l Massa, she responds, "What is you? An interloper? A spook crouching by the do' without thought to revolution and advancement of the cause? You got no regard for the plight of yo' fellow sistern and brethren?" The revolution might not be televised in this parody of life on the plantation, but Young Negress wins by turning the big house into a madhouse before fleeing to a high hill where a helicopter hovers overhead ready to bring the southern aristocracy to a bullet-riddled end.

The playwrights whose work is included in this book represent barely a fraction of the African American women who are writing plays that speak to our past, present, and future. It is my hope that this anthology will help inspire even more women playwrights to continue the work of putting their voices, their stories, and their people on the stage.

Notes

1. They are Charles Gordone, who won for *No Place to Be Somebody* (1970), Charles Fuller, who won for *A Soldier's Play* (1982), and August Wilson, who won for *Fences* (1987) and *The Piano Lesson* (1990).

2. Darwin T. Turner, ed., *Black Drama in America: An Anthology* [1971] 2d ed. (Washington, D.C.: Howard University Press, 1994), xxxiii.

3. *Black Enterprise*, "The New Look of Broadway" by Carolyn M. Brown (December 2011), 14.

4. Directed by Kenny Leon, who also directed *Stick Fly* and *The Mountaintop*, it won for Leon the 2014 Tony Award for best direction. Sophie Okonedo, who played Ruth Younger, received a Tony for best performance by an actress in a featured role.

5. Harry J. Elam Jr. and Robert Alexander, eds., *The Fire This Time: African American Plays for the 21st Century* (New York: Theatre Communications Group, 2004), xiv.

6. Turner, *Black Drama in America*, xviii–xix.

7. Margaret B. Wilkerson, ed., *9 Plays by Black Women* (New York: New American Library, 1986).

8. Elizabeth Brown-Guillory, ed., *Wines in the Wilderness: Plays by African American Women from the Harlem Renaissance to the Present* (New York: Praeger, 1990).

9. Sydné Mahone, ed., *Moon Marked and Touched by Sun* (New York: Theatre Communications Group, 1993).

10. Kathy A. Perkins and Roberta Uno, eds., *Contemporary Plays for Women of Color* (London: Routledge, 1996).

11. E. Patrick Johnson and Ramón H. Rivera-Servera, eds., *solo/black/woman: scripts, interviews, and essays* (Evanston, Ill.: Northwestern University Press, 2013).

Contemporary Plays by African American Women

TANYA BARFIELD

Born in San Francisco and raised in Portland, Oregon, Tanya Barfield began her career in theater as an actor. After receiving her undergraduate degree in acting from New York University, where she performed in many different plays, she soon realized that her opportunities in professional theater were limited. She therefore began writing and performing her own work in a solo show titled *Without Skin, Or Breathlessness*. She eventually grew tired of being herself on stage, as she commented in an interview, and turned to writing plays. An invitation in 1998 by the playwright Chiori Miyagawa to join a fellowship program she founded for emerging writers of color at the New York Theatre Workshop helped Barfield make the transition from actor to playwright. A workshop helmed by director Leigh Silverman followed and led to Barfield's being accepted into the prestigious Juilliard Playwrights Program in New York. Barfield received an Artist Diploma from Juilliard in 2002.

Tanya Barfield is a recipient of several honors and awards, including a Helen Merrill Playwrights Award (2003) as well as a Lilly Award and the inaugural Stacey Mindich Prize (2014). In addition to *Blue Door*, which has been produced in regional theater companies throughout the country, Barfield has written *Of Equal Measure, The Call, Bright Half Life*, and several solo and short plays.

Blue Door was commissioned by Playwrights Horizons with funds provided by the Harold and Mimi Steinberg Commissioning Program. It received its world premiere on August 23, 2006, at South Coast Repertory Theatre.

Director:	Leah G. Gardiner
Lewis:	Reg E. Cathey
Simon/Rex/Jesse:	Larry Gilliard Jr.
Set:	Dustin O'Neill
Costumes:	Naila Aladdin Sanders
Lighting:	Lonnie Rafael Alcarez
Sound:	Jill BC Du Boff
Stage manager:	Randall K. Lum
Dialect coach:	Philip D. Thompson
Dramaturg:	John Glore
Production manager:	David Levenworth

Original lyrics by Tanya Barfield. Original music by Larry Gilliard Jr. and Leah Gardiner.

BLUE DOOR

Generations of Black Men

A play for two actors.

CHARACTERS

Lewis (mid-life)
Simon, Rex, Jesse (young)

(There should be approximately a twenty-five-year age difference between the two actors. The actor playing Simon, Jesse, and Rex must be able to sing.)

SETTING

There are two spaces: the one Lewis occupies and a separate place. There is a door. The door is not to be actually represented, but it figuratively exists. There are no blackouts. Each man will remain on stage for almost the entire play. At only one point in the evening will one of the men exit. The play occurs between 1851 and 1995.

SONGS

The songs are to be sung a cappella. The melody of each song should be written in the musical style specific to the character, situation, and period.

A NOTE ABOUT THE MONOLOGUES AND CHARACTERS

The play involves storytelling, and in many cases one character will assume the identity of another during his story. As a general rule, if a new character name does not appear before the internal dialogue, then a total personification of the character may detract from rather than add to the story.

When Lewis speaks in the voice of his wife, he does not completely assume a feminine identity. Lewis's wife may have an airy façade, but she's also a smart and caring woman. As with all the roles (but particularly with the slaves), it is important not to play stereotypes. Simon is highly intelligent and he does not speak slowly. During even the most trying of circumstances, Simon is heartfelt but never sentimental, indulgent, or self-pitying. When Simon embodies the character of

Jonathan, he plays Jonathan as a complicated young man whose actions are hurtful but without intentional malice. Simon's mother's accent is Gullah: a Creole blend of Elizabethan English and the language of her African ancestry. Simon does not share his mother's accent.

Although Lewis and Rex often debate issues, the strife between them is not a social or political critique. Their opposing views are personal and familial, about both identity and sibling rivalry. There is a deep need between these brothers, and their relationship is one of great conflict but also great love. Jesse is performative and entertaining and he imbues his stories with humor. It is only through song that Jesse expresses the depth of his feelings.

> It is a peculiar sensation, this double-consciousness, this sense of always looking at one's self through the eyes of others, of measuring one's soul by the tape of a world that looks on in amused contempt and pity. One ever feels his twoness,—an American, a Negro; two warring souls, two thoughts, two unreconciled strivings; two warring ideals in one dark body, whose dogged strength alone keeps it from being torn asunder.
>
> —W. E. B. Du Bois

1995. It is night. Lewis, a refined, well-educated man in his fifties, is in the throes of insomnia. Hovering on the edge of Lewis's awareness, a young boy can be heard singing an invocation in Yoruba.

ANCESTOR:

Baba agba	Grandfather
Iya agba	Grandmother
Mo pe o	I call on you
Eniyan fo soke	Fly, people
Eye fo soke	Fly, bird
Idiran mi wa sile	Come down, my ancestor
Angeli wa sile	Come down, angel
Baba agba	Grandfather
Iya agba	Grandmother
Mo pe o	I call on you

LEWIS: A divorce. (*Lewis quickly pushes the reality of the thought away. He speaks to the audience, upbeat with a wry sense of humor.*) I won't go to the Million Man March and my wife says she wants a divorce. She doesn't want to offend me completely, so she hedges for a moment, then: "Lewis," she says, "Lewis, I was thinking . . . I think I'd like a divorce."

A divorce?

"Yes, a divorce."

A divorce?

"A divorce."

A divorce. Why?

"Well," she says, "you—I—"

Well? I say.

"Well, it's just because of that."

My wife and I have been married for twenty-five years. She says she's thought about it for quite some time now, about nine or ten years, and it seems that there's this resistance I have, to looking at myself.

"You won't go to the Million Man March," she says.

The Million Man March? Apparently, it's interfering with our relationship. I ask if there's someone else. She says it would be easier if there were someone else, less existential. But no, no there's not. She says there's a story to a person's life, a dimensionality, because each person has a greater "personhood" within them. But if a person compartmentalizes their life like I do, she says, they deny the dimensionality of themselves and that's difficult because you never feel like you're getting the whole person. A relationship is about total honesty and—

"You know, Lewis . . . you're black."

Yes?

"It's all about your father," she says.

I didn't go to his funeral. It's been a year, I haven't even visited his grave—

"What kind of a man wouldn't—"

I wasn't close to my father.

"What about your great-grandfather, Simon?"

He died when I was ten.

"You said you were very close."

When I was ten!

"You won't go to the Million Man March. A million black men are gathering in public and you won't go. And maybe it's because you're married to a white woman, but I don't think that you should use the fact that I'm white as an excuse to erase your history."

You want a divorce because I don't want to march on Washington, not as any form of protest but just to announce to the world that I'm black?

"It's also because of housework."

Housework? I never commit. I say I'm going to do the dishes or vacuum or fix the hinges on the door, and I just don't do it.

Feng Shui, that Feng Shui book her sister gave her, that's what this is about. That book is Chinese and she's white—Do you think, maybe, she's "denying *her* culture"?

"I've learned a lot from Feng Shui. Your house has to be in order. The fact that it came from the Orient is not the point!" (*Beat.*)

She leaves. The house is empty. Emptier than I can imagine.

I have the sensation of being watched. I watch my wife leave, and as she leaves, I divorce myself from myself. I become two selves—my self and the self that watches my self.

(*An apparitional Spirit watching Lewis appears.*)

SPIRIT:
> (*sings*)
> Run, boy, run, pattyroller come'n get ya

LEWIS: The sleepless specter, insomnia, descends.

SPIRIT:
> Run, boy, run, you best run t' get away

LEWIS: Stop.

(*A complete shift. With indiscernible ease, the Spirit transforms into Simon. It is 1863. Simon is a bright young man—good-humored—intelligent, and with the touch of a poet. Simon is 19 years old, although he refers to himself as 103. Upbeat, he speaks to the audience and occasionally to Lewis, who does not acknowledge him.*)

SIMON: Katie Maddox!

Before I tell you bout Katie, I best tell you bout me. My name Simon. I had a son, Jesse. Jesse got Charles and Charles begot Rex and Lewis. Lewis the one jes been talkin. Now, I already lived 103 years and got buried in the grave. But I come to be in this story. I don't know a word of play-actin. But I say, when I here, I jes tellin stories, jes handin down time-old stories. So you jes sit back and listen, real comfortable-like.

Here we go! Katie Maddox! Now. I'm nineteen years old.

Today the day I meet my wife, Katie Maddox, who be Lewis great-grand-mammy, and she make my heart jump. Katie lived over yon Tom Brady place, and I had heared before that "she jes the purtiest slave gal in walkin distance." I jes bout that age a young buck wanna see these things for meself, so I figure I make my way over t'Brady place, and I ain't gonna tell no-how bout my where-bouts neither.

Now I don't got no pass and no slave 'llowed to walkabout witout no pass, but that was no matter t'me, cuz I figure if I be catched by the collar, I plan on sayin to the patroller, "Mr. Pattyroller, suh, I jes out huntin up the root medi-cine" (as Mistis Betsy had fallen ill with a terrible fever and she'd jes begged us slaves to make a cure on her)—which was plain true. So in that case, Aunt Sally did sent me out to hunt up the primrose flower.

But then, if the patroller warnt in belief of this story, I planned on rollin my eyes and sayin "Please, suh, I jes a triflin boy." And I'd hold up the primrose and (for fear of lil Mistis Betsy's illness and her sad countenance) that pattyroller'd send me back home witout no lash. Now if he did that, I'd wait til he outta seein-distance, and then lickedy-split I'd turn off the other way.

So, wit the primrose flower in hand, I walk myself all the way over to Mr. Brady place to spy a look at Katie Maddox. And as luck would have it, I don't stumble cross no patrollers.

There a mighty bit of frolickin as everyone gather'd round a fire. The womenfolk shuckin corn and the younguns dancin round in a ring. Mr. Brady always grin and say, "My niggers just like family." And he paid no mind to

Saturday night parties, long as the corn ears be ready sun-up. So everyone jes gather round tellin stories and singin and makin up a pot of hamhocks, full merriment.

(*sings*)

> Come and shuck that corn tonight
> Come and shuck with all your might—

I spy Katie Maddox stirrin up a pot, my heart jump a beat like dancin. And 'fore I know myself what I doin, I march right on up to her and say, "Sweet Katie, you the finest gal I ever laid eyes on, and iffen you 'llow yourself t'get to know me then you gonna see I ain't so bad myself neither and I swear every Saturday night I come 'round this place and give you a primrose flower for your admiration; I'll be comin for however many Saturdays it take for you to figure me for a decent fellow and on that last Saturday, we to make up a fine party and jump over the broom."

Now I always been a man of my word, even back in m'boyhood, so now each Saturday I got to pick two flowers. One for Katie and one for a chance meetin wit a patroller. Well, it take a month and a half of Saturdays for Katie to make up her mind on me. A whole month to decide and another two Saturdays to keep me waitin. And on that last Saturday she say she be my wife and that's how us come t'be married.

(*Beat.*)

But you know what? The moment us was married, I knew right then and there that I didn't never want to live a day on earth witout Katie. Thinkin that took a lil joy out the celebration. Spose to be happy to be wedded. But I keep to thinkin that one thought, "What happen if the day ever come I lose my Katie?"
(*Simon glances at Lewis, who doesn't see him.*)

LEWIS: It all started when we lived in Greenwich Village, married two years, and my wife says she wants to take a vacation in the country.
Vacation in the country. Why?
We could go on hikes, we could read old books, she says, we could tell stories, analyze our dreams. She says my life is all about success, achievement, and it's great to strive, "But, Lewis, we need to be in nature."
Now, let's be clear: there are no delis in the country. She says that you don't need delis. Because you have the trees instead and that's all you need, the trees.
People lurk behind trees.
"No they don't."
Yes they do.
"They do not."
Yes, as a matter of fact, they do.
"Who?"
Crazy people. Mass murderers. Red-necks.
She doesn't miss a beat. "I think you're experiencing 'Tree Anxiety.'"

Tree anxiety?

"Yes," she continues, "I think you may be suffering from Tree Anxiety."

I ask her to elaborate on that, so I understand it properly. She says she's noticed that a lot of people here on the East Coast suffer from an irrational fear of trees.

Come on, I say, I'm not afraid of trees, I'm afraid of people lurking behind the trees, and I'm not afraid of them, I'm just cautious.

"That's a form of Tree Anxiety."

No it's not.

"Yes it is."

Look, I worry, a realistic worry, that there are people in the woods that wish to do harm to others. And, may I clarify, the country is filled with a bunch of racists and I believe the concern I have for racists is a realistic concern—

"Okay, so we won't go."

We can go.

"You're saying you don't want to go."

What am I saying?

I am *suddenly* aware of the difference between my wife and me. Not that this hasn't occurred to me before. But I am suddenly *aware*, in a very new and unsettling way. We live very different lives, and it isn't only because I grew up in a large metropolitan area, not because of Tree Anxiety but because I can't fade into the country. I can't take a weekend trip without a strained obviousness that I am there. There's no choice attached to my difference, I can't suppress it in order to grant my wife a weekend in the country. Even if I dress differently, cut my hair differently, speak differently. I can't slip into the expanse.

I want to say: I can't go, I can't take a trip to the country, I can't be a part of the trees—

I say nothing.

I can't *not* be black.

(*Simon quickly and effortlessly transforms into Rex, Lewis's charismatic, militant brother. Rex's presence completely dispels Lewis's awareness of the audience. At no point during this scene does Lewis acknowledge the audience.*)

REX: Why is this news to you?

LEWIS: (*thrown off-guard*) What—

REX: Why is this news to you?

LEWIS: Rex?

REX: Why is your blackness suddenly news to you? Why do you think that you are saying something new?

LEWIS: What are you doing here?

REX: Where the people?

LEWIS: What?

REX: Where all the people? The characters?

LEWIS: What characters?

REX: In yo' story.

LEWIS: What story?

REX: The story you in.

LEWIS: I'm in my house.

REX: In yo' house imagining your story.

LEWIS: No I'm not.

REX: Yeah y'are.

LEWIS: No I'm not.

REX: Yeah y'are.

LEWIS: No I'm not.

REX: Yeah y'are. Brother Lewis, ya can't shake the doppelganger—

LEWIS: What—Rex—

REX: You got to break this night down to the nitty-gritty, bro.

LEWIS: Rex, you're dead. (*Beat.*) What are you doing here?

REX: (*to the audience*) My brother watches the story of a black man.

LEWIS: I am in my own story—my life, and you have nothing to do with that life.
Besides, you're not even here. You're in my mind. Insomnia.

REX: Lewis, you a black man.

LEWIS: A waking dream—

REX: Not a person that *happens* to be black.

LEWIS: A nightmare—

REX: It's not an elective state of being.

LEWIS: Sleep deprivation—

REX: Who's the audience?

LEWIS: What?

REX: Who *is* your audience?

LEWIS: I don't have an audience.

REX: Who is your *intended* audience?

LEWIS: I'm not in a—there is no audience!

REX: White people.

LEWIS: What?

REX: White people, that's your audience.

LEWIS: I don't have an audience.

REX: You got a buncha white people sittin up in your head being your audience. You
livin under a White Gaze. And, to be clear, if you think black folks gonna wanna
haul their asses into this theater—I'm talking bout *this* theater—watch you deny
life, where they suppose to sit down and not talk back, then, brother, you are
sorely mistaken. And it's time to take a look at that.

LEWIS: This isn't an interactive experience—

REX: Don't want nobody signifying yo' testimonial. Don't want yo' story too black—

LEWIS: Black?

REX: My brother afraid to be black.

LEWIS: Is being black not liking Shakespeare, opera, quantum physics—

REX: You've been running away—

LEWIS: This attitude has always been your problem, Rex—

REX: Turning your back on everything that make you black—

LEWIS: I'm right here. And if I'm turning my back, I'm turning it on the excuse of failure, oppression—

REX: *Centuries* of oppression—

LEWIS: Oppression is not an excuse—

REX: Can't look at the future unless you look—

LEWIS: Unless you look at the misguided belief in past and present? "Causality" is a crutch—

REX: It time you take a look—

LEWIS: I've *looked*, we've all looked, we know all about slavery and the past and—

REX: What do you know?

LEWIS: I know enough to know that it's time to move on.

REX: Once again, my brother running away.

LEWIS: From the Black Mafia? The are-you-black-enough? blacker-than-thou—

REX: Your *people*—

LEWIS: While you were hanging out in the Mission cultivating your failed "authenticity," I was in college. Unlike some, I didn't want to go to jail, so I went to school. The first, the only person in this family that didn't want to spend his life in ignorance—

REX: Oh, *you* the only one?

LEWIS: I went to school—

REX: To learn how to assimilate wit The Man.

LEWIS: No. To become a professor. Philosophy of mathematics. To teach at a prestigious university. To become a man of social entitlement. To excel. I'm not ashamed to say that I've learned things that white people know all about. Even things they know nothing about. For example, it is impossible to count the *complete* decimal expansion of the number *pi* backwards. Wittgenstein.

REX: King of Your Kingdom and still a Slave.

LEWIS: Your mentality, illiterate victim mentality, you call Being Black. You want me to talk the talk, walk the walk, hang with the homies, gangsta-rap my way to the American Dream by bitch-slapping our people outta intellectual parity.

REX: Keep it real, Lewy-Sambo. He a White Devil in black skin, my bro. Go on, brother, defame my image, imagine your solitary, ariettic show. Tell Whitey bout your drunk of a daddy, how you reinvented yourself in yo' own image, pulled yourself up from your bootstraps, you American Dreamer. Tell em all bout after Malcolm and Martin shot, when I (your blacker bro) spiraled down outta The Movement. Ended up homeless and on crack. Why don't you tell Whitey how both our mama's boys (you the good son and me the bad) suffer the same sickness: self-loathing, the silent affliction, a plague of the skin. Both our daddy's sons suffer the phantom illness called self-hate.

LEWIS: Rex, you're not here.

REX: I'm here in spirit.

LEWIS: What do you want from me?

REX: This is a summoning.

LEWIS: This is insomnia!

REX: A Descendant of Ham. Like Ham, Lewis watched his own father backslide from faith, spiral into drunkenness. Dad watched his father consumed by fire. This is the mantle worn.

LEWIS: No, this is your manipulative—

REX: Noah begat Shem, Japheth, and Ham—Ham begat Cush, Mizraim, Phut, and Canaan. Great-grandfather begat Jesse, who begat Charles.

LEWIS: This isn't about—

REX: Charles begat Rex and Lewis. A servant of servants shall Lewis be! What did Lewis begat? Lineage extinct. You the last one alive from this family. So you gotta look back to the legacy—the last one remembered, born first under the curse of this continent. He was called Simon.

LEWIS: Stop it—

REX: The dead needs the livin just as the livin need the dead.

LEWIS: Go away, stop it! Just, just—

(*Rex instantly transforms into seven-year-old Young Simon. It is 1851. There is an almost apparitional quality to Young Simon—insomniac, delusional, and unnerving.*)

SIMON: (*to Lewis*) Every night 'fore sleep, I ax Momma, "Why us slaves?"

LEWIS: Just go away!

SIMON: Momma, why I don't got no daddy? Daddy shot down. Why my daddy shot? Shot for tryin run. Why my daddy run?

MOMMA, LEWIS: Shh!!!

SIMON: Momma, Momma, Momma—Momma, Momma—

LEWIS: (*to Simon, overlapping*) In my mind? All in my mind—(*Lewis moves away. The haunting aspect of Young Simon now fades as he speaks to the audience.*)

SIMON: Momma, why my daddy run? Why my daddy shot? Momma, Momma—
(Momma:) Oonah hush mout', chile—
(Simon:) But, Momma—
(Momma:) No one got no daddy, son. Buckrah Massuh own all we slave.

LEWIS: Think about math.

SIMON: One plus one is two.

LEWIS: An infinite sequence of numbers exist before zero.

SIMON: Momma say, before I born, me got four brothers and three sisters but them all been sold away. I ax why them been sold and Momma jes cry. Momma cry then I cry then Momma tell me not to cry.

Momma sing a song in the old language, bout once us people got us wings tore offa us.

(*Momma sings, gently, as a lullaby.*)

    Eniyan fo soke
    Eye fo soke

When I lil bigger than knee-high and Momma out pickin cotton, I back in the Big House pickin up chips, sweepin the yard, swattin flies offa the table, toten dishes from the kitchen, bowin m'head to Missy, drivin the cows to the pasture, toten dried up meat from the smokehouse, swattin at flies, toten the dishes back to the kitchen, not droppin any dishes, not spillin soup, not stealin sugar lumps out the kitchen, not makin any ruckus.

LEWIS: Success, achievement . . .

SIMON: (*as Momma*)

   Idiran mi wa si—

(*In an attempt to master his insomnia, Lewis picks up an old book,* Robinson Crusoe. *He reads:*)

LEWIS: The Life and Strange and Surprising Adventures of Robinson Crusoe.

SIMON: Book-learnin. Once'n I tall enough to Momma's elbow, she send me to fifteen-year-old Young Master Jonathan's a fair number of nights for book-learnin and arithmetic. It warn't legal to learn no slave to read and write, so Momma be powerful thankful on Young Master Jonathan's kindness, and I be sent every eve Sunday.

(*to Lewis*)

(Jonathan:) "Shall we try the next book, boy?"

LEWIS: (*picks up a different book*) Moby Dick.

SIMON: (Jonathan, *kindly*) "Boy, are you listening?"

LEWIS: (*reading* Moby Dick) "Chapter One. Loomings . . ."

SIMON: (*matter-of-fact*) Sometimes, be called useless boy, good-for-nothin picki-ninny, darkie, lil nigger, dumb nigger and "get-over-here-boy!" I start to think, don't I got no right name a'tall? Out from the big house, I say, (*calling to Momma*) "Momma, what my name be?" Momma draw her mouth like a smile, she say, "Honey-boy, yuh name be Simon, chile." Simon m'name? "Dat right, lil shug." Simon.

LEWIS: "Some years ago—"

SIMON: (Jonathan) Boy, are you listening! Huh? Oh.

SIMON, LEWIS: "Chapter One."

SIMON: "Call me Ishmael."

LEWIS: "Some years ago, never mind how long precisely . . ."

SIMON: I hold the book, stumble out the words. For weeks and weeks. Jonathan sit closer than breathin distance. Then, one night, his leg be press up 'gainst mine. Then his hand crawl across my stomach and down into my britches. He put his other hand in his own britches. I jes stare at the page, while Jonathan's hands fumblin in both us britches. Then Young Master Jonathan start to twitchin and shakin.

LEWIS: (*continuing to read*) "The thought of whiteness . . ."

SIMON: (*overlapping*) Should I keep to the readin?

LEWIS: (*overlapping*) "heightens that terror to the furthest bounds . . ."

SIMON: (Jonathan *overlapping*) "Get outta here, boy! We will continue the lesson next
week."

Should I keep to the—

(Jonathan:) "Please, please, boy, get out!"

LEWIS: "The thought of whiteness . . ."

SIMON: One week I beg Momma don't send me. But Jonathan still request me so I
have to go. Sometimes my eyes well up with a flood of tears and Jonathan got
his hand in my britches and I think what if he sell me 'way from Momma?

One night, I go out the door of the Big House and wonder how long it take
til Jonathan be grown and sent way to university. How long til I be grown?
One night, I don't got no spirit in me to carry m'self back to slave quarters. Jes
wanna trow m'self on the ground like a lil bumble-bee dyin. Wanna walk to the
river and put m'self like dead leafs on the water. One night, I lose my way and
can't find home.

Dark night, one night, night-soul night.

I look up, and there be a hundred blazin candles shinin down on Simon.

"How long," I ax them stars, "how long til ya paste my wings back on me?"

LEWIS: A constellation of moments. A Euclidean universe? Think about math.

(*Simon glances in Lewis's direction.*)

The past forever vying for the present. Near and near and nearer still . . .

SIMON: (Young Simon) Years later on, Jonathan sent way to university. (*Simon is now
twenty years old.*) I get grown. And Katie get wit child. Katie still by way of Mr.
Brady plantation and I still way of Massuh Davenport.

One night, I sneakin my way over to Katie plantation but first I stop by
Momma for a spot of grub, and Momma say to me, "Why ya don' come by no
mo? Me got some story fix t'pass down t'yuh." I say, "You know, Momma,
Katie wit child now." Then Momma say, "Next time, oonah best t'brung me
by lil Katie fo' a visit." And she look me down wit that look that mean no
back-talk.

(Simon:) Momma, I's too old for that look. (*Momma gives a mothering "no back-talk"
look.*) Even once I full grown, Momma give the look: no back-talk.

Now, Momma leg gone bad a few years 'forehand and she mostly bent-down
over when she walked. Massuh complained to high heaven and back that he
couldn't do nothin wit my mammy and if she didn't tend to her work good, he'd
send her sorry ass away. So the lastest thing I knew possible was for Momma to
get snucked out in the middle night to spy a visit on my Katie.

Momma keep starin at me: no back-talk. "Sho, Momma, I muse up a plan to
carry you the distance to Katie."

I scheme for a month a more, until I get the idea on how to steal some bottles
of milk and give one to each patroller us meet on the way. So, the day of the
night us set to go, Momma fallen ill wit a mighty cough and Massuh Davenport
come by and say tomorrow she to be sold.

My Momma to be sold?

(Davenport is oblivious and unconcerned with the effect his words will have on Simon.)

    "That right, Simon—Ruby being sent to auction. A man like me's better off gaining two dirty nickels sellin her now, than payin five dollars down the line to make a grave."

So that my Momma's last night.

That night, Momma quiet. Then she smile.

(Momma:) "Take dishyuh bucketa blue paint, honey-boy, paint up dis do'."

(Simon:) Now ain't no time to be paintin doors, Momma. Tomorrow you be sent to auction.

(Momma:) "Paint dis do'way blue. Keep d'good spirits in. Keep d'ghost out."

(Simon:) Momma—

(Momma:) "Eh! Eh! Paint dis do' blue. Da dey keep yuh soul-family watch over yuh."

(Simon:) Momma—this a door, Momma—

(Momma gives the look: no back-talk.)

I take the bucket of indigo and start on paintin the door.

(Momma:) "She carryin high or low, son?"

(Simon:) Katie carryin low.

(Momma:) "So what you g'wine name yuh boy, son?"

(Simon:) Us didn't choose no name yet, Momma. Waitin for you to fix the child wit your blessin.

Momma think for a spell. I keep on paintin the door.

(Momma:) "Jesse a fine name."

(Simon:) That what we call him then, Momma, us to call him Jesse.

Momma look at the blue painted door. She smile.

    When the wagon come next day sunup, I holler up a mighty ruckus, throwin punches and Momma shakin her head to hush me. Get dragged off and whipped down good like I never lashed 'fore. Whipped so bad, can't 'member the end of it, jes wake up the next morning. Momma gone.

    That day the worstest day in my born life, cuz that day word come that my Katie done got sent to auction too. That day a devil growed up in me and I break all the things in the room. I tear to shreds the corn-shuck mattress. I be standin, all covered wit dried up blood, I standin in the room alone wit a heap of old corn-shucks strown every which a way.

    The day be blazin full-sun wit shadows made purple from the heat. I walk down to the river and I keep walkin and I walk like a man that got no name and I walk til the sun jes a cold cinder fallen in the sky. I walk through the water and I walk and walk as night come over me and I walk past the light that wake tomorrow and I walk and walk til I can't tell the day from darkness. I don't hear the dogs barkin when they come. Don't hear the voice of dogs in the trees. Don't feel the dog teeth as they pull me down nor when the pattyrollers break all the bones my left foot got in it. Don't even hear myself cry the way a baby cries fo' the Lord to take 'im.

They brung me back to Massuh Davenport plantation. I don't 'member nothin much more bout them days cept I wake up and a shadow leanin over me and it Jonathan full-grown as a man.

Ain't seen Young Master Jonathan since he went up North, some years past. But before I can spit, I feel Jonathan put his kerchief on me brow, and he don't touch me no more than that. He say, "Simon."

Then Jonathan, his eyes bright like little stars, whisper,

(*contrite*)

(Jonathan:) "I've been to Boston and I heard Mr. Emerson speak—and, Simon, I can assure you that your bondage will not be eternal. I've learned of poetry and the theater and so many things. I've heard of a lovely Miss Dickinson. A lady poet, imagine that!" Jonathan keep goin on in that manner, tellin everythin he seent up North and the words be glimmerin like a storybook til I don't hear no more.

"Simon? Simon—would you fancy I recite Miss Dickinson's poem? I've committed it to memory."

Everythin in me fulla hate, so I don't say nothin and Jonathan don't neither. After some time, he begin the poem.

(*Lewis reads from a book of Emily Dickinson's poems. A feather moment. Each man remains in his own world but they have a mutual longing.*)

LEWIS: Will there really be a morning?
SIMON: Is there such a thing as day?
LEWIS: Could I see it from the mountains
    If I were as tall as they?
SIMON: Has it feet like water-lilies?
    Has it feathers like a bird?
LEWIS: Is it brought from famous countries
SIMON: Of which I have never heard?
LEWIS: Oh, some scholar!
SIMON: Oh, some sailor!
LEWIS: Oh, some wise man from the skies!
SIMON: Pleased to tell a little pilgrim
LEWIS: Where the place called morning lies . . .
SIMON: I fall from sleep into a bed of tears. Katie, my unbirthed child, and my momma all gone! I tell Jonathan to put me back to work, let me work til I get worked to death.

(Jonathan:) "Simon, I cannot speak for the whereabouts of your mother, Ruby, but I have heard about your Katie. Simon, Katie wasn't sold at auction. Mr. Brady never intended to sell Katie at all. Mr. Brady took Katie to auction only to mind the children, not to sell her. Only to mind the children that were slated for sale."

I can't barely hear the words he sayin. I look over at the blue painted door. Katie here?

(Jonathan:) "Katie gave birth, Simon. You and Katie have a baby boy."
Katie and my boy both here?
He nod.
Momma gone?
He nod again.

(*sings a spiritual*)

> My mudder build a house in Paradise,
> Ona build a house in Paradise . . .
> Build it witout the wood from a tree,
> Build it set her soul to free.
> Free—

(*Lewis was, for an instant, touched. But then he composes himself completely. He cuts off the song, banishing the Spirit of Simon. The sound of classical music wafts in.*)

LEWIS: We're all enjoying ourselves, laughing and carrying on. The dean's wife has just told what seems to be an unusually funny story. The dean's wife is hosting a departmental tea party in my honor. The dean's wife is named Deane, which is confusing, and she serves crumpets and cucumber sandwiches.

I have just received a job at a university. My wife and I are terribly in love. Married four years.

As we drive to the party, my wife asks why I am so quiet and I say I'm thinking about Tree Anxiety because we have to drive through a long corridor of trees. She laughs and proceeds to tell me the names of the trees, and I nod as if I'm listening. But, in actuality, I have a pit in my stomach; what if they don't know I'm black?

However, when we arrive it is instantly clear that they had been forewarned. They've been expecting me, and they are delighted to meet a black mathematician. I am, in fact, a rarity (like gourmet food that has been sent from abroad, ordered at an exorbitant price).

My wife goes off and talks to Deane, and I mingle throughout the party and find myself with a group of professors' wives. They are more than pleased by my presence. I feel like a movie star until I notice one of the women staring at my hands like they are strange objects and she twitches with nervousness. And I wonder, hasn't she ever seen black hands and seen the way our palms are lighter than the backs of our hands and I wonder what she thinks about this. Is she scared of my hands? I drop my hands into my lap (a non-threatening gesture that seems a little feminine). But maybe I've imagined her fear and my whole body tightens, not knowing where to put my hands. A part of me wants to take these strange objects and strike her—and then I become afraid for the woman and guilty.

The funny story continues. My laughter is now forced. Fight or flight. When will this terrible party be over? I hear the sound of my laughter rushing in my ears. I watch myself laugh. I observe myself observing myself trying to laugh. And the continual observation and self-consciousness seems to last a lifetime, but in fact it is only a few minutes. The woman's gaze darts off me as the circle of women's laughter hums in my ears—the chatter of the story deafening—and one of the laughing ladies exclaims, "Racism? That's the problem of race identity!"

Suddenly all eyes are on me.

"What do you think, Lewis?"

Think?

"About what he said."

Said what?

"My student."

He said?

"He asked, 'If you abolish the concept of race, will you abolish racism?' I said I didn't know. 'Perhaps in a manner of thinking. But I don't think so.' Is that assimilation? I just don't know how Afro-Americans would feel about that. So, I told my student that I would talk to you, Lewis, and get back to him. Because I'm not going to go bandying around socio-cultural ideas based on erroneous assumptions."

I say nothing, but my fork clatters onto my saucer. (I had been trying to sugar my tea with my fork.) Think about math. (*Rex appears.*)

REX: The Life and Strange and Surprising Adventures of a Black Man in the Theater of His Mind. (*Rex becomes the Woman at the Tea Party. She is innocent and sincere.*)

WOMAN AT PARTY: Is race the primary determinant of capacity? I just don't know. You see, each culture hands something down through generations. But what do they hand down? Poverty. Complaints. Blaming everyone else for their problems. And I'm not saying a person is a bad person if they're poor, but the thing is, often times there's a criminal element. So, when I'm on the street and I see one of them, a man, I'm frightened—that's my first reaction, fear. I can't help it; I've had bad experiences.

He's black, Lewis is, and—he's successful, intelligent and doesn't make excuses for himself, and I'm not afraid of him, I'm not. He's not like them at all, of course, but when he first came to the party—I'd never admit it, but—I saw him from a distance, so tall, and at first I thought it was one of them. Oh, that's an awful thing to say. I'm ashamed of that. That is such an awful thing to say. But isn't it the brain categorizing information? Identification and classification. It takes a moment. (*returning to the earlier moment as the question is repeated*) What do you think, Lewis?

LEWIS: Think?

REX: When you, Brother Lewis, think about our people, you think: "Why is everyone so ghetto, so poor? They ruin it for the rest of us." Because you can't—no matter how many polysyllabic words come out of your mouth—you can't never escape being one of them. Being black hangs over you like a shroud; you're shackled by blackness. No matter how many tweed suits you wear—you could've stole them, right?—you are just a black man like every other black man, and they brace themselves when they see you, "I hope he's not one of them that only knows monosyllabic words, one of them that harbors a criminal, violent element." (*to the audience*) Lewis tries not to look at the woman looking at his hands.

(*Rex vanishes.*)

LEWIS: At the tea party, a series of broken numbers cascade down on me. Air sucks itself out of my lungs. I must make myself indistinguishable, I think. I must distinguish myself. I must become the pale, chalk-drawn shadow of success. I contemplate the square root of negative one.

I wish I could vomit. I wish I could vomit on all of these two-dimensional cackling pointed-beak-people. But also I want to put them at ease so they won't be afraid of my black hands. And the desire to protect them from their own fear overtakes me. I watch my hands bring a cup of tea to my lips. I swallow the bile. (*brightly*) "Well, I'm here," I manage to say, "so I suppose we're moving beyond race. In a manner of thinking. Perhaps."

(*Jesse, Simon's ebullient and quick-witted son, appears. 1871.*)

YOUNG JESSE: Me here, my name Jesse. After slavery was ended, my momma (she be Katie) and my daddy (he be Simon) and me here (Jesse), we was rented a little parcel of Mr. Brady's land. My daddy the only slave learnt mathematics, and Daddy always complain Mr. Brady be reading the wrong numbers out the ledger.

Every month, Brady come by our cabin to collect rent money. One night, Daddy bowin his head to Brady, but then he say, "Mr. Brady, suh, I 'pologize but them numbers don't add right. Now I paid ya twenty-three dollars and sixty-seven cent last month and I sold ya five barrels of cotton. I bought three dollars fifty-nine cent wortha grocery, so how you figure I'm debted ya two and a half dollar?" (*With childlike animation, Jesse reenacts the conversation.*) Brady look at Daddy real steady-like.

(Brady:) "What you drivin at, Simon?"

(Simon:) "Suh, I learnt readin and arithmetic and them numbers you got don't add right."

(Brady:) "Simon, you mean to say that you, a nigger, know how to add up numbers better than me?"

(Simon:) "Suh, I only sayin if you rethink them numbers, you gonna see a error."

(Brady:) "You make a good wage by me, Simon."

(Simon:) "Truth be told, suh, I ain't makin nothin. All I doin is watchin your right hand give your left hand all my money."

I pipe up. "Daddy, votin day comin tomorrow. Yankees talkin bout elections. Say Freeman Bureau gonna protect sharecrop rights."

(Katie:) "Jesse, hush, chile—"

(Jesse:) But, Momma—

(Katie:) "Jesse, hush!"

Brady spit. (*Demonstrating, Jesse spits.*)

(Brady:) "Katie, you born on this land, my plantation. You practically my own. Now ya don't think you gotta involve the Freeman's Bureau in a little dispute between family, do ya?"

Mr. Brady grunt, take one of Momma's biscuits, then he leave. That night a knock come on the door.

(*Jesse stamps his foot, indicating the knock on the door.*)

Daddy tell Momma and me to get back behind the stove cuz that knock didn't sound like no knock he 'quainted with, and sho enough, he open the door and staring at us was six ghosts.

One ghost say,

(Ghost:) "Nigger, go get me some water."

Daddy get the ghost a cup of water, and the ghost slurp it down.

(Ghost:) "I just climbed up from hell and my throat's dry. Get me another cup of water."

Daddy bring another one and the ghost gulp it down.

(Ghost:) "Get me another one."

Daddy bring more water.

(Ghost:) "You scared?"

(Simon:) "No, suh."

(Ghost:) "As long as you uppity niggers don't fill out a tally sheet at the poll tomorrow, you and your family ain't got nothing to be scared of."

(Simon:) "Ain't scared, suh."

(Ghost:) "Ain't scared, Simon? Bring me another cup."

Daddy bring another cup of water. The ghost don't drink this cup. He pour the water out on Daddy's shoes. Daddy say,

(Simon:) "Ain't scared, suh."

The ghost stand perfect still.

(Ghost:) "Well, then, if you ain't scared, Simon, I bet after you go vote tomorrow—then tomorrow night, your woman and boy will be. Mighty scared, Simon. Awful scared."

Then he grunt, take one of Momma's biscuits and all the ghosts climb onto they horses and ride off. Daddy shut the door and Momma say, "Simon, you ain't going to vote tomorrow."

Daddy say, "That all right, Katie." Then Daddy grab his axe, go outside and start splittin wood.

All night long, Daddy just splittin wood. Every hour he sharpen his blade, then he split some more wood. Momma toss and turn in the bed and Daddy outside just splittin wood.

Next morning, Daddy say, "Jesse, go get ya momma a bucket of indigo. Paint that door up blue. Keep the night terrors out. Keep ya soul-family in."

"Daddy, once'n I get bigger, I gon' vote. I don't care if six hundred and sixty-six goblins, ghouls, and gargoyles show up at my door. I gonna vote!"

LEWIS: Mathematical structures and the repudiation of time. (*With the word "repu-diation," Jesse moves away.*) When I first met my wife, back when I worked as a tutorial assistant, I told her, "I'm going to write a book, you know. Someday, I'm going to write a great book."

My twentieth year at the university, I write *Mathematical Structures and the Repudiation of Time*. My wife is ecstatic. She throws a huge party in my honor. The entire department comes. So do my parents. My parents have nothing to say to the department. And the department has nothing to say to my parents. My Dad leaves early.

A few weeks later, I go to dinner at my parents'. (*Lewis sits.*)

My father is stone cold sober (an event I'd rather not repeat). My mother displays my book on the coffee table. "We're all so proud of you . . . aren't we, Charles?"

My father is not so proud. He reads the newspaper. The book reviews have not been kind.

(**Father/Charles:**) "My son, the mathematician! That party your wife threw. Your fellow co-workers didn't even dare speak to your family. Your mother sat in the corner the whole night."

I try to explain. "That's just the way it is in academe. It's a very insular world."

(**Father:**) Your mother said I oughtta rent a tux, for your party. Which I did, a tuxedo, for my son. And at that party, I was there in my tux, and a coupla of them professor types asked me to pour their drinks—

(**Lewis:**) Dad, it was a mistake.

(**Father:**) Oh sure, 'course it was, son. All the other tuxedos at the party that wore black skin were serving drinks.

(**Lewis:**) What did you think of my book?

My father ignores the question and turns to the review. He's studied it relentlessly. He reads with practiced precision.

(**Father:**) "Harlem-born professor examines the Big Logical Questions. One should, perhaps, applaud this new player in a field reserved for the intellectual elite."

He pauses for emphasis and then reads that section again.

(**Father:**) "—in a field reserved for the intellectual elite"—reserved for who?—the intellectual elite.

"Harlem-born professor-"

(**Lewis:**) I get it, Dad.

(**Father:**) "Unfortunately, the author does little to advance time-reality questions." My son, the PhD! His book does little.

(**Lewis:**) Did you even read the book, Dad? I wrote a book. And, by the way, not all the reviews are bad. A black publication called me a "scintillating mind."

Dad doesn't care. All he cares about are the high-profile—the white—reviews.

Dinner! Mom serves roast pork and collard greens. It's a formal dinner, in my honor; silverware scraping the good china. "Why not have a drink, Dad. Because you're much better drunk than you are sober. I worked my entire life to better myself. I did it for you. Success. Have you ever, even once, supported me?"

(Father:) "Supported you? Worked myself into the ground to put food on this table, didn't I. Supported you! Better a son take a beatin from his own father than take a beatin from the world. What's my son do? He goes out and embarrasses my ass. Goes out and writes some book that don't even sell. Seems to me if you can't write a book that people are gonna want t'buy—that people are gonna respect—then you shouldn't write a goddamn book at all!"

I am silent. I will divorce myself from my father. It's the last dinner we share. At home, my wife asks how was the evening. I go to the bathroom and vomit.

(*Jesse, now a young man and a bit of a trickster. 1890.*)

JESSE: Once I grown, I work in town. Day-time ringing till at the colored barber shop. Night-time sweeping floors at the white barber shop. Barely make ends meet. Weekends, Momma gets me in the field doing mule-work and telling me to quit my cussin.

Hardly got three quarters to my name, but I my own man. Sho' got tired of meeting up with ghosts, so I go out hoboing. And one day I stumble cross a church right longside a road wit nothin to the north and nothin to the south for miles and miles on end. Just a prayer house, really, and I figure it so small and runned to the ground it might e'en be a black folks church.

I creep up on closer and hear the preacher callin out,

(Preacher:) Come all ye down-trodden, heavy laden! Come one, come all! God calls all wearied with toil and blighted by misfortune into His Kingdom! God calls everyone into his sanctuary! In God's house, every sinner finds his home!

Been down on my luck since I started travellin and mighty pleased to hear that preacher's voice. I fling open the door of the fallin-to-pieces little church and sit right on down in the amen corner.

But once the service end, the preacher stomp up to me, gripin,

(Preacher:) Ain't no niggers allowed in this church, boy.

(Jesse:) My name's Jesse, not boy, and I didn't see no sign fo' whites only, sir. But I heared ya callin all God's children to his Kingdom.

(Preacher:) Ain't no niggers allowed.

(Jesse:) I just heared ya now, "all us find home—"

(Preacher:) Ain't no niggers allowed!

(Jesse:) And truth be told, Mr. Preacher, I been carryin around a whole floursack of sins that I bout ready to get unburdened from. See, I been on the road fo' more than a month of Sundays and I keep collectin things in this here bag, sins among them.

(Preacher:) Ain't no niggers allowed!!!

(Jesse:) Ain't no sign.

(Preacher:) Ain't no sign cuz halfa these folks never met no nigger in they whole life. Case you too stupid to see, there ain't nothin to the right and nothin to the left. None of em here couldn't even read a sign if it offered up a re-ward.

(Jesse:) Lemme tell ya, Mr. Preacher, sir, pretty soon Mr. Pullman himself's gonna put some rails 'long this road, so if ya want your little church to stay witout black folks, ya best fix up a sign.

(Preacher:) How I spose t'do that?

(Jesse, *with charm*:) For a hot meal, I spose I could scrawl it out for ya.

(Preacher:) You gonna write the sign?

(Jesse, *indicating a huge sign*) "Whites Only."

(Preacher:) That's right.

The little preacher calls after Delilah,

(Preacher:) Get this nigger some grub and paper and pencil too.

(Delilah:) Paper and pencil, where I gonna get that?

(Jesse:) Don't worry, I say. And I take both paper and pencil outta my bag. I write the sign. Slowly. To make sure the meal still come.

That's an awful nice lookin sign, Preacher say.

And you sho' gave an awful nice soundin sermon, I say. Lookee here, in some parts, I even heard whites and blacks be congregating in the church together.

(Preacher:) Whites and blacks?

(Jesse:) That's right.

(Preacher:) To-gether?

(Jesse:) They sho' is.

(Preacher:) Not my church.

(Jesse:) Suh, I made your sign kindly—

(Preacher:) Not my church!

(Jesse:) We broke bread 'mongst each other—

(Preacher:) Not my church!!!

The two of us stand outside that fallin-to-pieces little church til nighttime. Each step of darkness come, that little preacher get more and more contrary. Finally I say, "Mr. Preacher, maybe it time both us consult wit God and see what He recommend." The preacher like that idea and he storm off.

Now, God never in my whole life showed up for any sort of consultation or visitation. So I put it out my mind, creeped inside the church, laid my head down on a pew and felled asleep. No sooner than that am I yanked to my senses and the little preacher wavin the "Whites Only" sign and yellin "Trespasser, he a trespasser!" A crowd behind him drag me outta the church and throw me in a hog-pen, back of a wagon. I get carried like that fo' two days, no food, no water, and then I get dumped on the dust-footed steps of a courthouse.

(Judge:) Thirteen years hard labor! The prisoner will be rented to the stockyard at the premium rate of a dollar twenty-five per day.

And after alla that befall me, you know what? God did make his appearance. He say, "Don't worry that they wouldn't let ya inta the church, son. I've been trying to get inta that church for over fifty-five years, and I ain't been invited in yet!"

(*sings, a blues song*)

> Got sent to the prison-yard
> When the Lord forgot my name.
> I got sent to the prison-yard
> When the Lord forgot my name.
> Workin in the coal-mine,
> Stomping that turp'tine field,
> Just a poor black boy
> I'm prayin I get killed.

(*Hearing "killed," Lewis begins to write advanced equations in the air.*)

JESSE:

> Got sent to the prison-yard
> When the Lord forgot my name.
> Gon' hide my tears from eyesight,
> So the world don't see my pain.
> I'm gon' hide my tears from eyesight,
> So the world don't see my pain.
> So tired of livin, don't wanna
> Live this life no mo.'
> Time I spend on this earth
> Ain't nothin but a lonely war.

(*Lewis continues to write the equations, attempting to dispel the Spirit of Jesse.*)

JESSE:

> Got sent to the prison-yard
> When the Lord forgot my name.

(*Lewis relives teaching a class, the philosophy of mathematics, at the university. It is two months before this evening. Although disturbed by Jesse's song, Lewis is in his element, a great lecturer. The class, blackboard, and students are not to be actually represented. The Spirit of Jesse watches Lewis. Lewis does not see Jesse, but the unconscious awareness of Jesse's presence is unnerving.*)

LEWIS: Thomas Aquinas called the number *pi*, 1.618033—(*Lewis has embarrassingly recited the number phi, not pi.*) Excuse me. (*With "excuse me," Jesse is no longer visible.*)
    The number *pi*—3.14159265—a perfect, transcendental number. (*looking for raised hands*)
    What else did he call this number? Yes! "The eternal number of God." Now, reflect on Newtonian absolute time and absolute space. Is time mutable? (*Beat.*) Questions? Thoughts? Any—any questions at all? Are you there? Okay, a class of geniuses! Moving on . . .

(*Lewis sees a new student enter the room.*)

    Oh, welcome to class. You are? Leroy. Leroy, you're late. But have a seat.
    (*gesturing to the equation*) Examine the mathematical structure. Is there a causal relationship between past and present? Can we define the present moment independent of the past?

Yes? Question, Leroy . . . Leroy, did you read my book? I wrote a book. A black publication called—it was assigned. I suggest you glance over it before our next session. Very well, moving on.

(*Lewis quickly adds to the equation.*)

Now, then. Examine the equation. Set aside your perception of temporal reality. Mathematically, is our psychological understanding of time (referring to the present moment as the arrival of a sequential series of past moments) a valid or artificial concept?

Excuse me? Leroy. May I proceed? May I? (*repeating what the student has just said*)

Master class—Yes, this is advanced—

"House nigger?"

Leroy, this is math. Not basketball practice. And by the way, you might make some of those hoops if you understood word one of parabolic arcs. (*returning to the lesson*) Temporal sophisms—(*Lewis hears it said again.*)

"House Nigger."

Leroy, who is calling whom a nigger?

(*pointing to the equation*)

Very well. When Kurt Gödel added rotation to the stress tensor, here, he found a—

"Nigger."

Leroy! Open the book, open my book. Do you think—if you were to open one goddamn book in your entire life—that you would be acting white? Maybe you should act white because you're pathetic, stupid, nothing—an ignorant nigger! What? No, Leroy, you're dismissed. Get out of my class right now. I said, get out!

(*Later, the dean's office.*)

(**Dean:**) He never said that, Lewis. He did not engage in name-calling. You say he said "House" and then used the "N" word?

(**Lewis:**) House Nigger, that's right.

(**Dean:**) Your student said "Heidegger."

(**Lewis:**) He said—

(**Dean:**) Heidegger.

(**Lewis:**) I heard him. He did not say Heidegger. Heidegger isn't even on my syllabus. This kid has the audacity to say I've Uncle Tommed my way to the top.

(**Dean:**) It's a yes or no question, Lewis. Did you or did you not call your student the "N" word?

(**Lewis,** *bordering on the irrational:*) The question should be: is time quantized (unconnected uncontinous units—as matter is to atoms, light to photons)? And black people have to ask themselves precisely this question!

(**Dean:**) Lewis? I think you need some time off.

(**Lewis:**) I don't need time off!

(**Dean:**) This makes no sense, Lewis. Your father passing, the book, whatever else's bothering you—How about a vacation? A leave.

(**Lewis:**) I've done everything, everything I've done is to succeed because when you're black, you have to be better than better, the best. Why should I take a leave? I've spent my entire life striving to rise above the drudgery of existence, *apprehend the eternal verities*—and I'm not going to let some stupid nigger—

(**Dean:**) Lewis, I'm putting you on leave.

(**Lewis:**) I don't need—

(**Dean:**) You don't have a choice. Mandatory leave.

I don't tell my wife about the leave. In fact, I never tell her. I dress for work every day. I leave the house. I come home at the specific hour one is to come home. I retreat into my study.

She asks, but I say nothing. One day, she enters (cheerful the way you are cheerful when you want to cheer someone up).

"I think you should go to the Million Man March. In Washington."

(*Lewis becomes fragmented as the voice of his wife gradually merges with his own.*)

I say nothing.

"I was thinking, Lewis, it would be—"

Say nothing.

"fun—empowering—"

Fun? Look at the prison.

"Prison? What are you talking about?"

Say nothing—

"Lewis, what are you talking about?"

Nothing, nothing, nothing.

"All I was saying was the Million Man March could be empower—"

All *I'm* saying—I said—did you hear what I said?

"I can't continue, Lewis—you deny your self."

I said never nothing never mind.

"It's not a relationship; I want a *whole* person—dimensionality—a relationship is about total honesty—"

Why! Why would I *possibly* want to march around on Washington? Because I'm black. You don't know—

"I know living with you can be very lonely, Lewis."

Weeks pass, the march comes, and she waits. She waits for me to march. I don't.

(*Beat.*)

My wife leaves.

(*Lewis gazes into the shadow-darkness of Jesse, speaking to Jesse as if he is himself.*)

You've got demons, Lewis. You've got a whole lot of demons.

(*1890–1903. Jesse is on the chain gang.*)

JESSE: (*sings, a work song*)

> Devil came visitin me nightimes,
> Came when my head hung low,
> Devil came visitin me nightimes,
> Came when my head hung low,
> Devil said he'd free me,
> If I kill that so-and-so.
>
> I'm going home, Lordy,
> Lord, I wanna go home.
> I'm going home, Lordy,
> Lord, I wanna go home.
>
> Some men die of malary,
> Some men die of stroke,
> Some men die of scurvy,
> Some men slit they own throat.
>
> I'm going home, Lordy,
> Lord, I wanna go home.
> I'm going home, Lordy,
> Lord, I wanna go home.

After bout three year pass, new boy in our cage. He in for rape. Fact is, half the mens from five counties in for raping white ladies. I ask, how many white ladies is livin in these counties anyhow? He say quite a few. "Once you out," New Boy tell me, "if ya see a white lady walking down the street, ya best to cross to the other side." I say that near impossible on market day, can't every black man walkin criss-cross the road. Alla those mens be thrown in jail for stopping traffic! One day, year later, New Boy got a glint in his eye. He say to me,

(New Boy:) Jesse, I got one for ya: Two black mens in a automobile drivin down the road. A chicken is crossin the road. The driver slam on the brakes and both he and the passenger is thrown *thirty-seven* feet outta the car. Now, how come botha them gets put in prison with three charges 'gainst them?
I say I don't know.

(New Boy:) See, the first charge is fo' murderin a baby chick. Second one is fo' defacin the road with skid marks. Third charge is fo' fleein *thirty-seven* feet from the scene of the crime!

After that, New Boy and me tell each other a story every mornin.

Then there be Joe Denver, biggest man in our cage. He really is in for rape. And murder, too. Alla sudden outta no where, Big Joe turns to New Boy.

(Big Joe:) Gimme yo' breakfast.

New Boy moves to the side and Big Joe eats it up. Two weeks of this I tell New Boy he gotta learn to stand up for hisself. Next day, New Boy don't give his breakfast. Big Joe slam New Boy by his head against the bars of the cage and New Boy don't get up. Big Joe turn to me.

(**Big Joe:**) I be hungry tomorrow. So, now on, you got t'give me yo' breakfast. I sleep next to New Boy's body til it start to smell and get covered over in vermin.

(*sings*)

> Been livin here thirteen years,
> I've been livin the Devil's plan.
> Been livin here thirteen years,
> I've been livin the Devil's plan.
> Been livin without no future,
> Oh, brother—won't ya give me a hand?

> I'm going home, Lordy,
> Lord, I wanna go home.
> I'm going home, Lordy,
> Lord, I wanna go home.

Time I got freed from prison yard, I practically old. Marry a young gal named Selma. Selma born me a son, little Charley. All day long that boy whistling and rhyming, keep me in stitches.

One night, me and Little Charley in town at the General Store. Hear a white fella up in arms.

(**White Fellow:**) "The carpetbaggers nothin but trouble! Yankees come down here and rip up all our land. Votin day tomorrow! Now they want me to vote for 'em? Talk about Reconstruction! Freeman's Bureau. All they wanna do is protect nigger rights."

That night I say to Charley, "Votin day comin tomorrow!"

(*to Lewis*) My little Charley, he be your father.

I say, "You know what, son. Your daddy gonna vote. And I don't care if a whole crew of goblins, ghouls, and gargoyles show up at the door."

LEWIS: Not this . . .

JESSE: So, the next day, I march right on into town. But you know what? The closer and closer I get to that voting booth, the more and more white folks think I lookin like a rapist.

LEWIS: Not this memory . . .

JESSE:

> Some men die in a cage,
> Some men die on the rail.

LEWIS: Stop, time.

JESSE:

> Some men die real quiet,
> Some men die with a wail.

> Oh, brother
> Oh, brother
> Oh, brother

JESSE:

>Oh, brother—

JESSE, LEWIS:

>—won't ya give me a hand?

(In a quicksilver instant Jesse becomes Rex. Lewis is now completely disoriented, overwhelmed by the attrition of the night.)

REX: You just sang with your brother.

LEWIS: I—what?

REX: My brother—

LEWIS: We do not exist simultaneously.

REX: My brother—

LEWIS: Jesse?

REX: Just sang with his brother.

LEWIS: Rex? Rex—

REX: Oh, brother—

LEWIS: Stop it!

REX: Oh, brother

>Oh, brother

LEWIS: Stop time, . . .

REX: Engage with me, brother.

LEWIS: Leave me, be gone . . .

REX: *(overlapping)* Oh, brother—

LEWIS: Oh, please.

REX: Won't ya give me a hand?

LEWIS: *(overlapping)* Let me out of this night.

REX: You ain't getting outta this night, Lewis. This my memory, too. And I ain't gonna let you kill my memory.

LEWIS: This isn't *your* insomnia—

REX: Fine. Watch me do the damn story. Where Dad?

LEWIS: Dad's gone, and I want nothing to do with Dad.

REX: You stopped time on Jesse—now you cutting out a few chapters of Dad. This night ain't this night without Dad. I'm gonna play Dad. You can chill out over there. Time we had some fun up in this joint.

(to the booth)

>Yeah, can I get a little more light? This crew, man, won't do nothing to help a brother out.

LEWIS: *(trying to reclaim his ground)* Who's your audience?

REX: My what?

LEWIS: Your audience?

REX: You. You my audience.

LEWIS: This is my night. I'm *in* it.

REX: Well, you ain't in this night with me, so you ain't in it. If and when you decide to *get* in it, then the kind people sitting in the pews out there, then they gonna be the audience. But right now, I'm doing this baby all for you.

    The Abbreviated Life of Dad.

(*sings*)

        Ofay ofay ofay—

LEWIS: (*unimpressed*) Okay, fine.

REX:

        boss-man say okay!
        Ofay ofay ofay—
        boss-man say okay!

(*to the audience*)

    Here the back story. When Jesse's son, Little Charley, Dad, was twelve, he quit school and went to working in the fields. Then after a while, Great-granddaddy Simon, Great Katie, and Little Dad move up north. Dad grow up and marry Mom. Everyone live in a teensy-tiny apartment. You and me ain't born yet, so—so far, it ain't that teensy.

    Dad fancied himself a musician, and Dad used to SING!

(*Rex begins the song Charles used to sing, upbeat and jump blues. Rex's rendition is completely silly; he uses his hands as puppets.*)

        Two little lovebirds is sitting in a tree
        Blackbird say, won't you marry me
        Bluebird say, you best get to work
        Blackbird say—
        I'm so tired of that boss-man jerk-ing
        me 'round all day

LEWIS: This isn't how you tell a story.

REX: How's it go?

LEWIS: How's what go?

REX: Two little lovebirds . . . The song?

LEWIS: I have no idea what you're talking about.

REX: —is kissing in a bush

LEWIS: That's a rhyme, that's not—

REX: Blackbird say something, something, something—What's next?

LEWIS: When was Dad supposedly singing this?

REX: When he tucked us in bed.

LEWIS: Tucked us into bed?

REX: When he came home. When he was mad at Mom. When he was pounding the pavement. When he was sweeping streets, when he was cleaning toilets, when he was throwing rent parties, when he used be standing in the soup line, when he was wooing mom. Sang that song when everyone moved up north, when he and Great Simon and Katie was cheering the 369th march up Fifth Ave. Back when he snuck into speakeasies wanting to sit down at Fast Jack's piano, all part of everyday he was fumbling over melodies—that's when Dad sang that song.

LEWIS: You're right. Dad sang?

REX: Before he stopped singing he was singing that song.

LEWIS: Blackbird say . . .

REX: What's next?

LEWIS: Blackbird say . . .

LEWIS, REX: Blackbird say, oh I wish, I wish

REX:

> Blue take Black's ring
> And fling it in the air.
> Well, Blackbird cry,
> baby don't you care.
> Bluebird squeak,
> buster don't you dare.

REX: Sing with me, brother!

> I'm so tired of that boss-man
> jerk-ing me 'round all day.

LEWIS: (*speaking, simultaneous with song*) Jerk-ing me 'round all day.

REX:

> Ofay ofay ofay,
> boss-man say okay!

LEWIS: (*speaking, simultaneous with song*) Ofay ofay ofay, boss-man say okay.

(*As the bond between the brothers strengthens, from now until the end of the play, Rex will gradually begin to relinquish his self-constructed militant identity. He will become the brother that Lewis shared a bedroom with as a boy.*)

REX: 'Member when Dad was workin that janitor job downtown?

LEWIS: Was that that one boss?

REX: That ofay-boss-man? One day he say he want to open a janitorial service up in Harlem.

So Dad started working on 125th. We was all happy.

LEWIS: When was that?

REX: Couple times, Great Simon took me and you down to Central Park. Gave us little sailboats, sail around on the pond. You just sat on the bench, recite your times-tables.

LEWIS: I did?

REX: Then one day, you tell Dad,

(**Young Lewis:**) "Daddy, why you don't go downtown and say to that boss-man, 'Mr. Boss-Man, that janner service up in Harlem nothing but grief. If ya wanna sell it to me, I take it off your hands.'"

LEWIS: I said that?

REX: And Dad did it, just like you said. Boss man say okay. Great Simon go, "You got a smart boy, Charley."

LEWIS: Bright idea. Didn't work out, though. Dad was in way over his head.

REX: He tried.

LEWIS: (*bitter*) Tried?

REX: You go after school, help him count up the money.

(*The brothers piece together their shared past.*)

LEWIS: Second-grade arithmetic wasn't help.

REX: Then one day, the man from the city come and shut him down. And just like that, Dad was jobless.

LEWIS: That's when he started drinking.

REX: Wasn't long after that, Great Simon died.

LEWIS: That was a terrible day.

REX: You were the one that found his body?

LEWIS: Wouldn't wake up.

REX: That was the day before you and me brought home bad grades in school, wasn't it?

LEWIS: Was it?

REX: Simon died and the next night Dad beat you silly.

LEWIS: Didn't care about a thing but the grades. Was I hiding under the bed?

REX: You was under the bed, and Mom was going, "You got a demon in you, Charles."

LEWIS: He hit her, too.

REX: What'd you say?

LEWIS: I didn't say anything.

REX: You say, "Stop it—"

LEWIS: Daddy drags me out from under the bed.

REX: (*as Young Lewis*) You cry, "Daddy—"

LEWIS: (*as Charles*) Dad says, "Shut up, Lewis!"

REX: (*as Young Lewis*) You say, "Please, Daddy, please—"

LEWIS/CHARLES: "What did I say! Shut up, Lewis! I'll whip you good—Don't think I won't—I'll whip the hide right off ya. I'll beat you like a slave! Shame me! Don't you ever shame me!"

REX/YOUNG LEWIS: "I didn't shame you, Daddy, I didn't shame—"

LEWIS/CHARLES: "Shame yourself, shame your whole goddamn family! Your great-grandfather Simon's idea! You know how hard I been working for you to get into that private school!"

REX/YOUNG LEWIS: "I know, Daddy—I tried, Daddy—I tried."

LEWIS/CHARLES: "You tried? You tried? White people try, Lewis, black people fail. So you best not try. You best do more than try."

REX/LEWIS: "You ain't understand, Daddy—"

LEWIS/CHARLES: "Don't you talk back to me! I gave you everything I never had! You throw it in my face! I'll kill you, boy. Don't think I won't kill my own son, Lewis. I will kill you."

(*Both brothers collapse, shaken by the reenactment of the beating.*)

LEWIS: How come he only beat me?

REX: You brought home bad grades.

LEWIS: You brought home bad grades.

REX: But you were his favorite, the smart one.

LEWIS: He beat me 'til my blood drained out.

REX: 'Til you were white as a ghost.

LEWIS: Said he was gonna beat the black outta me.

REX: And he did.

LEWIS: Mom takes me to the hospital the next morning. Dad doesn't look at me, doesn't say a thing. Broke two of my ribs and snapped my collar bone.

REX: That afternoon, great-grandaddy's funeral.

LEWIS: I don't go. I put on my pajamas, crawl back to bed.

REX: You ever thought of askin after Great Simon?

LEWIS: I barely remember Simon.

REX: Late that night, after the funeral, Dad comes to apologize.

LEWIS: His breath stinks and he goes on and on, saying he's sorry.

REX: Then he tells us bout watching his own dad, Jesse, die.

LEWIS: After that night, we never speak of it again.

REX: But he tells us every detail.

LEWIS: Slurring his words. Then he just goes out of the room and shuts the door.

(*Beat.*)

REX: Lewis, tell the story Dad told us.

(*Lewis won't tell it.*)

REX: Grandpa Jesse went out hoboing . . . stumbled cross a Whites Only church . . . got put on the chain-gang.

LEWIS: I know how he died—

REX: After Jesse outta prison and Dad was little—One day, it was time to vote. So Jesse march right into town—

LEWIS: I remember, Rex—

(*Rex gazes out at the audience. He speaks clinically, without affect.*)

REX: He was stripped naked and chained to a tree. White families drove for miles and miles to watch. Photographers came, too.

LEWIS: There's no point in telling it again.

REX: They castrated Jesse. They lit a fire. The audience was fit for an amphitheater. Cameras clicked the whole time. Jesse was consumed by fire. Afterwards, charred organs and bits of bones were sold as souvenirs. Twenty-five cents apiece. Photographs cost ten cents apiece. He was hung and burnt for trying to vote. For trying to vote. But what'd they say? Lewis? Lewis?

LEWIS: What does it matter what they said?

REX: I can't remember.

LEWIS: So what does it matter?

REX: *Be* in this night, Lewis.

LEWIS: They said: Dad's dad, Jesse, was lynched for raping a white woman and killing her husband. Everyone called him guilty.

REX: Then what happened?

LEWIS: A reporter from many, many towns away came.

REX: He interviewed the "raped woman."

LEWIS: She said she saw Jesse march into town to vote.

REX: Her husband blocked his path.

LEWIS: They quarreled—

REX: —right outside the voting booth. What'd the reporter say?

LEWIS: (*as reporter*) "That nigger kill your husband?"

REX: (*as woman*) "Kill my husband? Oh, Heavens no! My husband was killed by Adam Stapleton. Those two been at each other for years."

(*Lewis continues to recite the reporter's lines, but he is unable to completely assume the role.*)

LEWIS: Do you feel any regret for the mistake?

REX: (*as woman*) "Kill a mule, buy another—"

LEWIS: Kill a nigger, hire his brother.

(*Beat.*)

REX: What d'you think it did to little boy Dad?

LEWIS: Little boy Dad.

REX: What do you think that did?

LEWIS: I don't know . . .

REX: Every once and awhile, Dad's grandma Katie sent Dad into town, to the General Store. And at the store, postcards hung in the window. Postcards of a man's burning body.

LEWIS: Ten-cent photos of Dad's lynched father for sale.

(*Beat.*)

REX: Time you free yourself, Lewis.

LEWIS: What about you, Rex, are you free? Did a drug overdose make you free?

REX: . . . No.

LEWIS: Both of us, then. (*A glimmer of Jesse can be seen in Rex as he begins to leave.*)

REX:
> I'm going home, Lordy,
> Lord, I wanna go home.

Don't clip your own wings, brother.

> I'm going home, Lordy,
> Lord, I wanna go home.

(*Rex completely exits the stage, leaving Lewis alone. All of the ancestors are now gone. Lewis "sees" his aloneness. One insomnia-filled night has passed. It is the pitch darkness before dawn.*)

LEWIS: Dad's gone; my brother's gone; my wife is gone. I am my own audience watching myself grieve.

Tonight, this ten-year-old night, Dad beats me; tonight he tells me the story of Jesse; tonight my great-grandfather dies. I am assaulted by the claustrophobia of trees tonight, trapped in a windowless box without walls, a silent prison; tonight my wife leaves me. This solitary insomniatic night of many nights— please, great grand-dad, please, Great Simon, please, great wise man from the skies, please take me out of this night, tonight.

(*For the first time in his life, Lewis has willingly summoned his ancestor. Lewis has called on the one that is most able to heal. In the separate space, Simon appears from the air in the seraphic glow of dawn. Simon tells this last story simply, without reenacting or completely assuming the role of the Union soldier.*)

SIMON: Thursday sun-up, I learnt it was, I hear someone blowing the bugle at the big house.

T'aint meal-serving time, but they blowing three long blows and that mean it time for us slaves to hurry on up to the house.

When I come inside, I see four white men sittin there with big brass buttons on they blue uniform. One of them white mens with a sun-creased forehead and turned-down lips look me straight in the eye and say,

"Do you know what day it is today, boy?"

I dunno so I say, No, suh.

"How are you coloreds going to take care of yourselves, if you can't even tell time?"

The man look at me and laugh.

I know how to tell time just fine, suh. I can tell it by the clock and tell it by the sun.

"And yet you don't know what day it is today?"

No, suh, I don't know the day of the week, cuz everyday but Sunday is the same day t'me, a working day. And I know today ain't no Sunday. What make this a special day, I say.

"Today is the day you're free."

Free?

I walk outta the house like a man that don't know he got two feet. I walk on over to Mr. Brady plantation. All sorts of chilrens spinnin in circles. Everyone throwin up they hats in the air. I walk down to the field and Katie seent me comin—and she flies out her arms like they's bird wings. Katie come runnin cross the field towards me—and I ain't never gonna forget how she runned that day—each foot slammin the earth, and wit each of them steps, she also glidin trew the air.

(*Lewis and Simon now occupy the same space. After an unsteady moment, Lewis decides not to question whether Simon is an illusion or reality. Simon is still a bright young man, the age of freedom.*)

LEWIS: . . . Great Simon?

SIMON: Lewis. (*Beat.*) What you doin all by your lonesome, Lewis?

LEWIS: I don't know. I . . . I have to get my house in order. Feng Shui.

(*Simon looks at the door. The door is not represented on stage, but it figuratively exists.*)

SIMON: You know, son, maybe us oughta do some work on this door. Fix the hinges.

LEWIS: Great Simon. I don't know where—who—why I am. All these years, I don't know why I am.

(*Simon understands what Lewis means. But he also knows that no words can answer this question.*)

SIMON: Great Son. How bout us paint up this door? Paint it blue.

(*Simon begins painting the door.*)

SIMON: Lewis, I ever tell you, back in slavery times, I learnt reading and arithmetic. Now, I wasn't keen on how it happened. But I awful glad to know books and numbers. Mighty proud of that.

(*sings*)

> *Eniyan fo soke*
> *Eye fo soke*

(*Simon teaches Lewis the song.*)

> *Idiran mi wa sile*
> *Angeli wa sile*
> *Eniyan fo soke . . .*

(*Hesitant at first, Lewis joins his great-grandfather.*)

LEWIS: (*overlapping*)

> *Eniyan fo soke*

SIMON:

> *Eye fo soke*

LEWIS: (*overlapping*)

> *Eye fo soke*

SIMON:

> *Idiran mi . . .*

SIMON, LEWIS:

> *. . . wa sile*
> *Angeli wa sile*

(*They continue to paint the door and sing together as the lights fade.*)

> *Eniyan fo soke*
> *Eye fo soke*
> *Idiran mi wa sile*
> *Angeli wa sile.*

(*There is a flutter of bird's wings.*)

ANCESTOR:

> *Baba agba,*
> *Iya agba,*
> *Mo dupe*
> *Mo dupe.*
>
> (Mo dupe: "Thank you")

END OF PLAY.

S. M. SHEPHARD-MASSAT

A dancer turned playwright, Sherry M. Shephard-Massat speaks with the rich Georgia accent she skillfully captures in writing for the southern-bred characters who inhabit her plays. Shephard-Massat was born in New York but raised in Atlanta. Her plays are inspired by her memories of her family and reflect her strong connection to her Georgia roots. She creates courageous characters, some of whom decide not to join the great migration north. They are determined to stand their ground in a place that represents the hard work, dedication, and sacrifices of their parents and grandparents. Their dreams of owning or holding onto the land they love keeps them connected to their roots and to each other in their small rural Georgia communities. Other plays by Shephard-Massat are *Waiting to Be Invited* and *Starving*.

Levee James received its world premiere on February 13, 2004, at the Bay Area Stage in San Francisco, California.

Director:	Israel Hicks
Lily:	Rosalyn Coleman
Wesley Slaton:	Steven Anthony Jones
Fitzhugh Martin:	George Wallace
Set:	Loy Arcenas
Costumes:	Michael J. Cesairo
Lighting:	Nancy Schertler
Sound:	Garth Hemphill
Dialect coach:	Deborah Sussel

LEVEE JAMES

CHARACTERS

Wesley Slaton—"Wes," early-to-mid-forties
Lily Grace Hoterfield—"Lil," mid-to-late thirties
Fitzhugh Marvin—mid-to-late thirties

DESCRIPTION OF INTERIOR

Furnished with the feeling of turn-of-the-century progress: a gramophone, jazz records, a radio, electricity. Indicates that a successful but modest rural family lives here. The kitchen is big enough for a good-sized family, with a large wooden table, matching chairs, and modern appliances of the period. It has an up-to-date cookstove and running water from the sink.

TIME

1923, Friday morning. Spring.

PLACE

Senoia, Georgia

Act 1

Scene 1

Lil Hoterfield and Wesley Slaton cross the stage arm in arm. Wesley is carrying a huge carpet bag. They stop in front of a prosperous farmhouse. Lil freezes; gazes at the house.

LIL: Wait a minute. Ooh, goodness calamity. How my sistah Clareesa woulda bragged up somethin' on this 'ere.

WES: Awh, Clareesa wouldn' ta nevah dun' no braggin' on this ole place. (*walks toward porch*)

LIL: Nawh, she wouldn' ta had to do tha' much. Anybody wit eyes can see fo' they-selves. Turned this lil' shotgun shack into a sacred sight to behold. (*Wes ascends the two or three porch steps.*)

WES: Ain't no church house nor nothin' near tha' important, Lily.

LIL: Jus' yo' home. Cain't git no moe sacred, can ya?

WES: Wann't nevah no shotgun shack neitha. (*laughs*)

LIL: Look like you dun' turned one house into three-foe' from the outside show, Wes. He dun' tacked on half-a-castle, honey. Wha' is you all 'bout these days, Wesley Slaton? Wha' is you tryin' to do?

WES: Jus' livin' prosperous as I can, Lily gal.

LIL: As you can.

WES: Jus' livin' prosperous.

LIL: Keepin' holt to it while you can.

WES: Sho' nuff. (*sets carpet bag on porch*)

LIL: (*laughs*) To thank I knew you when you wuz livin' off luv, nibblin' on my big sistah.

WES: How 'bout a cool drink, Miss Lil?

LIL: Why, thank you, Mistah Wes. (*moves toward porch; examines the landscape*) Much as I enjoyed tha' lil' stroll from the station, I am 'bout parched to the teeth, suh.

WES: Wouldn' ta let cha walk tha' far you hadn' insisted so hard.

LIL: Wannit ta bend down an' smell the honeysuckle e'ry otha' step; close as I could. (*bends down; smells a flower*)

WES: Well, come on in 'ere, then. (*laughs, opens the door*)

LIL: Like when I wuz a lil' girl.

WES: All tha' bendin' 'n' honey-suckin'.

LIL: But they sho' let cha go the way a' the raisin on transpo'tation. (*Wes moves into the yard, politely assists Lil to her feet. Lil stands.*)

WES: Shame on 'em.

LIL: Tha's why I'm workin' on gettin' me a motorcar, myself. Much goin' from ma'am to ma'am I do. (*Lil and Wes move toward the porch.*)

WES: A motorcar? Wha' chu need a motorcar fo'? Good as you look, I know mens'll take you anywhere you wanna go, girl. I'm 'ere to tell you. Nevah hafta git behind a single wheel in life.

LIL: Is tha' right?

WES: Actual fact.

LIL: Well, my new ma'am . . . (*Moves up a few steps onto porch. Wes picks up carpet bag.*) she got one all to 'erself. She swear by 'im. She say, "Lily, perhaps a woman's all 'roun independence may very well be tied to havin' a motorcar these days." (*Wes opens door to living room. Lil enters, stands gazing at the room. Wes enters, closes door. He takes off his hat, hangs it on nearby coat rack.*)

WES: Yeah. Ole cock-eyed Fitzhugh Marvin, he got a motorcar. (*Sets carpet bag down next to coat rack; moves into kitchen area. Lil follows. On the cookstove, a pot for coffee, a pot for stew, and a small basket of biscuits are present.*)

LIL: Fitzhugh Marvin.

WES: Yeah, ole Fitzhugh. (*Takes pistol off, puts it in kitchen drawer. Unbuttons cuffs, rolls up shirt sleeves.*)

LIL: Cock-eyed Fitzhugh.

WES: He be 'ere tomorrow lookin' ovah the lay a' the land, so to speak.

LIL: Well, I'd be glad to see 'im. Say 'e sporty?

WES: Lorr, tryin' leastways. Cock-eye an' all. We fishes on Sat'day mornins down at the creek. Afterwards, he gon' come by fo' a lil' fish fry an' say hey. How 'bout tha'? (*Lil nods and smiles.*)

WES: Good. Take yo' hat off, Lily gal. Stay awhile. (*Lil takes off hat.*)

WES: Yeah, he still cock-eyed, ole Fitzhugh . . . (*Wesley reaches for hat.*)

LIL: Still cock-eyed. (*She hands Wes her hat.*)

WES: But he got a brand new motorcar he drivin', tho'; yes, suh. (*takes hat*) Preacher tells folks to keep loved ones an' they livestock off the road when you see 'im comin'. Said he gon' be dun' knocked a hole in his own head or somebody else's one, but he drivin'. Yes, ma'am, he sho' drivin'. My ole truck suit me jam up, tho'.

LIL: If the tire ain't flat, don' fix it.

WES: Tha's right. Have a seat 'ere, Miss Lil. (*Lil continues looking around kitchen. Wes moves back toward coat rack in living room.*)

WES: (*from living room*) Now, Mamie Jane Brown, she got 'erself a motorcar too, but she needed one 'cause 'er pie 'n' cookin' bi'niss had jus' growed an' growed, an' a bi'niss woman's gots ta be able to git 'erself to 'n' fro', I tole 'er. (*hangs Lil's hat next to his*) Like a professional. Started a real good caterin' bi'niss, but carryin' aroun' all tha' hot food by hand wann't the answer. (*moves back into kitchen, goes to sink*) "Gon' put scars all up 'n' down yo' arm, Mamie," I said. An' a horse 'n' buggy ain't none too up-to-date 'n' prosperous in itself. Excuse me. (*washes his hands*) You 'membuh Mamie? She had a nice res'trant in town 'foe she left.

LIL: 'Foe she left? Where she go? (*Wes gets glasses from the cupboard next to the sink.*)

WES: Spivey Kaye, I suspec'.

LIL: An' you don' know where she went to?

WES: Tha's where all 'er peoples at now. (*wipes glasses out with nearby dish towel*)

LIL: How long she been gone?

WES: Not long. Week.

LIL: Oh?

WES: Ten days.

LIL: An' wha' about the res'trant doin' so good, you said?

WES: Well, you know. Thangs, personal sit'ations wann't workin' out. Didn' have nothin' to do wit 'er bi'niss, tho'. Oh, 'er bi'niss was boomin'. Matter a' fact, Fitzhugh dun' bought most a' 'er stuff off 'er on time. He gon' try to open up a fish 'n' chicken shack or some such. First, he got tha' car. Now, he interprisin' all ovah the place. (*goes to table with glasses*) She gon' hate she missed chu.

LIL: Me too. (*pauses, notices kitchen table*) Wes, you kept it.

WES: Why wouldn' I? (*Lil moves to table, touches it. She bows her head slightly.*)

LIL: God bless this holy article, an' all whose names are upon it; who have come 'n' gone befoe us. In Jesus name. A-man. (*runs her fingers along the edge*) We started e'ry meal wit tha' blessin'. There's mama's name, the date she wuz born an' the date she died. (*kisses her hand, lays it upon the table*) Daddy's . . . Clareesa . . . Yo's, Wesley . . . (*continues running fingers along edge of table*) The date I wuz born . . . Yo' girls . . . (*turns away from table full of emotion, sees icebox*) Ooh, look at tha' icebox! (*moves to icebox*) Wha' kinda thang is . . .

WES: Top a' the line. (*Lil opens the icebox door, looks inside.*)

LIL: Baby! A sacred sight to behold.

WES: Aw, I wuz jus' teasin'. Bet chu seen much fancier than tha' up in Atlanta.

LIL: Well, this 'ere is mighty big time indeed fo' these parts.

WES: Tha's the big city, tho'. E'rythang's bigguh 'n' better there.

LIL: You thank so? (*closes icebox*)

WES: Stands to reason. Bet e'rybody 'n' they step-daddy got a new icebox in Atlanta. Bet chu even got one. (*Lil goes to the table.*)

LIL: Don' bet too much upon it, Wesley. (*Wes moves to icebox.*)

WES: Here, down this cool drank, then. (*opens icebox, gets pitcher*) Tha's wha' chu need, city gal. A dose a' good ole spring water. (*pours water into glass*)

LIL: You jus' said the word, brain chile. I may have arrived by train but my back would swear to ya I come by covered wagon the whole eighty-somethin' miles. (*Grabs her back, sits. Wesley sets glass on table, pours one for himself.*)

LIL: Sis-in-law got a pain won' wait fo' man nor beast. Hand me my bag, Wesley. Would ya, please?

WES: Sho', Lil. (*Sets his glass down; exits into living room. Lil exhales loudly.*)

WES: (*calls*) You awright, gal? (*moves to coat rack, picks up bag*) I got some horse liniment out in the barn.

LIL: (*laughs, calls*) Not the horse liniment, now. I b'lieve I'll pass. (*Wes re-enters with bag, hands it to Lil.*)

LIL: Thank you kindly. (*reaches into bag*) Here I am in the flesh, y'all. (*takes out a flask, pours contents into glass with water*) Ooh, good ole spring water. (*Wes sits opposite Lil at table, holds his glass.*)

WES: You sho' you awright, Lil?

LIL: As right as the blue in the deep blue sea, brotha-in-law. (*takes a huge sip*) Ooh, baby! You sho' 'nuff said the word. (*Wes sips from his glass.*)

WES: Been foe' years, Lil. We thought you'd 'bout fo'got us. Matter a' fact, Eunice, she said soon as she graduated next year, she wuz gon' spend a lil' time, go find 'er auntee. (*Lil goes back into carpet bag.*)

LIL: Did? Bless 'er heart. (*takes out a small ashtray and cigarettes*)

WES: Make sho' you still wit the livin'.

LIL: Tha' so sweet. (*lights up*) Somebody woulda' let cha know if I wann't. (*blows out a smoke ring; Wes watches her expertise.*) Yo' girls awright?

WES: Yeah, you saw 'em. They awright. (*watches smoke ring disappear*)

LIL: Ain't nothin' wrong wit yo' girls down 'ere?

WES: I teach 'em how to talk back; protect theyselves. Why you ask?

LIL: Cain't nobody tell yo' girls wha' to do, can they?

WES: My girls know how to knock a man's teeth out, Lil.

LIL: Yeah.

WES: Tha's wha' chu wanna know? Say?

LIL: They rock-chunkin', an' ball-playin' up a storm, I hear. (*casually picks pieces of lint off dress*)

WES: You hear? (*smiles, leans back in chair*)

LIL: Mmmm-hmh.

WES: Yeah. How 'bout it? (*sips*)

LIL: Well, them boys' games, Wes. You cain't git no decent, grown man husband knockin' hell out of 'em wit no rocks an' no baseballs. (*flicks ashes into tray*) I know you don' expect 'em to hang in 'ere wit chu fo'evah now, do ya?

WES: No, I don'.

LIL: Good, 'cause folks gits ta thankin' 'n' talkin' too damn much. (*takes a puff*) An' speakin' a' which, bet chu an' Mizz Mamie Jane Brown wuz makin' a pretty successful coupla somethins 'roun 'ere fo' a minute, huh? You wit the castle. Her wit the new motorcar.

WES: How you know 'bout me an' Mamie?

LIL: Same way I know 'bout tha' baseball an' them rocks. I ain't s'pose to?

WES: You sho' got a mouth full a' the hap'nins fo' somebody been gone, tha's all.

LIL: The hap'nins? Three years, nevah even askt tha' woman to marry you. Nothin' hap'nin' 'roun 'ere ceptin' root rot. Say the railroad oughta be shame. Oughta be shamed a' yo'self.

WES: (*stands*) Lil, git tha' cigarette smoke out this house stinkin'. (*He fans the air over the table. Lil puts cigarette out in ash tray.*)

LIL: I s'pose all y'all did fo' three whole years is listen to the radio on Sundays, an' read the Sears Roebuck Bible. (*Wes coughs, goes to window, pulls curtains back, looks out.*) You hear me, Wesley. Wha' wuz you waitin' on? The Second Comin'? Quit tha' bobbin' an' weavin' an' play coughin'.

WES: Now look now, I can bring a pig in 'ere, sit 'im down at tha' table, an' dare 'im to smoke his own poke. Tha's wha' I can do where I put the roof up at.

LIL: I know who pay these bills, boy. Why didn' you marry Mamie Jane, I say?

WES: How you know I ain't askt 'er? How you know all this stuff?

LIL: 'Cause I'm a genius, tha's how. I read the dawg-gone tea leaves, honey. I got a crystal ball in this bag 'ere.

WES: Or is the lil' ole nosey grapevine dun' put a bug in yo' ear? Huh? Maybe found chu up in Atlanta an' writ' chu a letter or two sometime.

LIL: Nobody writ' me nothin'.

WES: (*laughs*) Who was it, girl? Keepin' tabs on me.

LIL: Listen, nevah mind. Humph. Pretty as she is . . .

WES: (*faces Lil*) Now, how you know how pretty she is if you ain't seent 'er? Ain't heard from 'er?

LIL: Heck, she wuz always pretty, man. Foe' years ain't no time. Her kinda pretty don' go nowhere. She still a young woman. Shoot, I went to school wit 'er. Boys an' mens flockin' all ovah her an' Clareesa.

WES: An' you too, as I recall.

LIL: Anyway, pretty an' successful, she'da been a fool waitin' aroun' fo'evah on you to stop plowin' an' take a bath. (*Wes laughs harder, takes sip from glass.*) Glad to see she beat it 'way from 'ere. Hard as you laughin'. You wann't the only one had yo' eye on 'er neitha; guarantee. I could be gone twenny-foe' years 'n' know tha'. Fitzhugh Marvin pro'bly had a cock-eye on 'er. Only thang, most a' 'er good play dun' seent big-time Wesley Slaton in the way, takin' up all the space an' moved on. Three years. Humph.

WES: You drunk, Lil.

LIL: Ain't tha' drunk, tho'. Shoot, I know mens. You better quit fanger-poppin' 'n' take heed.

WES: Ain't nobody poppin' no fangers.

LIL: You ain't poppin' no fangers, then git on down to Spivey Kaye an' marry Mamie. Go tell 'er you love 'er. Did chu tell 'er you love 'er?

WES: Ask yo' crystal ball.

LIL: You got to tell 'er you love 'er. Tell 'er it 'bout kills you not to talk to 'er once a day. It ain't got to be the truth. Jus' care enuff to try to lie. The girls is darn near grown, Wesley. I don' wanna see you up in this ole half-a-castle by yo'self.

WES: You ain't been 'ere five minutes, Lil. You got it all tied up in gold-plated Merry Christmas paper.

LIL: Wit a big ole red bow big as yo' head, fool.

WES: How you gon' argue wit me ovah who an' when I marry again, Sis-in-law?

LIL: (*stands*) Ain't nobody arguin' wit chu, Brotha Wesley. Who arguin' wit chu? Jus' need to git yo' bi'niss in order.

WES: My bi'niss is in order.

LIL: In wha' way?

WES: I got enuff jobs 'roun this place to keep me hoppin', like I say.

LIL: Meanwhile, you gon' work it 'til the bottom fall out of ya? Is tha' the plan? (*Wes takes both glasses, rinses and dries them with dish cloth at sink.*)

LIL: Well then, you ain't gon' need a woman. You gon' need a mama, 'cause all a woman can do fo' you afta' the fact is change yo' diapers an' spoon-feed chu. Ain't none a' this fair to neitha one of ya, Wes. Think about it. Wha' say?

WES: Look 'ere, you an' Mamie ain't gon' kill me wit all this thinkin'.

LIL: My daddy workt chu sun up to sun damn down on this place when he had it befoe' an' afta' you married my sistah, an' tha' ain't kilt chu not nayah' day.

WES: Twenny years ago.

LIL: An' made two babies wit 'er then so, wha' chu tryin' to say now? You beat up at fo'ty? Cain't think? You tired out? Chile, ain't no dumb bunnies 'roun 'ere. E'rybody know there's always somethin' to do runnin' a farm. A cow to buy, to milk e'ryday, chickens to feed, a barn to raise, an' so fo'th. Tha' ain't news.

WES: Wasn' nobody tryin' to pull no fast one on Saint Mamie.

LIL: Don' git funny, now. Tha' woman was runnin' 'er own bi'niss. She didn' need chu. She wannit chu.

WES: I know Mamie a good woman. (*puts glasses back in cupboard*) She steady, got a
smart head on 'er shoulders . . .

LIL: But didn' nevah askt you fo' nothin' outright. Tha' there was the problem.

WES: Look at it this way.

LIL: A big, robust man an' a good-lookin' woman. Both of ya in yo' prime. I swan.
(*sits again at table*)

WES: If I had married 'er, if I married 'er tomorrow, you wouldn' have no bi'niss
down 'ere, would chu? Gon' show the girls how to be wha'? How ta be ladies? I
knew wha' chu was hintin' at. (*reaches for flask on table*) Wha' is tha' chu drinkin',
Mizz Lawd an' Lady 'Erself? Some kinda fanciness you dun' learnt up the street
somewhere.

LIL: You mus' want a taste. (*She stands, reaches for flask. Wes takes flask from her playfully;
Lil laughs.*) Git out the way! (*She moves around table toward Wesley, attempts to take
flask. Wes grabs Lil around waist from behind.*)

WES: (*laughs*) You worried 'bout us. You come back home, see to yo' fam'ly, luv up on
yo' nieces some. Show 'em wha' they miss from they mama. I like tha'. (*Lil pulls
away. They face each other. Lil goes to window, looks out.*)

LIL: I'm wonderin' where it is they runned off to wit ma good trunk. (*Wes goes to
window beside Lil, looks out.*)

WES: They'll be along. Runnin' a coupla' errands is all. (*Lil goes to table, sits.*)

LIL: Who was tha' biggun' again? Lord luv 'im. Tha' boy wha's helpin' wit the luggage.

WES: (*sits at table*) Call 'im Big O fo' short.

LIL: Well, I sho' wouldn' know why 'cause ain't nothin' short about tha' big boy.
Him 'n' Opalee, they so cow-eyed ovah each otha, you'd hafta be a blind, crazy
so-an'-so not to see tha'. Did chu see 'im? Opalee, she nudged 'im fo'ward.
(*stands*) He all nervous. He took in a deep breath an' he say, "Olysses Robenzene
Pullman. Tha's my name, ma'am. Pleased to make yo' acquaintance." Then, he
bowed at the waist like he been practicin'. (*bows*)

WES: Sho' nuff?

LIL: "Well now," I say. "Why do I feel like I'm in the presence a' exiled royalty?
Mighty pleased indeed, Mistah Pullman," and I give a lil' curtsey back. (*curt-
seys*) He bowed again. (*bows again*) "Why, you jus' a big ole King a England. Tha's
who you are." Tha's wha' I say. An' Opalee standin' 'ere jus' a smilin'. Jus' a
beamin'. Showin' all the teeth. (*PAUSE.*) You let tha' big boy be 'ere on a Sat'day
wit yo' girls when you ain't aroun'?

WES: He awright, Lil. He work fo' me.

LIL: Say do?

WES: Twenny-foe'-seven, ceptin' church an' choir on Sundays.

LIL: Church duty, is it?

WES: Yes, ma'am.

LIL: He is a mighty big man, tho'; still. This Big O. Could squash lil' Opalee, couldn'
he? Man big as 'im. You know wha' I mean. She'd hafta' chunk a mighty hard
rock to knock tha' Goliath down.

WES: O wouldn' nevah do nothin' to hurt 'er like tha'.

LIL: Fine, 'cause the ole Wesley Slaton wouldn' hardly let 'im live behind it.

WES: Wouldn', won', an' will not. You right about tha'.

LIL: An' Auntee Lil pack a mighty sharp straight razor 'erself, baby. Hate to hafta whip it out on somebody.

WES: You packin' wha'?

LIL: I ain't playin', boy. Lets 'em know from the word GO, honey. (*takes razor from bag, stands, opens it*)

WES: (*stands*) Now Lil, now . . .

LIL: Y'all listen to yo' auntee. Men folk sniffin' 'roun? Make it clear. No monkey shines. Do? Me an' whoevah it is gon' have us a misunnerstandin', unnerstand?

WES: Lemme see tha' thang. (*moves toward Lil*)

LIL: You dun' seent it befoe. (*hands razor to Wesley*) Used to be Clareesa's. B'lieve tha's how she got chu to marry 'er fin'ly afta' all them hy-jinks in the barn when my papa wann't lookin'. I'm mo' mail it to Mamie in Spivey Kaye soon as I git thu'. (*Wes fondles razor as though in memory of . . . Lil moves to window, looks out. PAUSE.*)

LIL: Ole Sneed ain't dead yet?

WES: Nawh, but he on his way to it. Had a bad stroke last Decembuh. Been bed-ridden evah since. He mostly struck at the th'oat. Cain't make a sound but umph, umph, umph. Anytime he want somethin', he hafta bam on the floe' wit a stick. (*puts razor back in Lil's bag*)

LIL: Well, some folks shouldn'ta nevah got issued vocal cords in the first place. Tha's my opinion. (*takes freshly washed glasses from sink area*) It's good God saw fit to shut 'im up. He had a foul mouth an' foul ways, Sneed did.

WES: Tha's fo' darn sho'. Now, his younges' son, Synn. . . . He got all the mouth an' the ways. Jus' like his daddy.

LIL: Maybe God'll see fit to strike him at the th'oat. (*sits at table with glasses, pours into them from flask*)

WES: He don' like much neitha. He like Fitzhugh car, but he don' like Fitzhugh.

LIL: They don' try to botha y'all, do they?

WES: Ole Sneed cain't do much a' nothin' layin' on tha' bed. (*Lil hands a glass across the table to Wes.*)

LIL: Did, I'd break tha' stick ovah tha' ole man's head crippled or not. (*sips from her glass, sits*)

WES: Young Sneed, he jus' a whole lotta imbecile craziness most a' the time. (*sips*)

LIL: Most a' the time.

WES: Unfit to go to school, be 'roun people. Stuff like tha'.

LIL: Imbeciles need watchin' too; closely. (*sips*) So, where this 'ere Robenzene, this Big O? Where his peoples from?

WES: Miss'sippi.

LIL: Like you. Know 'em?

WES: His daddy workt wit me on the levee 'side my daddy 'foe tha' flood, an' I made my way here to Georgia. His mama an' daddy both got put down by the influenza, tho'. He come 'ere to me.

LIL: Anotha' motherless influenza chile. I swan.

WES: Opalee an' him.

LIL: If it ain't the influenza, it's the polio. Clareesa, Clareesa. Both a' them killers jus' go on in, take who they want an' back on out, don' they?

WES: He cain't even read nor sign his own name is wha' I mean, Lil.

LIL: (*sips*) Wha'd you expect? His daddy befoe 'im workin' on the levee. Half a step away from bein' a complete farm fool his own self. Heck, me 'n' my sistah taught chu how to read 'n' write; how to act in public.

WES: Me?

LIL: You.

WES: No such a' thang.

LIL: Couldn' even read.

WES: I had manners.

LIL: You the one leave 'im work 'ere, roam roun' yo' house much as he want to too, if you worried so to death 'bout tha' chile's non-readin' an' writin' skills. You shouldn'ta let a good-lookin' item like tha' be wit yo' babies twenny-foe'-seven ceptin' church duty on Sundays, then. You was askin' fo' it.

WES: He wanna take 'er up no'th. (*turns up glass, finishes drink*)

LIL: Up no'th?

WES: Git married an' go up no'th. (*puts glass on table*)

LIL: Well, you mus' be crazy 'bout tha'. How ole is he?

WES: He twenny-one.

LIL: Twenny-one? Ain't no boy then, Wesley; a man. Shoot, way grown.

WES: But she jus' fifeen. She ain't ready fo' none a' tha'. (*stands, moves to sink with glass*)

LIL: Clareesa was fifteen an' you was twenny-two, Wesley. Come on.

WES: Tha' was a lifetime ago. You got two, three moe opportunities now since back then. (*sets glass in sink*)

LIL: Like wha'?

WES: A girl wit some education . . . wit some half-way decent education . . . she could do some college. She could go up no'th an' do some college first befoe she tie 'erself down.

LIL: Here we go again wit the up no'th. (*stands, moves to stove*) Listen, e'rybody goin' up no'th, but up no'th cain't hole e'rybody. So many colored folks up no'th now, they arms an' legs be jammed up, hangin' all out the windows an' doe's.

WES: How you know? You nevah been near up there. (*picks up Lil's glass from table*)

LIL: You don' know where I been, numbuh one. You sendin' yo' daughter to come find me. (*lifts lid on pot on stove*) An' numbuh two, ain't enuff black folks singin' the praises a' up no'th fo' me to b'lieve it's too far dif'rent from wha' I jus' said. (*tastes contents*) They workin' you overtime up there. (*adds seasoning from nearby shaker*) Tha's wha' I know 'bout some up no'th. Up no'th ain't the only place a body can work hard. (*She tastes again, nods approval, places lid back on pot. Wesley places glass in sink.*) Shoot, I'm quite sho' you work like two mules right 'ere on this place e'ryday still. You an' my papa workt like foe' mules on this place. E'ryday I watched ya, you did. Up no'th. Livin' an' breathin' in each otha's faces day in, day out. Tha's wha' they doin'. Them streets ain't so paved wit gold but, oh yeah, they is filled wit education. I promise ya'. Riots an' whatnot. Least-ways down 'ere, you can grow yo' own food when you git hungry. An' don' men-tion it, not talkin' 'bout the peoples cross the hall wit they nine, ten chirrun. If it ain't Dom, it's Deter cryin' all night long. Peoples you don' even know an' don' wanna know. Peoples carryin' the influenza an' the polio. (*Wes picks up flask from table.*)

WES: O say he got two, three cousins up there. 'Magine they still aroun'. Could look out fo' 'em. Got neitha influenza nor polio.

LIL: 'Magine? Gon' take yo' baby somewhere to some peoples he jus' imagine?

WES: Intends to find 'em, he say. He know 'bout where they stay at. In New Yawk City.

LIL: Well, which a' way you want it? Stay or go, Wesley? First, you soundin' like it's a bad idea fo' 'em to git married. Now, you talkin' 'bout findin' some long-lost cousins-in-law they can stay wit while they married. In New Yawk City. Lemme tell ya, tha's a whole dif'rent ball game, brotha. New Yawk City. The slicksters is slicker than slick. They'll chump you quick an' make you thank YOU crazy. Meanwhile, tha' boy cain't even read nor write.

WES: Cain't even read a sign say, New Yawk City. (*opens flask, takes a sip*)

LIL: I see it's botherin' you. They wouldn' be the first bumpkins to hit town. Won' be the last. Ain't nobody gon' hardly botha' 'er too fast nowhow they see tha' big levee farmhand shadow standin' 'side 'er. (*Lil washes out glasses in the sink with a wet cloth.*)

WES: (*sits*) She ain't prepared, tho'. Gon' spend all they time searchin' 'roun a city lookin' fo' two, three stray Miss'sippi negroes, in a city full a' Miss'sippi negroes, an' Alabama negroes . . .

LIL: An' Georgia negroes, Tennessee, Arkansas . . .

WES: See? Wha' chance they got, Lil?

LIL: She luv 'im enuff, she can read 'n' write fo' 'im, I guess. Shoot, if they goin', they goin'. (*sets glasses face down at sink area to dry*) Chance or none. You cain't hog tie 'em to ya, Wes. They gon' wiggle loose. I'm tellin' ya. (*wrings out cloth*) Both of 'em. One way or the otha. Happens e'ryday. Wit somebody or by theyselves. Maybe it's jus' her time fo' tha'. Her due season. (*cleans sink area with cloth*)

WES: She don' know wha' it take to be a proper wife to somebody is wha' I'm sayin'.

LIL: I know wha' chu sayin'.

WES: Mama to a chile.

LIL: It ain't easy.

WES: An' wha' if someday she gotta be both the mama an' the daddy like I did? Is it her time fo' tha'? Her due season for tha'?

LIL: Was it yours?

WES: (*stands*) She spoiled. She don' know how to do nothin' but be spoiled.

LIL: (*pauses*) Did chu know how to take care an' raise chirrun by yo'self foe' years ago? No, but chu did it anyway, an' you did it right. They two fine girls. (*folds cloth*)

WES: Listen, she can go to nursin' school then, cain't she?

LIL: I don' know. Do she like sick people? (*places folded cloth near sink*)

WES: Lil, I wanna send 'er to you in Atlanta right now, Lil. Take 'er. Take both of 'em, hear? Hear me?

LIL: I jus' stepped off the . . .

WES: I'll pay fo' e'rythang. You can put 'im both in a fine . . .

LIL: Maybe she don' even like sick people, Wes.

WES: She could teach school, then.

LIL: Wha' she wanna go wit me fo'?

WES: Eunice can keep up wit 'er music . . .

LIL: You they daddy. Why would they wanna leave you to be wit me?

WES: I'll pay for it, Lil. Dammit, I tole ya. I'll pay fo' it.

LIL: Wesley, maybe she don' wanna teach nobody's brats. Did chu ask 'er? (*takes flask from Wesley*)

WES: She have some 'erself, she gon' hafta teach 'em. Babies start comin', ain't no turnin' back.

LIL: Wes, maybe the only man Opalee wanna nurse fo' is tha' one. Maybe the only babies she evah wanna teach be theirs. (*puts cap back on flask, puts it in bag*)

WES: She ain't ole enuff to know wha' she want; wha's bes' fo' 'er.

LIL: Wha' chu tole my papa when you askt 'im fo' Clareesa? I heard e'ry word. You say, "Mistah Poole, I don' know too much myself, suh, 'bout education. No book-learnin' to evah speak of in my fam'ly; nothin'. My daddy, he workt on the levee all his life. Got kilt workin' on the levee. They called 'im Levee James at his grave 'cause James was his name, an' he got kilt on the levee. Give his life in a flood. I was workin' on tha' levee long 'side of 'im soon as I was ole enuff to walk by myself. Now, I ain't stupid 'n' dumb but, truth be tole, the most useful part a' me is always been jus' big an' strong, Mistah Poole. So, tha's wha' I got goin' or had 'til I met yo' daughter. I cain't hardly b'lieve she wanna be wit me, but she do. You know I works hard. I ain't gon' nevah quit. She gon' always eat, suh. We'd like to have yo' blessins, Mistah Poole." (*sits at table*) Plus, I ain't ready to leave noway, but I'd go tomorrow first thang you find Mamie. You want somebody to go somewhere, you can take 'em both wit chu an' Mamie. How 'bout tha'?

WES: You don' unnerstand, Lil.

LIL: I'll leave when all y'all pack up fo' Mamie's mama an' daddy's house in Spivey Kaye. Tha's wha' I'll do. They got a nice, big place 'ere. Lots a' room fo' a weddin'. Fo' two weddins. Her daddy an' all his sixteen brothas built it. Nuff room fo' a army.

WES: Lil, I cain't.

LIL: Dammit, you a tough nut to crack. (*slams hand on table*) I didn' figure there was this much work to do. (*stands, faces Wesley*) You listen 'ere, Wesley Slaton, go find tha' woman, marry 'er an' cut this single man foolishness out right now. I'll put my bags back on tha' train right behind yo's an' e'rybody can go on livin' happily evah afta'.

WES: Exac'ly wha' Mamie tell you in them letters, Lily Grace?

LIL: You know wha' she say, man. One letter one month ago an' the same thang she was tellin' you in person. That's wha'. She want chu to cut yo' ties wit this town an' y'all go 'way somewhere. Simple. She thought if you went where some fam'ly's at, a place to start ovah fresh, it might could be awright. Say she heard the white folks talkin' 'bout chu in the rest'rant, Wes. They said you dun' fo'got how to act an' you know wha' tha' means. One minute they sayin' who need to learn wha' lesson. Next thang, the lesson been taught. Dixine's boy, Tommie Mathias. His medals was still hangin' off his uniform when they cut 'im down Christmas day in '19. (*Wesley stands; moves DOWN LEFT.*)

WES: I was one of 'em tha' cut 'im down.

LIL: Speck Kimbrough got it in '20.

WES: I was 'ere.

LIL: David an' Malcom Teasley tha' same year.

WES: Know 'bout tha' too.

LIL: Toolie, Raymond's mama.

WES: I know.

LIL: Yo' friends don' wanna see y'all hurt; kilt. Did you know tha'?

WES: I ain't scared to die, Lil. (*Lil moves closer to Wesley.*)

LIL: Good, Wesley. That'll come in real handy fo' you, but do yo' chirrun feel the same way? How 'bout tha' big boy? They take 'im too jus' fo' bein' in the wrong place . . .

WES: I ain't gon' be run off. I'm not gon' do it.

LIL: Wesley, you know wha' I'm sayin' is true.

WES: Man work a place ovah twenny-somethin' years deserves wha' good come from it. Tha's true too. America say tha'. Sneed got a nice home. Why cain't I have one? This property is paid fo' now. It's mine.

LIL: Git tight-lipped an' deaf if you want to.

WES: My sweat. Poole's sweat.

LIL: Darin' Mamie to say anything to the girls about it.

WES: I'm mo' keep it.

LIL: She tried goin' to 'em anyway . . .

WES: I'm gon' keep still right 'ere on it long as I draw breath. (*sits stoically*)

LIL: But, if you say too much, they git scared, tell you, an' 'ere you go bent outta shape wit her permanently an' fo' all days. She didn' want tha'. So wha'? Tha's my two cents. Let 'im be bent outta shape. Tha's wha' I writ 'er back. You tryin' to save his life, Mamie, an' his girls. Tha's a thang you don' smoothe ovah.

WES: An' she tried e'ry kind a' smoothin' 'ere was too, Lily. B'lieve me.

LIL: Oh, I b'lieve you. I b'lieve tha' woman darn near kissed yo' feet, man. Up one toe, down the otha'. You rock-headed, tho'. An' then some. (*Wesley circles around, stands at sink. Lil continues to face him as he moves.*)

WES: I ain't gon' jus' up an' go an' leave all this married an' nothin'. I could have fifteen cryin' wives. Twenny-somethin' years, I ain't wrong. I do have a right.

LIL: They don' care nothin' 'bout cho right or yo' wrong. They say . . .

WES: They say.

LIL: Y'all so uppity now, Hard-head . . .

WES: I don' care 'bout wha' they say.

LIL: Why he go way to Tynin County to do bi'niss? Mistah Taylor dun' seent ya ovah there numerous a' times.

WES: I can do bi'niss where I wanna do bi'niss. It's my labor.

LIL: Look 'ere, Wes, sell it. Sell it, Wesley. Will ya'? Sell this place. Sell all of it.
(*Fitzhugh Marvin appears in back doorway dressed loudly and wearing an eye patch. He dusts himself then knocks on door.*)

FITZHUGH: (*calls*) Wha' ch'all tryin' to sell up in 'ere?

WES: Nobody sellin' nothin', Fitzhugh.

FITZHUGH: In tha' case, I'm comin' on in anyway. (*enters*) Hey, there!

WES: Hey yo'self. (*Lil gazes at Fitzhugh's suit.*)

LIL: Ooooh, chile. God be wit us in Jesus name, A-man.

WES: Where you goin' to all spiffied up?

FITZHUGH: To heaven, if I live right. (*strikes a pose CENTER STAGE*)

LIL: How many pockets you got on tha' thang, darlin'?

FITZHUGH: It's Fitzhugh Marvin, Miss Lil! (*does smooth soft shoe shuffle and turn*)

LIL: I see who it is.

WES: Ain't no work fo' you nowhere today, Soft Shoe?

FITZHUGH: Not today.

WES: Hmph. (*moves to window*)

FITZHUGH: I'ma peekin'. (*Fitzhugh cuffs his hands around his eyes in Lil's direction akin to looking through binoculars. Lil shoos him.*)

LIL: Gone', boy. (*Laughs. Wes goes to back door, looks out.*)

WES: This ain't the hangout. Where yo' car at? I ain't heard cho reg'lar zoom up. (*moves back into kitchen*)

LIL: Maybe he come by foot. (*Fitzhugh dusts himself again.*)

WES: He don' even walk to the outhouse no moe. Know he ain't walk no two miles.

FITZHUGH: Might did. (*takes off hat, hands it to Wes*) Come to gaze an' make 'miration.

WES: Make 'miration?

FITZHUGH: On Miss Lily Grace, thank you kindly.

LIL: On me?

WES: Oh, Lorrr. (*hangs hat on kitchen chair*)

FITZHUGH: (*to Lil*) On you a minute or two.

LIL: Tha's wha' chu all fixed up fo'? Have mercy. Thank you, Fitzhugh. (*Wes pulls Fitzhugh's eye patch.*)

WES: Do gracious.

FITZHUGH: (*flinches*) Watch out now! (*Adjusts eye patch. Wes gets coffee mug from cupboard near sink.*)

WES: You cain't but half see on a clear day. How you gon' do some gazin' an' makin' 'miration wit one eyeball?

FITZHUGH: Tha's fo' you to watch an' learn, Question Man. (*Wesley moves to stove, pours coffee from pot. To Lil:*) Turn it aroun' fo' me, Heartstring.

WES: You keep talkin', fresh-mouth . . .

FITZHUGH: Awh, shucks now. Fresh-mouth . . . (*laughs*)

WES: She gon' heartstring you somethin' good in tha' there bag yondah. (*sips, crosses back to table, sits*)

FITZHUGH: Well, wha'evah you got good fo' me, I'm read' ta see.

LIL: You ain't gon' fall out then, is you? You so dawg-gone ready. (*Turns, moves to stove. Fitzhugh takes Lil's hand.*)

FITZHUGH: Shoot, I'm 'bout to cut the buck, cool as I feel. Atlanta ain't doin' you no harm, Lily Grace. (*kisses Lil's hand*)

LIL: (*laughs*) Awh, leave tha' alone an' come hug my neck, man. (*pulls hand away, extends arms*) Ain't no game 'ere. (*Lil and Fitzhugh embrace.*)

FITZHUGH: Yes, ma'am. Yes, ma'am. Cain't fool you wo'th a dime, can I?

LIL: Nawh, suh.

FITZHUGH: Cain't even give it to ya.

LIL: Not on a golden platter wit a apple stuck in yo' mouth. (*They let go of embrace.*)

WES: Wha' chu want, Spote?

FITZHUGH: A cup a' coffee maybe. Have a' ole friend tell a man 'bout Atlanta hap'nins. (*twirls Lil around once*) I likes to be up on my news. (*Hums. Lil picks up pot from stove, moves to sink.*)

WES: Git chu a newspaper, then.

FITZHUGH: (*to Lil*) Now tha' I got my motorcar . . .

WES: Runnin' 'roun beggin' coffee off workin' folk.

FITZHUGH: I'm mo' be up on all the stuff. (*Lil gets mug from cupboard, prepares to pour from pot into mug.*)

WES: Ain't no free coffee up in 'ere fo' no free-loader wearin' a' ole eye patch. (*Lil pauses. Wesley stands with mug, exits out back door. He sits on porch steps, sips.*)

FITZHUGH: (*calls*) Tha's so's peoples'll stop callin' me cock-eyed.

LIL: Is it workin'? (*continues to pour*)

FITZHUGH: They have stopped callin' me Cock-eyed Fitzhugh.

LIL: Tha's good.

FITZHUGH: Now, they callin' me Cock-eyed Fitzhugh wit a Patch. (*Lil laughs.*) But I'm tryin' hard to change my image, Miss Lil.

LIL: Change yo' image.

FITZHUGH: Ole Cock-eyed Fitzhugh don' wanna' be Cock-eyed Fitzhugh no moe. No respect in tha'.

LIL: Uh-huh . . . (*puts mug with coffee on table for Fitzhugh*)

FITZHUGH: 'Sides, I ain't nevah had no cock-eye in the first place. See? (*Lil sits at table.*) Still ain't. Y'all knowed me all my life. (*holds up patch*) Is I evah had a cock-eye, Miss Lil? Say?

LIL: (*looks*) Nawh, you right. Not a truly cock-eye. Jus' a sleepy eye.

FITZHUGH: Yeah, a sleepy eye; yeah. (*takes jacket off, hangs it over back of chair*) Plus, ain't even ole neitha. Ole Cock-eyed Fitzhugh. Tell you wha'. From now on, I jus' wanna be plain Mistah Marvin, or Mistah Fitzhugh, or Mistah Fitzhugh Marvin.

LIL: (*picks up small basket of biscuits on stove*) Want a biscuit 'ere, Mistah Marvin?

FITZHUGH: I'm tryin' to fix my mind on upliftstation. (*Lil hands basket forward.*) No
  thank you on tha' biscuit, Miss Lil. Coffee's jus' fine an' dandy. (*sips from mug*)
LIL: (*takes biscuits back to stove*) Uplift who?
FITZHUGH: Upliftstation. Lookin' up. Lookin' upwards. Progressin'. Like you . . .
  (*calls*) Big Wes On The Back Porch! I been waitin' on the right sit'ation. (*Lil sets
  another coffee mug on the table.*) The right opportunity to present itself, reveal itself
  to me like out the Bible. (*Lil picks up coffee pot from stove, goes to table, pours.*) Like
  the Word say. Say you s'posed to wait on 'im to tell you where you s'posed to go,
  an' when an' how. Wait on 'im. Then, move yo' one foot fo'ward one step so's he
  can take the two moe he promised. You wait on 'im, he say. Wait on 'im an' he'll
  make you a fisher a' men. (*He exits onto back porch. Lil watches Fitzhugh exit, places
  coffee pot back on stove.*) Look at cho yard, Wes. I look. I think 'bout wha' kind a'
  flowers bloom this time.
WES: Them Clareesa's flowers. She planted 'em.
FITZHUGH: E'ry year, it be dif'rent. Somethin' amazin'.
WES: They come up 'er way.
FITZHUGH: Exac'ly. This yo' dream show place. Yo's an' Miss Clareesa's. I try not to
  work too hard fo' anybody outsides a' myself. Save the best a' wha' I got fo' me.
  Tha's awright too, ain't it? (*Lil gets cigarettes, exits through back door, lights up, stretches.*)
WES: (*stands*) We saved our money 'stead a' spendin' it on clothes an' troublesome
  junk we didn' need. Where yo' car at, Fitzhugh? (*moves into back yard*)
FITZHUGH: Loaned out.
WES: Said we gon' surprise Lil, ride 'er ovah to the church dinner tonight innit. How
  we gon' do tha', Fitz?
FITZHUGH: I'm mo' have it back way 'foe night this time, Wes. Promise.
WES: Loaned out to who? Like I don' already know.
FITZHUGH: Then, why you ask me?
WES: He gon' give it back this time?
FITZHUGH: He gon' give it back. Don' he always give it back?
WES: Wit moonshine an' who knows wha' else all ovah the back seat. We s'posed
  to wash it up an' clean it out this afternoon. Darn near need new upholstery
  an' you ain't had the car three months. He dun' borrowed it foe', five times. Tell
  'im to go buy his own. He like yo's so much, Clipper got fifteen moe in his yard
  read' to sell. Them two, three dollars he give you to borrow it, he oughta save,
  buy his own. Git his daddy to buy 'im one. In fact, his sick ole daddy got one he
  ain't usin'. Go drive it. Pour shine on it. Tell 'im to go to hell next time he ask.
  You scared a' tha' lil' imbecile.
FITZHUGH: I ain't scared a' tha' boy.
WES: I'll tell 'im tha' fo' you. He IS a boy. Ain't nobody scared a' him. Not him, or
  his sick daddy AN' they redneck friends. Them two, three dollars he tho' at cha,
  you buy them cheap clown suits wit. How 'bout they call you Mistah Circus
  Clown, then?
FITZHUGH: They ain't cheap.

WES: He didn' even wanna pay you the last time, did he? I ain't havin' Lil ride in no . . .

FITZHUGH: (*calls*) Nothin' wrong wit my suit is it, Miss Lil?

LIL: Nothin' a good brushin' down won' cure. (*Fitzhugh goes back into kitchen. Lil puts out cigarette, re-enters kitchen.*) Wha' kinda work do you do, Fitzhugh? (*Wes moves onto porch; stands at door, sips from mug.*)

FITZHUGH: Oh, I run errands. Odd jobs man. A piece a' this. A lil' bit o' tha'. I'm gon' do some high-toned food servicin', Lil Grace. Some big-time appetite quenchin'. Yes, ma'am. I got all kinda plans in the works an' it's gon' hap'n, too. It's gon' hap'n. I got me a motorcar an' three good suits. I dun' took my step.

LIL: Tha's the step God tole you to take.

FITZHUGH: Miss Lil, if you know you goin' to church on Sunday mornin', you bes' wash yo' dirty neck, an' the bottoms of yo' feet on Sat'day night. I'm ready, I say. An investment in my own blessins. (*finishes coffee, puts mug in sink*)

LIL: Okay, wha' chu know 'bout some cookin', then? (*sits at table*)

FITZHUGH: Well . . . (*sits at table*) I know if it ain't burnt completely up, it's awright. It ain't gon' kill you.

LIL: You cain't serve awright-won'-kill-you to nobody. Most folks can git better than tha' at home.

FITZHUGH: I b'lieve a plate a' burnt food from time to time is good fo' the digestion. (*Wes laughs.*)

LIL: Since when? Wha' fool tole you tha'?

FITZHUGH: I b'lieve I heard a bona fide doctor said tha'.

LIL: You tryin' to kill somebody, boy.

FITZHUGH: No, I ain't.

LIL: I workt fo' a doctor an' his wife an' he ain't nevah askt th' cook to burn up the dinner.

FITZHUGH: I can fry a mean fish tho', Miss Lil.

LIL: Not one time.

FITZHUGH: I can fry a mean fish; tasty. Cain't I, Wes?

WES: Yes, he can at tha'.

FITZHUGH: An' you tole 'bout the big fry tomorrow, didn' you? (*Wes nods, sips.*)

LIL: He didn' say it was no BIG fish fry.

FITZHUGH: All fo' you.

LIL: Gon' kill up a whole bunch a' folks wit some burnt fish all fo' me. (*laughs, goes to back door, takes Wes's mug, goes to sink*)

FITZHUGH: Oh, it's gon' rip. It's gon' roar. You'll see. Gon' git a gal to do the cookin', tho', anyhow. I ain't worried 'bout tha'. I'm mo' hire me somebody good when I start my enterprise. How 'bout chu, Miss Lil? Want the job? (*Lil washes out mugs, dries them.*)

LIL: Me? I ain't nevah been crazy 'bout a cookin' sit'ation. (*Wes re-enters the kitchen.*)

WES: Listen to the rest a' the scheme, Lil. Tell 'er 'bout it, Fitz.

FITZHUGH: Well, my thought is maybe I git married an' she do all the cookin' fo' free.

LIL: Tha's a pitiful, fool excuse fo' gettin' married, Fitzhugh honey. I'm surprised. You a stunt-puller after all.

FITZHUGH: Nawh, nawh . . .

LIL: Who wants a stunt-puller?

FITZHUGH: A good church girl wha' ain't gon' steal from me, 'cause wha's mine is already hers, an' wha's hers is already mine, see? An' wha' make it so sweet is somethin' happen to me, she git the whole deal. She got a ready-made bi'niss 'cause I had it 'foe I had her, unnerstand?

LIL: I unnerstand stunt-pullin' all day long.

FITZHUGH: Nawh, now. Look, now. Listen, she git me, an' the bi'niss . . .

WES: An' yo' clothes.

FITZHUGH: An' my car! (*Wes laughs, moves to Fitzhugh.*) HAH! I'm darn near the answer all way 'roun, ain't I? (*Wes puts his arm around Fitzhugh's shoulder.*) She might not git vast rich off of me, but she won' be no pauper. Not unduh my care an' jurisdiction. Not wit wha' I got to offer.

WES: An' maybe y'all git vast rich at tha'.

FITZHUGH: Maybe. (*to Lil*) But I don' want no ugly girl, now. Cain't wake up to it. Lawd no. She gots ta cook an' be easy on the eye, see? I'm mo' go ovah 'ere to the church meetin' tonight an' check out the talent.

LIL: Tell you wha'. If God do indeed take care a' all fools an' lil' chirrun, Fitz, then you an' me gon' be jus' fine. (*Fitzhugh strokes his suit, laughs.*)

Act 1

Scene 2

LIGHTS DIM indicating night. SOUND OF crickets; the peace of natural nightlife is underscored by a honky-tonk tune playing in the distance. Lil hums the tune, stumbles slightly through front door barefoot, carrying her hat and shoes, hangs hat on rack at door, drops shoes on floor, makes her way into kitchen. Wes sits at table bare-chested. His fingers fondle an empty shot glass and a half-smoked cigar. He stands when he hears Lil enter.

WES: Where you been, Lil?

LIL: Nowhere special, Wesley. Alley Pats. (*goes to back door, cleans sand from her feet with hands*)

WES: Them roadhouses dangerous. It's Friday night.

LIL: I know wha' night it is.

WES: We been wonderin' 'bout chu, Lil. One minute we standin' 'ere talkin' to the Rev'rend Sykes. The next e'rybody look up, you dun' walkt off wit Ftizhugh, they say. Coulda' stayed at the house, if you wann't comf'table.

LIL: Seein' as how all them Christians wuz waitin' on me, tha' wouldn'ta been a very Christian-like thang to do. Y'all dun' talkt me up so to e'rybody.

WES: We drove all ovah lookin' fo' ya. Girls so worried, they didn' wanna go to bed. Had to make 'em go to bed.

LIL: You ain't gon' make me feel bad, now. Ooh, don' it feel good to walk bare. Fitzhugh car run outta gas, motor broke down; somethin'. I tells 'im fo'git it. Go on. Don' worry 'bout me. I'm mo' walk home an' tha's wha' I did. He couldn' stop me. Stretched my toes out. Skin on the ground. On the cool, white sand. On the cool, cool ground. (*gets broom, sweeps sand out of back door*)

WES: Folks git juiced up an' crazy-actin' . . .

LIL: Wha' you comin' afta' me fo'. I'm awright.

WES: You drunk, Lil.

LIL: (*stops sweeping*) An' all you got in tha' there glass is fresh spring water. (*puts broom away, goes to sink, pumps water into her hands*) Hey, 'membuh wha' my papa say when we pulled up on you on the road tha' day? He say . . . (*to Wes*) Wha' he say? (*laughs*) He say, "Boy, you need some decent work?" An' you say, "Mistah, I didn' thank I was doin' somethin' indecent but yes, suh. I b'lieve I could use a piece a' steady work at tha'. Do wit ma' hands. Git down in the dirt." You wannit to work wit cho hands on his daughters.

WES: I didn' know nothin' 'bout y'all. I ain't seen but one, an' tha' one was you.

LIL: I wann't the answer tho', was I?

WES: You was too young, Lil.

LIL: When you seent my sistah. Now, Clareesa woulda' sho' nuff cut chu up then, you took me ovah her, wouldn' she?

WES: Who you gon' show how to act like a lady when you reelin' in the street yo' own self? Huh?

LIL: Maybe there ain't no such thang as a lady, Wes. Maybe it's jus' mens an' wom- ans havin' sense enuff to know when somethin' right need doin', figgerin' out jus' wha' tha' right thing is they need to do an' then, havin' the courage to do said same right thang. (*gets glass from sink, sets it on table*) Mamie is a lady. Faith- ful, heart-givin'. Yeah . . . (*goes to icebox, takes out water pitcher*) I'm glad she left, 'cause if you was evah gon' askt 'er to be yo' wife, you'da done it by now. A man know wha' he wants when he wants it anyway. Y'all stand firm on tha'. (*pours water into glass, puts pitcher on table*) An' if he don' know, he ain't wo'th bein' both- ered wit nohow. (*picks up glass*) Wastin' all yo' valuable time. 'Specially a rock- head like ole Wesley Slaton. (*Lil sips.*) Miss Mamie wit the motorcar. (*puts glass on table*) How she wind up chasin' you is wha' I wonduh. You was sniffin' 'roun 'er dress tail, correct? She wann't payin' you no dif'rence. No moe than a hi an' a good-bye on Sundays. But time she put a smile wit it, show some teeth, let chu start holdin' 'er hand in public, let peoples see ya sittin' wit 'er in church, step- pin' out wit 'er, stayin' ovah an' whatnot, you start pullin' away, talkin' 'bout bein' busy. Wha' chu tell 'er? You not clear? You confused? Yeah, you don' know wha' day it is when it comes to HER but, when it comes to this farm place, you'll lay yo' life down. You know you got ta hit it e'ry mornin' 'foe daybreak an' you git right on up to it too. Don' chu see, Rock-head? E'ry woman wants somethin' special, Wesley. Somebody that'll put his hand on yo' foe'head, check yo' tem- perature when ya don' feel so good. Pick you some honey-suckle sometime. Fix you a cup a' coffee when the day been extra long. Tha's wha' special mean. Tha's all it is. Nothin' fancy. Somebody you ain't got to beg to be nice to you 'cause tha's wha' they live fo'. (*sits*) You knew 'bout tha' when you married Clareesa. I know you did.

WES: I did. It wann't gon' nevah work out wit me an' Mamie, Lil.

LIL: Why?

WES: I was walkin' aroun' wit the thought in my head fo' months. Askt 'er. Askt 'er. She'll help you wit the girls full-time, be the mama they need. Explain thangs I cain't, but somethin' . . . somethin' . . . missin'. Selfish. I know I was selfish. (*sits*) But cookin' an' makin' pies ain't the answer to all thangs. Tha's not a woman. Tha's a hound dawg waitin' on you to come home, layin' on a rug by the doe wit its tongue hangin' out, wishin' you would bless 'er wit yo' presence; waitin' on some scraps. Tha's not a woman.

LIL: Mens comp'ny. (*stands*) Wha' ABOUT mens comp'ny? I ain't met a one could look past his own ego long enuff to claim the great prize tha' is me. I don' know wha's wrong. I don' thank I rise too high, nor fall too cheap, but I expec' I mus' give 'em too much hell to pay anyway 'cause I'm by myself. See, I'm the type give my whole heart an' it comes back on me in a thousand lil' broke glass pieces e'ry time. Guess it jus' ain't fo' me, 'cause I cain't. I won' do it. I will not give myself away like a sack a' ole potatoes. I cain't do tha'. I am wo'th some effort still. Even now. There is somebody somewhere in this world who sees an' unnerstands tha'; who know a good woman on sight, an' will vow to keep 'er come wha' may. I was sho' you could use a new wife by now, but I thank you dun' up an' married this house. I b'lieve tha's it. I b'lieve you thank it's all right 'ere in this kitchen, in this backyard, upstairs in the bed wit yo' baby girls in they flannel drawers, an' they long, to-the-floe, stainless steel night gowns buttoned clean up to they hairlines, an' you gon' let the white folks kill you behind it ta boot.

WES: I'm not runnin' from nothin' an' nobody.

LIL: WALKIN' 'roun 'ere on yo' pride, then. Prince Wesley. KING Wesley. You fool. Watch 'em stomp it right into the ground.

WES: Not gon' have my girls see me run.

LIL: I have heard an' heard. You a man. You ain't runnin'.

WES: I'm mo' be a man in they eyes long as I live. Lose e'rythang me an' they mama workt fo'? E'rythang yo' papa workt fo'?

LIL: Don' put my papa in this. He'd tell you to git thee the hell on.

WES: (*stands*) No, he wouldn'. Poole stood his ground. This place belong to my girls, an' they chirrun', an' they chirrun's chirrun. Tha's fair. Tha's jus'. Tha's how it's gon' be . . .

LIL/WES: Long as . . .

LIL: You draw breath. (*PAUSE.*) I don' rightly know wha' to do 'bout chu after all. Wha' the hell is I'm doin' down 'ere? Gon' git myself kilt. I'm gon' pack my bags . . . (*moves to exit kitchen*)

WES: I ain't like you. I ain't runnin'.

LIL: When ole man Sneed come at me, I had to run. Eitha tha' or have his chirrun'. Tha's why I ain't lived 'ere since foe'teen years ole. He come up on me. He say, "Do it right, I leave Poole alone." (*Wes moves closer to Lil.*)

WES: You didn' nevah tell nobody tha'.

LIL: We dun' cut enuff a' our peoples down out the trees.

WES: We thought chu runned off 'cause a' me an' Clareesa, then 'ere come a new baby, an' e'rythang takin' up extra space.

LIL: How I'm mo' begrudge a baby two inches wo'th a' room?

WES: So, tha's why you . . .

LIL: Wha' chance I have? I fetch an' carry fo' rich white women. I fix they hair, an' keep they clothes, an' hear they crap 'bout how they husbands dirty low-down, but they got the bank account so, they the ones laughin'. I been e'rywhere; e'rywhere. If I'm runnin', an' I been so many places, how come I ain't no furtha' way than Atlanta now? No chirrun'. No husband to luv' me proper. Heck, I can go an' stay wherevah it is I want to long as I can wash some ma'am's clothes but, I'm tired, an' I'm lost. I'm lost. An' I want some peace. Nevah nothin' but clean up an' cook an' wait on people. I can read. I can write. I can count. Wha' else could I do, could I be if I had the chance? Wesley? Wha' is there fo' me to do wit my life? Huh? You knowed me when I was fresh, an' not patched an' half put back togetha' like I am now. Was I pretty? Really? Was I? Was I smart? Sho' nuff? I was, wann't I? Oh, the music I coulda' made. Why didn' you choose me? (*moves DOWNSTAGE CENTER*) "Do it right," he whispered. Leaned down to me in my childhood an' whispered, "I let cho daddy live. I let cho sistah have 'er baby; keep 'er man. Let cho mama keep 'er house. Do it right." Trapped. Outside. Roadhouse ain't no dangerous place fo' Lil; nawh. Open fields. Now, them places is dangerous. (*Wesley moves up behind Lil. Lil turns to exit, faces Wesley. Wesley caresses her face in his hands.*)

LIGHTS DIM

Intermission

Act 2

Scene 1

Early morning the next day. Wesley chops wood in back yard while singing in gandy rhythm.

WES: (*sings*)

> Met a girl . . .
> Name Lil Grace . . .
> Met a girl . . .

Got a pretty face . . .
Got brown eyes . . .
Got round hips . . .
Got rosy cheeks . . .
An' red lips . . .

(*Lil appears on porch in a robe. Wes continues singing.*)

She got a razor . . .
Gon' cut chu up . . .
Got a razor . . .
But she's a baby pup . . .
'Cause she ain't mean . . .
Not mean to me . . .
She ain't mean . . .
Couldn' nevah be . . .

LIL: Man, wha' chu doin'?

WES: Thought somebody might like a lil' gandy wit the mornin' coffee, woman.

LIL: Where you pick up gandy from? (*She descends stairs into yard. Wes drops the axe, moves toward Lil.*)

WES: Oh, I did some a' e'rythang fo' I landed 'ere. Railroad, rag-picker. Sellin' Apple Jack, Pomade, beggin', driftin'. (*kisses Lil, cradles her in his arms*)

LIL: Wes, you wann't lookin' fo' my sistah last night, was ya? I didn' disappoint cha, did I?

WES: How you talk.

LIL: But, chu want me, tho'?

WES: Want chu? Wann't it e'rythang you thought it oughta be?

LIL: Was it e'rythang you thought it oughta be? I'm askin'.

WES: Didn' the sky open up an' the clouds start circlin' 'roun goin' whoop-de-whoop, girl?

LIL: This ain't funny to me.

WES: I'm not laughin'. I promise you.

LIL: I don' mean jus' fo' one night, Wesley. I mean fo' a long time. A lifetime. You want me? Say it so I know where I'm standin'.

WES: Yes, I want chu. (*They embrace.*) Hole up a minute. (*He goes to gramophone in living room, checks record, gives it a good crank. SOUND OF music playing.*)

LIL: (*calls*) Now I'm really wonderin' wha' it is you s'posed to be doin'.

WES: (*calls*) Waitin' on you. (*He dances about the room. Lil enters. Wes pulls her toward him.*) Waitin' on you. (*They move together slowly. Wes twirls Lil. She giggles.*)

LIL: Where the girls at?

WES: O took 'em shoppin'. They makin' up a special dessert fo' the fish fry tonight. (*tries to pull Lil close again*)

LIL: (*stops*) You tole 'em? (*gasps, steps back*) They heard us?

WES: Well, wit all tha' there hollin' you was doin' in the backyard last night . . .

LIL: Me?

WES: Like somebody found heaven on earth.

LIL: Who the one hollin' fo' they heavenly fatha?

WES: I don' doubt somebody heard somethin'.

LIL: Awh . . . maybe they'll thank they dreamed it.

WES: Maybe they'll thank two wild dawgs was out back doin' laundry in the moon-light, an' callin' fo' Jesus to come hep' 'em wit the clothes line. (*Wes laughs, hugs Lil.*) Calm down, baby. O somewhere wit 'em pickin' berries an' whatnot.

LIL: You a heathen an' a half, Sir Wesley. I swan. (*buries her head in his chest*)

WES: An' you a roadhouse dollie, Lady Lil. (*Lil swats Wes playfully.*) Awh, wann't nothin' they didn' already know was comin' the minute chu stepped in 'ere, Auntee. You was home. Who couldn' see tha'? Home fo' good.

LIL: Wha' I see, wha' I hear, Clareesa kickin' the covers off us.

WES: Nawh.

LIL: The ghosts gon' ramble wit me, I tell ya.

WES: No ghosts waitin' to haint chu, honey.

LIL: Mama's pots 'n' pans rattlin'.

WES: Not 'ere.

LIL: Daddy.

WES: No, ma'am. Not in this house. If it's yo' mama an' daddy, an' Clareesa callin' to ya, they only tellin' you not to run from me, Lil. (*He takes Lil around the waist, pulls her toward him.*) Don' run from me, baby; don'. Togetha' we got time. Togetha' we strength. (*They dance. The record stops. Wes continues to hold on to Lil.*)

LIL: Wes, the gramophone. . . . You better go on outta 'ere 'n' meet Fitzhugh.

WES: Where he at?

LIL: (*leading Wes into kitchen*) Any later all the fish'll be gone. (*goes to sink, picks up sand-wich wrapped in brown butcher's paper*)

WES: Tell Fitz to meet me at the spot, okay? (*moves to back porch. Lil follows.*)

LIL: Okay. (*Wes picks up fishing tools from porch. Lil hands Wes the sandwich bag. Wes takes it, exits stage whistling. Fitzhugh enters through the front door disheveled. He leans on sofa, attempts to straighten his appearance. Lil hums in the kitchen. Fitzhugh makes his way to kitchen.*)

FITZHUGH: Hey, there.

LIL: (*looks up*) Well, hey there yo'self. Dad-gum, boy. Wha' chu do? Sleep in yo' car? Come on, sit down 'ere. (*Fitzhugh moves slowly toward table, eases into chair.*) Man, you need some a' this right quick. (*Lil gets a mug, pours in coffee from stove.*) Nice 'n' hot.

FITZHUGH: Jus' like I need it, Lil. (*She puts the mug on the table in front of Fitzhugh.*)

LIL: I see. (*She gets the sugar bowl and a spoon from sink area, puts them on table. Fitzhugh opens sugar bowl, gets a spoonful out. His hand shakes.*) You better eat somethin' too, hear? (*He puts sugar in coffee, stirs slowly.*) No sense in you fallin' out, sittin' in the hot heat, fo' no fish fry. (*She gets a small plate of biscuits from stove, puts it on table in front of Fitzhugh.*)

FITZHUGH: No, ma'am. No sense. Thank you. (*sips coffee slowly*)

LIL: (*sits at table*) Ooh, but we got full last night didn' we, Fitz? (*Fitz nods, takes a bit of biscuit. Lil laughs.*) Lorr, how country folk do luv to look at a pulpit all day an' night long. Shoot, the whole Sunday ain't even enuff fo' 'em. They got to pick on Tuesday, Wednesday, Thursday . . . They'da whooped 'n' hollered 'til the wee hours if Rev'rend Sykes hadn' fell asleep 'n' started slobbin' on hisself. An' wha' about tha' Rev'rend Sykes, tho'? He 'bout kilt me. (*stands, mimics*) An' now, sponsored by our good, sanctified neighbor an' holy friend Mistah Wesley Slaton, I humbly present to y'all our sweet 'n' angelic sistah, Lily Grace Hoterfield, who is visitin' wit us this evenin' from Atlanta, where she has been livin' an' enjoyin' a righteous, biblical life in Christ. Yes, yes! Fresh outta the pages a' both testaments I'm sho'. In the name a' Jesus. A-man. (*She sits. Fitzhugh laughs, sips.*) Tell me somethin', Fitz. How they feel about Wes 'roun 'ere?

FITZHUGH: Who?

LIL: Wesley. How they feel about 'im?

FITZHUGH: How who feel about 'im?

LIL: You know the group.

FITZHUGH: Folks look up to 'im.

LIL: Them tha' don' want chu to have nothin' wo'th nothin', Fitzhugh.

FITZHUGH: Oh, you mean Taylor an' them othas. (*sets coffee mug down*)

LIL: How many othas?

FITZHUGH: A few moe a' the type. They already tryin' to build some new government roads thu' two or three peoples' places right now.

LIL: (*stands*) How come tha' ain't the clue fo' y'all to start lookin' fo' somethin' new to do, then?

FITZHUGH: But, we don' wanna' leave, if you talkin' 'bout leavin'.

LIL: Wha's so fab'lous 'bout this place? Huh? How many hints do y'all need? Shoot, they didn' hardly wanna' leave neitha, did they? Them two or three peoples. But push come to dawg-gone shove. Pushers 'n' shovers. Bullies. See? They forcin' you out anyway. Forcin'. A lil' bit a' relocation money out of it if at all. Jus' two, three dollars apiece, right? Why do y'all put up wit this?

FITZHUGH: Ain't nobody puttin' up wit nothin' now, Lil. The otha mens, Wes included, we been meetin' in secret to plan out some sort a' strategy against it.

LIL: Wha' kinda strategy?

FITZHUGH: Stand our ground. Be firm. Calm 'til we see wha' they next move gon' be.

LIL: Oh, Lorrr. Tha's why the car bi'niss?

FITZHUGH: I mean . . .

LIL: Have mercy on my soul. Being calm but firm . . .

FITZHUGH: I don' own no land now but . . .

LIL: I don' know why they ain't swooped down in 'ere already . . .

FITZHUGH: Someday soon, it's gon' be about me too so . . .

LIL: An' cleaned you all out like they did Rosewood.

FITZHUGH: Tha's why you ain't been back 'ere in foe' years? Since Clareesa died?

LIL: You don' know wha' chu doin'. There are some places you can go to where they don' pull you thru the streets at least.

FITZHUGH: Like St. Louis? Florida? Oklahoma? Where is it dif'rent, Lil? Chicago? Atlanta?

LIL: Meetins' in secret. Strategy, my ass. Y'all thank y'all in charge down 'ere. Y'all ain't in charge.

FITZHUGH: Washington, D.C. where the capitol is? Where the President of the United States live?

LIL: Yes. Take yo' lil' chicken 'n' fish shack up to the President a' the United States. Tha's wha' chu do.

FITZHUGH: Tell us where it be better. I'll be the first one in line to go, pullin' my good buddy an' all his wit me. In the meantime, seem like givin' up one hard time fo' anotha is all we'd be doin'. Tough to choose by me. By Big Wes. This our home. These our friends.

LIL: You can git some new friends, an' people leave home all the time, Fitz. Cain't suck on yo' mama's teet all yo' life.

FITZHUGH: I nevah knew my mama.

LIL: I didn' mean it like tha'. I'm sorry.

FITZHUGH: See, it's enuff to say, "How 'bout us all pack up an' go way," but you askin' a man like Wesley to work in somebody's factory. Somebody's shoe shop. Somebody's fish 'n' chicken shack. Tha's a long way down fo' a man like Big Wes. Who he gon' be if he cain't be Wesley? Our lives in this town, an' the history of this world have always been push you 'ere, pull me there. Some folks go an' come back. If wha' chu want ain't 'ere, then why you do tha'? Why you give up the free life in Atlanta? I know you not goin' back. Yo' heart not innit an' I'll tell you why. 'Cause this a place where you can crawl up in its arms, let e'ry bit of it cover you like a blanket an' close yo' eyes an' say, "I'm not invisible e'rywhere. Somebody knows an' cares about me right 'ere."

LIL: You luv yo'self some Wesley, don' cha?

FITZHUGH: I listen to 'im. I don' always heed 'im 'cause, at the end a' the day, a man's got to take his own stand in life. He got to go 'head an' do wha' he got to do to make his own world go 'roun.

LIL: Wes thank a lot a' you too.

FITZHUGH: Treat me like a lil' brotha or somethin'. I ain't nevah had a brotha, or a sistah or nothin' but tha' ole, low-down cousin raised me 'n' beat on me; broke up my eye. So, I 'preciate bein' kinda watched out fo', even if he do talk gruff at me now 'n' then.

LIL: Lil' Fitzhugh. I swan. I can see yo' low-down cousin draggin' you by the collar thu' the street like yesterday. You know, I couldn' nevah stand tha'. In fact, I cursed 'er out one time.

FITZHUGH: I know.

LIL: A lil', sawed-off nothin' wit no teeth. I wondered afterwards if I had made it any worse on ya.

FITZHUGH: Couldn' ta got no worse.

LIL: Hmph. I askt papa. I said, "Fitzhugh got tha' ole, mean, nasty cousin, Papa. Cain't he come stay wit us?" Papa say, "Fam'ly's fam'ly, an we ain't gon' meddle in they bi'niss, but don' worry. One day real soon, young Fitz gon' grow up an' beat the hell outta HER an' that'll be the end a' tha' right quick."

FITZHUGH: I'da been pleased an' proud to join y'all's household. I thank you fo' the good thoughts. Used to see you too. Watch chu watchin' Big Wes. He'd be totin' some big somethin', an' I'd thank, "No chance wit Lily Grace."

LIL: Wha'?

FITZHUGH: "Lily Grace in luv."

LIL: No such a' thang. Wha' chu talkin' 'bout?

FITZHUGH: Ain't nobody mentionin' 'bout hard times no moe at this table today. The draggin' is ovah, say Lil? Lily Grace back in town. To stay. Hope you of a mind to have a nice time tonight.

LIL: Watch yo'self wit tha' car sit'ation.

FITZHUGH: I'll be awright. God takes care a' fools 'an' lil' chirrun.

LIL: Then you 'n' me gon' be jus' fine. (*hugs Fitzhugh*)

FITZHUGH: Well, I'm mo' git on down to the fishin' now. Thank you so much fo' the breakfast.

LIL: Ooh, wait . . . (*goes into icebox*) Y'all got somethin' to drank? (*Fitzhugh stands, steadies himself, holds his side, sways.*) Fitz? (*Fitzhugh collapses on floor.*) Fitzhugh?! (*Goes to Fitzhugh, opens his jacket. It's blood soaked.*) Oh . . . Fitz, wha' . . . (*Fitzhugh tries to get up.*) No, don' chu move. I'm goin' to git a doctor or somebody . . .

FITZHUGH: Nawh, don' git nobody. Ain't no doctor. Help me to the chair. I'll be awright. I git cleaned up, I'll be awright. (*extends his arm*)

LIL: You need moe than cleanin' up. Don' chu move, I said. I need some bandages. Don' chu move, now. Don' chu move. (*Lil exits from living room through doorway OFFSTAGE RIGHT.*)

SOUND OF wild whooping coming from a car passing rapidly. Fitzhugh stands, gets Wesley's shotgun from behind the icebox. He stumbles out the back door. Lil enters kitchen with a clean shirt and assorted rags, pauses, goes into back yard.

LIL: (*calls*) Fitzhugh! (*circles around the house, calls*) Fitzhugh!

WES: (*enters back yard, calls*) Yeah, where is Fitzhugh? I know who was makin' all tha' noise. (*He puts fishing gear on back porch, wipes his feet on mat, and enters the house.*)

LIL: (*calls*) Wes!

WES: (*calls*) Lil! Where you at, girl? (*sees blood around the room*) Cut yo'self? Lil!? (*He pulls another shotgun from behind the icebox, exits front door. Wes heads Lil off in the front yard.*) I thought chu wuz . . . Wha' hap'ned 'ere?

LIL: Fitzhugh. He shouldn' be stumblin' aroun'. He need a doctor bad.

WES: Stumblin'?

LIL: Bes' we can do is git 'im to a doctor quick as we can! (*SOUND OF gunshot*)

WES: Fitzhugh! (*He runs offstage. Lil follows.*)

LIGHTS DIM

Act 2

Scene 2

Lil enters carrying a large carpet bag in each hand, sets them down at front door. SOUND OF truck horn beeping loudly twice. She looks out of the window.

LIL: Thank God they're back. (*She stands at front door. Wes pushes past, carrying both shotguns.*)

WES: Y'all got to git outta 'ere today. (*He moves toward kitchen; Lil follows.*) E'rybody in the truck.

LIL: Fitzhugh too? Did chu find Fitzhugh? (*Wes drops shotguns on the table.*)

WES: Fitzhugh dead.

LIL: Nawh . . .

WES: Here, buy 'em wha'evah they need. (*takes out money tin*)

LIL: Wha' hap'ned?

WES: I buried 'im.

LIL: Buried 'im? Who . . . ? (*Wes hands Lil the tin.*)

WES: Here . . .

LIL: No, tell me!

WES: Take this money. NOW! Hear me? (*Lil pushes money tin away.*) Now! You got to git chu an' them chirrun' outta 'ere! They waitin'. (*puts money tin on table*)

LIL: Tell me! (*Wes moves DOWNSTAGE, faces audience in SPOTLIGHT.*)

LIGHTS DIM on kitchen area.

WES: I followed tire 'n' blood marks off the road 'n' down to the shallow end a' the creek. The tracks were familiar, 'n' the trail was hot. Still full a' half-flyin' dust-dirt an' hibiscus bushes been runned ovah, pulverized then whipped up wit the fast motion a' tha' foe'-wheel, trail-makin' contraption. There young Sneed sit in Fitzhugh car head cocked, legs crossed 'n' barefoot justa' swingin'. Fingers knitted behind his bump-knotted head, lookin' at the twisted red a' his neck like a game a' good luxury earned offa hard day's work, whistlin' 'n' singin' some kinda crazy, devil tune.

(*SOUND OF a tune whistled*)

I recognized my good shotgun layin' high 'cross the thigh part a' this monkey lap. How he git it, tho'? "Dammit," I reckon. "Fitzhugh dun' give this boy my property," I think. Wit MY stuff. Wit Fitzhugh's equipment. This devil's monkey layin' back, tellin' time wha' to do 'n' time seem't willin'. It oughta be ashamed the way time look like it 'low 'im so much; sit at ease wit stink, moonshine fumes scapin' thru the very holes a' his lizard skin. Whippin' 'roun time' nose an' time beggin', chompin' at the bit to smell it. Sneed, he dictatin' to time an' all, "I am in charge a' how the world TURNS." It don' even mean nothin' to 'im tha' somethin' or somebody might be watchin'; approachin'. 'Cause he was satisfied, I tell you. I touched the rail a' tha' mobile an' noticed a foreign color startin' to spill inside the water a' the creek, fillin' it fast. It's thick, an' I think it's a flower buddin' up. Moe hibiscus. But I ain't nevah seen one like tha'. It ain't right. Some kinda crazy, new hibiscus flower springin' fo'th. In my creek. My creek is the devil's own mouth now, I think. From a crazy devil tune from tha' devil's mouth. I think it's a crazy, devil flower 'cause it's just a-flappin' an' a-flappin'. It's got two, three big ole leaves just a-flappin' wit this crazy color leakin' out of it. Then, I see it's on to somethin'. Attached. There's somethin' attached to it. There's a . . . Fitzhugh. There Fitzhugh be. Face down. Blood circlin' 'round 'im from the bud a' the flower where he been hit. Attached to this flower which is his skull an' his brains which is been gapped open wit tha' shot from my good gun. This piece a' evil used a thing a mine to do this, an' right then, right there, all my blood 'bout to boil ovah an' spill out thu' my fingertips. My heart 'bout to beat itself to its own last breath thu' my ears. My lungs was on fire. The soles a' my feet melted away. I heeve in the chest an' then I go limp. I went down. Fo' tha' second a' eternity, I am on my knees fo' breath where there is none evah. My scorched, blind eyes pull at blades a' mad grass in the shadows tryin' to find out who I am. I'm confused, an' know, an' confused, an' know jus' tha' fast an' then, I know and I stand. I am Speck Kimbrough, an' I am Tommy Mathias wearin' them meddles from Europe pinned upside down an' in the linin' a' my tired heart. Comin' back from doin' such good works ovah there. I am Dixine goin' insane. I am lil' David an' Malcolm pitchin' horse shoes in my grandmama's yard. I am Miss Toolie, Raymond's mama. Wha' I do but try 'n' keep 'em from takin' my boy? I am yo' daddy Poole behind tha' plow, an' my daddy James like a Hebrew slave on tha' levee. I am me right beside 'em all pullin' wit e'ry tug. Me, my neighbors cuttin' our neighbors out the trees an' I ain't laughin'. I refuse. I ain't whistlin'. I refuse. I ain't singin' no tune. I refuse. He don' even hear me comin' but he know I'm comin,' 'cause he better know it. He better not be tha' stupid, tha' crazy today. He better know somebody care 'bout this man, Fitzhugh. Face down in the water where he fish on Sat'day. Sneed better know this man Fitzhugh got a friend. Wann't all tha' alone in this world an' somebody's comin' fo' 'im. Somebody's comin' 'bout 'im. Somebody's comin' to fix this, an' tha' somebody was me, an' I took tha' devil from tha' car mid-whistle, mid-laugh, mid-moonshine drunk. I turned his pinched red devil face to mine, let 'im see me 'foe I snapped his scrawny, evil imbecile's neck in two. In two. Now. Now. Back in the busom a' the evil tha' made cha. I left Sneed fo' the snakes an' the sun to burn up.

LIGHTS UP

(*Wes moves into kitchen, pulls out another rifle and a box of bullets from behind the icebox, puts them on the table, checks and reloads the rifles.*)

LIL: Listen to me, Wes. Wesley, you got to leave wit us, then.

WES: Nawh.

LIL: Yes an' let the stink a' Sneed's carcus rise up all ovah this rotten town.

WES: You think I'm gon' run off now?

LIL: A reason is a person, Wesley. Yo' people, yo' fam'ly.

WES: Fitzhugh was fam'ly.

LIL: Cain't git 'im back tho', can ya? Cain't take it back, can you?

WES: I tole you I meant to kill tha' devil. Didn' you hear me?

LIL: Meanwhile, tha' creek's on yo' land, Wesley. Taylor, the Sneeds, they gon' all come straight fo' you.

WES: I know they will. Let 'em come. I ain't runnin' from none a' tha'. I start runnin', when I'm gon' stop, Lil? When? From the influenza, an' the polio, an' the floods!

LIL: An' gov'ment roads, an' dead white boys, an' the rope!

WES: Why cain't chu unnerstand this? (*puts rifle and pistol on table*)

LIL: Why cain't chu?

WES: I decide when I get up outta bed accordin' to wha' I hafta do from day to day. Nobody rides me. I answer to no one's back doe. I want fo' nothin'. I provide an' have provided fo' my fam'ly from right 'ere. If I go from 'ere, I am nothin'. I am no one. A Mississippi rag-seller pushin' Pomade on backwood gravel again. Faceless! You above all else oughta git wha' tha' feels like. (*checks and loads the pistol*) Wha' good it do I become anotha nobody now?

LIL: They'll say you kilt both of 'em.

WES: Then, tha' would be a lie. Get out. Go. They waitin', I said. GO! Git outta 'ere! GO!

LIL: Listen to me, please . . .

WES: Hear!?

LIL: Listen, now. You stood by yo' daddy, didn' ya'?

WES: I'da died fo' 'im.

LIL: Long as you could, right?

WES: I'da died wit 'im.

LIL: Wit all yo' might to help keep them waters back but yo' daddy, he wouldn' let go. Y'all wouldn' let go an' the waters took 'im.

WES: Tha's right. Goin' nowhere if it ain't my time.

LIL: Was it awright fo' 'im to stand 'ere when it wann't no hope?

WES: I stood there next to 'im an' I'm still 'ere.

LIL: Wit a wife an' fam'ly waitin' fo' 'im at home? Please hear me. A wife prayin' 'er son an' 'er man come back to 'er? Was it? You livin' in a world wit'out 'im now. Wit'out yo' daddy. Yo' mama, watch 'er standin' in the middle a' the floe wit empty hands outstretched, tears streakin', wailin', sayin' wha' am I supposed to do wit this? Wesley, there's got to be anotha way. (*She grabs Wes's arm. He breaks away.*)

WES: Wha' way? There ain't no way, but les' say there is anotha way. We take it to the courthouse. Then, we tell the sheriff wit our hats in our hands. Young Sneed jus' conked Fitz on the head wit my gun barrel or somethin' by mistake. I tells 'em I lost my temper a lil' bit. Tried to put a lil' grease on young Sneed's neck but he slipped, I sing the sheriff a song. Whistle him a ole slave tune. Do a lil' soft shoe. Ole Sneed shake my hand from the sick bed. Mizz Sneed hug my neck. We all excused fo' the misunnerstandins. Fo' ole Sneed takin' advantage of ya. Fo' all the piss an' the shit. Fo' ole an' new. (*Lil grabs Wes again.*)

WES: GIT AWAY!

LIL: You gon' stay, I'm gon' stay too. We'll all stay. We can all go to the sheriff an' tell 'im e'rythang. Or, maybe we say I did it, huh? I come from Atlanta. Ain't no tellin' wha' I might do. (*Wes slaps Lil across the face. Lil picks up the pistol and cocks it. Wes turns toward Lil.*)

WES: Gimme tha'.

LIL: Touch me again an' I'll kill you myself.

WES: Gimme tha', I said.

LIL: I'll blow yo' damn head off. Don' no som-bitch hit Lil. (*points the gun at Wes's head*) Tricked me so's I'd luv you, do wha'evah you want me to do, you thought. (*moves toward him, pushes gun into Wes's chest*) Show the girls how to run. Be broken-hearted an' run, but when I'm gon' stop?

WES: Give it to me, then.

LIL: I'll kill you, man. I swear I will.

WES: You do tha'. You do it. I brought Lil in my house. Tole 'er how safe it was to luv me. Let Lil be the one break tha' levee. Run tha' flood thu' 'ere, Lil. Run it.

LIL: Don' let 'em . . .

WES: Do it, Lil . . .

LIL: Don' let 'em have you like this.

WES: Do it or git the hell outta my way. (*He grabs the gun barrel and moves it from his chest. Lil lets go of the gun. Wes takes it, moves back to preparing the second rifle at the table.*)

LIL: Wesley, I nevah begged fo' nothin' but I'm beggin' you. I'm beggin', Wesley. Don' stay 'ere. Don' stay 'ere. Don't. (*They face each other. Wesley kisses Lil and finishes loading the rifle. She picks up the money tin.*) You git two or three of 'em fo' me, an' foe' or five of 'em fo' yo' girls, an' six or seven of 'em fo' Mamie, an' Dixine, an' Tommy an' Toolie an' Fitzhugh. You git 'em. Git 'em right in they manhood. (*exits house through front door*)

(*SOUND OF truck cranking, idling, driving off. Wes checks the windows and blows out the lamp light. He takes a knife and begins to carve into the table. Lil re-enters the house. Wes hears her, cocks the gun, and points it. Lil moves into the kitchen.*)

LIL: I give the girls the money tin. (*Wes lowers the gun.*) Big O's takin' them to Mamie. (*picks up a shotgun from the table*) They gon' wait 'ere 'til we come fo' 'em. (*She sits at the table. Wes picks up other shotgun and sits at the table. They hold hands across the table.*)

LIGHTS DIM

BLACKOUT

The End

Glossary

a'	of
an'	and
alla	all of
'bout	about
chirrun / gran-chirrun	children / grandchildren
cho	your
cho'self	yourself
chu	you
don'	don't
drankin'	drinking
dun'	done (in place of *have* as an auxiliary verb)
'ere	here / there
e'ry	every
'em	him / them
evah	ever
fo'	for
foe'	four
'foe	before
I'm mo'	I'm going to
jus'	just
I swan	I swear
moe	more
nevah	never
'n'	and
otha	other
ovah	over
sho' / sho'ly	sure / surely
sit'ation	situation
thang	thing
tha' / tha's	that / that's
thu'	through
unnerstand	understand
wann't	wasn't
wha' / wha' s	what / what's
wit	with

KATORI HALL

Katori Hall was born and raised in Memphis, Tennessee, the setting for several of her plays, including *Hoodoo Love* and *The Mountaintop*, a two-character play that imagines how Dr. Martin Luther King, Jr., spent his last night at the Lorraine Hotel in Memphis. A graduate of Columbia University in New York, where she majored in African American studies and creative writing, Hall initially had no intention of becoming a playwright. Her goal as an undergraduate was to pursue a career in journalism. That all changed when she took an acting class and was given an assignment along with her acting partner, another young African American woman, to find a two-character scene that was appropriate for them and to work on it together. They couldn't find anything, so Katori wrote one and has been writing plays ever since.

After graduating from Columbia in 2003, Hall enrolled in the American Repertory Theater's Institute for Advanced Theatre Training at Harvard University where she earned her M.F.A. in 2005. She also studied at the Juilliard School's playwriting program. In addition to seeing her play *The Mountaintop* produced on Broadway during the 2011–2012 season, Katori Hall lists among her numerous awards the prestigious Laurence Olivier Award for Best New Play for *The Mountaintop*, which she received in 2010, making her the first black woman in the British award's history to be so honored. Other plays by Hall include *Remembrance, Saturday Night/ Saturday Morning, Our Lady of Kibeho, Childen of Killers, WHADDABLOODCLOT, Hurt Village, Pussy Valley,* and *The Blood Quilt*.

Hoodoo Love received its world premiere at the Cherry Lane Theatre, in New York City, where it opened on November 1, 2007.

Director:	Lucie Tiberghien
TOULOU:	Angela Lewis
CANDYLADY:	Marjorie Johnson
ACE OF SPADES:	Kevin Mambo
JIB:	Keith Davis
Set:	Robin Vest
Costumes:	Rebecca Bernstein
Lighting:	Pat Dignan
Sound and musical arrangements:	Daniel Baker and the Broken Chord Collective
Production manager:	Paige van den Berg
Assistant stage manager:	Joan Cappello
Technical director:	Ian Grunes
Fight director:	David Debesse

HOODOO LOVE

CHARACTERS

TOULOU—a young black woman who runs away from the cotton fields of Mississippi to the bluesy streets of Memphis. In stature she is tiny, but her presence makes her seem taller than she is.

CANDYLADY—a former slave and the Hoodoo Madame of Beale Street with a timeless essence, yet with the quick tongue of a young'n.

ACE OF SPADES—a young, sexy, ramblin bluesman with a "behind like a caboose" and hands that can play the blues out of any woman's back.

JIB—Toulou's older brother, a born-again Christian missionary.

PLACE

A cluster of shacks along a cul-de-sac next to Beale Street. Memphis, Tennessee.

TIME

Great Depression.

Prologue

Day. Toulou's shack—a measly wooden one-room shack with a sagging front porch and a squeaky screen door. Toulou is looking through her mojo bag in front of the shack. The dress she wears encases newfound womanly curves.

TOULOU:

> Two teaspoons graveyard dust
> One toenail for safe keepin'
> A lock of yo' hair for luck
> Yo' guitar string for prosperity

(The train sounds.)

> "Here lies he who dared to love again."
>
> Gotta catch that train
> Ride it like a maine
> Gotta catch that train

It's comin' in
My heart will die just to
Ride on that train
Gotta catch that train
Ride it like a maine

(*The train sounds.*)

CANDYLADY: It's time. (*Toulou picks up her guitar as the train sounds again.*)

Act 1

Scene 1

One year earlier. Lightning strikes. Train sounds. Pitter-patter of rain on a corrugated tin roof. Ace and Toulou are making passionate love. Beneath the soft candlelight, the sweat trickles from their bronze bodies. Their groans and moans create beautiful cacophony with the creaking and squeaking of the wrought-iron bed. Finally he climaxes on top of her. Silence. She sighs. She gets up to light the lantern.

ACE: Where you goin'?

TOULOU: I'll be back.

ACE: Unh, unh.

TOULOU: Unh, hunh.

ACE: I wanna come with you.

TOULOU: Baby, I gotta pee.

ACE: You always gotta go pee after.

TOULOU: Hell, don't you?

ACE: No.

TOULOU: I felt it all up in my gut that time.

ACE: Well, I'm a big boy.

TOULOU: Who tolja that?

ACE: You just did.

TOULOU: Honey, I'm short.

ACE: Ohhhh! You'se a mean one! (*Toulou urinates in a corner bucket.*) Why you don't go outside to do that?

TOULOU: 'Cause I got to squat and ain't no haints jumpin' up in this hole here. That's how Miss Lucie got possessed. Say she walked outside and some whisper jumped clear up into her crotch.

ACE: Who done told you that lie?

TOULOU: Unh, unh. That ain't no story. Lola Faye got it from Dot Jean, who got it from Uncle Charles, who heard it from Lilly Lynn who—God know she hear everythang standin' on that street corner—got it from Big Mama Bell who heard it from LaSalle who got it from Cornbread who heard it from Frayser Boy who got it from Tinky, Punkin, and Miss Ida who helped Miss Lucie throw down the demon. (*She walks away from the pot.*)

ACE: If she woulda just laid down a trick she wouldna' ran into that mess. I be tellin folks now . . .

TOULOU: Don't talk that shit 'round me!

ACE: Why not? It's true!

TOULOU: Mama told me not to believe in that voodoo, hoodoo or whatever-you-do mess.

ACE: It's *hoodoo,* and I done seen't some things that had me believe it. One time my mama let her girlfriend plait up her hair. "Yo' hair so long. Look like lynch ropes fallin' down yo' back," her girlfriend say. Mmm, hmm. When mama went home her stomach started hurtin' her somethin' terrible . . .

TOULOU: She prolly was wit child.

ACE: Naw. Her stomach was bubblin' so much she couldn't hold nothin' down. Just got sick as a dog. Madea asked if somebody had been playin' in her hair. Mama say, "My girlfriend." Madea slapped her clear 'cross the face and say, "That's why you sick!" Madea made mama lay down, and that's when they saw it.

TOULOU: Saw what?

ACE: Live thangs in her.

TOULOU: *Live* thangs?

ACE: *Live.* Madea took her to the hoodoo lady down the street to get a bag of tricks. Mama drank them herbs and sat on the pot. Say a million lil' white snakes came fallin' out of her. Just wrigglin' round in that pot. She never let nobody play in her hair after that. Live thangs inside her . . . (*Ace points behind Toulou.*) What's that?

TOULOU: Ahhhh! Don't do that to me, Ace!

ACE: Just joogin' ya. Hush now. We don't wanna wake Candylady up, my lil' Scary Mary.

TOULOU: My name is Toulou, thank you very much. Too lil' for my skirt. Too lil' for my shoes. Too lil' to leave Byhalia, Mississippi. Too lil' to live. Too lil' for every-thang, but I did it. Toulou . . .

ACE: Well, go on, Miss "Too lil' for this. Too lil' for that." Like the way it roll off yo' tongue. (*He kisses her deeply.*)

TOULOU: I ain't never seen it done like you did last night.

ACE: Quit joogin' me.

TOULOU: Nah, Ace . . . I wanna see it. Up close.

ACE: You might be scared of it.

TOULOU: No, I ain't. I couldn't see it good last night 'cause the lights was low.

ACE: You sho'll was starin' at my mojo—

TOULOU: I wun't *starin'* at yo' mojo!

ACE: You was!

TOULOU: Let me see it again!

ACE: You sho' you'se ready, nah? (*He puts his hand beneath the covers.*)

TOULOU: I'll show you mines, if you show me yours . . .

ACE: I done already seen yours. (*She hits him on his shoulder. Ace pulls out a harmonica from beneath the covers, then plays a sharp blues progression, wiggling his hands around the airbox of the harmonica, making it wail. Toulou looks on in awe.*)

TOULOU: Sound like it sound when you tryin' to get away. (*A train sounds in the distance. He jumps up to get dressed.*)

ACE: I gotta get on her.

TOULOU: Where you off to next?

ACE: Wherever the wind take me. If I'm passin' through a city and I gets a feelin, that's when I jump off that boxcar.

TOULOU: Take me witchoo.

ACE: What?

TOULOU: You heard me . . . Take me witcha.

ACE: The others might get mad.

TOULOU: The others?

ACE: See, that's why I like you; you don't give me no mess like the others. Every time I leave they start cryin', cussin' and carryin' on, but you . . . you'se a strong one. Might couldn't tell it from lookin at you, but you is.

TOULOU: There are others?

ACE: You thought you was the only one? Baby, I'm a one man travelin' band. I'm searchin' for that one song that gone put me on the map. Have everybody screamin' my name. If I poke under enough skirts, I'ma find it. See, I'm a lucky nigger. You don't know how it feel to have folk eyes on you, waitin for that magic to flow from yo' lips. Ooooooo, honey-baby, it's a beautiful trip.

TOULOU: Them others ain't got nothin' on me. They ain't worth pickin' a fist-full of chitlins! I bet you get more shit out of 'em than somethin' to eat.

ACE: Can you sang?

TOULOU: Whatchoo talkin' 'bout? "Can you sang?" Hell, every Southern girl raised in a church can sang.

ACE: Well, sang me a song then.

TOULOU: Where? Here? Right now? This a shack, not a juke joint.

ACE: Every hole-in-the-wall got shack in they name. Shuga Shack, Tacky Shack. Now sang me a damn song.

TOULOU: You just scared I might open my mouth and blow you and ya lil' funky, pootie, tootie harmonica—

ACE: Jezebel!

TOULOU: Jezziebelly—or whatever—out my house—

ACE: I'm waitin'. (*Toulou breathes in and breathes out and begins to sing but stops.*)

TOULOU: I don't see why you don't believe me. (*Ace begins to play a blues progression on Jezebel and motions for Toulou to sing. Reluctantly, Toulou sings a song, "Flow Up South." A poor, meek, off-key voice flows out of her mouth.*)

> From Memphis to Chicago
> From New Orleans
> On up to Harlem
> Flow, flow honey
> Flow up south—

ACE: (*Laughing hard*) How you gone shake the shack sangin' off-key like that? No wonder nobody'll let you up on they stage.

TOULOU: Sangin' ain't 'bout bein' on key. It's 'bout makin' you feel somethin'.

ACE: Well, I feel like it's time for me to go.

TOULOU: Awwww, hell!

ACE: Baby, I got a reputation. I been workin' the Cotton Belt for ten years now. Blowin' in them clubs from Memphis to Chicago, myself. Hell, I got so many songs that a white man down from Chicago gone put me down on them shiny circle thangs. Make me a bona fide star! I'm 'bout to be bigger than Hambone Newburn, Charley Patton, Washboard Sam . . . Even Robert Johnson his—Wait! Who wrote that there though?

TOULOU: I did.

ACE: You did? Hmmph.

TOULOU: I wrote it on the ride up here from Mississippi, yeap. You ain't the only one who got a behind like a caboose.

ACE: A real backwater Delta darlin'. Somehow I could tell.

TOULOU: You might thank I'm country, but this lil' girl got some big city dreams. Soon everybody in Memphis gone know my name.

ACE: Is that right?

TOULOU: Yeah, if you just let me come witcha . . .

ACE: I thanks you gone have to stay home.

TOULOU: If you don't let me come, by the time you get back somebody else might be lyin' in yo' bed.

ACE: Betta not be no 'nother nigger up in my bed—

TOULOU: Doggone it! Just take me!

ACE: Not this time. What would the others say? (*Ace tries to kiss her. She doesn't want to kiss him, but he ends up convincing her—somehow. The train sounds again.*) See, you done made me miss my train. (*And he's gone. Toulou runs over to the quilt they made love in and smells it. She sings her song. Her voice is louder, stronger. She is surprised by it.*)

TOULOU:

> My man got bowlegs
> Like the Mississippi
> No matter what I say
> He won't come back to me
> Gotta heart like a train
> Run straight to the sea
> My man always runnin'
> Like my old man river,
> The Mississippi
> From Memphis to Chicago
> From New Orleans on up to Harlem
> Flow . . . Flow . . . , honey
> Flow up south!

(*Her voice shakes the shack.*)

Scene 2

Next day. Toulou is hanging clothes on a crude makeshift line outside the shack. The voices of children can be heard offstage chanting.

RHONDA'S CHILDREN:

> Goofer dust! Goofer dust! On yo' head
> Gonna sprinkle goofer dust all over yo' bed
> Wake up in the mornin' and find yoself dead
> Goofer dust! Goofer dust! On yo' head.

TOULOU: Them chilun' gone burn in hell for singin' that shit. Rhonda, keep yo' rascals out my outhouse! We ain't got no more petro unless you gone buy me some! (*Candylady, an old, round woman, steps out of the shack next door.*)

CANDYLADY: What's all this carryin' on out here? I didn't get no sleep durin the slavery days. Let a old lady catch up!

TOULOU: You know you wun't no slave!

CANDYLADY: Shee-it!

TOULOU: It's Rhonda and 'nem chilun . . .

CANDYLADY: Yessa, chile. They stole some of my sour pickles. You'd thank they'd have some good sense to steal some coats as bare as they brown bottoms is.

TOULOU: It sho'll do feel like it 'bout to snow.

CANDYLADY: Rhonda don't be feedin' them chilun'. That's why they stealin'.

TOULOU: She must keeps her a man around. Wit all them. I need to learn somethin' from her.

CANDYLADY: She know a baby keep a man around, or make him run out the door. Hell, if she woulda done took that root I made for her, she wun't have all them half-buck-naked chilun runnin 'round. I mixed her up some black cohosh osha root! Woulda had two lil' niglets 'stead of five! (*Beat*) Them clothes ain't never gone get dry, you hang 'em out in the cold like that. You tryin' to find somethin' to do since he left. (*Toulou begins to pull the clothes off the line.*)

TOULOU: Whatchoo talkin' 'bout?

CANDYLADY: I know how a woman looks when she done got her some.

TOULOU: Some what?

CANDYLADY: Oh, you thank the Candylady ignant! I might can't read, but you ain't messin' wit no fool. (*The train whistles in the background. Toulou looks off into the distance.*) When he comin' back?

TOULOU: Who knows?

CANDYLADY: Dealin' with the ole Ace of Spades. They say he got a woman in every town that train stop in.

TOULOU: They's a goddamn lie.

CANDYLADY: Say he makes a woman's kitchen knaps curl tighter than a noose 'round a innocent nigger's neck.

TOULOU: Now, whoever *they* is—they tellin' the truth 'bout that one.

CANDYLADY: Say he got a strong back, and it ain't from pickin' cotton.

TOULOU: Where you hear all that from?

CANDYLADY: The river told me.

TOULOU: Ohhh, there you go speakin' in riddles again.

CANDYLADY: Chile, the river flow deep with the spirits of our ancestors. You betta go speak witcho mama's daddy.

TOULOU: I don't believe in all that.

CANDYLADY: It believe in you.

TOULOU: Do it tell ya how to keep a man like that? Always comin' and goin'. Got a behind like a caboose.

CANDYLADY: Honey, he'll always be in the wind.

TOULOU: Well, how you make him love you when you ain't there?

CANDYLADY: Well, you can try yo' way. Get on yo' knees and pray to God or you can steal him, ya know? Put him inside here . . . (*She pulls out a blue crushed velvet bag and tries to hand it to Toulou, who just stares at it with great fear.*)

TOULOU: That's yo' mojo. I can't touch it.

CANDYLADY: Sho you can! Woman can touch another woman's nation sack. She gain some strength. Leave a lil' bit of hers behind. It's the man that can't. 'Cause he usually the one we carry inside. (*Candylady tries to make her touch the bag.*)

TOULOU: Stop it, now!

CANDYLADY: Just look at it!

TOULOU: It gone make my eyes fall out.

CANDYLADY: Touch it, crazy chile! This here hold some good memories and some candy for yo' dreams. (*Toulou overcomes her fear and touches it.*)

TOULOU: What's inside yo's?

CANDYLADY: All my mens. Got my first husband in here: Winky. We wouldn't never married though. Not in the white way. Massa wouldn't 'low it. I 'member he used to throw a lil' bit of cotton in my sack when we was in the fields. I couldn' never pick the 'mount I was suppose ta pick. "You slow gal!" he useta say. He knew he was a fast picker. Had a fast hand. Could play him some guitar, honey. They sold him off up river. I never saw him again after that. But I know he loved me, still love me. His guitar strang be shakin' in that bag on our marriage birthday. My second husband was a sweeeeeeeet muthafucka'!

TOULOU: Ooooooo, tell it now!

CANDYLADY: Called himself Suede! Kisses smooth one way and rough the next. He worked next to the blacksmith, makin' the animal skin into saddles, clothes, whatever them crackers wanted. He was the only nigger 'round here wearin' animal skin pants. He had eyes round as peach pies and a manhood as long as that river.

TOULOU: Ooooooo!

CANDYLADY: I'm tellin you, chile, that man was fierce! 'Til one day he caught one of them white boys down the street funnin' his sister Mae Jean. Suede struck him down in one blow. He was fierce, I tell ya . . . They strung 'em up on that oak tree at Auction Street. He burned bright red. Never heard him scream. I gotta piece of that noose in my bag, chile. I gotta piece of my third husband, my fourth one, my fifth . . . Yeah, I been good at makin' men into memories, chile. As long as they don't make a fool out of me.

TOULOU: I can always keep him by puttin' him inside here?

CANDYLADY: Just be sure it's his memory you want. It ain't always fo' sho', but faith ain't neither. (*Beat.*)

TOULOU: What might I do if . . . I happened to . . . to decide . . . ya know?—uhm—"lay down a trick?"

CANDYLADY: (*Smiling.*) Mmmmhmmm. Now, you speakin' my language. Let's goofer him. Make him *sick* ta love ya!

TOULOU: I don' wanna make 'em sick!

CANDYLADY: Nah! A mojo bag'll just have 'em thankin' 'bout ya, draw him to ya, but if we fixed up a root . . . well, he'll always be rooted to yo' side.

TOULOU: Mama useta say even love can't possess a ramblin man. I don't 'spect a trick'll do neither!

CANDYLADY: You ain't always gotta play with the cards you dealt. Remember, the man who got two Queen of Hearts in his hand is a cheat. But the woman wit two Jokers in her hand—

TOULOU: Got too damn much to handle!

CANDYLADY: Alright, I'm tryin to learn ya a lil' somethin', nah . . . You'll learn to play cards like a man one day. I know I have.

TOULOU: This ain't no card game. This my life.

CANDYLADY: You'd be surprised; ain't no difference in the two. (*A train whistle blows in the background. They both look up. A man dressed in a suit enters with a small carpet bag over his shoulder.*) Who is that fine hobo man comin' up in here?

TOULOU: Who? (*She freezes.*) Oh, my God! Hide me! (*Toulou hides behind Candylady.*)

JIB: Is that my Toulou I see o'er yonder playin' hide-go-seek?

CANDYLADY: Look more like duck-the-lynch-mob to me.

TOULOU: Hide me, nah!

JIB: She ain't changed since we was chilun. Two years. Two whole years! Come give yo' big brother a hug. I bet you wun't 'spectin' to see me, huh? (*Toulou stands still with her mouth hanging wide open.*)

CANDYLADY: This the first time I'm hearin' 'bout a brother.

JIB: Awwww, you didn't tell folks 'bout yo' favorite brother?

TOULOU: My only brother.

JIB: Gurl, quit stallin' and give me a doggone hug!

TOULOU: I been warshin' clothes all day. Don't wanna get you wet. Look at that suit you got on.

JIB: It fine, ain't it?

TOULOU: Sho'll is.

JIB: If I'm gonna be a preacher I got to dress like one, don't I?

TOULOU: Followin' in Daddy's footsteps, huh? Well, I'd be 'fraid to wash a suit like that on my hands. 'Fraid I'd tear it or somethin'. Howja find me?

JIB: How I caught ya? Awwww, I remember when you was just yah-high, runnin' 'round in 'nem fields, you used to dream about livin' pretty top a bluff. Memphis, the Bluff City!

CANDYLADY: Now, what a fine man like you doin' bein' a preacher?

JIB: Who this heathen?

TOULOU: Where my head at? Candylady, this Jib. Jib, this—

JIB: What kind of name Candylady?

CANDYLADY: What kind of name Jib?

JIB: You got me on that one.

CANDYLADY: They call me Candylady for one simple reason. Everybody need a lil' honey now and then. Ain't that right, Toulou?

TOULOU: She got all we need—grits, corn meal, sour pickles with peppermint sticks in the middle. Folk come all the way down from Ripley to get some of the sweet stuff she got.

CANDYLADY: And I does a lil' rootwork now and then. (*Jib takes his holy oil vial and makes a cross on Candylady's front step.*)

JIB: "Depart from evil—hah—and do good; seek peace—hah—and pursue it." Psalms 34:14. I ain't sho' I'd be right proud of that.

CANDYLADY: You want salvation, go to church. You want somethin' done, come to me.

JIB: Guess you can't change folk evil ways, but folk come all the way down from Ripley! Whatchoo sellin' fo' free?

CANDYLADY: Oh, nothin' don't go fo' free, but my mouth.

JIB: Oooooooweeee!

CANDYLADY: I thank I likes him, chile! Yo' sister won't give you a big welcome? I will.

JIB: That's awright. I'm sure she'll give me a right good welcome later on.

CANDYLADY: Well, it was so nice to meet you. I'm fixin' ta get my store together. You stop by for anythang you want. (*Candylady exits.*)

JIB: Look a' here! Look a' here! My sister! Done run away from home to the big city. Me and Daddy didn't know what to do when you left. Hard to find somebody that don't write ya, let ya know where they at. But "Seeketh—hah—and ye shall find." We done really missed you.

TOULOU: Folks up here talk too much.

JIB: They sho'll do, Toulou. You 'bout the only person round up here wit that name.

TOULOU: So when you leavin'? Ya betta get goin'. It's hard to catch the train after sundown—

JIB: Whoa! Whoa! Slow down that horsie 'tween yo' legs. Where's yo' hospitabletality at? I just wanted to visit you for a day or two.

TOULOU: Mmmmhmmph . . . So how the church down there?

JIB: Well, you know after Mama pass, all Daddy could do was throw hisself into that church. You should come back and see it. Membership gettin' so big now. Everybody need some savin' specially them niggers runnin' round out here. You see, I might be startin' me up a church. Daddy say we need to spread our seed. Plant it everywhere and watch it grow like cotton in the Mississippi mud. If you do it right, it grow fast. Just need the right man to take care of it.

TOULOU: Ya sho' you'se that right man?

JIB: Yes, Pastor Jib is. See, I gots goals. What them high falutin' blue-blood niggers call asp-er-ations!

TOULOU: Well, look at you. Been readin' more than the Bible I see.

JIB: I thought I'd be able to stay with you awhile. Maybe I can get that church runnin...

TOULOU: Jib... I don't know, now.

JIB: We kinfolk. I *am* yo' big brother.

TOULOU: It's a lil' tight up in here nowadays.

JIB: Who you livin wit? A man? You shackin' up? So you'se a fornicator. "Let the woman—hah—learn in silence—hah—with all subjection." First Timothy, chapter 2 verse 11.

TOULOU: You might as well be talkin' jibberish for all these folks up here know. These folks don't go to church 'round here. Whatchoo need to open up is a joint, a hole-in-the-wall. That's where you'll make you some money. (*Jib sneaks up and hugs his sister from behind.*) Unh, unh, Jib! Wharcha doin'?

JIB: Just wanna hug my sister, that's all. (*Jib hugs her tightly and looks into her eyes. Toulou tries to push him away.*) That's all. (*He lets her go. Straightens his suit, wrinkled from the tussle.*) Which one of 'em yourn? (*Toulou reluctantly points to her shack. Jib walks into it. Toulou stands watching him.*)

Scene 3

Morning. The shacks. Candylady sits on her porch smoking a pipe, while Toulou combs her hair.

TOULOU: I thanks I need one of them.

CANDYLADY: Not before you go to work. They get rid of you soon they smell you.

TOULOU: Ain't this a trip! I spend all day warshin' my clothes, cleanin' my house, and now I gotta go do the same thang in somebody else house. Hell, ain't no rest for the weary!

CANDYLADY: Don't you get tired of bein' sick and tired?

TOULOU: I'm sick and tired of my brother.

CANDYLADY: Already? He ain't been here but a minute.

TOULOU: But a minute! Shee-it. He been here a whole month! Can't barely go to the clubs no more. Can't tell 'em I'm goin' down on Beale. He be wantin' to come wit me every time I go off.

CANDYLADY: Don't worry. You know how nigger folks is; he'll be gone 'fore you know it. (*Train whistle sounds. Toulou stares down the path off into the distance.*)

TOULOU: The only way I can talk to Ace sometimes is in my dreams.

CANDYLADY: That's the best place to keep yo' man.

TOULOU: Why?

CANDYLADY: That way you can control him. But that mean he thankin' 'bout you.

TOULOU: That man ain't thankin' 'bout me.

CANDYLADY: How come he ain't?

TOULOU: He prolly laid up with some other woman.

CANDYLADY: (*Pause.*) He is.

TOULOU: You ain't suppose to tell me that.

CANDYLADY: The devil's a liar; I ain't.

TOULOU: You gonna give me a puff of that or what?

CANDYLADY: Getcho own!

TOULOU: Ohh stingy woman! (*They laugh, then settle down.*)

CANDYLADY: You and Jib, close?

TOULOU: Too close sometimes.

CANDYLADY: I see. Well, thangs get too crowded over there, you know where I'm at.

TOULOU: Yes, ma'am. Well, I'm off.

CANDYLADY: Ohh, don't call me "ma'am."

TOULOU: I's sorry.

CANDYLADY: Make me feel too old.

TOULOU: Well, how old is ya?

CANDYLADY: Honey, I'm so old I bleeds dirt. Come by later on, though. I got a lil' somethin' for you.

TOULOU: Whatchoo got for me?

CANDYLADY: Oh, a lil' candy to catch a fly.

(*As Toulou exits, Candylady sings her a song, "SHUGA WOMAN BLUES."*)

> You want some a' my shuga babay?
> I got the best candy in town.
> You want some of this shuga babay?
> I know how to really put it down.
> But I done gave 'way all my shuga
> Ain't got no mo' fo' this old clown.

(*A harmonica blasts from behind the shacks. Ace enters playing a wailing solo blues riff.*)
Play on, Ace. Play on!

ACE: But I want some yo' shuga babay.

CANDYLADY AND ACE: The best shuga this part a' town.

CANDYLADY: You want some of my shuga babay?

ACE: Sho'll do!!!

CANDYLADY: You bets know how to put it down.

ACE: Wooohooo!!!

CANDYLADY:

> 'Cause I'ma tell everybody
> I'm gone get mine this time 'round.

(*Ace finishes their impromptu jam with a riff on his harmonica. They hug.*) Back in town, huh? You just missed lil' Toulou.

ACE: I thought you was her for a minute there. I was gone take you right on up to Dyersburg with me!

CANDYLADY: I'm too old, baby. But I bet I could tear it down!

ACE: Tear that roof right off! (*Jib enters, awakened from his sleep.*)

JIB: Now who is playin' that blues shit on a Sunday mornin'? Didn't yo' mama teach you no better?

ACE: Well, I'll be goddamned! Toulou been coatin' on me?

CANDYLADY: Boy, this her brother Jib. Done come up from Mississippi to start hisself a church.

ACE: She didn't tell me her brother was a preacher. Matter fact, I'dn know she had a brother.

CANDYLADY: Honey, me neither! Niggers be so secret nowadays.

ACE: Sho'll do.

CANDYLADY: Well, I'm so glad you finally poked in on us. We done missed ya.

ACE: I done missed yo' sweet chew root. Can I have some? Pretty please? I'll give you a penny.

CANDYLADY: A penny? Baby, my shuga worth a dime. (*She switches her hips into her shack. The two men stare at each other. Silence.*)

JIB: From what I heard so far, you pretty good on that harp.

ACE: Yeah, this here my Jezebel. So you a man of God?

JIB: "Thou sayest that I am a King—hah. To this end was I born, and for this cause—hah—came I unto the world, that I should bear witness—hah—unto the truth." John 18:37 . . . Yes. I'm also her big brother, and she from a respectable family. Whatchoo do?

ACE: I'm what they call a bedtime baptizer of men. Me n' you 'bout know the same folks. 'Cause the same niggers dancin' in the joint on a Saturday night is the same niggers dancin' in the aisles on a Sunday mornin'. Ace of Spades, Beale's best blues blower.

JIB: Awww, so you the Ace of Spades? . . . So I guess you familiar with these parts. (*Beat.*) Where's a place a maine can get a burnin' shot of whiskey?

ACE: Hmmph. You might jus be my kind of preacher! Where yo' church at? (*Ace brings out a deck of cards and starts shuffling them, intricately.*)

JIB: Not only can you play the blues, but you'se a gambler? That's a damn shame!

ACE: Ain't we all out here gamblin' for somethin'? Tell you what. Play ya? I win; you buy me a drank on Beale. You win; I buy you a big ole' bottle of Jack. Whatchoo gone do?

JIB: A bottle of Jack? How you gone 'ford that?

ACE: I'll figure that out. (*Jib looks around to see if anyone is coming. He thinks for a moment.*)

JIB: Deal!

ACE: Whatchoo play? Bid-whist? Cracker tonk?

JIB: Two-man spades.

ACE: Aww, shit! That's my game. They don't call me the Ace of Spades for nothin'! You sho' you can throw down wit me? Two-man spades?

JIB: We the only men here. Deal, nigger! (*Ace laughs and begins dealing. Jib pulls out a dented metal flask and drinks.*) So you know my sister, huh?

ACE: I come see her from time to time.

JIB: Nah, what I'm askin' you is do you know my sister? Like Samson know Delilah. Oh, you don't read the Bible do you?

ACE: You trumped my card. I prolly know her 'bout as well as anybody else.

JIB: Do ya? (*Jib plays the first card.*)

ACE: Yep.

JIB: That's my book! I'd like to travel like you some day.

ACE: You might be able to with all that mission work you preachers do.

JIB: Word is, you got a woman in every county. Got you some black diamonds stashed away in all these clubs. Breakin' these broads' hearts.

ACE: Nah, they lyin'.

JIB: Nah, a spade's a spade. Why you ain't out on the road right now? My sistah's biscuits keep you 'round?

ACE: They taste real good.

JIB: (*Interrogating.*) Oh, so you done had some of her biscuits, huh? (*Beat.*) Oooooooo! I bet womens be wantin' ta sop yo' gravy up with they lil' biscuits. You know, 'cordin' to some folks, you done had 'bout hundred women. That true?

ACE: Folk don't know what they be talkin 'bout—Ay, you is takin' my book! Diamonds cuts hearts when the spades run out!

JIB: Take the book then. Damn! I ain't say nothin' when you reneged two books back.

ACE: Maine, I ain't no cheat!

JIB: "Forsake not the works of thine own hands—hah." So my sister . . . she number one hundred and one?

ACE: You drunk? Why you joogin' me like that?

JIB: Joogin'? Joog? Now, I likes that word! Hell, I'm just "joogin" you. We mens, ain't we? We can "joog" like that. Nah, I'm just tryin' to welcome you into the family. Hell, we might be kinfolk this time next year. (*Pause.*) Yo' book.

ACE: I ain't never gettin' married again.

JIB: Damn, maine. Can't believe some broad tied you down.

ACE: Got left.

JIB: But a nigger like you got plenty to choose from. Every good man need a wife to make a house a home. Keep that heifer prone so she won't get gone! That what I say.

ACE: You ever been married?

JIB: Nah.

ACE: I can tell.

JIB: Like I was sayin'. You need to have the one at home then you go runnin' 'round. That way you can have every color in that chocolate rainbow. You got yo' sapphire. Oh, they a rare breed. Sang notes so pretty blue make you wanna make love to the sky. You got yo' hoodoo whores. Beware of them bitches. You make 'em mad, you liable to wake up the next mornin' walkin' on all fours. I saw a man in Lil' Rock got poison by his wife. He ain't never turn back right. Then you got yo' church women. They pretend they so tight you can't stick a chew root up they box, but slip them some lil' moonshine, and they'll be wailin' louder than two trains runnin'. See my sister, she like them church women.

ACE: How you know what kind yo' sister is?

JIB: Hmph? (*Jib ignores the question and counts his cards instead.*) Well, looks like I got sixteen books to yo' ten. Where my Jack at?

Scene 4

The shacks. Toulou dances in from the alley, singing. She has stars in her eyes and lipstick on her lips. Her voice is more mellifluous. Even stronger than the last time we heard. She sings "Sunday Morning Man." Candylady is on her porch, listening.

TOULOU:

> I got one man for Monday
> Two for Tuesday
> Three come in on Wednesday
> Four, five for Thursday, Friday
> But I got one fine man
> Just for Saturday night
> 'Cause he the only one
> Can glaze my Sunday ham right.

CANDYLADY: The butt of yo' ham 'bout to burn up.

TOULOU: Leave me 'lone!

CANDYLADY: Where the hell you done been! You smell like you been smokin' a turkey! I told you 'bout goin' to work wit all that ciggie smoke on ya. You gone lose that warshih' job!

TOULOU: They can take it from me for all I care! Folks 'round here can't 'ford to eat, and crackers still payin' Negroes to wash they clothes.

CANDYLADY: And wipe that whore paint off yo' lips—

TOULOU: Ohhh, they look so pretty up there on Beale Street!

CANDYLADY: Don't tell me ya hookin' from the plantation?

TOULOU: They let me off a lil' early and Beale on my way home so—

CANDYLADY: So?

TOULOU: The Tacky Shack lookin' for an openin' act for the jug band tomorrow night! Miss Lucie son, Jerry, own it now. He had all these gals up there standin' in a line on the corner near Schwab's 'bout to sang for him. Ole Bug-Eye Jerry would open the door and one girl would walk out blowin' kisses at him—or cryin'—then another girl would walk in, then me—

CANDYLADY: Let me tell it. You walked out blowin' kisses?

TOULOU: I ain't walk out! Bug-Eye call me to the stage. "Who Taloola?" he say, and I says, "That's Toulou to you!"—I hope I'd make him mad—I strolled up with my heels clickin' 'long that wood floor. I planted my feet, opened my mouth and this gut-bucket voice came tumblin' out—

CANDYLADY: You gone sang tomorrow!!!

TOULOU: Nah. It wouldn' me! Nothin' was comin' out of me, but somethin' was comin' from the back door 'cause that's when Lillie Mae Glover, Memphis' Baby Ma Rainey herself, walked in. Just beltin' and bendin' blue notes right there. Can you believe it? I ain't never seen no star before, but here she was in the flesh wit all her parts just a' jigglin'. Folks in the club stood up when she strolled in. She walk like a peacock.

CANDYLADY: Girl, you ain't never seen one of them in yo' lil' life.

TOULOU: At least I thanks a peacock walk like she walk. I ain't never seen no woman switch her hips like that. Almost like her hips floated in front of her and the rest of her body just followed. One day, I'ma strut like that.

CANDYLADY: Did you ever sang?

TOULOU: They forgot I was even there.

CANDYLADY: Shee-it. Well, at least you got in for a minute, but yo' legs too short to strut like a peacock.

TOULOU: One day, watch! You said you was gone give me somethin' when I got back from workin' . . . (*A drunken Jib and Ace stumble in singing a hymn.*)

ACE AND JIB: *AMEN! A-MEN!*

CANDYLADY: (*Overlapping*) My mojo already workin' for ya, and I ain't even gave it to ya yet . . .

ACE AND JIB: *AMEN! AMEN! AMEN!* (*Toulou runs like a child just let loose from church and embraces Ace. Jib, who can hardly stand up straight, watches.*)

TOULOU: When didja get back?

ACE: The first wind that blew in from St. Louie, I caught it, and here I am. But we need to getcho brother in the house. Looks like he gone be sick tomorrow.

JIB: (*Snapping*) I'm gone be fine!

CANDYLADY: He need a cup of parched rice and bay leaves. Take away that headache 'fore it come—and that attitude. (*Candylady exits.*)

ACE: He might can play some spades, but he can't hold his liquor worth shit.

JIB: (*Drunkenly mumbling*) Ace in love witchoo Toulou.

ACE: He gone need a ice rag. Some fellah knocked him down 'cause his gal didn't take kindly to Jib's "layin on of hands" trick.

JIB: I was tryin' to heal her.

ACE: And that nigger *heel* landed right up yo' ass!

TOULOU: Still mannish as ever. Get in the house, Jib.

JIB: See, my sister gone take care of me.

TOULOU: Get, Jib! (*Jib stumbles into the shack. Ace fixes the red flower sticking out of his lapel.*)

ACE: Yo' brother is a plum fool! Did you miss me?

TOULOU: Hell, nah.

ACE: Quit tellin' a story.

TOULOU: I ain't! Why you have my liquor-lovin' brother out on Beale I just don't know! Hell, you ain't even took me drankin'.

ACE: No woman like you need to be up in them hole-in-the-walls. You come from a respectable family.

TOULOU: I'm surprised I didn't see y'all down there.

ACE: Down where?

TOULOU: On Beale. 'Cause that's where I was tryin' to get me a job at wit Ole Bug-Eye Jerry.

ACE: Girl, you know you ain't suppose ta be down there walkin' 'round by yoself!

TOULOU: Well, it wun't nobody 'round to take me so I gotta do what I gotta do. Them jug stompin' boys was lookin' for them a boogie woogie woman.

ACE: I know they was. Lillie Mae suppose to be singin' there tonight with her fine tail.

TOULOU: That ugly thang! Walk like a chicken rolled over by a trolley car.

ACE: You seen't her? Well, you lookin' at the wrong woman. Even if she was ugly— which she ain't—it don't matter. A woman who sang like a canary can have a face like a cow ass.

TOULOU: Well, her songs is bad. I can come up with some better shit than that. Can prolly come up with some songs that better than yo' stuff.

ACE: Ain't nobody better than me.

TOULOU: So why don't you sang me a song then?

ACE: I ain't got no songs to sang you.

TOULOU: Calling me scared? Shee-it.

ACE: I got a lil' somethin' cookin' on the stove, but it ain't ready to be ate up yet.

TOULOU: (*Mocking*) "Ohh, I'm the best. Look at me! I can sang better than Robert J. Hambone Newburn—"

ACE: Quit it, now—

TOULOU: "Wilson Jackson Jefferson—"

ACE: I ain't never said that! Quit—

TOULOU: "Washboard Punkin, Tinky Robinson, and yours truly—"

ACE: Quit it, Abby! (*Silence*)

TOULOU: Oh, that her name. Who that there flower for? (*Beat*)

ACE: You?

TOULOU: (*She snatches it from him.*) Can always tell when a man lyin' 'cause they be slow in answerin' ya questions.

ACE: You ain't catchin' feelins for me, is ya?

TOULOU: Ever since I met you you always been gone.

ACE: Not true. I play here most the time. This where the blues is born.

TOULOU: You got that right. (*Pause*)

ACE: Toulou . . . look how that evenin' sun make yo' skin shine like a brand new penny.

TOULOU: A empty wagon make a lot of noise . . . Abby . . . that's a pretty name. Don't sound nothin' like mine, but it sound good. How she look?

ACE: Like you! You even joog me like her—

TOULOU: How she act?

ACE: She wink her eyes at me like Candylady—

TOULOU: Where she live?

ACE: Elmwood Cemetery. Abby been dead a year now. I visits her grave and puts me some flowers down every time I come back. But today special—the anniversary of her death. She . . . died givin' birth to my baby. Baby gone, too. Was a girl.

TOULOU: I's so sorry to hear that.

ACE: Ya smell like her. Ya got crook teeth like her. Ya hands rough like her. You the kind of woman a man wanna meet sooner, but Abby—

TOULOU: Beat me to yo' lil' roamin' heart, huh?

ACE: Look, every blues man lookin' for somebody to sang they song about. Abby my song.

TOULOU: Well, there you go. You actually do have a heart. It just don't belong to me.

ACE: I been runnin' back and runnin' back ever since she passed. Hell, feel like a dog that been chained to a stake. Only thang is, the chain gone now, but I still keeps comin' back to that ole cemetery. Well, I ain't gone be comin back no mo'.

TOULOU: Whatchoo mean?

ACE: (*Gathering his things*) I done worn my welcome out like a sharecropper's work clothes. You can see my knees and they bucklin'.

TOULOU: No, no, no, don't leave. Stay at least one more night.

ACE: What 'bout yo' brother?

TOULOU: Oh, he ain't gone hear nothin' as drunk as that fool is. I'll put him on the floor. One more night? Let me give you somethin' to remember me by . . .

ACE: I would like somethin' of yourn. To keep on me at all times. Whatchoo got to give me, Toulou? (*She takes his hand and begins to lead him inside her shack.*)

TOULOU: What I really wanna give ya, I don't thank you can handle right now.

Scene 5

Next day. Early afternoon. Toulou and Candylady are sitting in front of their shacks washing greens in a bucket.

TOULOU: How you cook yo' greens?

CANDYLADY: A lot of salt and a lot of fatback.

TOULOU: And a lot of love.

CANDYLADY: Awwwwwww, shee-it. Ole Ace of Spades done put it down right again.

TOULOU: Shhhhh! He still sleepin'!

CANDYLADY: (*Quietly*) Hmph. Must be getting' a lil' tight over there. What Jib be doin'?

TOULOU: Just actin his color. Hell, darker! Luckily, he still sleep hard. (*Giggling.*) Done got 'customed to them night trains so he ain't hear one peep.

CANDYLADY: Now, I ain't wanna know all that. I guess he had a surprise this mornin. I heard 'em stompin off in a huff. Mmmph, mmph, mph. Is Ace gonna stay for a while at least?

TOULOU: He leavin' tonight like he always do.

CANDYLADY: You don't want him to.

TOULOU: I don't need no kind of man.

CANDYLADY: That's not what Toulou was tootin' a few days ago. You sho' you don't need a man 'round no mo'?

TOULOU: Sho' as the blue in the mornin'. (*Candylady takes a brown paper bag out of her apron pocket.*)

CANDYLADY: Well, I guess you don't want this here—uh, recipe I got for you? Here you was screamin' 'bout wantin a man—(*Candylady dangles the paper bag in front of Toulou's face.*)

TOULOU: Give it here! (*Candylady snatches it back.*)

CANDYLADY: Oh, now you want it!

TOULOU: Whatchoo got for me? Whatchoo got? (*Toulou snatches the bag out of her hand.*)

CANDYLADY: They don't call me the Candylady for nothin'. (*Toulou opens it and looks inside. Beat.*)

TOULOU: Aww, this just a orange in a paper bag. This ain't nothin'. Where the roots at? The trickin'. The conjure!

CANDYLADY: Now, whatchoo thank! I can't go all way 'cross the ocean back to Africa to get the real conjure, so I gots to stand in the oranges.

TOULOU: What wouldja used?

CANDYLADY: Hell, I don't know. See, this whatchoo do. (*Candylady demonstrates with the orange.*) This whatcha call a "get-a-man" ritual. First, you get yo' salt bowl and yo' orange. You write the man's name on a piece of this paper bag nine times. Nine times, nah! Poke a hole in the lips of yo' orange. Pour a lil' gunpowder in. Just enough. Not too much. Then you find one of his foot tracks in the dirt. Take that and sprinkle that on up in there with some cinnamon. Take a lock of yo' hair. Roll it up in that piece of paper bag. Then stuff it in the orange.

TOULOU: This don't sound right.

CANDYLADY: It ain't gone sound right at first, but when you see that man wit love in his eyes you gonna thank me. Now listen here. You find the house where he gone sleep at for nine days. You bury the orange with the hole end down. Make sho' it where the settin' sun can see it, outside of where he stayin.' Then you go inside that house. Put some red pepper in the stove and just when it gets to burnin' yo' eyes, you go to every corner of the kitchen and sprinkle salt—see, that's what the salt bowl for.

TOULOU: That ain't gone work.

CANDYLADY: Nine days later. Dig it up 'n you'll see. This rootwork here's some powerful shit!

TOULOU: Yeah and every Alice, Betty and Carrie's some powerful shit, too!

CANDYLADY: Why you ain't gone goof him?

TOULOU: 'Cause Ace don't stay nowhere. He don't never lay down in the same bed twice. I'm surprised he done laid in mine that many times. 'Sides, Ace in love with a ghost. I'm competin' with a dead woman.

CANDYLADY: Oh. Let me handle that. Put some of yo' menastration in his coffee . . .

TOULOU: What?!

CANDYLADY: Work every time.

TOULOU: Now, you just done caught a bad case of uncouth!!!

CANDYLADY: How you ever gone be a sanger if you don't get down and dirty? Gal, you betta throw that prissy shit on somewhere. Is ya sho' you just competin' with a dead woman? Hell, every man liable to have somebody else bakin' they jelly roll . . .

TOULOU: I'm the only girl he got 'round here—who alive. You done heard somethin?

CANDYLADY: Like I say before. They don't call me the Candylady for nothin'. (*Candylady dangles a small flyer in front of Toulou's face. Toulou takes it and reads it.*)

TOULOU: I thought you couldn' read?

CANDYLADY: Folk talk a lotta shit. I reads they lips.

TOULOU: (*Reads.*) "Hear the Ace of Spades play with Lillie Mae, Queen of Hearts on Beale. Lillie sangs the blues! All this week! Don't miss it." Huh! And he say he was gone leave tonight, but he sangin' with that old snagatooth broad!

CANDYLADY: Mmmmmm, hmmmmmh.

TOULOU: So you thank he gone lay up with this bitch?

CANDYLADY: MMMMMMmmmm, HMMMMMmmh.

TOULOU: So that mean, I gotta go to her house, bury the orange, roast red pepper in her stove, and salt her whole damn room?

CANDYLADY: Not if we keep him 'round here. I done heard you sang. You need to be on that stage with him. Not no Lillie, Queen of Hearts. That high yellah heifer ain't queen of nothin' but throwin' hissy fits.

TOULOU: Why you so keen on me sangin' with him for?

CANDYLADY: Every woman need a maine to make her dream come true. Shooo, I done had dreams before. I had dreams for my chilun.

TOULOU: I ain't never heard you talk 'bout no chilun before.

CANDYLADY: They all died off. My chilun was suppose ta bury me. I wouldn' suppose ta bury them. But life go that way sometimes, don't it? You remind me of the youngest one—Sarah. She was gone be a sanger, but she didn't get a chance to do that. You can—if you play yo' cards right. Pick up that Ace! You get that card, you done won the game.

TOULOU: Sarah . . .

CANDYLADY: Lil' just like you is. Didn't thank she was gonna make it when she came out. She made it for awhile, though . . .

TOULOU: So what I need to do?

CANDYLADY: First, you need the rule-yo-man root. (*Candylady takes a small green glass bottle out of her apron pocket.*) This here some dragon's blood. After you bury this orange, put this in whatever you cook him today.

TOULOU: He thank he gone leave . . .

CANDYLADY: Keep that nigger prone so he won't get gone.

Scene 6

Later that same day. Toulou's shack. Ace is on the bed covered with the quilt. He is moaning and shaking. Toulou brings a wet towel and a basin to the bedside. She wipes the sweat from Ace's forehead.

TOULOU: You just need to sit still and nap awhile.

ACE: Uggggggghhhhh! My stomach . . . my ass. I never eat before playin', but I did it anyway. I done broke my ritual! That's just somethin' I never—ugghh—do. I feel like I'm dyin'.

TOULOU: Quit actin' like a heifer. You know you ain't dyin'! At least . . . you betta not be.

ACE: I ain't gone make my gig tonight. God-doggonit! Lillie Mae gone be blowin' and I'ma miss it!

TOULOU: Honey, you ain't gone miss a thang. I done heard betta.

ACE: Oh, you ain't heard no betta than some Lillie! No ma'am! See, me and her go hand in hand. We play the blues like it's suppose ta be played.

TOULOU: (*With attitude*) Do you, really?

ACE: (*Moaning*) What I eat today?

TOULOU: I dunno.

ACE: Hell, my whole night shot to shit, and I ain't kiddin'. Ugggggggh. I know what I done ate! Some of that peach cobbler of yourn. You put in some bad peaches?

TOULOU: No. Even if I did, it would just taste nasty. Not have you runnin' to the out-house all day.

ACE: Well, somethin' wrong with me. Somethin' real terrible—ugghhh.

TOULOU: I'ma be back. I'ma go get some clean rags from the line out—

ACE: Don't go!!!

TOULOU: I need to—

ACE: Sang me a song. Please. Blues the best medicine.

TOULOU: (*Teasing.*) You sho' you don't want Lillie to sang it for you?

ACE: (*Growling.*) She ain't here with me right now, is she? It's just that . . . my mama used to sang me a song when I would get sick, that's all.

TOULOU: Well . . . um, just . . . um—er . . . Let me see . . . (*She clears her throat. At first, she is afraid to sing the song, but as she gazes into Ace's eyes she finds the courage to sing out loudly and proudly. Massaging his body with her notes she sings a soft tune, "Sloppy Heart Blues."*)

> I'm a young girl kinda sloppy wit my heart
> I confess, I'm a young girl kinda sloppy wit my heart
> E'er maine I give it to, either drop it or make it fall
> Baby I'm down on my knees
> Beggin' you please, baby please
> Don't you commit my sin
> Don't be . . . don't be sloppy wit my heart

ACE: (*Softly.*) Why, that's the bluest voice I've ever heard . . .

TOULOU: Really?

ACE: Mmmm, hmmm. I'm have to take you on up to the Tacky Shack wit me . . . (*He has fallen asleep in her arms. Toulou sneaks out of the shack.*)

TOULOU: (*Whispers, gradually getting louder.*) Candylady. Candylady! CANDYLADY! (*Candylady comes out of her shack.*) Are you tryin' to kill him or somethin'?! Whatchoo give me to give him!

CANDYLADY: Girl, a lil' dragon's blood ain't gone hurt nobody. Give 'em the runs—
that's all. Ain't nothin' magical 'bout it. He ain't dyin', just actin' like a bitch.

TOULOU: You sho'?

CANDYLADY: I do hoodoo, honey. I ain't like them other two-headed doctors in the
county. I does good with mines. It look like he stayin' though . . .

TOULOU: Yeah, but I can't talk to him with him runnin' to the outhouse every
minute.

CANDYLADY: He done heard you sang yet?

TOULOU: Yesssssssss. . . .

CANDYLADY: Chile, what he say?

TOULOU: That I got the bluest voice he done ever heard! He gone take me to the clubs
wit 'em, he say.

CANDYLADY: That's what I'm talkin' 'bout! Don't let that dream slip away! You just
make sho' you give him a dose of yo' voice every time you give him a slice of yo'
cobbler. Make him swallow it for the next nine days—(*Jib enters.*)

JIB: Good evening, ladies. How you been doin', Miss Candylady?

CANDYLADY: I'm doin' fine, darlin'. How 'bout yoself?

JIB: Could be grander. (*Jib cuts Toulou a look and goes to enter her shack.*)

TOULOU: Where you thank you goin'?

JIB: Get me somethin' to eat.

TOULOU: Ain't nothin' up in there for you. (*Ace moans from inside.*)

JIB: So he still up in there, huh? Thought y'all woulda had y'all fill of bumpin' bel-
lies. "Meats for the belly and the belly for the meats—hah, but God—hah—"

TOULOU: Oh, shush, bwoy!

JIB: You should be 'shamed of yoself.

TOULOU: What I do ain't none of yo' business.

JIB: You just wanna get hurt, dontcha? I'm tellin' ya. I know his kind. "For I am with
thee, and no man—hah—shall set on thee to hurt thee: for I have much people
in this city." Acts 10:18 . . . Wait a minute . . . 18:10? Yeah, Acts 18:10. I used to
be like Ace before I found the Lord again.

TOULOU: Ace ain't nothin' like you. And if you ask me, you ain't find God the first
time. (*Ace moans loudly from the shack.*)

JIB: You want this maine to come up in yo' house, put up his feet, eat up all yo' food
and take 'vantage of you?

CANDYLADY: Sound like somebody else I know.

JIB: Tell me what business you got shackin up?

TOULOU: I'ma go sang with him!

JIB: What! Girl, is you joogin' me? You can't sang. Now you can sang with the
choir, but you ain't no Memphis Minnie, Ida Cox, or Queen Bessie, for that
matter.

TOULOU: You don't know who I am and what I can do. And how you even know 'bout
Minnie 'nem?

CANDYLADY: I thought you was *sanctified*?

JIB: Never mind that! I know you ain't got no business out here coatin' in the streets with that no-good nigger.

TOULOU: Why you come up here? Seem like you do more layin' 'round than workin'. Tryin' to tell me how to run my life. Last time I checked, I'm the master of this plantation—small though it may be. (*Ace moans again.*)

JIB: I ain't gonna stand round 'n let you get nailed in yo' tail by some shiftless blues man. (*Jib goes toward the door. Toulou puts herself between her shack door and Jib.*)

TOULOU: Stop! He ain't done nothin' to you.

JIB: But stayed in this house one night too long.

TOULOU: Funny, I ain't asked where you been all day. Rhonda say she saw you comin' out a hole-in-the-wall.

CANDYLADY: And it wun't no club neither. (*Beat*)

JIB: I'm off. (*Jib exits.*)

TOULOU: Candylady, you got a conjure to get somebody *outta* yo' house, too?

CANDYLADY: I knew you'd be askin' for that one, sooner than later.

Scene 7

Night. Nine days later. Candylady and Toulou are gathered in the middle of their shacks. Cicadas sing.

CANDYLADY: You done dug it up? (*Toulou raises a mostly decomposed orange with the scrap of paper above her head.*) What it say? (*Toulou reads under the moonlight.*)

TOULOU: Ace of Spades, Ace of Spades, Ace of Spades, Ace of Spades—

CANDYLADY: Repeat after me. Nine times. "Earth root him near me. Earth make him stay. Earth root him near me. Never go away."

TOULOU: Why?

CANDYLADY: Just repeat the doggone thing, now! Remember this, once you turn the hands of it, ain't nothin' you can do. Gotta let workin' tricks lay.

TOULOU: "Earth root him near me. Earth make him stay. Earth root him near me. Never go away."

CANDYLADY: "Earth root him near me. Earth make him stay . . ." (*Candylady lights a small bundle of sage. She circles the flame around, smoke filling the air. Toulou and Candylady chant the slow prayer. They repeat it over and over again. It picks up speed and rolls into the wonderful sounds of soul and body making love. Candylady speaks in tongues. Toulou's body begins to shake. Their prayer climaxes and they stop. Something inexplicable has passed through them. Silence. Cicadas sing.*) Tell it exactly whatchoo want.

TOULOU: I wanna always have a piece of Ace heart. (*Crickets.*)

CANDYLADY: Now read it.

TOULOU: "He loves you." (*Candylady smiles. She takes a pink crushed velvet bag and places it in Toulou's hand.*)

CANDYLADY: Make sho' you hides this bag now. And don't never let no man touch it. He just might steal it away.

Scene 8

Next night. Toulou and Ace appear onstage in front of a crowd in a rowdy juke joint. They sing in perfect harmony together. Toulou dances beside him.

TOULOU: Welcome to the Tacky Shack! This Ace. I'm Toulou. And we got this here song for y'all.

ACE AND TOULOU:

      Bumblebee woman
      Bumblebee woman walkin' in
      Bumblebee woman
      Bumblebee woman walkin' in
      She done stung me
      Now I'm about to sin

ACE:

      She got poison on her tail
      That taste sweet as hell
      Watch her now, she buzzin' by
      'N she gone sting them men

ACE AND TOULOU:

      Bumblebee woman
      Bumblebee woman walkin' in
      She done stung me
      Now I'm about to sin

TOULOU:

      I got him crazy off my shine
      Tipsy off my wine
      Got ruby lips, hambone hips
      I ain't gone spend one dime

ACE AND TOULOU:

      Bumblebee woman
      Bumblebee woman walkin' in
      She done stung me
      Now I'm about to sin!

ACE:

      She got that high yellah skin
      That curly black hair
      Smooth wit a cup of water
      Hangin' down to there
      Bumblebee woman
      Bumblebee woman walkin' in
      She done stung me
      Now I'm about to sin

(*Lights shift, placing them back in Toulou's shack by the end of the song.*)

ACE: That there song for you!

TOULOU: (*Pissed.*) That song ain't for me. I don't look nothin' like that.

ACE: Awww, woman. That just give the song some flavor.

TOULOU: You sho' it ain't 'bout Light n' Yellah Lillie?

ACE: No, ma'am. That song's for you. That's gone be our first hit.

TOULOU: Lookie here! I got ya writin' songs and every thang.

ACE: You sho'll do! Sho'll do . . . I feel shame.

TOULOU: Whatchoo got to feel shame 'bout?

ACE: I was runnin' back and forth to the outhouse for I don't know how long!

TOULOU: Nine days . . .

ACE: Mmph, mmph, mmph. You gone be famous. You sang like a train rangin' in the midnight hour!

TOULOU: I *did* bring that house down tonight.

ACE: And Lillie had the nerve to try you. She ain't got no notes on you. It was all you.

TOULOU: You thank so?

ACE: What spell you done put on me, Toulou?

TOULOU: I don't know . . .

ACE: 'Cause I look at you sometimes like . . . sometimes . . .

TOULOU: Like what?

ACE: Like Daddy use to look at Mama. (*Beat*)

TOULOU: That's how you tell yo' women you sweet on 'em?

ACE: I ain't never told a woman much 'bout feelin'. I usually tell Jezebel that. She the only thang that catch my breath. But since I met you . . .

TOULOU: Whatchoo tryin' to tell me? (*Ace pulls out a broom decorated with flowers from behind the stove.*)

ACE: Whatcha say?

TOULOU: I ain't studyin' you!

ACE: You need to be studyin' me 'cause I been studyin' you. Marry me, Toulou. Jump over this broom like we jumpin' over the sky.

TOULOU: But you always movin' around.

ACE: Come with me to Chicago tonight! That white man up there waitin' on me to make a record. I'll blow the harp. You'll blow yo' lungs. We'll be a pair, baby. (*Ace sings from his core and dances her around the shack.*)

> Slipped her heart into my coffee
> It taste so sweet
> Slipped her heart into my coffee
> Taste good to me

Look baby, you got me rollin'!

TOULOU: (*Nervously laughing*) You just tryin' to make money off me!

ACE: I'm tryin' to make babies off you.

TOULOU: It's like I'm dreamin' while standin' . . .

ACE: Look at yo' pretty lil' mouth . . . (*He kisses her.*)

TOULOU: Where you learn to kiss so good from?

ACE: Watchin' my daddy with my mama. He never got to see Mama much. He was always out in 'nem fields. Made love to the night more than he did my mama. Daddy was a bluesman, too. Was the best man on slide Coldwater ever seent. Nobody could pull a bottleneck over them strangs like my daddy. His hands was so worn, every crack held a memory that would stream into that guitar, so buttery sweet . . . One day, Daddy was workin the field. Mr. Goldy said the nigger who split the most cotton that day would get a five cent raise, but my daddy wun't worried 'bout no pocket change—he had a new song to sing my mama. He was chuckin' quick 'cause he wanted to get on home and sang it to her. Daddy was shovin' cotton in that gin so fast until—until—that gin took off his hand. He died in that field alone, blood seepin' into that bale. I promised myself that if I ever got me a woman that I loved as much as Daddy loved Mama then I wun't gone be no fool. I was gone make our lives bend. If I'm gone be in that field, she gone be in that field wit me. If I'm gone be on the train, then she gone be on that train wit me. 'Sides every good bluesman need a woman to blow his blues 'bout . . .

TOULOU: What 'bout Abby? (*Beat*)

ACE: Who that? (*He acts as if he has never heard this name before. Toulou realizes that her spell has been cast over Ace.*)

TOULOU: (*Barely able to hold her pleasure.*) Never mind. Give me that broom.

Scene 9

Night. Toulou's porch. Toulou and Ace are kissing goodbye.

ACE: Remember where to meet me?

TOULOU: Where Auction meet the river.

ACE: 'Cross the trolley tracks and I'll be down there. Waitin'. (*They kiss again.*) I gots to go. Now remember, we can't miss that midnight train! That white man up there waitin'. Don't forget my guitar, nah.

TOULOU: I won't! You just make sho' you gets our money from Ole Bug-Eye.

ACE: Don't worry, girl. Soon, me and you gone be on 'nem records and e'er- body gone know our name. It's like you done put a spell on me, "Hoodoo Toulou." So tender, so blue. You mine. (*One last kiss. Ace exits. Toulou hurries inside to pack her things. Meanwhile, a tipsy Jib emerges from the shadows beside the shack. He enters the shack.*)

JIB: Where you thank you goin'?

TOULOU: (*Slightly frightened.*) Nowhere.

JIB: I saw you, "Too Lil'."

TOULOU: You ain't seen't nothin'.

JIB: I saw you. Sangin' that devil's music on the stage wit . . . yo' man. He ain't worth the salt in cornbread, that knotty-nappy-headed nigger that—

TOULOU: You drunk.

JIB: No, I ain't! Just a lil' stupid. Was down on Beale tonight tryin' to round me up some black sheep. Lord knows they need to be saved. I go into to the Tacky Shack, and guess who I's find? You and 'nat nigger . . . together. Daddy ain't raise you like that. (*Jib reaches out to Toulou, but loses his balance and falls onto the floor.*) You ain't gone help yo' big brother? I need yo' help. I need you to take care of me.

TOULOU: Why don't you get you a wife to take care of you?

JIB: You done wit me? How you gone do that? Oh, I see. You'se Ace woman now— one of 'em at least. You ain't got it all, "Too Lil'." But God take care of fools and babies.

TOULOU: Is that why you still alive?

JIB: Does he ever whisper "give me that sweet pussy" in the middle of the night? (*Jib pinches Toulou on her behind.*)

TOULOU: Stop, it Jib! I ain't playin witchoo tonight.

JIB: (*Mocking Ace's voice.*) "Toulou. Beautiful Toulou. Can I have some of your biscuits?"

TOULOU: You need to go to bed. (*Jib rustles through the cabinets of the shack. Toulou continues to gather her things.*)

JIB: You got some rubbin' alcohol? Some turpentine?

TOULOU: You don't need nothin' else to drank tonight! Lay down somewhere.

JIB: Well, I gots to give it to ya. You can sang! So proud of my lil' sister. I heard ya. Shit! Even got you a lil' guitar, now. Done came up to Memphis and became herself a blues sanger. Hmmph. Maybe I got some Jack left . . . (*Jib looks beneath the bed for alcohol and finds the marriage broom. He looks up to see Toulou, turned away packing a bag. Beat. It all clicks.*) Don't leave me.

TOULOU: Be right back. Gotta give Candylady her thangs back. (*Toulou begins to walk out of the shack with her bag.*)

JIB: Don't leave me. Stay wit me. You gone stay wit me? (*Jib breaks down into a maudlin sob.*) Promise you ain't gone leave me like Mama. Promise, Toulou! (*He holds onto her waist tightly. Beat*)

TOULOU: I promise.

JIB: (*Softly*) Tell you what, let's dance. (*He takes her into his arms. She struggles to free herself.*)

TOULOU: Jib, I don't wanna—

JIB: I just wanted to celebrate 'fore you leave, nah. I can't let you leave me again.

TOULOU: Whatchoo talkin 'bout? I was gone be back in a minute.

JIB: I don't wantchoo to go.

TOULOU: Jib—

JIB: I don't wantchoo wit him!!! (*Jib pushes her away, then goes under the bed and reaches under to pull out the marriage broom. He thrusts it into her face. Beat*)

TOULOU: I been sweepin'.

JIB: Who you thank I am? Sam sausage head? Why you ain't invite me to the weddin'? I know! Because you done did what them backwater country folks do. You ain't done it by God so the contract ain't worth shit! Jumpin over a broom! Hell, might as well go back to Africa for all that nothin' you believe in! (*Jib breaks the broom in half over his knee.*)

TOULOU: Nooo!

JIB: Gone and found yoself some hoodoo love!

TOULOU: You thank you know everythang 'cause you done been to some high falutin' preacher school that Daddy sent you to. Now, I'm sick and tired of yo' shit! You sit up here and lay around all day claimin' you puttin' up a church. Claimin' you goin' down to Beale to save some black sheep! You on the corner lookin' for some pussy just like the next one. Just like yo' Daddy! Always tryin' to "heal" somebody. Puttin' y'all hands where ya don't need to be puttin' 'em. Hell, if it wun't for me, you wouldn' have a pot to piss in or a window to throw it out of. (*Jib slaps her.*)

JIB: You just don't get it, do you? He don't love you! He can't never love you, like—

TOULOU: You?

JIB: Like . . . yo' family.

TOULOU: Mama dead, Jib! And as far as I'm concerned, Daddy dead to me.

JIB: You gotta forgive him for that mess.

TOULOU: "I'll show you mine, if you show me yours . . ." Ain't that one of y'all lines? He taught you more than scripture, I'll tell you that.

JIB: I know you ain't too good on forgivin', but I'm tryin' to make thangs right.

TOULOU: The apple don't fall too far from the fuckin' tree!

JIB: Don't talk about Daddy like that!

TOULOU: Y'all ain't shit! I'm gone, Jib. Bye. (*She begins to run out the door, but he grabs her.*) Let go a' me! Let go a' me! (*Toulou struggles against him. Jib pushes Toulou down on the bed. Toulou screams.*)

JIB: I ain't gone hurt you. Tryin' to make you feel good. (*Jib rips off her skirt. Toulou kicks and fights. He pins her down. Jib pulls down his pants. Candylady stumbles to her screen door.*) I'm tryin to make you feel good, like I useta. Remember?

TOULOU: Help me! Help me! Candylady, help me! (*Candylady opens her door, coming out to her porch. She stops.*)

JIB: I loves you. I loves you so much.

TOULOU: Help me!

JIB: I loves you. You mine. (*Jib finishes raping his sister. Candylady can't will her feet to move.*)

TOULOU: God. Please. Help. Me. (*A moment of silence.*)

JIB: God ain't got nothin to do with this. (*The midnight train sounds. Jib breaks down sobbing uncontrollably on top of her. Candylady stands there, in shock. The sound of the train in the blackout.*)

End of Act One

Act 2

Scene 1

Day. The shacks. Toulou emerges from her shack strumming Ace's left-behind guitar. She has the lean-back of a woman six months pregnant. Candylady emerges from her house and stands on her porch looking at Toulou playing "Misery."

TOULOU:

Gone on away from me baby
I don't want you no way
Gone on away from me baby
My heart ain't where you stay
I thought yo' name was Love
Now I call you misery

He was a tall drank of water
On a hot summer night
Looked too damn good
To e'va be right
He say, "Miss, howyado?
My name is Misery."
Who in hell's name
Done played this trick on me?

Gone on away from me baby
I don't want you no way
Gone on away from me baby
My heart ain't where you stay
I thought yo' name was Love
Now I call you Misery

Left me danglin' like a fish from a strang
You took my heart, you took everythang
Hook in my mouth, hook in my soul
The dreams of you that won't come true
In this big black hole

Gone on away from me baby
I don't want you no way
Gone on away from me baby
My heart ain't where you stay
I thought yo' name was Love
Now I call you Misery

CANDYLADY: You gettin' mighty good on that there.

TOULOU: How you know? Ya been eavesdropping?

CANDYLADY: Got thin walls. (*Beat*) Yo' fingers must be real sored over. (*Ignoring her, Toulou strums her guitar and sings again.*)

TOULOU:

> Gotta catch that train
> Ride it like a maine
> Gotta catch that train—

CANDYLADY: That's a new one!

TOULOU: Gotta have mo' than one song to sang when I finally get out on the road.

CANDYLADY: You will.

TOULOU: I know. (*Toulou tries to stand up on her porch.*)

CANDYLADY: You need some help?

TOULOU: I don't need nobody help . . . ma'am.

CANDYLADY: Ma'am? What I tell you 'bout callin' me ma'am? I ain't that old.

TOULOU: Shee-it! You'se old in yo' ways. I'm just tryin' to show you respect since you'se my elder and all.

CANDYLADY: No, I'ms ya friend.

TOULOU: Friend? Hmmph. (*Pause*)

CANDYLADY: I ain't seen ya in months seem like. You don't half come out the house. You been getting' them plates I been leavin' for you?

TOULOU: I give you yo' plates back, don't I? (*Pause*)

CANDYLADY: Well, thank ya for warshin' them. Rhonda had ta take ya job up on Davey's Plantation.

TOULOU: I guess she need the pocket change more than I do. (*Candylady sits on the porch beside her and brings out a metal flask.*)

CANDYLADY: Wanna lil' taste? I hears ya in the mornin's . . . (*She holds it out for Toulou.*) It'll make yo' tummy feel better. (*Toulou looks at Candylady cautiously then takes the flask. And drinks it. It's nasty; she spits it out.*) Crushed up charcoal and water. Keep it. The sickness ain't left you yet, but it will soon.

TOULOU: All yo' conjures and cures. You thank you got a cure for everythang. You got a cure for lonely? Hell, you got a cure for everything else. So you thank. You just one a' 'nem two-bit two-headed doctors. Don't nothin' you do work.

CANDYLADY: My rootwork *do* work—

TOULOU: It do? I sho'll is by myself right now.

CANDYLADY: I just start thangs out. It up to you to finish 'em. Sometime folk can taint the trick you lay. Can break the spell. Be actin' like backwards potions. Like, like—

TOULOU: Jib?

CANDYLADY: Yes . . . Like . . . Jib. Some folk so evil inside they can break the will of good. But there are ways to fix nasty folks like him—

TOULOU: I don't like the way you "fix" folks. Got a fish fryin' in the skillet, but steady lookin' the other way. Lettin' thangs get burnt.

CANDYLADY: I wun't always the best cook. But I ain't the one who burnt yo' last can of beans. You shoulda' just left when you had the chance. Met Ace down at them tracks that night.

TOULOU: How you know I was suppose ta meet him?

CANDYLADY: Like we say . . . these walls is thin. (*Silence*)

TOULOU: I called yo' name. (*Beat*) I called yo' name and you ain't come.

CANDYLADY: You ain't the only one been taken 'vantage of! Before you die you might be done in two or three more times. A man'll be a man, even if it is ya own brotha.

TOULOU: I bet' not never see the likes of him again. Heard he still 'round. Buildin' his "church"!

CANDYLADY: You done learnt the hard way. Bad mens stay and good mens go away.

TOULOU: Never mind all that! Whatchoo need to give me is the root Rhonda didn't take.

CANDYLADY: Can't. Hoodoo womens told ta heed the river, not stop it.

TOULOU: Well, I talked to the river yesterday.

CANDYLADY: And what she say?

TOULOU: It's mine! I'ma do with it what I please. Sooner I flood Jib baby out, sooner I can get gone!

CANDYLADY: You sho' you wanna take that chance? It might be Ace's, now—

TOULOU: I ain't lucky enough for it to be his.

CANDYLADY: Luck ain't got nothin' to do with it, the bones already been shook. (*Beat*)

TOULOU: You know what's inside me?

CANDYLADY: . . . I don't know nothin'.

TOULOU: Well, shake 'em, then. (*Candylady begins to go to her porch.*) I said shake 'em! (*Candylady stops. She turns around. She thinks for a moment, then digs under her dress, from which she brings out a fistful of animal bones. She throws down the bones in the middle of the two shacks and squats over them to read. Candylady is reading, reading, reading. She smiles, she reads more, then she freezes. She picks up the bones and begins to pace.*)

CANDYLADY: (*To herself*) No, it ain't supposed to be that way.

TOULOU: What? What did you see?

CANDYLADY: No . . . The bones . . .

TOULOU: Tell me whatchoo saw. What? Tell me!!!

CANDYLADY: No. They changed . . .

TOULOU: Candylady, you betta tell me what goin' on . . .

CANDYLADY: You can't know.

TOULOU: You ain't makin' a lick of sense, Candylady! Candylady, what did you see? Did you see . . . him? You tell me whatchoo done saw. You tell me now! (*Beat*)

CANDYLADY: It gone be a girl. Ya gotta keep this child if you want Ace's love. Let her grow. You say the only thang you needed in this world was a piece of Ace heart, well . . . be grateful. Most folk die never truly bein loved . . . as for Ace, he walkin' the line . . .

TOULOU: He ain't comin' back. Ain't it?

CANDYLADY: Whenever I throw them bones, they only tell me what most like to be possible, not what will finally *be*. The bones can always be changed by what we do and by what somebody else do. The bones can be changed by you—

TOULOU: I'm tired of this mess! All these goddamned riddles and tricks. I shouldna' never listened to you. Layin' down tricks. Gooferin'! Hexin'! Doin' this and that, forcin' folk hands! Thangs gone be the way they gone be and that that.

CANDYLADY: Now, it up to you, Toulou—

TOULOU: You was the one tellin' me I needed a man. That I needed to sang wit a man. I thought that was the way. Yo' tricks! Hah! Now, I ain't got no mens around. Nobody to hug me. Nobody to hurt me—

CANDYLADY: My lil' Sarah—the one that remind me of you—oh, them bones say she was gonna be a sanger chile. Just like you. She was my last one. Sarah was born July 4, 1865. The day didn't mean nothin' to me 'cause I was still shovin' cotton in sacks, chile. Still callin' the white man "massa." O'er the years I gots beat somethin' horrible. From massa to Daddy on down to my mens. My back got a web of welts that won't never heal. One night, I was feedin' Sarah from my tit, but she wouldn' go to sleep. Teeth was breakin' through the skin so she was up all night. My husband Wally come in screamin' and hollerin', "Quiet that baby down! Or I'ma kill it and you!" Just mad 'cause some cracker down the street talked down to 'em. I says to Sarah, "Shhhhh, Pappy need his sleep, baby girl. Shhhh!" And I pressed her as tight as I could into my tit so she'd just stop cryin'. "Suck that milk, lil' girl. Suck it." She finally got full. I put her to sleep beside me and we made it through the night—she didn' wake up once. The next mornin' I looked at her lips. They was blue. She was gone . . . You right. You don't need nobody. Especially nobody who gone make you smother the life that's yourns. Just make sure you ain't the one stealin' the wind outcho own dreams. (*Candylady reaches in her pouch beneath her dress and brings out a small red vial.*) You want what Rhonda didn't take? Here. One drop make the floods come for two weeks. It hurt hard. I know . . . Losin' a chile like losin' a part of yoself. Three drops take care of yoself. And nine drops . . . well . . . that take care of somebody else. (*They look at each other. Toulou takes the red vial from Candylady.*)

TOULOU: When did you make this?

CANDYLADY: I did it the night I heard you.

Scene 2

Next week. Night. Orion's belt burns bright blue in the sky. Beneath the starlight, Toulou looks at the red vial. She opens it. She smells it. It enchants her. The train whistle blows in the distance. Ace walks in all haggard and worn, playing a slightly out of tune guitar. He stumbles onto Toulou's porch and sits down. Ace plays a haunting song, "Auction Block Blues." His voice, teeming with booze and pain, stops her.

ACE:

> The road paved by cotton
> Is the road straight to hell
> I say, the road paved by cotton
> Is the road straight to hell
> I'm sittin' at this auction block
> Ain't got no mo' soul to sell
>
> I say my feet gonna lead me
> Down this crooked railroad track

> I done rode this broke rail
> And I can't find my way back
>
> Lookin' sideways, lookin' 'round
> Lookin' up and lookin' down
> Only thang I got is my heart
> On this old auction block
>
> I'm lookin' for my baby
> But she don't want me no more
> I'm lookin' for my baby
> To come and open her screen door
> I promise my purty baby
> I ain't gone leave Memphis no more
>
> I say my feet gonna lead me
> Down this crooked railroad track
> I done rode this broke rail
> And I can't find my way back
>
> Lookin' sideways, lookin' 'round
> Lookin' up and lookin' down
> Only thang I got is my heart
> On this old auction block

(*Toulou opens her creaky screen door. Ace doesn't look back.*)

ACE: I was hopin' you was dead. 'Cause at least that would 'xplain it.

TOULOU: I see you done got yoself a new guitar.

ACE: I had to. I left my old one.

TOULOU: That one sound ugly.

ACE: Won this one off a spades game up in Chicago. Lost a heap more than I won though.

TOULOU: Well . . . 'Least Jezebel got somethin' to 'company her. (*Ace turns around and finally sees Toulou.*)

ACE: Shee-it, you done got fat, gurl.

TOULOU: I been eatin' real good.

ACE: Folks been complainin' 'bout how there ain't no mo' food 'round. I guess you ate it all up!

TOULOU: You thank you so funny.

ACE: (*Laughs to himself*) You just a reglar remnant. Been followin' me in my days and in my nights.

TOULOU: You got a thang 'bout fallin' in love with ghosts.

ACE: I reckon I do.

TOULOU: I reckon you can't stop by and visit now and again. This the longest you done been away. A lot done happened.

ACE: I *sees* that.

TOULOU: You wanna come in?

ACE: Nah, just stoppin' by. I don't wanna wake yo' man up in there.

TOULOU: I ain't got no mens. I'm by myself.

ACE: Hmmph. (*Beat*) Jib ain't in there?

TOULOU: Hell, goddamn no!

ACE: Damn . . . Just askin'.

TOULOU: You sho'll is askin' a lot of questions to just be walkin' up in here.

ACE: Well, let me ask this one, since I sho'll ain't got no answer for it: Why you ain't come like I told you to?

TOULOU: Why you just didn' wait?

ACE: The world don't wait for nobody, 'cludin' me. So when it say move, I moves, no matter how hard I try to stay. I toldja that white man was tryin' to record me. Why you didn' come?

TOULOU: We didn't need to go up to Chicago! People dreamin' 'bout paradise up there, and we sittin' pretty top a bluff!

ACE: Hmph. You wun't never no lie . . . A song I wrote done made a thousand dollars. Ain't that some shit? That white man down from Chicago finally recorded me. But . . . he ain't like my voice. "We need a woman's voice. That's what's sellin'." I got drunk one night . . . was playin' some spades. Bettin' shit I didn' need to be bettin'. Well, that cracker must got one drop of nigger blood in him 'cause he play spades betta than me. I lost my song. Lost it 'cause I didn't know how much it was worth. One month later, I'm walkin' down the street and e'rybody up in Chicago singing my song. Hmmmph. Been ramblin' 'round with this stankin' guitar ever since.

TOULOU: Sound like the world ain't too keen on you.

ACE: It ain't never been. See, if you woulda been there. You coulda cut a record. Cut yo' own . . . That white man woulda loved you. But you ain't come. Why? I just wanna know why.

TOULOU: 'Cause . . . (*Silence. She refuses to answer.*)

ACE: (*Shaking his head*) Is that my baby?

TOULOU: Sho'll is.

ACE: You sho' you ain't been coatin'?

TOULOU: Nigger, please!

ACE: It just that some womens done say it mine, and it pop out and don't look nothin' like me—

TOULOU: Look in my eyes and see if I'm a lie. (*He does. She puts his hand her stomach.*) I got a lot of hope in my tummy. I got enough for you and me.

ACE: You gonna let me come back home?

TOULOU: If you sho' this where you wanna be . . . (*Beat*)

ACE: Ain't no use a' runnin' 'round no more. Ready to put all this silliness behind me.

TOULOU: You'll get back to it. Hell, when the baby pop out, I'm liable to come back on the road witchoo—

ACE: Nah, baby—

TOULOU: But I been writin' songs! You should hear 'em—

ACE: We done wit our nigger dreams—

TOULOU: Perk it up, baby! You gotta bring somethin' more than sorrow into this house.

ACE: Whatchoo mean by that?

TOULOU: You got some money on ya?

ACE: Awww, Toulou. I thought you was different from the others.

TOULOU: I am different. I got yo' baby.

ACE: Hell, whatchoo want me to do? Sell my guitar?

TOULOU: Well, this house too lil' for two guitars and like I say, that one sound ugly.

ACE: I ain't sellin' shit!

TOULOU: I thought you done gave up on it?

ACE: I just might wanna play on it every once in a while—

TOULOU: Like you play on me?

ACE: Ain't true—

TOULOU: If I let you come home, you gots to do right by me. More than you done ever done by anybody in yo' life.

ACE: I can't do right by nobody. Can't do right by myself. I done lost my song. I done lost everything—

TOULOU: You think that sad story gone get ya out of this puddin' you put me in? Slurp it up, baby. (*Ace looks down at his guitar.*) You ready? All I got in my tummy is . . . a lot of hope.

ACE: A lot of hope. Yeah. Yeah. Yeah . . . Woman, you betta cooks me somethin' real good tonight . . . Where my shuga at? Come on, give me a kiss. (*Ace begins necking this beautiful pregnant woman he hasn't seen in six months . . .*)

TOULOU: Yo' thang too long. It'll hit the baby in the head.

ACE: Yeah, put a big ole dent right 'tween the eyes. (*He tries again. She pushes him away firmly.*) What wrong?

TOULOU: I don't want—

ACE: But—

TOULOU: Not now. Just not now. (*She goes inside the screen door and it slams behind her.*)

Scene 3

Next week. Toulou's shack. Ace sits off with bottle in hand. Toulou stomps back into the shack with an oil canister. She sets it down by the bed.

TOULOU: That was yo' time to put some mo' petro in that outhouse out yonder. (*Ace grunts.*) Ya hear what I say?

ACE: No.

TOULOU: (*Cutting Ace a look*) It stanks to the high heavens out there. Them lil' niglets next door keep on usin' our outhouse. I told Rhonda to keep her chilun' away from there. Five of 'em just pilin' up the shit. How can lil' people make so much stank?

ACE: Well, we finna find out soon enough. (*Ace takes a swig from his whiskey bottle.*)

TOULOU: (*Eyeballing Ace*) I done told you' 'bout that drankin'. 'Specially on a Sunday mornin'.

ACE: Since when you done become sanctified? Hell, a shot of whiskey help a maine face the truth 'bout his life. (*Beat*) You gone get you somethin' to eat this mornin'?

TOULOU: Nah.

ACE: You need to.

TOULOU: You can have some of this catfish and grits over there. I'ma get some biscuits out of the oven in a minute—

ACE: You ain't gone eat?

TOULOU: I ain't hungry.

ACE: Toulou, it look like you carryin' "too lil'."

TOULOU: Ain't that why they call me Toulou? "Too lil' for this, too lil' for that." Hell, but I ain't too lil' to do everythang 'round here. (*Ace begins to practice on his guitar, ignoring Toulou. He then begins to sing "Hoodoo Toulou."*)

ACE:

> Slipped her heart into my coffee
> It taste so sweet
> Slipped her heart into my coffee
> Taste good to me
> Slipped her heart into my coffee
> Won't leave me be
> Slipped her heart into my coffee
> Got me on my knees—
>
> I's a hoochie-coochie ramblin' man
> Ain't never been caught
> Got this pecan girl from Memphis
> Runnin' through my thoughts
> Go by the name of "Hoodoo Toulou"
> Put a spell on me
> Cooked some love into my biscuits
> Then tricked me to eat
>
> Slipped her heart into my coffee
> It taste so sweet
> Slipped her heart into my coffee
> Taste good to me
> Slipped her heart into my coffee
> Won't leave me be
> Slipped her heart into my coffee
> Got me on my knees—(*Beat*)

"Toulou" . . . Jib say y'all daddy gave you that name. (*Toulou's body stiffens.*)

TOULOU: Whatchoo brangin' his name up in here fu'?

ACE: No reason. Ran into him last night down there on Beale. Still doin' his "layin on of hands" trick. Still needin' a beat down.

TOULOU: What the hell *you* doin' down there?

ACE: Just catchin' up wit folks, that's all.

TOULOU: You ain't supposed to be down there drankin—

ACE: There you go, naggin' again.

TOULOU: I ain't a' naggin' !

ACE: Oh, yes you is! Now it my time to nag on you, "Hoodoo Toulou." Would you ever call yoself lyin' to me? Huh? HUH, Toulou? (*Ace backs Toulou into the shack's corner.*)

TOULOU: That smell still makin' my tummy queasy. Look like I'ma need to put some mo' petro to take the edge off that stank. (*Toulou grabs canister, but Ace grabs Toulou's wrist.*)

ACE: I don't smell nothin' comin' from that outhouse, but somethin' sho'll do stank up in here. You ever smelt a lie, Toulou? Hmmph? Smell like my nails, my hair, a small bottle of Jack! All wrapped up in yo' lil' mojo bag. (*Ace takes her dusty pink crushed velvet mojo bag and dangles it in her face.*)

TOULOU: Where ya find that at?

ACE: Don't matter. I fount it!

TOULOU: You done broke the cardinal rule. (*Toulou scratches at him, but Ace holds her back.*) You ain't suppose ta touch a woman's mojo! You done messed up the power.

ACE: Whatchoo done did, gurl? Put a hex on me?

TOULOU: (*She pounds on Ace's chest.*) You gone make me lose my power!

ACE: You done trapped me in this goddamn shack! You done stole my goddamn soul!

TOULOU: You done stole my heart! (*Ace throws the mojo bag and she scrambles across the floor to get it.*)

ACE: Befo' I left for Chicago, I kept on havin' this dream. Me and you walkin' past oranges with pieces of paper bag bloomin' out them. You wun't let me step on 'nem. Said that I'd crush the seeds. But I wanted ta step on 'nem oranges so bad. They was so big and bright that I hadta cover my eyes . . . No wonder . . . you done laid a trick on me.

TOULOU: You was always leavin' me.

ACE: You ain't had to force my hand! You been crawlin' 'round at night for my toe clippins, the barber shop floor for my hair. You prolly got some of my man juice in that bag. (*Beat*) You do, don't you?

TOULOU: (*Nodding her head*) 'Cause you was always leavin' me.

ACE: They say a man ain't supposed to touch a woman's mojo. Well, we wouldn' have to touch the bag if bitches wun't tryin to goofer a nigger! You didn' have to force my hand, Toulou.

TOULOU: But I just wanted to know.

ACE: Know what?

TOULOU: How it feel. When somebody love you. Love you wit all they heart.

ACE: When I was on that boxcar all I could think about was you. Yo' waist fit in the crook of my arm like that last puzzle piece—snap. You was supposed to know that. Ya know . . . folks 'round here talk, Toulou. They *hear* shit and that make them know shit. I done heard some thangs that I don't wanna believe. But if you hexin' me then . . . I don't know *what* to believe . . . (*No response from Toulou*) Is that my baby?

TOULOU: It's yours . . .

ACE: If I love it, huh?

TOULOU: I got a lot of hope in my tummy.

ACE: Hope? We need a heap more than some fuckin' hope! I wanna kick you in yo' stomach so bad. Ya lucky you'se wit chile.

TOULOU: You wanna kick me in my stomach? Kick me! Kick me now! I swear, lovin' you like fallin' into a hole in the ground. I done come up missin' in my own mirror. It's like I done had a screen door between my legs and I just kept lettin' you come in and out, in and out, IN AND OUT! But you, you just kept on lettin' it slam. It's been slammed so much my screen door 'bout fallin' off its hinges!

ACE: Stop yo' yappin'! You wanted me more than I wanted you—

TOULOU: Hah! I can do bad on my lonesome—

ACE: You can't do shit by yoself! You ain't neva gone do shit, be shit—

TOULOU: Yes I is, Ace. I got me some songs. I got mo' songs than you could eva thank of. I'ma pop this baby out and put it on yo' lap. And you ain't gone see none of me no mo'. Unh, unh. The Toulou train gone choo-choo her way on down the river. I'ma sang my songs if it the last thang I do.

ACE: I'll throw this baby in the river, you leave it wit me.

TOULOU: And I'll help you. 'Cause I'll be damned if I'ma be the one left lookin' in the face of a mistake for the rest of my life.

JIB: (*Offstage*) Hey, there! Y'all up in there? (*Toulou freezes, Jib enters from the alley.*)

ACE: Speakin' of the devil . . .

TOULOU: What the hell he doin' here?

ACE: (*Watching her closely*) He say he needed a place to stay tonight 'cause he leavin' for Byhalia in the mornin'.

TOULOU: Ain't nobody tell you to be invitin' no folk up in my house.

ACE: This my house and that yo' brother! I'll tell you this, I'ma find out somethin' from somebody tonight. Leave potatoes in the dark long enough, even they grow eyes.

JIB: Hey, y'all up in there? (*Ace comes out onto the porch.*)

ACE: Hey, maine. Toulou just getting' ready for the day.

JIB: Awwww, I'll stand out here a bit. Catch some of that Sunday mornin' light. She been doin' good?

ACE: Yeah.

JIB: Baby prolly ready to bust out any second, now.

ACE: Nah, she got a lil' longer.

JIB: I wish I had a son to help me with this here church. Need more than one pair of hands.

ACE: She say ours—it—a girl. It's hangin' high, that's how we know.

JIB: Is that right? I bet she gone look like Toulou.

ACE: (*Under his breath*) At least we knows that fu sho' . . . We got some catfish n' grits on the stove up in there. Toulou, ya decent? (*Silence*) Come on up. Womens know they be takin' too long to do shit. (*Ace and Jib walk through the door. Toulou stares at Jib. He looks back. Pause*)

JIB: Hows ya doin', sister?

TOULOU: Fine.

JIB: I thought I'd surprise ya.

TOULOU: Almost like it's my birthday.

ACE: Fix us some plates, Toulou. (*Toulou goes to fix the plates.*)

TOULOU: Whatchoo want in yo' grits?

ACE: Butter and sugar.

TOULOU: You want some oranges, too?

ACE: (*To Jib*) So ya gettin' ready to get up on out of here, huh?

JIB: The one thing that would keep me here I done lost.

ACE: Well, runnin' a church is some risky shit.

JIB: That what I know. (*Jib brings out a gold glass-bottom metal flask.*)

ACE: Ooooooweee! Whatcha got there?

JIB: This here full of some premium Jack. That Gold Medal Series.

ACE: They got some Gold Medal?

JIB: Limited edition "Jack Flasks" they callin' them. Sellin' 'em out the Shuga Shack.

ACE: Damn, she sho'll look pretty. I guess preachers gots ta drank in style. Dress in style, too. I likes me them there wing-tips. (*Indicates Jib's shoes*) All that must a' cost a pretty penny.

JIB: Hell, I don't know how much it cost 'cause I can't counts my money.

TOULOU: Well, you wun't always the brightest penny in the pouch.

JIB: Oh, there go Toulou. Joogin. (*To Ace*) You might need to go get one for yoself.

ACE: I just might. So you tired of good ole Memphis?

JIB: Nah, seem like Memphis tired of me. But I got word from down Byhalia. Daddy sick, Toulou. Folk say he ain't got long. I ain't been too right in the head since I found out. (*Toulou slams Ace's plate on the table.*)

TOULOU: Hmmmph.

JIB: Thought I'd let ya know . . . Might need to go on down there and see him off. Well . . . Funny—what can happen in a year.

ACE: I'd say that myself.

TOULOU: If you grab the river up, you can fold a year back onto itself. The river speaks the truth. (*The men look at each other.*)

ACE: Toulou been hangin' 'round Candylady too long. Talkin' in riddles and shit. Sometime can't barely understand her.

JIB: Womens hard to understand. 'Specially when they wit child.

TOULOU: Womens is hard to understand 'cause mens can't treat 'em right. (*Toulou gives another plate to Ace.*)

ACE: What I'm gone do wit this?

TOULOU: Pass it on to Jib. I don't feel like walkin' all the way over there.

ACE: Toulou, if you don't act right—

JIB: That's alright. I done already had some biscuits this mornin'. You happy to see me, sister? (*Silence. To Ace*) I see you still playin' on that guitar.

ACE: Useta have two. Just got one now. Pawnt it for some pocket change, ya know?

JIB: Wish I could play a instrument. When you seen't me last night, I was lookin for a piano player for the church. Thought I'd find one real easy down there.

ACE: You ain't gone never change. I don't get down on Beale too much nowadays.

TOULOU: You was just there last night.

JIB: Oh, a man can do what he wanta. Me and you should go on down there again tonight.

TOULOU: Naw, he gotta go out to the Davey field today and tomorrow mornin' so—

ACE: I done tolt you ten goddamn times that I ain't pickin' no cotton.

JIB: Those hands made for pickin' strangs, not no cotton. If I was you, I wouldn't waste it, maine. Not me. (*Jib picks up Ace's guitar.*)

ACE: Yeah, you right 'bout that.

JIB: Whatchoo say, maine? I see ya lil' fingers itchin'. Let's gone on down there!

ACE: We gettin started a lil' early, ain't it?

JIB: It's my last day in Memphis . . .

TOULOU: You thank yo' Daddy'll like you runnin' out in the streets while he layin' on his deathbed?

JIB: He'd be the first one to say a man ain't perfect. (*Beat*)

ACE: (*Standing.*) Let me get my thangs together.

JIB: We off. (*Jib walks out of the shack and waits on the porch. Toulou stares at Ace, who grabs his guitar. He looks at her stomach, but doesn't say anything as the screen door closes behind him. Toulou goes back to clearing the plates they left behind. She goes back to the table and discovers that Jib left his metal flask on the table. She digs into her bra and pulls out the red vial. She dumps all of the poison into the metal flask and shakes it, leaving it on the table.*)

Scene 4

Later on that night. The shacks. Jib and Ace are drunkenly walking back to Toulou's shack. Jib has the guitar in tow. The broken broom adorned with dead flowers lurks in the corner.

JIB: Is she here?

ACE: Prolly. Toulou! (*They walk into the shack and discover that she's not there.*)

JIB: Prolly over Candylady getting' somethin'. See she still got that broom in the corner.

ACE: Oh, she sweep with it now.

JIB: I spect she would. It *is* a broom. (*Jib sees the metal flask sitting on the kitchen table.*) Oooooooo!

ACE: See, I told ya, ya left it here.

JIB: Ooooooo, boy! I was 'bout to cut up if it wun't here. Shee-it.

ACE: Wanna play cards?

JIB: Now, you knows I'm bad as hell.

ACE: I been on a losin' streak myself lately. Hell, I ain't even got nothin' to gamble for no mo.

JIB: How 'bout that there guitar?

ACE: My guitar? I don't know 'bout that, maine.

JIB: Hell, if I was you I'd take that guitar and leave. What a maine like you doin' holed up in this itty bitty old shack anyway? Freedom. That's the prize!

ACE: If I bet my guitar, whatchoo gone bet?

JIB: My Bible. (*They laugh heartily.*)

ACE: What if you won that one though? I'd run yo' church and you could be a travelin' bluesman like me. Preacher man, go see the world! You ain't prolly been nowhere but to Byhalia and back. The world got some colors you ain't even dreamed of.

JIB: Bet it got some womens, too.

ACE: Womens? I'll be the first to say I've had my share of 'em.

JIB: You a lucky one.

ACE: I always been good at givin 'nem what they need—for the moment. Does that make me a bad maine?

JIB: Nah, it just make you a maine. (*Ace picks up the cards on the table.*)

ACE: So . . . one last one for the road?

JIB: Why the hell not?

ACE: It's 'bout time I break that streak. I got some John the Conqueror in my pocket and a blue tongue. I'm ready Freddy!

JIB: Nigger, please.

ACE: Deal.

JIB: Nah, it's yo' deal.

ACE: You want me to deal the cards?

JIB: The cards already been dealt. I'm gone lose tonight, my boy, either way. I done already lost.

ACE: I don't know, Jib. Tonight might be yo' lucky night. So what we playin' for? Really?

JIB: I sees you been eyein' my Jack flask.

ACE: You right, you right . . . (*Jib pounds his flask on the table.*)

JIB: How 'bout it? (*Ace takes it into his hand and peers into its shine.*)

ACE: She says she want me to stop drankin . . .

JIB: Maine, quit it! You lettin' her control ya like that? What she done did? Put yo' manhood in her lil' mojo bag!

ACE: Quit joogin' me!

JIB: You'se a womanish bluesman if you don't drank, nah. (*They laugh—Jib heartily, Ace uncomfortably.*)

ACE: This Jack flask'll do it for me and if you win—

JIB: Yo' guitar'll do. If I don't win it now, I'ma come back for it later. I'm like Jesus. I comes like a thief in the night!

ACE: Guess I'll have to sleep with one eye open from now on!

JIB: Yeah, maine! I can't believe the Ace of Spades is still here. What she done done to get you so sprung? Surprised you ain't walkin' on all fours like Milford Jackson from Tupelo.

ACE: I thought you ain't believe in that.

JIB: I don't. But I believe what I saw—a man turnt to a dog!

ACE: I'm dealin'. The sooner I win, the sooner I'll be out of here. Plus, I want that there flask.

JIB: Whatchoo mean by that?

ACE: If I win, after tonight I'm movin' to Chicago. I'ma go up there and make some more records. I done already cut one song on a circle and everybody up in Chicago sangin' it. They like my songs already, maine.

JIB: Old Ace of Spades gettin' ready to move his itchy feet . . .

ACE: I'm famous 'round here, but I'm gone be world-class, maine.

JIB: You joogin' me?

ACE: What I need to joog a joker for? My book.

JIB: Damn, Southern dreams do come true.

ACE: Yeah, if you go up North. My book. Look's like I'm ahead.

JIB: So you ain't gone be studyin' these Memphis folks afterwhile?

ACE: Nope. Damn! Yo' book.

JIB: You should take Toulou witchoo. She sang.

ACE: Most nigra girls growin' up in the South can sang.

JIB: Must be somethin' in the water.

ACE: But I don't thank her maine would like that now, would he? My book.

JIB: Whatchoo talkin' 'bout? You her maine.

ACE: Sad to say it. But folk say she been funnin' somebody else. My book.

JIB: Nah . . .

ACE: Steppin' between midnite and day on me.

JIB: You drunk or somethin'? I can't believe that. She wound up tight on you.

ACE: Yo' book! Folk been talkin', specially at church. And I heard some thangs, but I'n believe it. I sho'll didn't . . . But I might believes it, now. Lookie here! Another book for me.

JIB: Play, nigger. Quit runnin' yo' mouth. (*Pause*) Whatchoo done heard?

ACE: Thangs. Need to change her name from Toulou to Loosie Lou. I can always feel when somebody been in my bed.

JIB: Really?

ACE: Can smell it in the sheets. Smell—like yo' color.

JIB: Well, ain't you got a hobo bag full of morals. Don't run that juke joint shit 'round here. And get yo' hand off my book.

ACE: Just joogin' you, man! But that's my book.

JIB: How that's yo' book?

ACE: 'Cause couple books back when I threw down a Queen of Hearts, you threw down a Deuce of Spades. Just then you threw down a Jack of Hearts so that mean you reneged so that mean I gets me three books.

JIB: You tellin' a story, bwoy!

ACE: I ain't lyin'. I been watchin' this game 'cause I want me that Jack flask. And that means I got se'teen books to yo' nine which mean I wins and you lose. Give me my prize, fool!

JIB: Hell, nah! I paid too many pretty pennies for this.

ACE: Re-nigger, you done made the bet. The cards been dealt. You gots to give me my prize.

JIB: Awright! Damn, man. I guess they don't call you the Ace of Spades for nothin'.

ACE: No, they don't. Give it. (*Jib goes over to the table where his flask sits. Jib thrusts the flask into Ace's face. Ace lets it linger, then reaches up to grab it just as Jib jerks it back.*)

JIB: Tell you what. Two out of two. You win.

ACE: What if you win? Then it'll be a draw.

JIB: Then we'll both get what we want.

ACE: That ain't no kind of game!

JIB: We gotsta play three games. You win two out of three, *then* you get everything: the flask, yo' guitar and you can get the hell out of here. That's only fair.

ACE: Well, life ain't fair.

JIB: But this game gone be. (*Beat*)

ACE: Well . . . we shoulda' been playin' that card since the beginnin'. (*Ace deals the cards quickly.*) You sho'll is a sore loser.

JIB: To lose is to know grace. (*Ace looks at his hand.*)

ACE: But it look like God's on my side tonight. (*They play faster and faster throughout.*)

JIB: My book.

ACE: Sho'll is! Yo' book.

JIB: I kinda want you to win. I'ma miss my shit, but I guess it's the lesser of two evils.

ACE: Is that right?

JIB: Yeap.

ACE: (*Laughing*) I brought you up here just to see if it was true.

JIB: See if what was true?

ACE: See what them folks been talkin' 'bout.

JIB: And what yo' conclusion?

ACE: That you look at her like my daddy looked at my mama. (*The game stops for a spell. Jib slams down a card to continue.*)

JIB: What, you thank you perfect? You ain't no different, no better than me, no better than nobody. See, I knows men like you. I been like you back in the day.

ACE: Back in the day? You still that way right now. Rhonda done told me number six on its way. (*Jib freezes.*) Just joogin' you! (*Ace laughs tauntingly.*) You was scared.

JIB: Now, I ain't been messin' round with no Rhonda.

ACE: She ain't *lil'* enough for you. (*Pause*)

JIB: Yo' book.

ACE: Well, look at that! We even so far.

JIB: Even. (*They begin to play faster. Ace seems to win every hand.*)

ACE: You know, I don't deserve her. Nobody does. She don't need nobody. She betta than you. She betta than me.

JIB: That's whatchoo got to tell yoself?

ACE: What do you tell yoself?

JIB: God forgives.

ACE: You'se a plum fool.

JIB: What? I ain't joogin'!

ACE: So you can do anythin' you want just as long as you get down on yo' knees at the end of the day and pray?

JIB: All sins can be washed away. He who walks in the mud, at some point must clean his feet. See, if you read Romans 6, you see we is forgiven even before we sin. "Sin shall not have dominion over you: for ye are not under the law, but under grace"—hah. What then? Shall we sin—hah, because we are not under the law, but under grace? God forbid."

ACE: Last time I checked with God, funnin' yo' sister is unforgivable. Ace of Spades. Does it everytime. (*Ace raises the last card. It is the Ace of Spades.*)

JIB: For all you know, that's my baby up in her belly. (*Silence*) Looks like you won. Yo' nineteen trumps my seven. But seven's a heavenly number. (*Jib hands over the poisoned Jack flask. Ace opens it and takes a long swig from the bottle to tame the anger down. He coughs.*)

ACE: That some strong shit. (*Ace begins furiously packing up his things. Just then Toulou walks back into the house.*) I thought I was gone be gone 'fore you got here.

TOULOU: Where you thank you goin'?

ACE: Lookin' like you been the one steppin' 'tween midnight and day—wit yo' own kin.

TOULOU: I ain't did nothin—

ACE: Seem like you done did e'erthang up under the sun! Ain't this some shit? Hexin' me, makin' me feel all womanish in front of you, coatin' on me witcho own brother!

TOULOU: No, that ain't what had happened. You gotta listen to—(*Ace raises his hand toward Toulou.*)

ACE: You shut yo' mouth! I hate you with a passion that can burn a hole through hell! Ooooweee, I just knew you was bad news. I felt it all up in my gut. It was all there. Well, I hope I never have this feelin' again. I can't even feel no more after today. From this day on I feel . . . I feel . . . I feel like I'm dyin'. (*Ace falls as the poison begins to take over his body.*)

TOULOU: Jib, whatchoo tell him!

JIB: I ain't tell him nothin!

TOULOU: You told him somethin', but you ain't tell him the truth. You ain't tell him whatchoo done did, you lyin' son of a bitch—

JIB: I ain't said shit!

TOULOU: Then what he talkin' 'bout?! (*Ace begins to writhe and shake.*)

JIB: He just drunk off that Gold Medal. (*She suddenly realizes. Toulou runs to the fallen Ace and searches him. She finds the flask.*)

TOULOU: Noooo! Go ask Candylady for the backwards potion!

JIB: Oh, Lawd have mercy. Whatchoo done put up in my flask?

TOULOU: JUST GO GET HER! NOW!

JIB: Candylady! Candylady! (*Jib exits to Candylady's house.*)

TOULOU: (*To Ace*) In a minute it's gone be alright. Candylady gone come back. Just hold on a minute. We just gotta get you the backwards potion, Thass all, Thass all.

ACE: The backwards potion?

TOULOU: Yes—

ACE: But blues the best medicine. (*Beat. He gazes into her eyes.*) Toulou, can you sing me a song?

TOULOU: Whatchoo want me to sing?

ACE: That song you sang to me. Yo' first song.

TOULOU:
> From Memphis to Chicago
> From New Orleans on up to Harlem
>
> Flow, flow honey—

ACE: I'm flowing Up South, ain't it? (*She nods her head "yes."*) You always had a song in you. You got a lotta songs. (*Candylady enters the shack and gives Toulou a look. There are no backwards potions for this.*)

TOULOU: This what Candylady saw. . . .

ACE: Toulou, sing me another.

TOULOU: Whatchoo want to hear, baby? Let me thank of somethin'. Oooo, I got a new song! A new song I know you gone like. . . .

ACE: (*Trailing off into a whisper.*) You still my wife . . . Abby. (*Ace dies in her arms. Silence. She closes his eyes. From the abyss of her gut, sorrow finds its way to her trembling mouth. She vomits forth a scream of a million tortured souls. The shack crumbles beneath the weight of her wail. Jib stands outside the shack, afraid to go in. All Toulou can do is sing through her tears.*)

TOULOU:
> Gotta catch that train
> Ride it like a maine
> Gotta catch that train
> It's comin' in
> My heart will die just to
> Ride on that train
> Gotta catch that train
> Ride it like a maine.

End of Act Two

Epilogue

Springtime. Morning. Ruby-lipped Toulou stands playing the guitar, continuing the song she started when Ace died in her arms.

TOULOU:

> I loved that maine
> And he loved me too
> But sweet love
> Don't do nothin'
> But give you the blues
> Mama useta say you gotta
> Know when to leave
> The road made by walkin'
> I'ma start my feet
> Gotta catch that train
> Ride it like a maine
> Gotta catch that train
> It's comin' in
> My heart will die
> Just to ride on that train
> Gotta catch that train
> It's comin' in
>
> A woman heart broke
> She break down and cries
> A man heart broke
> He take a train and rides
> But this lil' lady
> Got somethin' to sing
> I'ma shake this sky
> Til everybody know me
>
> Gotta catch that train
> Ride it like a maine
> Gotta catch that train
> It's comin' in
> My heart will die
> Just to ride on that train
> Gotta catch that train
> Ride it like a maine

(*The train sounds.*)

CANDYLADY: It's time. So you leavin' the ol' lady, huh? When you comin' back to visit us?

TOULOU: I'm gone play a couple of joints down the road. Be back soon.

CANDYLADY: Lil' Acie Mae, what Mama gone call herself? "Hoodoo Toulou"? Yes, Mama gone call herself—

TOULOU: Naw, I thank I'ma come up with somethin' else. Better. Name myself for once.

CANDYLADY: I's see. I's see. (*Toulou comes to peer over Candylady's shoulder.*) Ain't that face the face of yo' love?

TOULOU: She got his lips.

CANDYLADY: Mmmmmhmmm. People will stay in yo' heart much longer than in yo' days. But, we'll always have a lil' piece of him with us. Won't we? (*The train whistle blows.*) That's the last train to Clarksdale. (*Toulou picks up her bag and begins to walk away. Candylady grabs her hand.*) You know . . . ain't no backwards potions to them kinda thangs. (*Toulou nods her head.*)

TOULOU: They say, "When a woman heart broke, she break down and cries. When a man heart broke, he take a train and rides." I'ma catch that train. (*Toulou looks at Candylady. A look is all they need. Toulou walks away down the road. Candylady sings a lullaby, "The Story," while rocking the baby to sleep. The sounds of Rhonda's playing children can be heard.*)

CANDYLADY:

> And that's the way the story go
> On the bluff where blue grass grow
> That's the way this hoodoo tale end
> Where broken wings don't try to mend
> And that's the way the story go
> And that's the way the story go

End of Play

NIKKOLE SALTER

A native of Los Angeles, California, Nikkole Salter began her career in theater as an actor. After earning a B.F.A. in acting from Howard University in Washington, D.C., Salter continued her study of acting at New York University, where she earned an M.F.A. While in graduate school, she co-wrote with Danai Gurira *In the Continuum*, a play about two black women, one living in Zimbabwe and the other in Los Angeles, who are dealing with AIDS. The play won an Obie award in 2006 for Salter and Gurira, who also performed the roles of the two women during the play's 2005 premiere and two-year international tour. In addition to an extensive theater and film acting résumé, Salter lists among her accomplishments a 2012 Robert S. Duncanson residency at the Taft Museum in Cincinnati, Ohio, where she wrote and performed in *Of Great Merit*, a solo play inspired by the art of the African American painter Robert S. Duncanson. She has received a 2014 Map Fund Grant, New York Outer Critics Circle Award, Helen Hayes Award, and recognition from the Theatre Hall of Fame. Other plays by Salter include *Lines in the Dust*, *The Princess and the Paparazzi*, *Torn Asunder*, and *Repairing a Nation*. Strongly committed to community activism through the arts, Salter is the founder and executive director of the Continuum Project, Inc., which seeks to empower young people through the arts.

Carnaval received its world premiere in an extended run at the Luna Stages Theater in West Orange, New Jersey (Jane Mandel, Artistic Director), where it opened on January 30, 2013.

Director:	Cheryl Katz
Raheem Monroe:	Terrell Wheeler
Jalani:	Jaime Lincoln Smith
Demetrius:	Anton Floyd
Set:	C. Murdock Lucas
Lighting:	Jorge Arroyo
Costumes:	Deborah Caney
Sound:	Steve Brown
Projection design:	Jay Spriggs
Production manager:	Liz Cesario
Stage manager:	Mary Ellen Allison
Assistant stage manager:	Christina Balkovic

Carnaval received its New York City premiere at Barbara Ann Teer's National Black Theatre in Harlem, where it opened October 21, 2014. Jonathan McCrory, Director of Theatre Arts Programming, Sade Lythcott, CEO.

Director:	Awoye Timpo
Raheem Monroe:	Gabriel Lawrence
Jalani:	W. Tre Davis
Demetrius:	Bjorn DuPaty
Set:	Daniel Zimmerman
Lighting:	Alan C. Edwards
Costumes:	Latoya Murray-Berry
Sound:	Eric Sluyter
Projection design:	Emre Emirgil
Production manager:	Belynda Hardin
Stage manager:	Laura Perez
Assistant stage manager:	Taylor Carter Jones

CARNAVAL

SETTING

1996: John F. Kennedy International Airport, Long Island, NY—the departure
terminal; Rio de Janeiro, Brazil—a three-bedroom condominium

2010: Club Carnaval in the borough of Manhattan, New York, NY

CHARACTERS

DEMETRIUS

In 1996: a twenty-six-year-old police officer, husband, and father to a five-
year-old daughter, from the Bedford-Stuyvesant community in Brooklyn.
Overwhelmed with responsibility, he struggles to reconcile his moral conscience with his desires; who he wants to be, with who he is.

In 2010: a forty-year-old man suffering from insurmountable injuries sus-
tained while trying to make peace with the role he played in his own fate
and his need for reconciliation.

JALANI

1996: A twenty-one-year-old college student from Bedford-Stuyvesant.
The younger brother of the recently deceased Jared, Jalani is riddled with
insecurities that he tries to mask with sexual prowess and bravado while
striving for attention, recognition, respect, and individual identity.

In 2010: A thirty-five-year-old husband of a Dominican wife, and father to
an eight-year-old son. Jalani is spiritually evolved and is the lynch-pin to
any reconciliation Raheem and Demetrius may have.

RAHEEM MONROE

1996: a twenty-six-year-old educated yet failed entrepreneur, also from
Brooklyn, looking for a way to gain the necessary capital to launch his Manhattan night club. Unsatisfied with the outcome of mediocrity displayed by
his own parents and peers, and deathly afraid of poverty, he is willing to do
anything to make sure he rises to the top.

In 2010: the forty-year-old owner of Club Carnaval, a premier hip-hop night
club with the theme of Brazil's biggest cultural attraction, Carnaval. He is
shrewd and resourceful, and yet, because of his success, he is even more
entrenched in his "by any means necessary" mantra.

LANGUAGE NOTES

// indicates the moment the next line begins and overlaps the end of the line being spoken

— indicates that the next line cuts off the line being spoken

. . . indicates a trailing thought after which there should be a bit of a beat before the next line

The gestures written into the dialogue should not impede the flow of the conversation.

Prologue

New York, NY, February 2010. An empty Club Carnaval in Manhattan. Perhaps DJ Khaled's "All I Do Is Win" blares from monster speakers. Raheem, centered in light, appears onstage.

RAHEEM: What's up, y'all? If you seein' this message you must be real special, cause that means you're a VIP at the most exclusive party in the city: the opening of my club. Club Carnaval. Pick up that remote and press record to leave a message in my video guest book—don't be shy. Make yourself known. Then relax. Enjoy the ladies, the costumes, the music. Lift your drinks and count your blessings. 'Cause in Rio, carnival is only once a year. But here, carnival is every night, baby. E ai meu, tudo bem, to all my garanhaos and gostosas!

The music rises. The lights zoom. The sound builds into . . .

Act 1

Scene 1

Private VIP room, Club Carnaval. The club is in full swing. Perhaps Jay-Z's "Big Pimpin" plays. Raheem has disappeared while his message remains in a looped projection on the walls of the club. Demetrius is revealed sitting on a couch in the balconied VIP section watching Raheem's projection in the room. He is dressed slightly too casually for the occasion. Demetrius gulps down his drink, reaches forward, and refills his glass. Jalani, dressed immaculately, tastefully, erring on the side of church, enters with two drinks.

JALANI: Got you something.

(Jalani hands Demetrius a drink.)

DEMETRIUS: What took you so long?

JALANI: It was wall to wall. Famous people—

DEMETRIUS: *(gesture signifying, "I'm not impressed")*

JALANI: I got two words: Off the chain—

DEMETRIUS: That's three words.

JALANI: Line to get in is wrapped down the street. Remember this? I loved these. Caipirinha.

DEMETRIUS: Yeah.

(*They drink.*)

JALANI: You have to admit, he did his thing (*referring to the projection*). I mean, look at this cat.

DEMETRIUS: Tired of looking at it—

JALANI: Still kinda early. Other folks haven't left messages yet. You can record. See?

(*Jalani points to the camera hidden behind the wall.*)

DEMETRIUS: It just loops over and over.

JALANI: Leave a message.

(*Jalani hands Demetrius a remote.*)

DEMETRIUS: You see the sign outside? Raheem Monroe's Club Carnaval?

JALANI: He's building a brand—

DEMETRIUS: What's next? Raheem Monroe's foot fungus cream—

(*Demetrius tosses the remote to the side. He rubs his legs.*)

JALANI: You alright?

DEMETRIUS: I'm fine.

JALANI: He knows we're here. I told the hostess to make sure. Probably running around.

DEMETRIUS: Got work tomorrow.

JALANI: He's coming.

DEMETRIUS: It's been over an hour.

JALANI: He had me invite you. Set us up in VIP. Bottles. He wanted us to be here. Said he wanted to say something.

DEMETRIUS: (*gesture signifying, "Whatever"*)

JALANI: You know you want to hear what he got to say.

DEMETRIUS: I'm not waiting all night.

(*A moment passses. A classic hip-hop song plays, perhaps Mobb Deep's "Shook Ones."*)

JALANI: Aww, yeah. This is my jam. 'member this? (*beat*) They don't make good music like this anymore.

DEMETRIUS: You sound so old.

JALANI: I ain't old. It's true.

DEMETRIUS: I don't know. I can't listen to some of it no more. I mean, if you really listen—I can't—

JALANI: Used to rock it.

DEMETRIUS: Used to do a lot of things.

(*Jalani grooves to the music while looking out onto the dance floor.*)

JALANI: Man, it's been a minute since I—(*slight beat*) I think that shorty is pushin' up.

DEMETRIUS: Who?

JALANI: Her.

(*Jalani points. Demetrius looks.*)

DEMETRIUS: Oh, hell no.

JALANI: She cute.

DEMETRIUS: She's fat. Her hair.

JALANI: She cute. She's not—

DEMETRIUS: Would you mess with that?

JALANI: No. I'm married. And she's not my type—

DEMETRIUS: That's right, you don't mess with black girls—

JALANI: I don't mess with nobody. I'm married.

DEMETRIUS: That's some real self-loathing shit, you know that, right?

JALANI: Everybody has preferences.

DEMETRIUS: I'm just saying.

JALANI: I'm tryin' to help you.

DEMETRIUS: I don't need no help.

JALANI: Is that right?

DEMETRIUS: You'd be surprised.

JALANI: Anybody special?

DEMETRIUS: (*beat*) No.

(*Jalani gets a text message.*)

JALANI: Jessinia. She wanna know what time I'm coming home. Got church tomorrow.

(*A moment passes while Jalani replies to the message.*)

DEMETRIUS: That's the new 3-G-S?

JALANI: Yeah, man!

DEMETRIUS: Heard the service sucks—

JALANI: It has a compass—look. Right now we're facing—

DEMETRIUS: Why do you need a compass?

JALANI: And it takes video. And you can edit it right on the screen. And you can text it. It's the best phone I've ever had—

DEMETRIUS: You a dork.

JALANI: This is Jared at peewee practice.

(*Jalani shows Demetrius his phone. Demetrius watches the video.*)

JALANI: Watch: he's gonna catch the ball and—

DEMETRIUS: Is that a girl?

JALANI: Yeah. They let girls on the team when they're young. She's quarterback. She bad.

DEMETRIUS: She's eight. Wait 'til they move to tackle. She gets laid out once, she'll be happy to cheer from the sidelines.

(*Demetrius hands Jalani his phone.*)

JALANI: You should come next Saturday. It's funny to watch them. He made a touch-down today. Hilarious.

DEMETRIUS: If I'm not working.

(*Moments pass.*)

DEMETRIUS: Where is this nigga?

JALANI: I'm hungry. You hungry?

DEMETRIUS: No. I'm ready—

JALANI: Be patient. He's coming. He got something to say. (*beat*) I'm gonna go find that waitress. Get some wings or something. You good?

DEMETRIUS: I'm good.

Jalani exits. Demetrius looks at Raheem's message projected on the wall. He lifts the remote, unmutes the sound, and listens to Raheem's message.

RAHEEM: What's up, y'all? If you seein' this message you must be real special, 'cause that means you're a VIP at the most exclusive party in the city: the opening of my club. Club Carnaval. Pick up that remote and press record to leave a message. . . .

Demetrius presses record and the party ambiance becomes muted. He zooms into himself, and the lights contract around him. As he examines the image of himself projected on the wall, the lights shift and sounds of scuffling are heard. The lights begin to flash, and as they blink on and off Demetrius is revealed getting beaten up as he stands. The flashes increase in frequency and intensity. As they do, Demetrius is transformed and transported to—

Scene 2

The music from the club turns in to the sound of music coming from earphones—perhaps Tupac's "Whatz Ya Phone #." Day One: JFK Airport, New York. February 1996. It's extremely cold. Demetrius, twenty-six, stands in an airline terminal waiting. He has a book, some very smart, slightly expensive luggage, his passport, his ticket, and his itinerary in hand. The announcer for his airline pages a passenger. Jalani, twenty-one, enters the terminal. He wears an Avirex leather jacket, and carries a large military-type duffle bag and a Sony portable CD player with monster earphones.

DEMETRIUS: Jay! Jay!

(Jalani sees Demetrius and approaches.)

JALANI: What up, dog!

DEMETRIUS: Whatever, man, you're late. Y'all are the worst—

JALANI: Where's Raheem?

DEMETRIUS: He isn't here, either. We're going to miss the flight.

JALANI: Uh, Jalani will not be waiting for Raheem. J waits on no one. I will leave his black ass. No diggity. No doubt.

DEMETRIUS: You're trippin'. We can't leave Ra. He's the one with the connect. We can't just go down there, knock on some stranger's door, talking about, "Yeah, so, we're friends of a 'biness' associate of yours," and expect him to be like, "Oh, great! Come in!" I mean, we don't even know where we're going exactly, and no one there speaks English and I don't speak Portuguese—

JALANI: I do.

DEMETRIUS: You do?

JALANI: Absolutely. (*demonstrating*) "Come-ay, here-ay, mommy. Sit-ay, on my lap-ay. Open-ay your mouth-ay—"

DEMETRIUS: You stupid.

JALANI: "Pass-ay the Bacard-ay." That's the only thing I need to know how to say all week, dog. All week!

DEMETRIUS: I'm not getting on that plane without him. I'm not taking my black ass to a foreign country without a tour guide.

JALANI: He'll be here. Calm down. You sound like a bitch right now. The only thing you should be thinking about is whether or not you brought enough condoms and K-Y jelly. (*beat*) You did bring condoms, Demetrius, right?

DEMETRIUS: Dude. Really?

JALANI: Tell me you brought some condoms.

DEMETRIUS: That's not something you talk to a grown man about, Jay. I wonder about you sometimes.

JALANI: I'm tellin' you right now: I'm not giving you not one of mine. I'm using all mine.

DEMETRIUS: I wouldn't ask you no way.

JALANI: I'm just lettin' you know.

DEMETRIUS: Great.

(*Demetrius goes to look at the departure monitor.*)

DEMETRIUS: Talkin' 'bout, "I'll take care of it." Couldn't take care of nothing to save his—

JALANI: He's coming.

DEMETRIUS: Twenty bucks says he shows up talkin' 'bout, "What had happened was—", that's if he even shows up—I shoulda asked to see pictures.

JALANI: D. Relax.

DEMETRIUS: I took days off.

JALANI: Be easy. He's coming.

DEMETRIUS: Twenty dollars says he's not.

JALANI: Alright. Bet.

(*Jalani shakes Demetrius's hand. Demetrius returns to look at the departure boards.*)

DEMETRIUS: They've posted our gate. (*beat*) Watch: it's going to be all, (*imitating Raheem*) "My hook up was supposed to . . . and that's why we can't . . ."

JALANI: I'ma need you not to be all uptight this week. You gon' have some fuckin' fun for once.

DEMETRIUS: What you know about fun, youngin'?

JALANI: Whatever, man.

DEMETRIUS: I have fun.

JALANI: I'm talkin' 'bout real fun, not that bullshit you called a bachelor party.

DEMETRIUS: Here you go—

JALANI: Damn straight, here I go—

DEMETRIUS: That was five years ago, man—

JALANI: I know, and I'm still traumatized.

DEMETRIUS: You wasn't complaining at the open bar—

JALANI: I'm talkin' 'bout the entertainment. You should've been doin' yo' thang on your last night of freedom.

DEMETRIUS: My party was the shit and you know it. Started at the Tunnel—

JALANI: We used to go to the Tunnel every weekend—

DEMETRIUS: VIP at Limelight—

JALANI: Been there. Did that.

DEMETRIUS: Then a private room at Goldfinger. How many sixteen-year-olds partied 'til seven in the morning? If it wasn't for your brother—

JALANI: We're not talking about Jared. We're talkin' 'bout you. And the quality of your entertainment.

DEMETRIUS: There were girls.

JALANI: But you couldn't touch 'em.

DEMETRIUS: You had to pay them, with your broke ass. They work for money, J. Tips.

JALANI: I don't pay for pussy.

DEMETRIUS: Is that what you plan to do in Brazil? Not pay for pussy?

JALANI: That's different. They're prostitutes.

DEMETRIUS: And the chicks at my party were . . . church girls?

JALANI: They was uppity.

DEMETRIUS: You got problems. (*Beat.*) He ain't coming.

Jalani places his earphones on and listens to music. Demetrius reads, occasionally glancing around for Raheem or at the monitor of departing flights. The announcer from the airline pages another passenger and announces a flight has been delayed.

DEMETRIUS: Is that our flight?

JALANI: (*taking off his headphones*) Huh?

DEMETRIUS: (*looking through his documents*) She just said flight nineteen seventy-nine will be delayed. I think that's our flight. Is that our flight?

JALANI: (*looking at the departure board*) Only if we're going to Istanbul. Calm down.

DEMETRIUS: Oh.

(*Demetrius returns to his book.*)

JALANI: What you readin'?

DEMETRIUS: Oh. Uh . . . (*beat*) How . . . Stella . . . Got Her Groove Back.

JALANI: What?

DEMETRIUS: You laugh, but it's a good book. I read *Waiting to Exhale* too—

JALANI: Oh my God!

DEMETRIUS: They're good books. My wife—

JALANI: Stop. Stop.

DEMETRIUS: What? At least I read, nigga.

JALANI: First of all, the "W" word is banned from this point on.

DEMETRIUS: Wife?

JALANI: Yeah. You gon' keep all the honeys away flinging that word around—

DEMETRIUS: (*sarcastically*) Oh, certainly they've never met a married man.

JALANI: Let me see that.

(Jalani takes the book and gives it a once over. He pulls out the bookmark.)

DEMETRIUS: Don't lose my page.

JALANI: You use a family picture as a bookmark?

DEMETRIUS: Dana had them made for Christmas.

JALANI: My God—

DEMETRIUS: *(snatching the book back)* Give me that.

JALANI: *(beat)* So, what did you tell your, uh . . . ?

DEMETRIUS: My wife.

JALANI: Yeah, her.

DEMETRIUS: What you mean?

JALANI: What you tell her? About the trip?

DEMETRIUS: I told her the truth.

JALANI: The truth.

DEMETRIUS: I told her I was going to Brazil. With my boys.

JALANI: With your boys.

DEMETRIUS: A convention of men.

JALANI: A convention.

DEMETRIUS: Yeah.

JALANI: And she believed you.

DEMETRIUS: I don't lie to my wife.

JALANI: You mean she don't know.

DEMETRIUS: She knows—

JALANI: I mean she don't know the deal. The real deal. 'Cause if she knew, Dana would whoop yo'—

DEMETRIUS: She knows. *(beat)* She knows everything, remember?—

JALANI: Oh, she still on that?

DEMETRIUS: She don't need my "two cents."

JALANI: Knowledge is power, dog! Knowledge is muthafuckin' power.

DEMETRIUS: And ignorance is clearly bliss.

Raheem, twenty-six, appears in the terminal, decked out, with way too much luggage for a week-long trip.

RAHEEM: CooCoooooo!!!!

JALANI: Look at this nigga.

DEMETRIUS: Lookin' like a Fubu billboard.

JALANI: *(to Demetrius)* He's here.

DEMETRIUS: I ain't giving you twenty dollars.

JALANI: See—

DEMETRIUS: For all I know, he got us flying with the cargo.

(Raheem enters. They all bark to greet each other.)

RAHEEM: Gentlemen. Gentlemen.

JALANI: Yo!

DEMETRIUS: They already posted our gate. Where you been?

RAHEEM: I had to help one of my chicks with her car. She had me standing outside, fuckin' breath makin' icicles on my nose, trying to figure out why the bitch won't start. Turns out her California ass had water in the fuckin' radiator. Water!

JALANI: Water?!

DEMETRIUS: Gotta love California girls.

RAHEEM: Water. It's twenty-eight degrees and she got water in the radiator and she wonder why her car don't work. I got it towed then I had to run to the crib—shower, shave, get lined up, you know—that takes time. I think she did that shit on purpose—trying to get me to miss the flight.

JALANI: What you tell her?

RAHEEM: I ain't got to tell her nothing. She know what's up. If she don't like it, she can step. You know how I do.

DEMETRIUS: (*skeptical*) Right.

RAHEEM: Y'all ready to be blessed?

JALANI: I can't wait!

RAHEEM: I'm telling you, it's about to be like nothing you ever—once you cross over—

JALANI: Let's go!

DEMETRIUS: What's in all the bags?

RAHEEM: You know a nigga gotta look good.

JALANI: Fuckin' pretty boy.

DEMETRIUS: It's only a week, man.

RAHEEM: (*pointing to his bags*) Well, this is just my shoes. Jeans, khakis, plaid shorts. Polos, jerseys. Button-downs and my linen for when I be pimpin'. Here go my supplies—

DEMETRIUS: Supplies?

JALANI AND RAHEEM: Supplies.

RAHEEM: And some liquor for—

DEMETRIUS: You can't take liquor on the plane, fool. // Ghetto-ass—

JALANI: // (*teasing Demetrius*) It's the law!   RAHEEM: //No, your Gump-ass is
                                                    supposed to buy it. Players like
                                                    myself, on the other hand—

JALANI: I done already told him he ain't gon' be policing us all week. Leave your badge at home, overseer, I mean officer.

DEMETRIUS: Says the unemployed virgin.

JALANI: Who a virgin?

DEMETRIUS: Let's hurry. The line is long.

JALANI: I ain't no virgin—

RAHEEM: Demetrius, fall back. I got this.

DEMETRIUS: (*acquiescing*) 'scuse me.

RAHEEM: We ain't waitin' in that line. I told you, this week, I got this.

DEMETRIUS: (*doubting*) You got it.

RAHEEM: All I gotta do is page my man.

(Raheem looks for the phone number and pulls out his cellular phone.)

JALANI: See. It's happening. All he gotta do is page his man.

DEMETRIUS: We'll see.

JALANI: Where my twenty?

DEMETRIUS: We not on the plane. We got to make it there in one piece before—

JALANI: See.

DEMETRIUS: What?

JALANI: You just like the white man. Changin' the rules in the middle—

DEMETRIUS: Shut up.

(Raheem ends his call.)

RAHEEM: Let's do this.

JALANI: *(grabbing the cell phone)* Let me see that. This is nice. I'ma get me one.

DEMETRIUS: The plans are crazy expensive.

JALANI: How much?

RAHEEM: It ain't no thing.

DEMETRIUS: You just got it like that now, huh?

RAHEEM: *(to Jalani)* I'll hook you up when we get back. *(to both)* Y'all ready?

JALANI: "Does a bear shit in the woods and wipe his ass with a white rabbit?"

RAHEEM AND DEMETRIUS: What??

JALANI: Y'all ain't heard Tupac's new CD? That nigga said, "Does a bear shit in the woods and wipe his ass with a fluffy white rabbit?"

RAHEEM: You copped it?

JALANI: Yeah. Got my refund check. *(referring to the CD player)* Got this. *(referring to his shoes)* These kicks. Bunch of CDs.

DEMETRIUS: Ain't that your money for housing?

JALANI: I didn't spend it all.

DEMETRIUS: Did you pay for your dorm?

JALANI: *(to Demetrius)* Man.

RAHEEM: *(referring to the Tupac CD)* Let me see.

JALANI: *(referring to the Tupac CD)* That nigga is crazy.

RAHEEM: He ain't better than Biggie.

JALANI: Shit is still ill.

Raheem receives a page. He checks it to confirm.

RAHEEM: *(finishing his message)* Let's be out.

DEMETRIUS: Carnival, here we come.

They gather their bags. An announcer from an airline announces that a flight is boarding. Demetrius drops his book.

RAHEEM: *(to Demetrius)* Is that a book?

(Jalani and Raheem fall out laughing.)

DEMETRIUS: Forget y'all.

(Demetrius picks up his book and they all exit, bags in hand.)

Scene 3

Day One: Rio de Janeiro, Brazil. Jalani, Raheem, and Demetrius enter the common space of an ocean-view, three-bedroom condominium suite, luggage and coats in hand. The space is bright, tropical, and state-of-the-art. It has a small kitchenette with a bar and a balcony that overlooks the ocean. There is a huge mirror on the wall, perhaps over the couch.

JALANI: Yo-ho-ho!!

RAHEEM: Welcome to paradise.

DEMETRIUS: Wow.

JALANI: This is what I'm talkin' 'bout, son!

(Jalani drops his bags in the middle of the room and runs out to the balcony.)

DEMETRIUS: Wow. You really—

RAHEEM: I told you.

DEMETRIUS: I must say I didn't expect—

RAHEEM: I told you.

DEMETRIUS: You sure this is free? 'Cause I didn't budget—

RAHEEM: It's free. Just re-stock the fridge. Slip the maid some extra money.

DEMETRIUS: This would cost a grip in the City. How much does something like this cost?

RAHEEM: Here? You can probably rent something like this for—

DEMETRIUS: I'm not trying to rent nothin' no more, man. C'mon.

RAHEEM: *(beat)* You could buy it for like a "g" a month.

DEMETRIUS: Oh, I'm definitely going to have to buy some property out here.

RAHEEM: You're already coming back, man?

DEMETRIUS: Maybe.

RAHEEM: I told you. It's a bi-annual pilgrimage for me. I got this one shorty out here—

(Jalani re-enters.)

JALANI: Yo, check the view! We can see the beach from here!

(They all go out to the balcony to look at the view.)

JALANI: I think I died and gone to muthafuckin' heaven. Sunshine in February—

RAHEEM: Gimme props!

DEMETRIUS: You the man.

JALANI: —and fat asses. Did you see those chicks, D?

RAHEEM: I told you. I'ma take care of you.

DEMETRIUS: Yes, I did. See the asses.

(They re-enter the apartment.)

JALANI: From the minute we got off the plane! They all look like Mariah fuckin' Carey. All of 'em. Even the black ones got Chilli baby hair.

(Jalani begins to change his clothes.)

RAHEEM: Chilli baby hair?

DEMETRIUS: Chick from that group TLC. That's his thing, remember? Chilli.

RAHEEM: Oh, yeah. You stupid, Jay.

JALANI: Full lips. Tiny waist. Thick thighs. Mmmm-mmm. It's like the best of both worlds. White girl hair. Spanish girl skin. Black girl booty. And southern girl attitude. My boy was here last year and he said he had bitches cookin' for him. Cookin'! When's the last time you got a New York girl to cook?

DEMETRIUS: Other than my mama?

RAHEEM: All my ladies cook.

DEMETRIUS: (*doubting*) All your ladies . . .

JALANI: He said they treat you like a king down here. They do what you say, let you fuck 'em any way you want—

RAHEEM: That's how they train 'em down here. They know how to treat a man, make 'em feel special. They'll make your bed, wash your ass if you want them to— they're nice—

DEMETRIUS: Nice? Of course they're nice. You're paying them. That's not nice, that's good customer service. Don't get it twisted. Plus you got American dollars, which, given the conversion, makes you—

JALANI: I'm ballin' nigga!

RAHEEM: Even still. They're just—they're not always trying to prove they're just as good as you. They train them to cater to their men, and they like it. It's cultural. You'll see.

(*Jalani is completely changed, wearing shorts and Timberland boots and stuffing his pockets with "supplies."*)

JALANI: You know! Let's go, gentlemen. I'm ready to get it in. You heard the way they was talkin' to me downstairs, like, "Ooo, papi. I want you."

DEMETRIUS: They're not Puerto Rican. They're Brazilian. They don't say "papi".

JALANI: I bet you they will.

RAHEEM: Slow your roll, Jay. I got to take a shower first.

JALANI: For what?

RAHEEM: I just been on a plane for nine hours. You know I got to be fresh.

JALANI: Fine. Come on, D.

DEMETRIUS: I got to call my w—

RAHEEM AND JALANI: Don't say that word.

DEMETRIUS: I told her I'd call. (*to himself*) Where's my calling card?

JALANI: Alright. Bet. You gay bitches can stay here with each other, then.

(*Jalani goes to exit.*)

RAHEEM: Jay. Slow down, man. First of all, you ain't goin' nowhere alone.

JALANI: Raheem. I'm grown.

DEMETRIUS: (*to Jalani*) Boy, please—

JALANI: You ain't worried 'bout me when I walk down Myrtle Ave, but you worried about me on the beach?

RAHEEM: Naw, son, I'm telling you. I've been here before. You ain't in New York. It look all Gilligan's Island, but there are some rules, some codes of conduct, I got to break down to you, if we're going to have a good time.

DEMETRIUS: Where's the phone?

RAHEEM: You got to hear this, too.

(*They sit.*)

RAHEEM: Rule number one. Don't go nowhere alone. Niggas get jacked all the time when they by theyself. There's just as many Brazilian dudes out there lookin' to come up as there is women. They will jack you. Rule number two. Stay on the strip. Dudes will come talkin' 'bout, "there are better chicks for better prices further in the city" and that if you just go with them—uh, uh, don't go with them. It's a set-up. You'll get there and there will be a bunch of niggas. They'll get you for all your money, your shoes, your jewelry, your passport—which brings me to rule number three. Don't carry all your cash. Leave most of it here, in a safe place. Just in case you get jacked, they won't get you for everything. Don't carry your passport with you, neither. The goal is to get here and to be able to get back home. It would be different if we lost our passport and we was white, but we ain't. We black—

DEMETRIUS: Still?

RAHEEM: Still, nigga. It ain't no different here. You all exotic 'cause you American, but fuck up and see how quick you just black again. Rule number four. Arrange the price with these chicks before shit jump off. A lot of 'em don't speak English, but they do speak money. Be real clear. The last thing you want is to be done tryin' to smoke a cigar and shit, and the chick screamin' you didn't pay her. It ain't worth it. She will go to the police, and they more corrupt than a muthafucka. (*looking at Jalani*) I do not want to spend my trip in the fuckin' police precinct. I could've stayed in New York for that.

JALANI: What you lookin' at me for? I ain't never been to jail.

RAHEEM: Just give her what she ask for and send her on her way. You can always buy another one. And rule number five—

JALANI: This a lot of rules, man.

RAHEEM: Don't go home with no bitches listening to no sob stories about how poor they are or how their daddies ain't got no legs or some shit. It's all a game. Bitches will be trying to cling to get you, trying to make you feel sorry for them and pay they rent. Fuck 'em and send 'em on they way. Don't get attached.

JALANI: We don't love them hoes!

DEMETRIUS: Is that it?

RAHEEM: That's it. We each have our own rooms. Here are your keys. Don't lose 'em.

JALANI: (*to Demetrius*) Let's go!

DEMETRIUS: I'm with you. Let me make my call.

JALANI: D. D, look at me. Look at me, D. Call her later.

(*Raheem prepares for a shower; to Raheem*)

You too. Put your faggot nigga sandals on and c'mon. We're in Rio, baby! Let's go.

DEMETRIUS: (*laughing*) Sandals . . .

RAHEEM: I got to take a shower, man.

(*Raheem gathers his bags.*)

DEMETRIUS: (*to Jalani*) I always say—Just give me a sec—

(*Demetrius exits with his phone card and his bags. Raheem starts for the bathroom.*)

RAHEEM: Don't worry, son, the bitches ain't goin' nowhere. Trust me. They a dime a muthafuckin' dozen.

Raheem exits with his bags. Jalani goes out to the balcony. He re-enters and sits down. He picks up Demetrius's book and tries to read. He checks himself out in the mirror on the wall. He gets frustrated with the waiting.

JALANI: Fuck this.

(*Jalani leaves.*)

Scene 4

Day Two: The next day. The Rio condo. Jalani enters from the bathroom in a towel (or boxers, whatever the quick change permits) with a bottle of lotion. He goes through his bag, pulls out a CD, and puts it in the condo CD player. He looks in the mirror. Perhaps he sings along to the beginning of R. Kelly's "Bump and Grind" as it streams from the speakers.

*Jalani is singing voraciously while lotioning his body. The feel of this moment should resemble the tone of the beginning of R. Kelly's "Bump and Grind." Demetrius enters, fully dressed. He carries a book—*The Ultimate Travel Guide to Brazil—*and a camera.*

DEMETRIUS: What is you doin'?

JALANI: The instant replay, baby!

(*Jalani demonstrates how he "performed" on his first night out.*)

JALANI: Smacked it, flipped it, rubbed it—

DEMETRIUS: You stupid.

JALANI: The Adventures of Pablo!

DEMETRIUS: Who is Pablo?

JALANI: That's the name I be givin' the chicks. Pablo got three down—

DEMETRIUS: You wasn't with no three women last night. Is that my lotion?

(*Demetrius grabs his lotion bottle.*)

JALANI: Swear to god. They was juicy. Mmm. They was so fine. No hair on they coochie. Them suntan lines. And all up on me. Chasing *me*. They smelled so good—so clean—

DEMETRIUS: Your brother would've been proud.

(*Jalani's jovial mood quickly becomes somber.*)

DEMITRIUS: (*long beat*) You alright? We can talk if—

JALANI: I'm alright. I'm good.

DEMETRIUS: (*a gesture signifying, "You sure?"*)

JALANI: (*beat*) For real. (*beat*) I'ma fuck one a day for him.

DEMETRIUS: (*with hidden condescension*) That's very nice of you. To share.

JALANI: We should all do that. One a day for Jared.

DEMETRIUS: (*half-heartedly*) Sounds like a plan. (*beat*) What time you get back?

JALANI: Who's countin' time? I'm countin' pussy. How many you bag?

DEMETRIUS: (*beat*) None.

JALANI: None?

DEMETRIUS: I wasn't feelin'—

JALANI: If you not gonna get none, why you come down here?

DEMETRIUS: I came down here to pay homage to my boy Jared—

JALANI: What, you prefer to watch? I can get with that.

DEMETRIUS: (*sarcastically*) Yeah, I like watching.

JALANI: You better stop frontin' and get with the program. What's the problem? (*earnestly*) Your dick broke?

DEMETRIUS: My dick is fine. I . . . (*beat*) A bitch just gotta be a certain way.

JALANI: And what way is that?

DEMETRIUS: Clean. Sober. And the ladies last night—I could wait.

JALANI: That's why you use condoms.

DEMETRIUS: I can't just fuck anybody, Jay.

JALANI: Why the fuck not? What kind of man are you?

DEMETRIUS: A real man.

(*Jalani begins to dress. Demetrius struggles to load film in his camera.*)

JALANI: There is a lot of dudes down here, right? Dudes from all over. You see those Norwegian dudes with their suntan lotion on, scared of the sun—

DEMETRIUS: In their man thongs—

(*They laugh.*)

JALANI: (*remembering*) Yo! I saw that nigga, Murray, from up the block, in the club—

DEMETRIUS: Tamika's little brother?

JALANI: Why he always got to be known as Tamika's little brother? Like that nigga ain't got a name—

DEMETRIUS: What's he doin' down here?

JALANI: The same thing every other man down here is doin'. He came down here with like twenty niggas from Harlem.

DEMETRIUS: That's who you was with last night?

JALANI: I know, right! Halfway around the world to end up with niggas from around the way—

DEMETRIUS: Small world.

JALANI: We had Moet flowin' all night, son. Ahh. I think I'm still faded. I didn't know it could actually be like this. Like for real. It's so live down here!

DEMETRIUS: Yeah—

JALANI: There was this one Urkel-dude with James Worthy goggles, hilarious, he was poppin' penicillin all night. And I was like, "Whatchu poppin' pills for?" Turns out, that nigga like to eat pussy, but he was scared of gettin' herpes or some shit, so he figured that if he took one pill each time, before he went down, he'd be alright.

(*They laugh.*)

DEMETRIUS: That's crazy!

JALANI: Niggas is stupid!

DEMETRIUS: Why would you eat any bitch's pussy down here? You know how many dicks she's had? The only pussy I ever ate is my wife's—

JALANI: (*teasing*) You know how many dicks she's had? (*beat*) I'm just playin', I'm just playin', I'm just playin', damn. Loosen up. (*beat*) Yo. I heard that the best time to get a chick is if you wait 'til late. Some of these chicks ain't got no way back home if it's too late and they'll fuck for free just to have a place to stay.

DEMETRIUS: You need help.

JALANI: (*à la Payless*) Why pay more, when you can pay less?

DEMETRIUS: You know Ra is going to kill you, right?

JALANI: What he gon' do? Please. (*beat*) What y'all end up getting into last night?

DEMETRIUS: Ra was doin' business deals all night. I ended up at this restaurant—

JALANI: (*teasing*) Reading your book?

DEMETRIUS: Fuck you. Just to get a drink while I waited for Ra. Take in the scenery. I was sittin' at the bar and this little boy came up to me. Like nine years old. And he was like, "Mister. I see you alone. I get woman for you." And he pointed to this woman on the beach. And I thought, "Ain't this about a bitch. Brazil even got the children pimpin." So I was like, "I'm good, thank you." And he was like, "You don't like her. You want black one?" And I was like, "No, no. Thank you." And he left with this dumbfounded look on his face like he just didn't understand that I didn't want a woman. So, I was chillin' with my drink, waitin' for Raheem, and like twenty minutes later, the kid comes back and he says, "Mister. You still alone. I got woman for you. You want her." And he pointed to this girl. This little girl. She was like twelve or something. No boobs. No ass. A girl, dog. And I was like—(*demonstrates his reaction*)—and I thought about my little girl, man—

JALANI: Why?

DEMETRIUS: The idea that she—I don' t know. So I said, (*emphatically*) "No. No." And the boy starts crying. I realized them women he was pointing to didn't know him. He just got hip to the game. He was hoping I was interested and I'd give him money. He was hungry. I felt bad, so I took him to dinner.

JALANI: Why *you* feel bad? He was trying to jack you.

DEMETRIUS: He was just a kid. (*beat*) I told him I was from New York and he was asking me if I know Biggie—like everybody from Brooklyn knows Biggie! I was trying to tell him, but he wasn't trying to hear me. He was telling me his dreams and—this is the crazy part—I looked up from our conversation, I saw that little girl walking with some old white dude off the beach. And I just lost my appetite. For everything.

(*Jalani pulls a video camera from his luggage and prepares it for recording.*)

JALANI: (*sarcastically*) That's real sad, man.

DEMETRIUS: You have no heart.

JALANI: For all you know, that man could've been her father. That little girl, that little boy, even, they ain't your problem. We ain't committin' no crime, the shit's legal here—

DEMETRIUS: Not for children—

JALANI: No sob stories. We're not supposed to get attached, remember? Focus.

DEMETRIUS: Oh, now you wanna follow the rules?

JALANI: Look. I got a cure for your broken heart. (*He hands him a condom.*) Take one of these. And call me in the morning.

(*Jalani grabs his camera and beach towel and starts to exit.*)

DEMETRIUS: Where you going?

JALANI: Fuck somebody, D.

DEMETRIUS: Hold up—

(*Jalani exits.*)

JALANI: (*from offstage*) And not another man!

DEMETRIUS: Fuck you!

Demetrius turns off the music. He grabs his lotion and lotions his hands. He fingers his wedding ring and pulls it off. He looks at it. Raheem enters from the back entrance from a morning workout. Demetrius puts the ring back on.

RAHEEM: What up?

DEMETRIUS: (*head nod signifying "What up"?*)

RAHEEM: (*calling for Jalani*) Jay! (*He waits for a reply.*) (*To Demetrius*) That nigga leave?

DEMETRIUS: (*shrugging of shoulders signifying "I guess."*)

RAHEEM: Why didn't you go with him?

DEMETRIUS: (*shrugging of shoulders signifying "What could I do?"*)

RAHEEM: You gotta watch him. Where'd he go?

DEMETRIUS: (*shrugging of shoulders signifying "I don't know."*)

RAHEEM: I'ma kill— (*referring to Jalani's luggage*) Does this nigga always leave his shit everywhere? Dirty muthafucka. Why can't he put his stuff in his room? He has his own room. That's what it's for. His shit.

(*Raheem starts to move Jalani's stuff into a pile. A moment passes.*)

RAHEEM: You not gonna believe what I got planned for y'all today. Boat ride, nigga. Picture this: Sunset. Like sixty women. Fine women. Video vixen, topless women. On a yacht. With like twenty men.

DEMETRIUS: (*a glare signifying "I'm not impressed."*)

RAHEEM: Open bar. Dope DJ—

DEMETRIUS: (*a dismissive eye roll signifying "So?"*)

RAHEEM: Just a hundred and fifty dollars.

DEMETRIUS: I'm cool.

RAHEEM: You're paying for the ratio. And first-grade liquor—

DEMETRIUS: I'm good.

RAHEEM: Don't act like you don't want to go. It's only a buck fifty.

DEMETRIUS: Only?

RAHEEM: You got a job.

DEMETRIUS: I got mouths to feed.

RAHEEM: Dana works.

DEMETRIUS: I hold it down.

RAHEEM: You can't afford a buck fifty?

DEMETRIUS: I thought you had the hook up.

RAHEEM: I said you had to pay for the ladies. I said your own food, your own chicks, your own—

DEMETRIUS: I'm good. I'll do my own thing. (*beat*) Like I did last night.

RAHEEM: (*beat*) When I went back to the bar, you was gone—

DEMETRIUS: Oh, so you *do* know you were fucked up for—

RAHEEM: I sent you a chick to keep you company. She said you were gone—

DEMETRIUS: I wasn't gonna be waiting around—

RAHEEM: I was comin' right back—

DEMETRIUS: I was sittin there for almost a hour, Raheem.

RAHEEM: It wasn't no hour—

DEMETRIUS: I'm not your groupie. I ain't impressed by all—

RAHEEM: It was business. I was conducting—

DEMETRIUS: So why couldn't you come back to say it was takin' a little longer than you thought? Why couldn't you do me that courtesy? (*rhetorical*) Why couldn't you do that? 'Cause you a inconsiderate bastard—

RAHEEM: It wasn't no hour—

DEMETRIUS: And why can't you just say, "sorry," nigga? "my bad—"

RAHEEM: 'Cause I ain't sorry. This is a vacation for you, but dudes like me don't get vacations. Ain't nobody givin' me two weeks paid nothin'. This is my business. I'm making moves 24/7. And I ain't sorry for that. I ain't never sorry for handlin' my business. I ain't sorry.

DEMETRIUS: You selfish—

RAHEEM: Stop bitchin', nigga. Grow some balls.

DEMETRIUS: Yo' mama wasn't complainin' 'bout my balls last night.

RAHEEM: Oh, my mama?

DEMETRIUS: Yeah, yo' mama.

RAHEEM: Well, at least my mama pretty enough to get fucked. Yo' mama so ugly she joined an ugly contest and they said, "Sorry, no professionals."

(*They stare at each other for a few moments, then fall out laughing.*)

DEMETRIUS: You've been savin' that one.

RAHEEM: I got more.

DEMETRIUS: You stupid. Well, *yo'* mama—

(*Raheem's pager goes off.*)

RAHEEM: (*referring to his pager*) Damn, this nigga is impatient.

DEMETRIUS: Who's that?

RAHEEM: Business // associate—

DEMETRIUS: Associate. Right. (*beat*) So, what's the deal? You ain't nickel and dime baggin' or no shit like that are you?

RAHEEM: What I look like?

DEMETRIUS: Then what is it? What's all this?

RAHEEM: It's legit.

DEMETRIUS: What is it?

RAHEEM: It's . . . tourism.

DEMETRIUS: Tourism?

RAHEEM: Guys like it here. They work hard, and they need a place to go where they can relax as men. And they're willing to pay for a quality experience. So I help 'em get down here. I coordinate it for them.

DEMETRIUS: I'm listening.

RAHEEM: Like today. We're going on a boat ride. For you, it's an excursion. For me, it's a business opportunity—to meet with the guys that run it to see if I can guarantee a certain amount of men to come every so often, if they'll give me a discount. And I just do like that. Put together packages with activities for seven days, two weeks, whatever. Set shit up for niggas, and get paid doin' it. My associate—

DEMETRIUS: Right—

RAHEEM: Yeah, he lays the groundwork. And I get the clientele. And run it from New York. This right here, this is one of my luxury suites.

DEMETRIUS: You own this?

RAHEEM: No, not—

DEMETRIUS: Oh.

RAHEEM: But I can use it any—

DEMETRIUS: Right.

RAHEEM: Like a time share. So, this is a business trip for me, really. To put things in place. It's a fantasy for y'all, but this right here is 'bout to be just how I do. And then, when I get the VIP shit set up, wooo hooo! It's gonna be off the chain. Ballers, rappers, execs, niggas with benjamins—then we can go international—

DEMETRIUS: So, you're like a travel agent.

RAHEEM: Yeah.

DEMETRIUS: With a agency?

RAHEEM: No. This is *my* shit.

DEMETRIUS: Oh.

RAHEEM: I don't need no partners. No investors telling me what to do.

DEMETRIUS: How much you bring in?

RAHEEM: More than the police department pays you to get shot at.

(*Moments pass. Demetrius prepares his camera.*)

RAHEEM: What did you end up getting into last night? You get you a little taste?

DEMETRIUS: No, I . . . it's a long story.

RAHEEM: What's wrong? (*earnestly*) Your dick broke?

DEMETRIUS: My dick is fine. I . . . I went out.

RAHEEM: Where?

DEMETRIUS: A club.

RAHEEM: Help?

DEMETRIUS: Ain't nothin' wrong with my—

RAHEEM: That's the name of the club. Help.

DEMETRIUS: Oh . . . right . . . I . . . I didn't remember . . . the name—yeah . . . yeah . . . got my drink on, you know—

RAHEEM: It was probably Help. It was crowded?

DEMETRIUS: Yeah . . . crazy. But, the women, they wasn't right, so . . . (*beat*) The whole situation—

RAHEEM: What—

DEMETRIUS: It . . . It scares me.

RAHEEM: You mean like, AIDS and whatnot?

DEMETRIUS: No. I mean, like—you wouldn't understand. If Jared was here . . .

RAHEEM: Try me.

DEMETRIUS: I'ma be real. On the real. Okay. When Dana got pregnant, I was twenty-one. Don't get me wrong: I love my daughter. I wouldn't trade her for nothing in the world. But back then, all I was thinking about was seeing the world. I didn't want to have no baby. I wanted Dana to have an abortion so bad, 'cause . . . I was just gettin' in the world. And I knew me. I'm not the type of dude to have a baby sittin' up somewhere while I ran the streets. So, when she said she wanted it . . . my whole world got real small . . . but I stepped up. I took that piece of me, and I put it in a box. While everybody was out partying, I went to night school. Went to the academy. Worked. Held her down while she finished. I wasn't no baby daddy. I was a faithful husband. I did everything right. And I was a father. Deja knows me. We live in the same house. Take her to school. Tuck her in. I'm her everyday father, you know. I love her more than my life. But I always felt . . . this—thing. Like I was missing out. That part I put up, never went away. It kept growing and now it's pushing at the sides of the box—and now, here, I can let it out. But I'm afraid that if I let it out, I won't be able to put it back. I'm trying to hold on. I feel guilty—

RAHEEM: For wanting to live your life? Man, please. Think about Jared. Died at twenty-seven. And what was his life? Going to school. Punching the clock. Paying bills. Trying to get at wack-ass females who think they all that. That's not living. Living is like a—"I'm free, I can do anything, go anywhere, conquer the world"—kind of feeling. There are grown-ass men who never had that. Always penny-pinchin'. Never get props. Afraid to speak their mind, 'cause somebody could take something from them. They ain't never walked into a store with their pockets so fat that they could buy anything. Every man deserves to know what that feels like. At least once. You only live once. Do what the fuck you wanna do. Go let these fine-ass women appreciate you. Nothing wrong with that.

DEMETRIUS: (*beat*) Yeah.

RAHEEM: (*beat*) Tell you what. I'ma take y'all to a place tonight, off the strip. Where all the women is like Halle Berry, swear to God. It's where all the ballers go. Discreet. You're going to be sitting next to lawyers, doctors. Last time I was there, I look over—dude from the Miami Heat—what's his name—he was gettin' served at the bar.

DEMETRIUS: At the bar?

RAHEEM: Balls and all, son.

DEMETRIUS: Yo . . .

RAHEEM: That's all you need. We'll go to that spot tonight, after the boat.

DEMETRIUS: Yeah.

(*Demetrius looks at his ring.*)

RAHEEM: Live your life, D.

(*Demetrius removes the ring and places it in a vase of flowers. He picks up his camera.*)

DEMETRIUS: I'm gonna go get Jay, grab something to eat—take him with me to go check out Corcovado Mountain. Maybe do that cable car thing. Take some pictures. Get some culture for his ass. (*beat*) What time we have to leave here to make the boat?

RAHEEM: Three.

DEMETRIUS: Okay. Meet you here.

(*Demetrius goes to leave.*)

RAHEEM: Don't worry about the money for the boat. I got you.

DEMETRIUS: (*beat*) Alright.

(*Demetrius exits.*)

Scene 5

PASSAGE OF TIME: Perhaps Wreckx-N-Effect's "Rump Shaker" plays. Lights flash in a photo-graphic montage of the guys having fun on the boat, at various Brazilian cultural attractions, on the beach, clubbing, popping champagne, etc., perhaps dramatized live or flashed onto screens surrounding the audience. The snapshots (of course) never include women but should indicate their presence, for example, someone holding a bra or panties in his mouth so that we understand that the women they're with are naked and that he took them off with his mouth. The passage should also include displays of Raheem wielding money, Jalani filming others and himself with his camera, Demetrius protesting being filmed, and Demetrius calling home with his calling card.

Scene 6

Day Four: Two days later. Night. Keys rattle outside the condo suite. The door opens.

RAHEEM: (*off stage*) Get yo' ass in here.

(*Jalani enters the apartment. Raheem follows.*)

JALANI: I—

RAHEEM: Don't say shit to me right now, Jay. For real.

JALANI: My daddy's gone and my brother's dead. I don't need you clockin' me. I'm grown. Recognize.

RAHEEM: Sit down.

Jalani sits. Raheem goes to the kitchenette and gets two cold beers. He returns to the living room and gives one to Jalani, who applies it to his face. Raheem drinks and nurses his hand with the beer. A moment passes.

RAHEEM: Every day it's something. On the first day you leave right after I tell you not to go nowhere alone. Then it was when you pushed the girl off the boat 'cause she said she didn't wanna fuck with your drunk ass. Destroyed my whole deal. Now you fightin' niggas? What the fuck was you thinkin'?

JALANI: I hate them niggas from Harlem. He was frontin' on me. And I just—

RAHEEM: And you just thought it was a good idea to throw a right hook at a 250-pound nigga? How did you think that shit was gonna turn out?

JALANI: I wasn't thinking—

RAHEEM: I know! 'Cause you don't never think before you do nothin'. When you gon' grow up? (*looking at his pager*) Now we gon' have beef with these muthafuckas!

JALANI: What was I supposed to do? He disrespected me. I had macked that girl—bought her a drink and everything—and when I came back this nigga got her. And I know he seen me with her. I had picked her from the time we walked up in there—

RAHEEM: You hit a 250-pound nigga over a bitch—

JALANI: She was mine—

RAHEEM: Jalani! She was a whore!

JALANI: Still—

RAHEEM: Do you know how many bitches is out there?! You want a bitch?! I got a bitch. I got twenty other bitches. I could get you a bitch.

JALANI: What you mean, you got twenty other bitches?

RAHEEM: Now I'm involved in this shit. And people know me down here. I got relationships with these people, Jay. You messin' with my business.

JALANI: What you mean, you got twenty bitches?

RAHEEM: Just what I said, nigga, I got twenty bitches.

JALANI: Like what? You pimpin'? (*long beat*) You pimpin'? (*beat*) You pimpin', Raheem? (*beat*) She was yours?

RAHEEM: Yeah, she was mine.

JALANI: What!?

RAHEEM: Jay—

JALANI: You're a pimp? You's a real, live, muthafuckin' pimp!

RAHEEM: Shut up—

JALANI: Oh, shit! How long you been pimpin'?

(*Muted sounds of a woman's moans come from Demetrius's room, not words.*)

RAHEEM: Shhh . . .

JALANI: You fuck for free?

RAHEEM: No—

JALANI: You could give me a discount?

RAHEEM: Shhhh. Shut up. (*longish beat*) You hear that?

JALANI: What?

RAHEEM: I hear—

(*Muted sounds of lovemaking come from Demetrius's room, not words.*)

JALANI: (*whispering*) Is that . . . ?

RAHEEM: (*whispering*) It's D.

JALANI: (*whispering*) Aw, shit!

(*Jalani grabs his camera and starts to go to Demetrius's room.*)

RAHEEM: (*whispering*) Where you goin'?

JALANI: (*whispering*) I wanna see—

RAHEEM: (*whispering*) Leave that nigga alone—

JALANI: (*whispering*) Naw, I wanna see.

Jalani continues to Demetrius's room and Raheem, overcome by curiosity, follows. Muted sounds of love making continue to emerge from the room, then:

JALANI: (*off stage*) Beat that shit up, dog! Drill that—

DEMETRIUS: (*off stage*) What the fuck—

JALANI: (*off stage*) Get it, D! Get it, D! Get it!

Raheem runs back to the living room laughing. Jalani follows, clutching his camera, doubled over in laughter. A moment passes. Demetrius enters the living room in his boxers and socks.

DEMETRIUS: Where is that muthafucka?

RAHEEM: D, calm down.

DEMETRIUS: I swear to God—

JALANI: Was that a glow-in-the-dark condom, dog?

DEMETRIUS: Give me that! I told you I don't want no pictures of me—

Jalani taunts Raheem with the camera. Raheem and Jalani laugh. Demetrius lunges for Jalani.

RAHEEM: Calm down, D.

DEMETRIUS: I'ma kill—

JALANI: I'ma call that nigga light bright! From now on, that's yo' new name! Light bright!

RAHEEM: What, you couldn't find your way? You needed a glow stick?

JALANI: I thought you only did that with your wife, light bright!

DEMETRIUS: Shut up. She can hear you.

JALANI: She don't speak English, D.

DEMETRIUS: She can speak a little. She understands—

JALANI: Yo, is that that same girl Ra introduced you to that night at the club, after the boat ride?

DEMETRIUS: Yeah.

JALANI: You still with the same bitch?

RAHEEM: You like her, huh?

DEMETRIUS: She's—

JALANI: This nigga is in love. I saw him. He be takin' her shoppin'—

DEMETRIUS: She needed some stuff for her house—

RAHEEM: I told you bitches will be trying to cling, trying to get you to finance they lives—

DEMETRIUS: I'm not.

JALANI: Besides, the bitch got a job to do. I mean, if she's hemmed up with you, she sho' can't be makin' her pimp no money—

DEMETRIUS: She ain't got no pimp. Pimpin' is illegal in Brazil, dummy.

JALANI: (*beat*) Oh, really? I did not know that. Did you know that, Ra?

RAHEEM: It's been like three days with the same chick, D?

(*Jalani picks up Demetrius's travel guide.*)

JALANI: Was that in the travel guide? No pimpin'?

DEMETRIUS: Fuck you.

RAHEEM: Don't you want something new?

JALANI: Pablo already got sixteen down—

RAHEEM: You ain't been with no sixteen girls—

JALANI: I try to average four a day—

DEMETRIUS: I like her, okay.

JALANI: Here we go—

DEMETRIUS: She's showing me stuff about the country. Teaching me the language.

JALANI: Digging for gold—

DEMETRIUS: Look: Olá! Meu nome é Demetrius. Pode você fazê-lo com galinha?

JALANI & RAHEEM: What?!

DEMETRIUS: (*to Jalani*) It's better than that sign language shit you be usin' to talk to the ladies.

(*Demetrius demonstrates.*)

RAHEEM: You do be lookin' like you tryin' to land a plane.

JALANI: I don't be trying to talk to a bitch—

DEMETRIUS: She needed a little help, so I helped her. It's my money. It don't hurt me none. And, she's teaching me about the culture, the food. Capoeira—that it's from Africa, Angola actually. And—come here—

JALANI: Talkin' 'bout my game is weak—

(*Demetrius leads them out onto the balcony. Raheem and Jalani reluctantly comply.*)

DEMETRIUS: Come here. I paid this taxi driver to take us around all day and she took me to her neighborhood—Rocinha, Rochina, something like that. A favela. Like a ghetto. It's right—maybe you can see it from here. (*He strains.*) You can't see it, but it's over there. Behind that Jesus statue. She showed me where Michael Jackson shot that video . . . How's it go?

(*trying to recall but getting the words and melody wrong*)

"They don't give a damn about who we are . . ." Remember that? It's crazy crowded, yo. I mean, like even more than New York crowded. Worse than Marcy. It's on this steep hill and the streets are narrow. And the buildings have flat roofs and are built literally on top of each other, but not in one shot. Like over time. It's like, when people want to buy property, they buy somebody's roof and build on top of it. And you look out from the top of the hill, and you see all the mismatched buildings and then you look further and see all the wealth on the coast. It's crazy. She said a lot of people who live in the 'hoods come from African blood—ex-slaves—and that, back in the day, the masters used to free the slaves for the three days of carnival to do whatever they wanted. It was a way to keep them pacified, you know, give them something to look forward to so they wouldn't revolt. So slaves would wait all year for these three days where they could drink, dance, worship, play music, whatever. Dress up. Imitate the rich. Live the dream. And that's how Carnaval got to be so big in Brazil. Everyone so excited to celebrate three days of freedom. Excited to live the dream. Even if it was only for three days.

JALANI: (*beat*) You are really killing my buzz right now.

DEMETRIUS: Don't you wanna know that?

JALANI: No! We've got to get you another girl. Fuckin' talkin' 'bout slavery—

DEMETRIUS: Next time I come, she's going to show me Bahia, São Paulo—

JALANI: The next time?

RAHEEM: You forgetting about your wife, man?

JALANI: (*teasing*) Dana who?

DEMETRIUS: No. I mean, if I come again—

JALANI: I'm telling you, his nose is open—

DEMETRIUS: Me enjoying Zeze's company ain't got nothing to do with how much I love my wife. I love my wife. This is just new and—

JALANI: (*scoffing*) Zeze.

DEMETRIUS: She's been telling me about her situation—

JALANI: Oh, really?

RAHEEM: What she tell you?

JALANI: (*taunting Raheem*) Yeah, what she tell you?

DEMETRIUS: She has kids. Two boys and a girl.

RAHEEM: Oh.

JALANI: How you know? That story could be part of her game—

DEMETRIUS: She took me home.

RAHEEM: You went to her house?!

JALANI: Breakin' all the rules—

DEMETRIUS: She said she needed some stuff for her house. I bought them some sandals. I saw a picture of her husband and was like—

JALANI: She married?

RAHEEM: That's why you can't trust bitches.

DEMETRIUS: She said he knew what she does. I couldn't imagine. Knowing that your wife is hoe-ing every carnival 'cause you can't hold it down.

RAHEEM: One man's wife is another man's hoe.

DEMETRIUS: But it's like . . . the only way we can come down here and trick on them like this is because they're at the bottom here. If they had money she wouldn't . . . And I was standing there. And it was funny. Ironic. I mean, because, if God had changed his mind, if we were born in Brazil, we'd be them.

(*They are all silent. Raheem drinks.*)

JALANI: (*to Raheem*) Let me get some of that.

(*Raheem passes his glass. Jalani drinks. A moment passes.*)

RAHEEM: Tonight's the night.

JALANI: I know.

DEMETRIUS: Jared would've liked this.

RAHEEM: What you think he would be like if he was here?

DEMETRIUS: I could see his ass now—it would be a harem up in here—

RAHEEM: He probably would've been fuckin' with that midget lady—

DEMETRIUS: You saw her too! I see her like every day—

RAHEEM: (*considering*) I don't know. She got a big ol' booty—

DEMETRIUS: He did always like the weird ones. Variety—

RAHEEM: 'Cause he could bag any chick he wanted, pretty nigga.

JALANI: No he couldn't. Every time somebody die they become like, invincible. Even he couldn't have chicks like this. Chicks like this only go to dudes with money, and he was broke. Fifty dollars in New York will only get you a crackhead. Don't no nigga got a life like this.

RAHEEM: Unless he got loot.

JALANI: And how many niggas you know with that kind of loot?

DEMETRIUS: Remember that bald chick Jared was fuckin' with?

RAHEEM: She was beautiful—

DEMETRIUS: She was so sexy—

JALANI: She was bald! Lookin' like a middle aged man—

DEMETRIUS: Naw, shorty was bangin'. When you're that pretty, you don't need hair. Most women can't do without hair. They'd be lookin' all alien-like.

JALANI: You stupid.

RAHEEM: Remember the white girl he had?

DEMETRIUS: Wooo, weee! She was fly for a white girl.

JALANI: She was fly. And she knew it. Uppity bitch. (*beat*) I'm sick of uppity bitches. You try to be nice. They don't want nice. They don't want good. It's like they

look for the niggas that gon' treat them bad, then complain that niggas is
treatin' them bad. Then when you wanna treat them good, they look down they
nose at you—like you shorter than them. (*beat*) 'Cause they got it too easy. All
they have to do is sit back and wait for you to approach them. Then you got to
prove why you worthy or some shit. You got to check these chicken heads. Be
like: I'm the man in this. You the woman, and I'm the man. (*beat*) Jared didn't
have that problem. He ran through these hoes. They fought over him. He dissed
them and they still fought to be with him. To this day, I never understood that.
I hated him for that. He was good in school. Hated him for that. Good at sports.
Tall. Hated him. His shadow was so long. Then he died. And his shadow grew
into a fuckin' eclipse. I remember sitting in the pews, looking at the people
bawling, thinking, "How am I gonna top this?" (*beat*) I'm fucked up, huh? (*long
beat*) I miss him.

DEMETRIUS: He's looking down right now, man. Always.

RAHEEM: I can't believe it's been a year.

DEMETRIUS: He'd be proud of you, man. Doing good in school. About to graduate.
Get a good job. Have a family.

JALANI: Why, so I can be miserable, like you?

DEMETRIUS: I ain't miserable.

RAHEEM: You ain't happy neither, nigga.

DEMETRIUS: I love my family. I'm just . . . I feel like—there's got to be more, you know
what I'm saying?

RAHEEM: This is more.

DEMETRIUS: Is it?

RAHEEM: Hell, yeah. Look around. Tell me you don't feel like the man right now.

JALANI: That's why I'm livin' it to the fullest, up in here, you heard.

RAHEEM: You should!

JALANI: And I'ma get mine up front 'cause you never know—

RAHEEM: Life's a bitch—

JALANI: And then you die.

RAHEEM: Ain't that the truth. Get or get got. Pimp or be pimped. That's the way of
the world.

DEMETRIUS: (*beat*) Let's pour his liquor out for him.

(*Jalani retrieves a liquor bottle from the bar. He hands it to Demetrius, who pours liquor off the
balcony.*)

DEMETRIUS: I know you're lookin' down, man.

(*Demetrius passes the bottle to Raheem. Raheem pours.*)

RAHEEM: Play on, playa.

(*Raheem passes the bottle to Jalani. Jalani pours.*)

JALANI: I miss you.

(*A moment passes. There is commotion in a foreign language from people below.*)

JALANI: Oh, shit!

RAHEEM: I think we—

(*Jalani pours a little more.*)

DEMETRIUS: (*stopping Jalani*) What you doin'? (*looking over the balcony*) Sorry! We're sorry! Uh. . . . pesaroso!

(*They laugh.*)

JALANI: We still going out tonight, right, to celebrate?

RAHEEM: That's what we came to do. Drinkin' his drink. And fuck all the weird ones. Live for him.

JALANI: (*to Demetrius*) You gonna send that barnacle on her way, right?

DEMETRIUS: I'ma put her in a cab.

JALANI: 'Cause it's boys night tonight, nigga! Let's get it in! "Tonight on the Adventures of Pablo—"

RAHEEM: Who is Pablo?

Jalani and Raheem exit the balcony. Demetrius stays and takes in the view, perhaps straining to see the favela. Jalani and Raheem confer and decide to lock Demetrius on the balcony. Demetrius hears the lock and turns.

DEMETRIUS: Alright, alright. Ha, ha, very funny. Open the door.

(*Jalani and Raheem taunt him and exit to their rooms.*)

DEMETRIUS: (*beat*) Raheem! Jalani! (*beat*) Open the door! Open the door! (*beat*) Y'all play too much! (*beat*) Zeze!

Scene 7

Day Four/Five: Later that night/morning. Jalani sits on the couch playing a Nintendo Gameboy. Hip-hop music is blaring from the stereo, perhaps the chorus from Dr. Dre's "Bitches Ain't Shit" or something incredibly vulgar, violent, and bitingly misogynistic. Raheem and Demetrius enter.

RAHEEM: (*laughing to Demetrius*) . . . Oh, my God, you—(*to Jalani*) You just got the door all open.

DEMETRIUS: (*to Jalani*) Turn that shit down before they kick us out of here.

(*Demetrius turns the music down. Raheem goes to make a drink.*)

RAHEEM: Jay, Demetrius took that bitch—

DEMETRIUS: Her name is Zeze—

RAHEEM: He took her to a movie! Did you know that? Like, on a date!

DEMETRIUS: It was a good movie.

RAHEEM: It was in Portuguese!

DEMETRIUS: It's just like watching a foreign film.

RAHEEM: But there are no subtitles. (*to Jalani*) This dude was whipped—

DEMETRIUS: We have a connection—

RAHEEM: Everybody has a connection with her, D! She's a prostitute! You're killing me right now. (*to Jalani*) Yo, you missed out! There was mad people, son—the floats, costumes, feathers and shit.

DEMETRIUS: It's like Labor Day times twenty. I got Deja a—what did they call this? Talked the guy down to five dollars—

RAHEEM: Like topless. Literally. Painted golden skin. Just a little leaf covering their—what's wrong with you?

JALANI: Ain't nothin' wrong with me.

DEMETRIUS: Nigga drunk outta his mind.

RAHEEM: How was that piece I hooked you up with? It was good, right?

JALANI: Your girl was trippin', Ra. You need to check her.

RAHEEM: What happened?

JALANI: Bitch tried to rob me.

DEMETRIUS: What?

RAHEEM: Whatchu mean?

JALANI: Rob me, nigga, whatchu think I mean? I brought her back here. I told her what I wanted, like you said. Make it clear before shit jump off. I told her that I wanted her to dance and strip. I wanted her to suck my dick. And I wanted to fuck her in the ass. I never had that before. And she was like, "I don't do ass," and I was like, "fine." And I paid her. I paid her fifty dollars up front. She danced and stripped and I asked her if she wanted something to drink and she said, "Yeah." So I come out here and mix us some drinks and when I walk back in the room, she jumpin' and shit. Like I caught her doin' something she wasn't supposed to be doing. Like she was scared. And I said, "What you doin'?" And the bitch trying to pretend that she don't understand English no more. And I look over and I see the top drawer of the nightstand wide open and I'm like, "No, this bitch ain't going through my shit!" Then, she must've seen my eyes, she got all scared trying to grab her clothes to leave and shit. And I was like, "Where you goin'? I paid you already." And she tried to keep going, and I grabbed that bitch by her hair like, "Where you think you goin'?"

DEMETRIUS: Jalani—

JALANI: She was trying to leave! And she started to fight me, and I—

RAHEEM: Where is she?

JALANI: And I hit her.

DEMETRIUS: What?

JALANI: She was trying to play me! I hit her.

RAHEEM: Ughhhh!

JALANI: And I fucked her. 'Cause I had paid her already. And she left.

RAHEEM: Where'd she go?

JALANI: I don't know.

DEMETRIUS: You're hitting women, Jalani?

JALANI: She was trying to play me. I don't play that—

DEMETRIUS: But she's a woman.

JALANI: I don't give a fuck about that hoe.

RAHEEM: I told you not to make a scene. Just let 'em go if they start trippin'. It's not worth it. You can buy another one. Didn't I say that!

DEMETRIUS: You don't hit no woman, Jay—

RAHEEM: Didn't I tell you that?!

JALANI: Fuck her. What's she gon' do? Run to her pimp? She don't even know my name.

RAHEEM: She'll run to the police.

JALANI: And say what? She was trying to rob me.

RAHEEM: You think the police give a fuck about—

JALANI: She was trying to rob me. That's the truth.

RAHEEM: The police won't care, Jalani.

JALANI: Well, it's her word against mine.

RAHEEM: You think they're going to believe you? They're not going to believe you. You're just a nigga to them. An American nigga.

JALANI: She's not going to go to the cops. If anything she'll go to you—

DEMETRIUS: Why would she go to Raheem?

JALANI: Raheem is her pimp.

DEMETRIUS: (*beat*) What?!

JALANI: Raheem is her pimp. That's what he's been doing. That's his business.

DEMETRIUS: What?!

RAHEEM: Which way did she go?

JALANI: So I'm good.

DEMETRIUS: Where are you going?

RAHEEM: To try to find her before—

JALANI: Yeah, go check that hoe.

RAHEEM: Shut up, Jalani. *Shut up!*

JALANI: Who the fuck you tellin' to shut up?

RAHEEM: You nigga! God! You *stupid fuck!!* If she does go to the police, you think she's just going to tell on you? No, nigga. She's going to tell them about me too. On the whole operation. Did you think about that? Of course you didn't. 'Cause you don't never think. You didn't think when you pushed that girl—my girl—off the boat. You didn't think before you threw that punch at Big Boy from Harlem—a dude who's part of the group that I brought down here! Got Armando questioning whether or not he wants to fuck with me—why? Why?! Because of you! Because of you, man. If it wasn't for your brother, man, I swear—if I didn't promise him I'd watch over you—I wouldn't even bother, nigga. You ain't worth it.

JALANI: I don't need you to watch over me—

RAHEEM: Fuck you, Jalani.

JALANI: I don't need nobody!

(*Jalani exits to his room mumbling. Raheem prepares to leave.*)

DEMETRIUS: Wait, nigga—

RAHEEM: I got to go find her.

DEMETRIUS: Wait a second.

RAHEEM: I don't need no lecture from you, Demetrius. Not right now.

DEMETRIUS: You brought me down here and you were pimping? Pimping, nigga?! I'm a fuckin' cop, man! A law enforcement officer. I can't be caught up in no mess. I got a family, Ra. A house—people who depend on me—and you brought me down here—you're messing with me and mine now, nigga.

RAHEEM: No, no, no, no, no. You brought yourself down here. Nobody had a gun to your head. You made the arrangements. You bought the plane ticket. You, nigga. You came, just like every other man from all over the world came down here— to get your dick wet. So you can get off your high muthafuckin' horse. Talkin' 'bout your house. And your job. And your family. You just a pink slip away from unemployment and a paycheck away from food stamps like everybody else. You're fuckin' a hoe, just like every man down here. At least I ain't lying about it, pretending it's something that it ain't. At least I ain't lying to my wife. At least I'm real with mine.

(*Jalani re-enters.*)

JALANI: She got my money!

DEMETRIUS: What?

JALANI: She got me for my money! All my cash—

RAHEEM: What?

JALANI: She got my money! My refund money for school!

DEMETRIUS: Where did you have it?

JALANI: Under the matress.

DEMETRIUS: You didn't check before she left?

JALANI: What am I going to do?

RAHEEM: Ughhh!

JALANI: What am I going to do?

DEMETRIUS: Calm down!

JALANI: I'ma kill that bitch!

RAHEEM: Armando's going to kill me—

DEMETRIUS: Y'all! Calm down!

(*Raheem heads for the door. Jalani follows.*)

DEMETRIUS: (*to Jalani*) Where you going?

JALANI: Going to get my money—

RAHEEM: Y'all stay here. *I'm* going to find her—alone. Don't leave—

JALANI: But—

RAHEEM: Alone, Jay!

DEMETRIUS: (*to Jalani*) Fall back.

RAHEEM: I got to go find her before—

(*There is a strong knock at the door. They all go silent.*)

RAHEEM: Shit! Be quiet.

DEMETRIUS: Who is that?

RAHEEM: Shhh!

Long beat. There is another strong knock. Raheem goes to answer the door. He puts his hand on the door knob and looks back at Demetrius and Jalani. He opens the door and light pours in.

BLACKOUT

End of Act 1

Act 2

Scene 1

Club Carnaval, 2010. Raheem appears at the DJ booth at the now-crowded club. Perhaps the chorus of Kanye West's "Good Life" streams out of huge speakers. Raheem pumps the crowd.

RAHEEM: (*chanting*) Where Brooklyn at?! Where's Brooklyn at!? Where Brooklyn at!?

(*There is a surge of affirmative responses from the crowd. Raheem gestures to the DJ to lower the music.*)

What's up, y'all! Y'all look so beautiful right now. I know y'all are enjoying the atmosphere. I wanted to take a moment to thank you for being here tonight for the beginning—you can brag that you saw the start, 'cause you know this 'bout to blow up, right?

(*There is a surge of affirmative responses from the crowd.*)

From the moment I had the idea, I knew it would be something y'all would appreciate. It's like, sixteen years ago—I was like a kid—I had this vision— and ain't nothing like seeing something you've dreamed about come to life. This right here is a beautiful thing. To look out and see all y'all having a good time—it's what's up. I know there are some very important people out there that's been down since the beginning—I see you, Q. I see you, Rus—people who always had my back. But there are a few people that I'm especially glad to see— my boys, Jay and D—where y'all at?

(*Raheem points to the VIP section, where Demetrius and Jalani are.*)

Them right there—them are my dogs—my fam. These the type of dudes—like, you can always find new friends, but you can't never find new old friends, know what I'm saying? We've been through some loss. . . . And I'ma tell you, success is sweet, but ain't nothin' like sharing your success with folk who know where you come from—from the Bed-Stuy gutter—I'm talkin' the realness, not this gentrified shit, you heard? Bed-Stuy do or die, baby! Needless to say I'm havin' a ball. So y'all enjoy y'all selves tonight. Get out your phones and tweet this to your friends. Get your drink on. Get your groove on. And leave me a message. It's Club Carnaval, baby!

Raheem gestures for the music to resume. The lights flash in pictures/snapshots of the three of them separately in the club—Raheem enjoying his guests, Jalani looking to Demetrius from the bar, and Demetrius picking up the remote. The snapshots quickly transport us back to . . .

Scene 2

Rio de Janeiro, 1996. Day Five: Police station. Jalani and Demetrius are in an interrogation room. They sit in silence for some time. Raheem enters, and the door closes behind him. They are silent for a moment.

DEMETRIUS: What happened?

RAHEEM: They're talking about charging us with encouraging prostitution.

(Raheem sits.)

JALANI: *(beat)* That doesn't make any sense. Prostitution is legal here.

DEMETRIUS: But encouraging it ain't.

(A moment passes.)

DEMETRIUS: What did you tell them?

RAHEEM: Nothing. They said she accused me of pimping and I said I didn't do it. She said that the apartment was a whore house, and I told them that it isn't. That they can go check it again. That it's just us there, vacationing. *(making sure)* You don't have weed or nothin' in the apartment, do you, Jay? We might make it out of encouraging prostitution, but they won't let us go for drug possession.

DEMETRIUS: Oh, my God. . . .

JALANI: No. No.

RAHEEM: Good.

(A moment passes.)

JALANI: They said pimping has a fifteen-year jail sentence.

RAHEEM: They're not going to put us in jail. They'd deport us before—

DEMETRIUS: And then they'd put us in jail.

JALANI: I can't go to jail, man, I—

DEMETRIUS: Shut up, Jalani.

(Silence.)

RAHEEM: *(to Jalani)* She said you forced her.

JALANI: *(beat)* I didn't force her to do anything. Did you tell them she stole my money?

RAHEEM: They said she said you did her in the ass even though she told you no.

DEMETRIUS: You raped her?

JALANI: Rape her? I paid her.

DEMETRIUS: Assault, pimping, and now rape. I can't believe this.

RAHEEM: How is that helpful, Demetrius? We're all in here together. Let's just focus on getting out together.

(*A moment passes.*)

JALANI: Okay. What are we going to do?

RAHEEM: They're going to talk to each of us alone. So the first thing is to get our story straight.

DEMETRIUS: We're just here vacationing.

RAHEEM: Exactly. It's just us three here from New York for a week for Carnaval.

DEMETRIUS: That's the truth.

RAHEEM: Exactly. Just tell them the truth.

(*A moment passes.*)

JALANI: What are they doing out there? What's taking so long?

DEMETRIUS: That's part of the game. They're just trying to put us on edge.

JALANI: Well, they got me. I'm on edge.

DEMETRIUS: I get the feeling that, if they were going to charge us, they would've charged us by now, though.

JALANI: I know, it's been like eight hours. What time is it?

DEMETRIUS: Longer than that. And what are they waiting for? Think about it. We've only seen and talked to the same officers that picked us up. They haven't separated us, or fingerprinted us, or made us write a statement or anything like that. I feel like, if we just slip them some cash, they'd let us go.

RAHEEM: Or accuse us of trying to bribe the police.

DEMETRIUS: We'd have to fish around first, to see if they're the type to go for it. But I get the feeling—

RAHEEM: This coming from a cop.

JALANI: (*to Demetrius*) How much money you got on you?

DEMETRIUS: A couple hundred.

JALANI: Ra?

RAHEEM: The same.

DEMETRIUS: (*beat*) You've been pimping for five days and all you got is a couple hundred dollars?

RAHEEM: (*beat*) I got a thousand or so.

DEMETRIUS: Really, Raheem?

JALANI: Demetrius, stop.

DEMETRIUS: We're sitting in jail and he's trying to hold out?

RAHEEM: I'm not holding out. This is all I got. I'm not going home to no nine-to-five—

JALANI: Okay, you guys, chill. We can't do this now. Okay? Now, how much money do we need to get home?

RAHEEM: We only need money to pay taxes on the way out, and whatever it costs for a cab to the airport.

JALANI: Good. Y'all got that at the crib. So that means we have a thousand to offer.

RAHEEM: A thousand?!

DEMETRIUS: A thousand! I wanna get out of here.

JALANI: That's like two thousand reais—

DEMETRIUS: Good. So, the next one to go in has to fish around to see if they're open to it. Alright?

RAHEEM: Yeah.   JALANI: Okay.

DEMETRIUS: That's the plan.

(*A moment passes.*)

JALANI: We should pray.

(*After a beat, Jalani reaches for their hands. They, in their own ways, and in their own time, comply.*)

JALANI: Our father, who art in heaven, hallowed be thy name. Thy kingdom come—

JALANI AND DEMETRIUS: Thy will be done—

(*Raheem's pager goes off. He looks at it.*)

On earth as it is in heaven. Give us this day our daily bread and—

JALANI, DEMETRIUS, AND RAHEEM: Forgive us our trespasses as we forgive those who have trespassed against us. And lead us not into temptation, but deliver us from evil. For thine is the kingdom, and the power, and the glory forever and ever. Amen.

(*Moments pass. The door opens. They look up.*)

JALANI: (*pointing to himself*) Me?

(*Jalani starts to leave.*)

DEMETRIUS: (*whispering to Jalani*) Fish around—

JALANI: (*whispering to Demetrius*) I know!

(*Jalani looks at Demetrius and Raheem and then exits the room.*)

DEMETRIUS: I just pray he doesn't fuck it up.

RAHEEM: He won't. He's wild, but he ain't dumb.

(*A moment passes.*)

DEMETRIUS: Tourism, nigga?

RAHEEM: I didn't lie.

DEMETRIUS: You didn't tell the truth, neither.

RAHEEM: You knew what that shit was.

DEMETRIUS: How I knew?

RAHEEM: You could've figured it out. Jalani did. You saw me that night at the restaurant. You saw me on the boat. At the club. You saw me makin' drops. You knew. But you didn't want to ask 'cause you were reaping the benefits. And that's how you've always been. Never wanting to kill the chicken, but the first one at the table with some hot sauce.

DEMETRIUS: I asked you what you were doing and you stood there in my face and said—

RAHEEM: How you think the condo was free? How you think you made it on the boat? Where you think that cash was comin' from? How did you think I knew Zeze? You thought she was my Brazilian friend from back in the day? I hooked that up for you.

DEMETRIUS: She's yours?

RAHEEM: What you think? You bagged a chick like that 'cause she liked your personality?

(*They are alone and silent for a moment. The door opens and Jalani re-enters.*)

RAHEEM: What happened?

DEMETRIUS: That was too quick—

JALANI: They got me in the room, and they asked me what happened.

DEMETRIUS: Yeah—

JALANI: I told them, we were just here vacationing. And they said that I was the one she identified—the one who . . . the one who hit her. And I explained that I did hit her.

RAHEEM: Why would you say—?!

JALANI: I told them I hit her because I lost my temper when she stole my money. See, they can understand that—man to man.

DEMETRIUS: That's still assault, Jay. Why would you admit—

JALANI: 'Cause they didn't care about her. I could tell. And I knew they didn't because after I said that, one of them said, "That's a shame. How will you get out of here without any money?"

RAHEEM: Bastards.

DEMETRIUS: No, this is good. So you think they'll go for it?

JALANI: Yeah. He basically told me, in so many words.

DEMETRIUS: Good. Good. I'll go next. I'll make the offer.

JALANI: Yeah.

RAHEEM: Why him? Why you?

DEMETRIUS: 'Cause I'm next. Give me the money, Ra.

(*Raheem hesitates.*)

JALANI: Give him the money, Ra.

(*Raheem reluctantly hands his money over. Demetrius pulls out his own money, combines the stacks, counts and arranges the money, and puts it in his pocket. Moments pass.*)

JALANI: Snoop just got acquitted. I saw on TV. They were out there watching videos. Mistrial technicality. Deadlocked jury. Something like that.

RAHEEM: Money will keep even a thug nigga outta jail.

DEMETRIUS: Y'all ain't Snoop.

JALANI: I know I'm not Snoop, I was just saying—

DEMETRIUS: Snoop ain't even Snoop. The nigga's name is Calvin. Calvin. That's y'all's problem. You don't know the difference between fantasy and reality 'cause you ain't got no responsibilities. This shit you got me wrapped up in right here, Jalani, this is reality.

RAHEEM: Here we go with the lectures.

DEMETRIUS: And you. At least he's young. There's hope for him. He could grow the fuck up at any moment. But what's your excuse? You're pimpin'?

RAHEEM: I don't need this shit right now.

JALANI: D—

DEMETRIUS: Had your moms and your dad. Went to college. But instead of a job, you want a hook up—

RAHEEM: What are you now, a psychologist?

DEMETRIUS: Where's your hook up now, nigga? Got me out here—both of you!

RAHEEM: Oh, you're the innocent one?

DEMETRIUS: He's beatin' bitches and you're //prostituting—

RAHEEM: I'm stimulating the muthafuckin' economy.

JALANI: Stop, // y'all—

RAHEEM: Naw, I'm sick // of—

JALANI: Stop. We got a plan. Stick to the plan.

(*The door opens. They look up. Demetrius rises and leaves the room without looking back. The door closes. Jalani and Raheem sit in silence.*)

RAHEEM: That nigga would sell us down the river. Fuckin' pig.

JALANI: He just mad. He's a cop. He knows what to say to them. He's going to go in there, talk some cop talk, pay the man, and come get us out. He's going to walk back in here and we'll be free. So be easy.

(*A moment passes. Raheem's pager goes off. He silences it.*)

JALANI: This place is Sodom and Gomorrah. Fuckin' Twilight Zone. My friends are not going to believe, when I tell them—this is some crazy shit, right? It's like a bad episode of *NYPD Blue*. Nobody's gonna believe—

RAHEEM: We're not out of here yet.

JALANI: But we will be. (*beat*) What time you think it is?

RAHEEM: I don't know.

JALANI: We might get out of here in time to catch the club, dog! What you going to do on your first day as a free man?

RAHEEM: Catch the club? This a joke to you? A fuckin' Great Adventure ride or some shit?

JALANI: I'm saying, this ain't got to ruin everything—

RAHEEM: You did ruin everything! Every fuckin' thing is ruined. And you owe me money, nigga! And I want my shit, or you might as well stay here.

JALANI: Who are you talking to?

RAHEEM: You heard me.

JALANI: What's the problem? So what, we spent a day in this room. We were probably gon' be sleep half the day, anyway—

RAHEEM: Shut up, Jalani.

JALANI: So, whatchu bitchin' about? You ain't lost nothin'. Your hoes still makin' money out there, right?

RAHEEM: You don't get it. Jalani, you fucked with my entire business. I had a goal. I was savin'. I wasn't doing this shit alone. I had business associates.

JALANI: So, // get some new associates.

RAHEEM: So? // So, nigga?

JALANI: (*playfully teasing*) You probably shouldn't be pimpin' anyway. It don't seem like you're that good at it. I mean, you wasn't makin' no money off of Zeze. This is just the cost of doing business, partner.

(*Raheem attacks Jalani. They fight. Jalani tries to stand on his own, but he is overwhelmed by Raheem. Raheem gets Jalani in a headlock.*)

JALANI: Raheem—

RAHEEM: *This* is the cost of fuckin' with my business. And you got to pay that cost. So, I tell you what: you come up with my money, or I'll pimp *your* ass on the block. Since you like ass fucking. Then we'll see how good a pimp I am. (*Raheem releases Jalani.*) 'Cause I ain't going home broke 'cause of your ass, Jay. I'm not. Fuck that.

(*A moment passes. Jalani cowers. They are silent. The door opens and Demetrius returns enraged, in tears. The door closes.*)

RAHEEM: What'd they say?

DEMETRIUS: I could kill that nigga!

(*Demetrius goes to attack Jalani. Jalani runs as Raheem tries to hold Demetrius at bay.*)

RAHEEM: What happened?

DEMETRIUS: (*to Jalani*) You know how much shit I've done for you?

RAHEEM: What happened?

DEMETRIUS: You was taping the girls, Jalani?

RAHEEM: What?

DEMETRIUS: This muthafucka was taping the girls.

JALANI: So—

DEMETRIUS: So? They went through the apartment and found like ten of them joints! They're holding them as evidence, 'cause they added a charge: pornography with the intent to distribute. The price just went up.

RAHEEM: No—

DEMETRIUS: Or they're going to book us.

RAHEEM: I can't believe this.

JALANI: I wasn't going to sell them. I wasn't even gon' show—they was for me to watch—to remember—

RAHEEM: They don't care.

JALANI: (*beat*) Now what are we going to do?

DEMETRIUS: We? We, nigga?

JALANI: How much money you have at the apartment? We can—

DEMETRIUS: You think those cops raided the apartment, but left our money there? That's it, nigga! They got everything! I saw it! Our passports! Our cash! Everything! That's it!

RAHEEM: NO! Ughhhhh!

JALANI: Everything?

RAHEEM: *Shut up*!!! That was my money! All my fuckin' money! All my—! (*beat*) Oh my God . . .

(*Raheem breaks down. Moments pass.*)

DEMETRIUS: (*beat*) They're talking six thousand reais to get us out of here. So we're looking for two thousand dollars. That's not that much money. We can find two thousand dollars. We can see if they'll let us make a call. And you can call your connects and—

RAHEEM: I can't call them. They're probably lookin' for me now. I didn't make the drop last night.

DEMETRIUS: Well, you can call your parents.

RAHEEM: (*beat*) Excuse me?

DEMETRIUS: Call your parents and get them to wire us—

RAHEEM: We ain't got that kind of money. We from Marcy. Call *your* mom.

DEMETRIUS: I can't.

RAHEEM: Oh, it's okay that my parents know but—

DEMETRIUS: I can't have people knowing I—

RAHEEM: Fuck you, Demetrius.

DEMETRIUS: I got a family.

JALANI: Guys—

RAHEEM: Ain't you got a credit card?

DEMETRIUS: I only got four hundred on that card.

RAHEEM: You only got four hundred dollars' worth of credit?

DEMETRIUS: I'm maxed out.

RAHEEM: I know y'all got savings. College fund. Some shit. Call Dana and tell her to wire it.

DEMETRIUS: (*beat*) I'm not calling my wife.

RAHEEM: What?

DEMETRIUS: I'm not calling my wife.

RAHEEM: Why not?

DEMETRIUS: I'm not calling—

RAHEEM: Then what's it going to be, 'cause (*referring to Jalani*) this nigga ain't got nobody but us. It's either you call her now and get the money so we can get out of here, or you call her later and tell her you got arrested for pornography with the intent to sell. And I don't think that's going to go over too well with your job. (*Demetrius considers.*) What else we gonna do?

DEMETRIUS: Fuuuuuck! What am I going tell her?

JALANI: Tell her we got jacked—

DEMETRIUS: But how am I going to explain—

RAHEEM: Tell her we got jacked. (*beat*) What?

DEMETRIUS: I can't—she's going to—

RAHEEM: Call her, D.

DEMETRIUS: (*beat*) Ughhh!

(*Demetrius goes to the door, pulls the calling card from his wallet, and knocks.*)

Scene 3

Day Five/Six: Police station, Rio de Janeiro. Hours later. Jalani and Raheem sit in the interrogation room.

JALANI: (*beat*) What's taking him so long? Maybe they booked him. What if D didn't get the money and they booked him? What if they keep us another day? What if we miss the flight?

RAHEEM: Stop, man. Just—chill.

JALANI: We leave early in the morning. If they don't let us go today, we're going to miss it.

RAHEEM: You know why Jared never let you kick it with us? 'Cause you were a little bitch. Like a little chihuahua barkin' behind a Rottweiler. Shut the fuck up so I can think. Please.

(*Moments pass. Raheem's pager goes off.*)

These niggas is looking for me.

JALANI: Your associates?

RAHEEM: I was supposed to meet them every night.

JALANI: Oh. (*beat*) Maybe you should try calling them. Just in case Dana doesn't—

RAHEEM: They're not going to be trying to hear me. They want their money.

JALANI: How much you owe?

RAHEEM: Including yesterday and today? Twelve thousand.

JALANI: Dollars?!

RAHEEM: Yep. And I ain't got it. And these niggas keep blowin' me up. (*laughing*) This shit is hilarious. Ah, man. It took me nine months to orchestrate this shit. And it took you five days to fuck it up.

JALANI: (*beat*) I'm sorry, Raheem.

RAHEEM: Shut up.

JALANI: I don't be meaning to fuck shit up.

RAHEEM: Shut up, Jay.

JALANI: You can tell those guys, tell them it was my fault. That I wild-out. Call them—whatever you want me to say, whatever you want me to do to make it right. I'm sorry.

RAHEEM: You got twelve thousand dollars?

JALANI: No.

RAHEEM: Then there's nothing you can do.

(*They sit in silence. The door opens. Demetrius enters. The door closes.*)

JALANI: What took so long?   **RAHEEM:** What did Dana say?
I thought they booked you.   Did you get the money?

DEMETRIUS: I, uh . . . I called, but she . . . she didn't pick up, so I left a message.

RAHEEM AND DEMETRIUS: A message?!

JALANI: Go call her back.

RAHEEM: I thought you said she goes straight home from work.

DEMETRIUS: She does. That's why I waited to call, to make sure she was home. She leaves the bank at two, picks Deja up from day care, and goes home. She likes to change her clothes.

JALANI: Why didn't you just call her at work?

DEMETRIUS: She'll be madder if I called her at work.

JALANI: It's an emergency—

DEMETRIUS: She leaves work, picks up Deja, and goes home. That's her routine. She'll get the message.

JALANI: Then why hasn't she called?

DEMETRIUS: She probably stopped off at the store. I don't know. She'll get it.

RAHEEM: What did you say on the message?

DEMETRIUS: I said, "Dana, baby. It's me. I need your help—"

JALANI: Did you say it was an emergency?

DEMETRIUS: I said it was serious, I said, "It's serious, and I need your help." And I . . . And I left the information to call back here.

JALANI: Why didn't you tell her to wire the money?!

DEMETRIUS: Just let me handle this my way.

RAHEEM: We're going to run out of time!

JALANI: Our flight—

DEMETRIUS: I can't leave a message and say, "I got arrested. And I need you to send all of the money we got in Deja's account to get me out. Oh, and by the way, I'm not upstate camping, I'm in Brazil." If I leave that on the machine she's liable not to call back. Just let me handle it. She's going to call back, and I'll talk to her. It will be better if we talk live.

(*A moment passes. Jalani and Raheem start laughing.*)

JALANI: Camping?

DEMETRIUS: I lied.

RAHEEM: Camping, though?

DEMETRIUS: Yeah.

RAHEEM: And she believed you?

DEMETRIUS: So she wouldn't ask for a number or try to call—

RAHEEM: That's priceless. I'ma have to use that.

JALANI: Do we look like some dudes to be pitchin' tents—

RAHEEM: Rubbin' sticks together—

JALANI: Wait. I think I see the North Star.

RAHEEM: Nope. That's the Chrysler building, nigga!

(*They laugh.*)

JALANI: What are you going to say when she calls?

DEMETRIUS: I'll say: "I love you. I'm sorry. I need you to send me two thousand dollars." (*beat*) *Two thousand dollars?!?* It's serious. *You hurt?* I'm sorry. *What's happening, Demetrius?* Just get a pencil. I need you to wire it to . . . to Brazil.

JALANI: (*beat, teasing Demetrius with a Dana caricature*) And why would I do that, Demetrius?

DEMETRIUS: Just—baby, please.

RAHEEM: Tell her ass, shut the fuck up and send the dough.

JALANI: No, Demetrius, tell me now. Why would I do that? Why would I send our money to Brazil when you're upstate? 'Cause you are upstate, right? That's what you told me.

RAHEEM: (*muffled, spoofing Demetrius*) No, I'm in Brazil.

JALANI: What's that? Speak up.

RAHEEM: (*spoofing Demetrius*) I'm in Brazil.

JALANI: What? I know you didn't just say—what?!

RAHEEM: (*spoofing Demetrius*) Listen—

JALANI: I knew you wasn't campin'!

RAHEEM: (*laughing*) Camping!

JALANI: Tellin' me you're going to celebrate Jared. That nigga is dead! Are you even with Jalani and Raheem? Put them niggas on the phone. Are you with some hoe, Demetrius? Are you with some hoe in Brazil?! I can hear her breathing. You think I don't know what goes on there?

(*Jalani and Raheem laugh loud and long. Demetrius doesn't respond. They are silent for a long moment.*)

DEMETRIUS: (*to Jalani*) Fuck you. Nobody cares about you, so you think care is a burden. To have someone to be accountable to, someone you care about, someone who cares about you—that's family. I'm about to use my daughter's tuition money on y'all, and y'all got jokes? And we brothers? Y'all don't know what a brother is. So fuck y'all.

JALANI: We was playin'—

DEMETRIUS: Both of y'all owe me a thousand dollars. When we can leave here, we go back to the apartment. I'ma get my shit. Get on the plane. And I'm done. Send my check in the mail.

JALANI: We sorry.

RAHEEM: I ain't sorry.

(*Demetrius moves to the far end of the room.*)

RAHEEM: And we can't go back to the apartment.

DEMETRIUS: Why not?

RAHEEM: I told you—them dudes is gon' be lookin' for me.

DEMETRIUS: I'm not you.

RAHEEM: They'll be there waiting, I'm telling you. They've been blowing me up. They're going to be waiting and they're going to cut into whoever walks through that door. They want their money. And I ain't got it.

JALANI: Say you got locked up.

RAHEEM: They don't care. I wasn't at the designated place at the designated time and I ain't got it. For all I know, she blew us all up and they'll think I snitched and stole their money.

DEMETRIUS: No—

RAHEEM: They don't negotiate. They don't accept payment plans. They gonna have you in a basement, leave you in a ditch in the Amazon somewhere. Ain't nobody gon' find you. Yo' ass just gon' be missing. We can't go back.

DEMETRIUS: But my ring—

RAHEEM: Leave it.

DEMETRIUS: I can't leave my ring.

JALANI: I thought you said they took everything.

DEMETRIUS: It was in that vase.

RAHEEM: No.

DEMETRIUS: I'm not leaving my ring.

RAHEEM: You'd risk your life for a ring?

DEMETRIUS: My family. My daughter. My house. My job. And yes, my wife.

RAHEEM: What—

DEMETRIUS: I'll risk my life for my life.

RAHEEM: Well, I don't risk my life for nobody. I'm not going back there.

DEMETRIUS: I don't need you to go with me.

JALANI: You can't go alone.

RAHEEM: That's on you. I'm not going back. Fuck that.

DEMETRIUS: (*beat*) Naw, fuck you. Fuck you, Raheem. Matter of fact—

(*Demetrius rises, knocks on the door.*)

JALANI: Wait a minute, y'all. (*to Demetrius*) D! (*to Raheem*) Ra, say something!

RAHEEM: When we get back, it's going to be cold.

(*The door opens and Demetrius walks out.*)

RAHEEM: (*beat*) Make sure to take some blankets from the plane.

JALANI: You for real 'bout to let him go alone?

RAHEEM: We're going to have to take the train, hop the turnstile—

JALANI: Are you listening to me? That's our man. We should have his back.

RAHEEM: Why? That nigga ain't got my back. I've been carrying his ass, both of y'all, since we got down here. Hooked all this up. He ain't never had no shit like this before in his life. But did he show me some fuckin' appreciation? No. Always looking for something wrong, or why something I'm trying to do can't work. Always complaining and throwing bitch-ass tantrums 'cause some shit ain't go his way. And I'm supposed to have some loyalty? I'm the one holding out? He the one would have us stay up in here rather than call—

JALANI: But he *did* call.

RAHEEM: And now he expect me to—?!

JALANI: It's his wife.

RAHEEM: No, it's a ring. Get another one.

JALANI: It's his wife.

RAHEEM: Get another one.

JALANI: But—

RAHEEM: I'm not going back.

JALANI: We're not going to let him go alone.

RAHEEM: I told him not to go.

JALANI: It's important!

RAHEEM: To who?

JALANI: To him! Don't you care about nothing? (*Raheem is silent.*) Raheem—how many beat downs did they take for some stupid shit you got into. Shit you shoulda got beat down for, shit that was your fault—

RAHEEM: Like when!?

JALANI: When!?! Like when you sold them Queens niggas leaves thinking you wasn't gon' see them again, and they came back 'round with like seven more muthafuckas looking for you. D didn't wanna fight. My brother didn't wanna fight. They jumped in with you 'cause they wasn't gon' stand by and watch you get beat down alone. And that's what you promised. You and D. Looking down at Jared's—at the funeral, looking down, you swore to God. We ride together. So how—? (*beat*) That's your man out there, 'bout to get run up on by dudes looking for you. You gon' let him take that by hisself? (*beat*) Raheem? (*long beat*) Wow. Alright. (*beat*) You . . . you, man . . . you ain't nothin' like my brother. Jared's probably turning over in his grave.

Jalani moves to the side of the room far away from Raheem. Lights flash as we see Demetrius in a theatrical montage like the one in the beginning of the play. As the lights continue to flash, Demetrius is "beat" back down into . . .

Scene 4

February 2010. Club Carnaval. Demetrius sits with the remote in his hand. Raheem stands at the entrance to the section. It is silent. Then muted sounds of the club creep into our awareness.

RAHEEM: You trying to leave me a message? (*Demetrius sees him.*) What's up, brotha?

DEMETRIUS: 'sup.

(*Raheem crosses to give him a customary greeting, dap, a fist shake/one-armed hug, pound, etc. Demetrius does not stand.*)

RAHEEM: Glad you made it.

DEMETRIUS: Yeah.

RAHEEM: You havin' a good time? My people taking care of you?

DEMETRIUS: Yeah.

(*Moments pass.*)

RAHEEM: You lookin' old—

DEMETRIUS: Old?

RAHEEM: I guess you always stayed twenty-six in my mind. (*beat*) Jalani told me Deja graduated. With honors, right?

DEMETRIUS: Yeah.

RAHEEM: She going to college?

DEMETRIUS: Spelman. Didn't want to leave her mother.

RAHEEM: Got her a graduation gift. Just a little something from her uncle R'heem. Ain't that what she used to call me?

(*Raheem hands Demetrius a small jewelry box. Demetrius places the box on the table.*)

DEMETRIUS: Jay said you wanted to see me? That you had something you wanted to say to me?

RAHEEM: Where is Jay?

DEMETRIUS: Went to get some food.

RAHEEM: They didn't bring you no wings? I told them—

DEMETRIUS: Raheem. I'm good. Say what you got to say, man.

(*Jalani enters with a plate of food.*)

JALANI: I got—oh. Hey!

RAHEEM: What's up, Jay?

JALANI: What's up, man! Congratulations!

RAHEEM: Thank you.

JALANI: It's real nice out there. We were saying how off the chain it is. You playin' with the big boys now.

RAHEEM: Always knew I would.

DEMETRIUS: Raheem was just saying what he brought me here to say.

RAHEEM: I wanted to bring both y'all here. I wanted you to see this. (*beat*) Tonight's the night.

(*Raheem reveals a plaque. It's a dedication to Jared.*)

JALANI: Oh, wow. Wow.

RAHEEM: This is my first American venture. It's special to me. So, I'ma put this up at the entrance. I wanted y'all to see it first. So we could bless it.

(*Raheem pours some drinks and passes them to Jalani and Demetrius.*)

JALANI: (*reading*) "For my brother, who left too soon. I ride for you. Rest in peace." That's nice, man.

RAHEEM: Fifteen years ago, when Jared died, it changed the way I saw everything. It made me see that, one day, I was gonna die, and that it could be possible that I hadn't even lived. I promised myself I was gonna get mine. Before I went, I was gonna have the world. And we promised him we'd take him with us on the ride. This is just the first step. I'm 'bout to take over. Represent!

(*Raheem raises his glass and drinks. Jalani follows.*)

DEMETRIUS: (*to Raheem*) That's what you brought me here for?

RAHEEM: I thought you'd appreciate it.

DEMETRIUS: (*to Jalani*) That's what you brought me here for?

JALANI: I didn't know what he was—he said he had something to say.

DEMETRIUS: Let's go.

JALANI: Wait a minute.

DEMETRIUS: That wasn't for me. That was for him.

RAHEEM: What did you think I was gon' say?

DEMETRIUS: I expected something, nigga. You owe me!

RAHEEM: Owe you?

DEMETRIUS: Yes! You owe me! Me! You brought me here for this!? This—

(*Demetrius lunges for the plaque but loses his footing and falls off of the couch, revealing his paralyzed legs. Jalani goes to help him.*)

DEMETRIUS: Don't touch me! Don't clean it up. (*to Raheem*) This is what you did. This is why you owe me. I lost everything fuckin' with you. You owe me. Every day you owe me. When I see a cop on the street, and think about how I would've out-ranked him by now, you owe me. When I go to the doctor, 'cause I got bed sores on the backs of my legs, you owe me! When I had to call my daughter to tuck her in 'cause her mama took her to Atlanta—when I foreclosed on my house—I lost my life fuckin' with you and you bring me here on some dedication?! Flossin' like anybody give a fuck about this shit!! Fuck you—!!

Demetrius knocks the plaque onto the ground. It breaks. He reaches for the jewelry box and throws it at Raheem, missing him completely. Jalani and Raheem watch while Demetrius begins to tear apart anything within his reach—food, furniture, liquor—in a frenzy until he becomes exhausted. He begins to cry a painful-to-watch cry. Moments pass. Demetrius settles.

RAHEEM: I'm sorry.

DEMETRIUS: Fuck you.

RAHEEM: I'm sorry, man.

(*Jalani helps Demetrius up.*)

RAHEEM: (*really long beat*) I'm going to DR next week to take care of some business. Come with me. I got a little club. Gorgeous little private beach. Beautiful women. Whatever you want.

JALANI: You own a club in DR?

RAHEEM: I don't own it. I use it. I can use it anytime I want. Like a time share.

DEMETRIUS: (*beat*) You still pimpin'.

RAHEEM: (*a gesture signifying a mixture of "You caught me" and "Yeah, so?"*)

JALANI: You still pimpin'?—after everything—you ain't learned?

RAHEEM: I learned. I learned that you pay off the local officials first, get them invested in your success, then you won't have no problems.

DEMETRIUS: (*to Jalani*) Let's go.

JALANI: You pimpin' in DR.

RAHEEM: I'm providing economic empowerment opportunities—

JALANI: By pimping them?

RAHEEM: I ain't pimpin' them. Everybody participates on their own.

JALANI: But it ain't right.

RAHEEM: Why do you care? You don't know them.

JALANI: What you talkin' 'bout? My wife is Dominican. Her whole family—how you know—

RAHEEM: I'm not pimpin' your family.

JALANI: Everybody there is somebody's family. It ain't right—what if your mama—

RAHEEM: What if my mama what?

JALANI: How is what you're doing any different from any other exploitation? From sharecroppin' or—

RAHEEM: What are you talking about?

JALANI: Them people are poor—that's what white folks do, Raheem.

RAHEEM: I know. I got more clients from Wall Street than Harlem. Niggas ain't got no money.

JALANI: Them people are like us. You know what it's like to be broke. You know how we grew up.

RAHEEM: Exactly. And I'ma make sure I don't never go through that shit again.

JALANI: They're people, Raheem—God wouldn't—

RAHEEM: I don't care about them. Shit, they don't care about me. They'd do the same. You tryin' to paint me out to be some kind of monster. I'm not some dude kidnappin' bitches, holding them hostage, threatening to kill their families and shit. I ain't got to force them chicks. I ain't no slave master. They come to me asking me if they can work, if their friends can be down. They come to me 'cause they can't afford to pay they rent, 'cause somebody needs medicine, or just 'cause they sick and tired of working fourteen hours a day for some company with nothing to show for it at the end of the week. And I'm the one pimpin'? They come to me 'cause the world would fuck them every day if they let it. And they stay 'cause at least with me, they get something for it. And in the end, that's all that matters. The one standing with the last dollar wins. Pimp or be pimped. Play or be played. Now, would it be better if the world was different? Yeah. So you waste your life crusading to change the world. I'm too busy gettin' paid.

DEMETRIUS: Let's go.

RAHEEM: I can't believe y'all would hate on me like this. They said people change—

JALANI: Naw, nigga, we grew up. We grew up.

RAHEEM: (*beat*) Man, get the fuck out of here.

(*Jalani stares at Raheem.*)

DEMETRIUS: Jay, let's go.

(*Jalani helps Demetrius into his wheelchair.*)

RAHEEM: That's why I ain't got no wheelchair access, you punk bitch. Wheel your cripple ass on outta here—broke bastard—stupid, pussy bitches—

DEMETRIUS: Let's go! I'm done.

(*Jalani wheels Demetrius out.*)

RAHEEM: Pussy punk bitches.

Raheem stands alone. The ambient party sounds rise, and the lights isolate him on stage. He plops down onto the plush sofa and props up his feet. He sees the remote and presses play. He sees Demetrius's image projected onto the wall.

DEMETRIUS: I can't tell you how many times I played this day out in my head. What I'd say to you. How I'd say it. I've been processing what happened in Brazil relentlessly. I'd play those days over and over in my mind. Sometimes with alternate beginnings. With alternate endings. But no matter what details I changed, I always blamed you. I blamed you for everything. It was easy to do. But it wasn't all your fault. No one forced me to go to Brazil. And you told me not to go back to the suite, but I went back for the ring anyway. I was desperate. (*beat*) I . . . I had cheated on Dana before we went down there. She caught me and shit was never right after that. So, I knew when I had to ask her for the money, my daughter's tuition, when I had to tell her I was in Brazil . . . I knew what she was going to say. When I called—I didn't leave a message like I told y'all. I spoke to her. She was home. She always left work, picked up Deja, and went home. She liked to change her clothes. She said she wouldn't leave me in jail in a foreign country, but she was leaving me. It was over. And I . . . I knew I couldn't go home to beg her forgiveness without my wedding ring. I deluded myself into thinking that it would make a difference. She left. She left me because of me. Not because of you. And I'm sorry I blamed you . . . for that.

This right here is what's up, man. I'm glad you made it. At least one of us is doing it big. I'm glad I'm here to see it. Jared would be proud. I think he'd be proud to see us back together again. It's been too long. I missed you. I must say I am a little upset y'all don't have no wheelchair access up in here. Inconsiderate bastard. Thank you for inviting me here tonight so that you could . . . could apologize. I love you, man.

The message loops. Perhaps DJ Khaled's "All I Do Is Win" plays in the club. Raheem watches. He breaks. Lights contract around the projection on the wall.

BLACKOUT

End of Play

Portuguese-to-English Translations

Raheem should be proficient in his Portuguese use and pronunciation in the video guest book message in the prologue. Demetrius should be much less so with his Portuguese use and pronunciation.

"E ai meu, tudo bem, to all my garanhaos and gostosas!"
Slang from São Paulo meaning "Hey. What's good (or what's up) to all my stallions and sexy chicks."
"Olá! Meu nome é Demetrius. Pode você fazê-lo com galinha?"
Hello. My name is Demetrius. Can you make it with chicken?
"pesaroso"
Sorry.

LISA B. THOMPSON

A native of San Francisco, Lisa B. Thompson juggles two careers, one as a playwright and the other as an academic. In both her scholarship and creative writing she's interested in exploring unconventional performances of black identity. She has an M.A. in African American studies from UCLA and a Ph.D. in modern thought and literature from Stanford University. Thompson is an associate professor of African and African diaspora studies at the University of Texas at Austin and the associate director of the John L. Warfield Center for African and African American Studies. Her work has received support from several institutions, including the W. E. B. Du Bois Institute for African and African American Research at Harvard University, the Office of the President at the University of California, the Five Colleges Inc., and the Michelle R. Clayman Institute for Gender Research at Stanford University. Thompson's plays include *Monroe*, *Dreadtime Stories*, *The Mamalogues,* and *Underground*. Her short works, *Mother's Day* and *I Don't Want to Be,* were included in the anthology shows *Black Women: State of the Union*, and *Black Women: State of the Union—Taking Flight*. She published the first scholarly study about contemporary representations of middle-class black women, *Beyond the Black Lady: Sexuality and the New African American Middle Class* (University of Illinois Press, 2009). Thompson's critically acclaimed comedy, *Single Black Female*, evolved from her research. The two-character play has been produced throughout the United States and Canada.

Single Black Female was originally produced in New York City by New Professional Theatre (Sheila Kay Davis, founder and artistic director) at the Peter Jay Sharp Theater on June 15, 2006.

Director:	Colman Domingo
Assistant director:	Corrine Neal
SBF 1:	Riddick Marie
SBF 2:	Soara-Joye Ross
Set:	Scott Aronow
Costumes:	Raul Aktanov
Lighting:	Russel Drapkin
Sound:	DJ Crystal Clear

SINGLE BLACK FEMALE

SETTING

The present. A comfortable, yet stylish brownstone in Harlem, New York. The main room is furnished with chairs, a sofa, a television, a stereo and a coffee table. The stage also has a walk-in closet and/or a dresser that stores various props (clothing, hats, shoes, surgical gloves, etc.) to help the actors create each vignette and character. Musical selections by female musicians and singers, a video monitor, voice-over audio, and slides provide an electronic component that supports a fast-paced, surreal environment.

CHARACTERS

> SBF 1: A thirty-eight-year-old African American woman. A literature professor with dreadlocks and a bookish, androgynous style accented with "afrocentric" accessories. She wears clogs and eccentric eyeglasses.
> SBF 2: A thirty-five-year-old African American woman. An attorney who sports a flowing perm or hair weave and wears high heels and sexy business suits, she is SBF 1's best friend, confidante, and alter ego.

Prologue

SBF 1: We are often asked what SBF stands for. Those three letters represent many things.
SBF 2: Sistas black and free.
SBF 1: Sincere blissful friend.
SBF 2: Saucy brazen freak.
SBF 1: Staying black forever.
SBF 2: Soulful, bold, and fierce.
SBF 1: Sad blue funk.
SBF 2: Sweet bangin' fuck.
SBF 1 & SBF 2: (*In unison*)
> We be
> Us be

Single
Black
Female

SBF 1: Diva.

SBF 2: Bitch.

SBF 1: Goddess.

SBF 2: And nobody wants to hear us. (*Beat.*) You undoubtedly heard of the black male crisis—well, there is also a very serious crisis for the black woman.

SBF 1: (*as PowerPoint lecture*) The National Center for Health Statistics informs us that "the marriage rate for white women is 76 percent higher than the rate for black women."

SBF 2: Teach!

SBF 1: According to the U.S. Census, 41.9 percent of black women in America have NEVER been married.

SBF 2: Damn!

SBF 1: And 57 percent of black children reside in single-parent homes.

SBF 2: Now what if a sista has a college degree or two—

SBF 1: Or three? She's more likely to be hit by a meteor than find a husband!

SBF 2: What happens to the black family if we don't find love? What will happen to the African American legacy?

SBF 1: Tonight let us introduce you to the world of the single black female.

SBF 2: Wait! This ain't sex in the inner city! That's another show. Let's be more specific, welcome to the lives of single middle-class black women.

SBF 1: Remember Ellison's *Invisible Man*? Well, we are the invisible women. Black professional intellectual leftists with conservative fiscal ideologies—

SBF 2: Except for a sale at Barney's!

SBF 1: We're the New Negro African American Black Colored Girls who only consider therapy. And even though nobody wants to hear us—we are tired of being ignored! We will no longer be QUIET!

SBF 2: You're anything but quiet. Sullen, or remote when angry—but never . . . quiet!

SBF 1: You're right about that.

SBF 2: Still nobody wants to see us, let alone really think about us.

SBF 1: But it's about time we get some accurate press.

SBF 2: We must thank Supreme Court Justice Clarence Thomas for putting us on the map.

SBF 1: Right, before his dreadful Senate confirmation hearing nobody thought we existed.

SBF 2: We STILL believe you, Anita!

SBF 1: And now we have sweet little Condi Rice to thank for making us popular the world over.

SBF 2: Isn't she single, too? Maybe if the child could get her hair right!!!

SBF 1: Don't talk about Condi now! That might prove a little too dangerous.

SBF 2: True.

SBF 1: People, before Ms. Oprah Winfrey became a media icon, the image of black womanhood was a bit stale and not very complex.

SBF 2: Yes, who can forget the long reign of Aunt Jemima, Sapphire, and Jezebel?

SBF 1: Now, we concede there were a few bright moments, especially during the late twentieth century. The seventies gave us Julia—thank God for Lady Diahann Carroll. The eighties gave us attorney Claire Huxtable, a Cosby creation. But the nineties gave us—

SBF 2: —Thee supreme ringmaster, Jerry Springer!

SBF 1 & SBF 2: (*Ad-lib typical talk show guest fight scene complete with hysterical dialogue.*)

SBF 2: We still haven't recovered from that hot ghetto mess. And we cannot neglect those hoochies shaking their rumps on BET. (*SBF 2 does booty shake.*)

SBF 1: Why would anyone go on those shows? Dance in those videos? I can't understand it.

SBF 2: Now, we do get some occasional exposure to remind us that black middle-class women are part of the American dream.

SBF 1: But, even in the twenty-first century the networks still won't cast a black woman as The Bachelorette. And no, *I Love NY* does not count!

SBF 2: That's because they believe no man would want us, even if we come with a million bucks! All we can get is *Flavor of Love*! Flavor Flav! That's some bullshit! No, we're not in style.

SBF 1: And we are not all the same, but we are looking for the same thing. To put it simply? Love. Unfortunately our generation is more single than double. This is her story and mine . . . and hers, and hers, and hers. (*Pause.*) And maybe his, too. Our story.

SBF 2: Well, at least what we are willing to share tonight.

SBF 1 & SBF 2: (*in unison*) Come on in.

Act 1. A Week in the Life of an SBF

Scene 1. Identity

SBF 1: There are obvious signs if you get beyond the door.

SBF 2: Once invited inside her cozy home it's easy to detect.

SBF 1: You spot the kitchen and dining ware.

SBF 2: On her shelves sit numerous Pottery Barn ceramic bowls and serving platters of every hue.

SBF 1: Don't forget the stemware—

SBF 2: Champagne flutes for every celebration. Only the French do bubbly, right?

SBF 1: But thanks to hip hop, Cristal has gone so ghetto!

SBF 2: You are wrong for that. Old-fashion highballs for a shot of Glenfiddich single malt after a long day in court.

SBF 1: Four martini glasses with pitcher.

SBF 2: Dry, very dry.

SBF 1: Wait! Don't forget those four jelly jars for the ethnic touch! (*Both laugh.*)

SBF 2: Damn! We sound like alcoholics.

SBF 1: A SBF typically owns an impressive collection of cookbooks.

SBF 2: As well as a healthy stack of take-out menus for those nights she doesn't cook.

SBF 1: Like six out of seven nights? Please. Who has the time? I order Chinese or Thai take-out for those evenings in front of the HDTV. And, for those down home nights? (*Southern blues music starts to play.*)

SBF 2: Amy Ruth's, baby! Soul Fixins! AMEN!!!

SBF 1: For dessert? Raven the Cake Man's red velvet cake.

SBF 2: Sock it to me!

SBF 1: SBFs also keep current subscriptions to *Essence, The Nation, Metropolitan Home,* and *Vibe—*

SBF 2: You read *Vibe?*

SBF 1: Oh yes, I must keep up with my students.

SBF 2: Clothing depends on whether she's an artsy boho—

SBF 1: Or a classy hoho?

SBF 2: Hey! Hey now! Watch it.

SBF 1: She's always well draped and politically—

SBF 2: And culturally—

SBF 1: Sophisticated. In the summer you'll find her at the Studio Museum of Harlem sporting flawless white linen.

SBF 2: She's got to have her Kente cloth bumpin' in February for Negro History Month.

SBF 1: Must be head to toe in deep dark chocolate for that night on the town. I read in *Vogue* that chocolate is the new black. Doesn't anybody realize that black folks have been chocolate for years?

SBF 2: Talk, girl! By the time an SBF reaches about thirty years old, she's found her style—now she's just trying to find somebody to like her style.

SBF 1: Where to meet us?

(*SBF 1 and SBF 2 start to fan themselves with local funeral home fans and mime greeting other parishioners.*)

SBF 2: At Abyssinian Baptist Church.

SBF 1: Or at Brooklyn Tabernacle's eleven A.M. service. Amen!

(*Sound of gospel music. SBF 1 and SBF 2 start to dance around like they have got the Holy Ghost.*)

SBF 2: Praise Jesus! Glory! Glory!

SBF 1: Wait! Who has all day to spend in church? It's the twenty-first century! This is not the South, you know. We are in NEW YORK CITY!

SBF 2: You can also find us at the bank—

SBF 1: Telling the manager to go to hell.

SBF 2: Or at the video store. You can usually find several single black women deep in on Friday and Saturday nights.

SBF 1: Lines? Please, I got Netflix! Yes, you can also find us at the stylist all day, any day.

SBF 2: No more beauty shop for me! I'm a spa girl. A facial every two weeks. A manicure and pedicure once a week and an organic herbal seaweed body wrap at least once a month. It's the role of the black middle class to integrate.

SBF 1: The spas?

SBF 2: Yes, the revolution—one massage at a time. Each of us has a role. I'm doing my part. I love the look in the eyes of those old Upper East Side society matrons when they see my naked black ass sauntering towards the sauna.

SBF 1: Somehow I don't believe that's what Martin, Malcolm, nor Huey and Bobby had in mind.

SBF 2: (*quietly*) Don't judge, I'm just doing what I think is right. You know what Audre Lorde taught us: "the personal is political!" After all, we are all women who come from fine stock. Our mothers and grandmothers were strong black matriarchs.

SBF 1: Who we've learned to forgive for not being stronger. Not to mention forgiving Daddy.

SBF 2: Hooray for therapy!

SBF 1: We are three paychecks away from being on welfare and two art openings away from being culturally insignificant.

SBF 2: We all have a constant preoccupation with our bee-hinds and hairlines.

SBF 1: We are mirrors for each other. (*Beat.*) A typical SBF carries—

SBF 2: In her Marc Jacobs purse—

SBF 1: Or her Coach briefcase—

SBF 2: A healthy supply of that Mango body butter. Don't wanna sport ashy elbows.

SBF 1: She also needs stylish business cards and a trusty iPhone. Don't forget the one thing she cannot leave home without—American Express!

SBF 2: Platinum. In case of depression, crack open wallet and spend, spend, spend!

SBF 1: In her closet an SBF can never have too many—

SBF 2: Seven Jeans, or St. John suits, or shoes.

SBF 1: During her lifetime an SBF can never have too many—

SBF 2: Dates.

SBF 1: Stocks.

SBF 2: Season tickets for the symphony.

SBF 1: And flowers.

SBF 2: Don't forget the condoms. These days it's BYO!

SBF 1: But an SBF better be careful if she has—

SBF 2: Too much weight. Too many wrinkles. Too much debt.

SBF 1: Or too much unresolved anger? Relax. Breathe, breathe, breathe.

SBF 2: Thank you, girl. After all, being single is a middle-class black thang! You need to understand.

SBF 1: Wait! Do you think looking for an appropriate partner is only a black middle-class woman's obsession? Why worry about what a person does for a living as long as they give you good lovin'?

SBF 2: Class makes us different. I can't really explain. You try.

SBF 1: Explain difference? Difference as defined by Derrida, or Henry Louis Gates Jr.?

SBF 2: Here we go! I don't want to deal with Gates. What do you think this is, *The New Yorker?* Are we on *Charlie Rose?* Turn the channel! This is our subconscious, damn it!

SBF 1: Okay, you pick the theorist.

SBF 2: Let me tell you like my mother would. There is something wrong, folks, when both Mike Tyson and Evander Holyfield were able to marry black women who have M.D.'s! Those women are medical doctors, for God's sake! As for me? I can't do the "he's a plumber why can't you love him" thing. I tried it several times. Don't hate me but my panties get wet when I weave my basket through the aisles of Whole Foods picking up organic cranberries and shiitake mushroom soup.

SBF 1: In the morning she brews a South American blend of coffee from Dean and DeLuca. Her last man? Bro went to heaven at the local 7-Eleven.

SBF 2: He grabbed a fast cup of joe from McDonald's with his Egg McMuffin. I wind down in the evening with a glass of Pinot Blanc and—

SBF 1: Didn't he think Pinot Blanc is a light-skinned Filipino?

SBF 2: The last one I dated woke up every morning to 3–6 Mafia's "You Know It's Hard Out Here For a Pimp."

SBF 1: Girl here likes the hopeful nuances of Rachmaninov's "Prelude No. 2118 in F Major B Minor." As for cuisine? I recall that boyfriend wrapped his lips around a fried chicken wang and could not let go!

SBF 2: I like turkey breast sliced thin on rye with a whisper of Dijon mustard.

SBF 1: She has to have her *Wall Street Journal* every morning. He reads the back of the cereal box!

SBF 2: And his idea of "must see TV?"

SBF 1: *Cops*!

SBF 2: My favorite show of all time? *The Sopranos*.

SBF 1: That was not TV—that was HBO!

SBF 2: My dream dinner? Scallops and fettuccine in a white wine garlic and butter sauce. His dream? Fried chicken, black-eyed peas, corn bread, and greens.

SBF 1: Hold up! Wait! Wasn't that you at the family reunion chowing down on a pig's foot doused in hot sauce? We ain't got that much class or that much education. What about our people? Our community? Maybe that's why we're alone.

SBF 1 and SBF 2 turn and look at a slide show of various black family photographs intermingled with pictures of single women. The photos reflect diverse families: big and small, urban and suburban, gay and straight, middle-class, and working-class. The montage ends with a rapid succession of single women's photos until they are the last image. Lights fade down.

Scene 2. Rappin'

SBF 2 window shopping at the Time Warner Center.

SBF 2: Brothas love to run game.

SBF 1: Yo! Yo! Shortie! Can I spit at you fo' a minute?

SBF 2: There are times when I want to say, NO! But if I do, they are guaranteed to say—

SBF 1: Fuck you then, bitch! You ain't all that. I didn't want to holla at you NO way. I was just trying to make you feel better, you—

SBF 2: Fat, skinny, stupid, stuck-up, bald, weave-wearin'—

SBF 1: Stank ghetto hoe!

SBF 2: But they don't always come at you like that. Some men can be smooth.

SBF 1: Baby, you sure look good. I just wanted to tell you that. Have a wonderful day. (*wide grin*)

SBF 2: (*blushing bashfully*) Thank you.

SBF 1: No, thank you, goddess. Your very presence has made me whole again. Besides, you remind me of my wife.

SBF 2: WHAT?

SBF 1: Would you like to join our family? What? You got a problem with polygamy? On the continent this is how the original black man gets down. What? Don't get sassy with me. The ratio is not in your favor, my sista. Come on home to your African king.

SBF 2: Brotha, I'll pass on joining your harem. I doubt you can handle the women you've got now. (*Beat.*) Don't get me wrong. There are times when I really want a man to rap to me. (*catches the eye of an eligible bachelor*) Hey. (*to audience*) Oh, my God, he's amazing!

SBF 1: (*as ideal man, interested but polite and reserved*) Hello.

SBF 2: Don't we know each other?

SBF 1: No, I don't think, wait. Yes. It was at that conference in Seattle. That's right. Good to see you again. How's your work coming?

SBF 2: Work? Work is good I—

SBF 1: Great. Well, that's my train. I really have to run. You take care now. (*hurriedly walks off*)

SBF 2: Wait! Wait! Damn, maybe I should have been more direct. "Hi, I'm looking for a husband. Please marry me!" My friends tell me I should try a more subdued, gentle approach. (*bats her eyes and speaks in a southern dialect*) Naive and charmin'. (*back to normal voice*) In fact, several of my girlfriends told me—

SBF 1: I will never get married! Never! Never! Never!

SBF 2: Or, I believe in serial monogamy.

SBF 1: I don't believe in the institution of marriage.

SBF 2: Marriage is stifling.

SBF 1: It oppresses the female gender!

SBF 2: Marriage is outdated; people should just live together.

SBF 1: I couldn't live with anyone. (*prances around dramatically*) I need my space, to live, breathe, laugh, work, create—(*freezes mid-sentence*)

SBF 2: I admit. For a long time I admired those women. I even envied their bold, carefree attitudes. I tried to emulate their style. Until? They get married. Invariably those are the ones who get hitched. None of them is even divorced yet, not that I'm waiting.

SBF 1: You know what they say, ambivalence pays.

SBF 2: If I knew then what I know now? I'd have traveled another route. More nonchalant.

SBF 1: Less honest?

SBF 2: No. I think it's important to be authentic. I believe at my age I need to put my cards on the table. After all, I'm not getting any younger.

(*Loud sound of clock ticking*)

That ain't the Monday morning 6 A.M. wake-up call. I'm listening for the sound of my future husband.

SBF 1: Hey, sexy, I like those lips.

SBF 2: Really, sugar, you haven't even seen them yet!

SBF 1: Woman, you sure look nice. Can I get me some of that?

SBF 2: Why would you say something like that to a stranger? On the street? At 11 A.M. on a Tuesday? We've got a long way to go as a people.

SBF 1: Hey, can I just talk to you for a minute, damn!

SBF 2: I was just going to ask you the same thing, young man. Do you know your maker? Is Jehovah in your life?

SBF 1: Oh, my God.

SBF 2: You see, going Evangelic on a man hasn't failed me yet. They all run for the hills.

SBF 1: Woman, are you nuts?

SBF 2: Yes, I am. You want to go out sometime? I like Italian!

Scene 3. Shoppin'

SBF 1 and SBF 2 shopping at the Gap in the Woodbury Common Premium Outlets.

SBF 1: Remember when the Gap sold Levi's?

SBF 2: Damn, girl, you are getting old!

SBF 1: Don't you mean we're getting old?

SBF 2: Look at that salesgirl. Every kid that works here has tan skin, naturally curly hair, low-cut jeans, and frosty blue eye shadow. Not everything needs to come back into style.

SBF 1: There's little Jennifer now in her too-tight tee shirt and those wedge shoes. She unleashes her insipid persona on everybody who crosses the store's threshold.

SBF 2: (*vapid*) Hi, welcome to the Gap. I'm Jennifer. Can I help you?

SBF 1: She's like a dope pusher pushing organized nostalgia.

SBF 2: It's called leisure wear for those "dress down" days at the office.

SBF 1: What is a gap? A gap is nothing, an erasure. A gap is a space waiting to be filled. An opening, absence, silence, emptiness, a fissure between all things relevant and—

SBF 2: A credit card.

SBF 1: Now Missy Elliot and LL Cool J pitch doo-wop-hip-hop promoting Gap-style black culture. Is black culture a gap?

SBF 2: Let's not go down that road, Miss Professor. I want to discuss something really important, like the mirrors the Gap uses.

SBF 1: Clearly Gestapo tactics. I look like a fat pig in those dressing rooms. I know I need to work out more, but damn!

SBF 2: Hey, girl, don't worry about it, shopping is a sport. You've been to a sale at the Barney's Coop? (*SBF 1 nods.*) All right, then. Besides, these clothes aren't made for our bodies. Those are for white girls. Hello? Mr. Designer Man, we have thighs, hips, and booty!

SBF 1: When I don't feel like being followed by some salesgirl, I shop online. One day my pleasure was ruined when I needed to confirm my order by phone. I got one of those customer service reps that spoke to me in a way that left a bad taste in my mouth.

SBF 2: You can't even hide in cyberspace! It's like they have a nigga detector on the phone! No matter how much education or money you have, they still know.

SBF 1: They speak with such distaste and disrespect that it makes me want to—

SBF 1 & SBF 2: Go the fuck off!

SBF 1: They request my address and it's fine until I get to my zip code—

SBF 2: Hmm. Where is that?

SBF 1: Manhattan.

SBF 2: Yes, of course. But what part?

SBF 1: Harlem.

SBF 2: What did you say, ma'am?

SBF 1: My place is in Harlem.

SBF 2: I'm sorry, ma'am, I couldn't hear you. Did you say HARLEM?

SBF 1: Yes, yes I did. HARLEM, Bill Clinton? Sylvia's? You know, the Upper Upper West Side!

SBF 2: Can you hold, please? Thank you. Call security, Marge. Must be a case of identity theft. This Negress is telling me she's lives in HARLEM . . . with Bill Clinton!

SBF 1: Thanks a lot. (*hangs up*) That always takes the fun out of my sprees. Being African American can be so inconvenient.

SBF 2: Remember that time when you had to call all your creditors because you didn't have enough money to pay bills and you had to ask for a payment plan?

SBF 1: I recall no such incident.

SBF 2: Well, I do, honey. Remember, we were still roommates back then.

SBF 1: Yes, and you encouraged me to get a little help.

SBF 2: I advised you to find some of those no good ex-boyfriends who owed you cash.

SBF 1: But thank you, Jesus, I was bailed out by my true and powerful role model, an institution, a living legend, Ms. Oprah—

SBF 2: (*as Oprah*) When we received your fax, you confessed that you were desperate. You acknowledge that you have a problem, is that correct?

SBF 1: Yes, but I'm ready to start over.

SBF 2: I have a check for fifty-eight thousand, two hundred ninety-five dollars and seventy-two cents. Oprah's Angel Network is giving you a new life, debt-free.

SBF 1: (*rips the check from SBF 2's hands*) Listen, Oprah, I appreciate the bailout, but trust me, I know deep in my heart that I will do this again. I love to shop and I won't stop for anyone. Not even you. That's my program.

SBF 2: You are such a shopaholic.

SBF 1: Don't talk about me, Ms. DKNY.

SBF 2: I'm proud of myself. I know who I am and what I want without a doubt. Besides—

SBF 1 & SBF 2: (*in unison*) I can stop shopping at any time. I just don't want to yet!

SBF 1: I am only shopping because I need to find something brutal for our twentieth reunion.

SBF 2: Girl, how many kids DO you have?

SBF 1: That's a good one, but they always unleash their lethal question.

SBF 2: You haven't had children yet? You better get started. You're not getting any younger.

SBF 1: I smile. (*under her breath*) Asshole! No, not yet, but Hannah, Amber, Megan, Kyle, Dylan, and Owen are just adorable. You look great. Call me!

SBF 2: Text me!

SBF 1: We will all get together real soon. We sat at that table and talked bad about EVERYBODY. Especially those AKAs.

SBF 1 & SBF 2: (*in unison*) Skee wee!

SBF 2: Look! That's Kelly!

SBF 1: Is she still writing for *Essence*?

SBF 2: Maybe she can do an article on you. West coast scholar goes East coast still looking for love.

SBF 1: Thanks. I won't hold my breath. Oh, my God. That's Priscilla. Wave!

SBF 2: Wow, five foot six and not an ounce over one hundred twenty-five pounds.

SBF 1: She does look great. At least I try to work out—aerobics, spinning, yoga, Pilates, and swimming—

SBF 2: Heifer, you do not swim. That thing is called a whirlpool!

SBF 1: Whatever.

SBF 2: Wait, didn't Priscilla marry that neurologist?

SBF 1: No, no, no. He's a novelist.

SBF 2: Hah! So she's broke!

SBF 1: Nope. He just had his third national bestseller. They own an apartment in the east village, a house in Santa Fe, and oceanfront property near Monterey.

SBF 2: Bitch! (*Both wave and smile.*)

SBF 1: Oh, yes, I'm fine. Things are great for us. I'm working out, when I can—

SBF 2: And shopping.

Scene 4. Sisterhood

SBF 1 and SBF 2 compete for space to primp in the club's bathroom mirror.

SBF 1: It's no secret. On some days I hate black women. We can be so damn EVIL! Just mean.

SBF 2: I particularly despise the way we turn up our lips, suck our teeth, and roll our eyes.

SBF 1: E-V-I-L! Evil!

SBF 2: Tell it, girl.

SBF 1: One night after teaching, I was standing in line at a sandwich shop on Astor Place, and the sister ahead of me starts going off. Like she was crazed. Just tore back and off the chain! She told this poor woman—

SBF 2: Look! You needs to make sure my order is done right. And yo, let me get some of them jal-e-peños with that!

SBF 1: I'm most embarrassed when other people of color witness or receive the brunt of these outbursts.

SBF 2: Señorita! Señorita! You needs to learn to speak American.

SBF 1: What are you doing? She's making our food, fool! She's your sister in the struggle. Of course I don't say that to her face. She might beat me down. But I think it real loud. (*Beat.*) One weekend I saw an older black woman give a particularly gratifying performance. While walking down the street she stopped me dead in my tracks. She stood before me, serene and regal—this gray-haired angel.

SBF 2: Baby?

SBF 1: Yes, Ma'am?

SBF 2: You're not her. I thought you was her.

SBF 1: I'm sorry. Who?

SBF 2: That actress, the black woman with the hair. No. You're not her. You look just like her, but you're not as ugly as she is. Whoo-whoo.

SBF 1: You mean Whoopi Goldberg.

SBF 2: That's right. But you're not as ugly as her, but you do look just like her, though.

SBF 1: Thanks, Ma'am. It never occurred to her that Whoopi is a beautiful black woman. No, that never occurred to her at all.

SBF 2: When people see us they assume—single, welfare, no education, and tons of babies. I'm not her.

SBF 1: We are all invisible to them and we don't even see each other.

SBF 2: I remember when I was the new sista at my firm. During my first day I was introduced to the staff. The senior partner made it a point to tell me a little something about every black woman who works there—all six of their four hundred thirty-two employees. I knew not one of them liked me.

SBF 1: Who does she think she is? That broad thinks she's cute. Hmm, she ain't all that. Bet she won't make partner!

SBF 2: That's not me.

SBF 1: Have you ever realized that there's a way that a black woman can say "girl-friend" that actually sounds nothing like a term of endearment.

SBF 2: That's because "girlfriend" is usually followed by "you need to . . ." or preceded by "excuse me,—girlfriend." Or, "girlfriend, let me tell you—"

SBF 1: I just want to say—

SBF 1 & SBF 2: Shut the fuck up, you EVIL bitch!

SBF 2: The last club I went to was the 40/40, and let me tell you, I nearly started a riot. The women's bathroom was crowded. So I rolled up on a sista who was standing in the mirror primping and just tightin' up her thang when I got bold and told her, "You look nice." She almost pissed on herself.

SBF 1: What?

SBF 2: Your outfit—it's really nice. (*Pause.*) That dress becomes you. (*to audience*) She just stood there looking. Then she moved away from the mirror and all her girls walked out behind her one by one by one. The bathroom was empty.

SBF 1: Quiet.

SBF 2: I stood there with my toes pinched in my high, high heels, startled by my reflection in the mirror.

SBF 1: A black girl.

SBF 2: An African American queen.

SBF 1: A sista.

SBF 2: I kept looking for all that evil in my face and eyes. I stared for what seemed like hours. My trance broke when the black woman in the reflection blew a kiss to me from the mirror and softly whispered—

SBF 2 & SBF 1: (*in unison*) I love your evil black bitch ass.

(*SBF 1 and SBF 2 grab hands and begin dancing with each other to Cheryl Lynn's "Got to Be Real" as they clear the stage and change their clothes for the next scene.*)

Scene 5. Computer Love

Zapp's "Computer Love" plays while they type away on their Apple MacBooks.

SBF 2: How can a woman find the love of her life using a cold piece of technology? How can you find passion through an inanimate object that crashes, freezes, and God forbid, gives you a virus! Am I putting all my hopes and trust in a plastic box with motherboards and computer chips? What have our lives come to?

SBF 1: Internet dating is cool, I'm telling you. Trust me.

SBF 2: What kind of self-respecting black man looks for a woman on the Net? They don't need to use a computer. Brothas are the most desired piece of equipment on this planet! Everyone wants dark meat, Asians, Latinas, Afghanis. . . . Black men are the hottest thing on God's green earth, and I believe that far, far away, on a distant star in the galaxy, some purple women want them too. So what am I to do?

SBF 1: Just try it—it's not like men are lining up outside your door right now.

SBF 2: Nice. Okay. Okay. Which site?

SBF 1: I've done the research. The selection is overwhelming. I'm delirious about the plethora of choices. There's a site for every taste, category, and proclivity. Of course, there is the tried and true, Match.com. That's where I posted my profile.

SBF 2: Anything promising?

SBF 1: Well, after I got past the dozens of profiles that made it clear that they were looking for anything BUT a black woman, I met a few interesting characters. Let me warn you, I did unearth several crazies, but I can say this: it has been an amusing distraction from writing lectures and waiting around for the phone to ring. I'm still very hopeful. But we're here for you. Here is another site, The Right Stuff, for snobby singles who attended the Ivy League.

SBF 2: Hmm, what about eHarmony?

SBF 1: Have you seen their questionnaire? It's longer than *War and Peace*. We don't have that kinda time! Just try Match.com. You'll need an enticing screen name.

SBF 2: Single sista.

SBF 1: That's taken!

SBF 2: Of course. How about Diva?

SBF 1: Too predictable.

SBF 2: Cocoalawyer!

SBF 1: (*types*) Yes! We're in. Age range? Thirty to forty. Weight?

SBF 2: No they don't. Those mothafuckas!

SBF 1: Calm down. Fit, a few pounds, or chunky monkey?

SBF 2: Fit!

SBF 1: Fit?

SBF 2: I said fit!

SBF 1: Okay, okay. What other essential info do you want to include?

SBF 2: Tell them I've got a New York mind, L.A. face, Oakland booty, and Vineyard cash! Sign me up for thirty days.

SBF 1: That's a bit too optimistic. How about one year?

SBF 2: A year of this? Remember, my clock is ticking!

SBF 1: Okay, how about six months?

SBF 2: That should be just enough time to find the love of my life.

SBF 1: What are you looking for?

SBF 2: Well, last time I checked, Barack Obama was taken. So I'll take anybody breathing within a five-hundred-mile radius. That ought to take care of the Tri-State Area, and most of the Eastern seaboard and Atlantic City too!

SBF 1: Come on. The point is to be more selective. We've already tried the "everybody" plan and that didn't quite work for the past thirty some odd years. We can do a search by age, race, education, weight, religion, and location—

SBF 2: Okay, I want someone who likes to cook, travel, read . . .

SBF 1: That sounds a tad generic.

SBF 2: Listen, you want to know what I really want?

(*spoken-word style*)
Give me a roughneck nigga with a law degree
Who pulls my hair and spanks me.
Talkin' 'bout a brotha who understands Hegel, Fanon, and slappin' bones
Who knows better than to sit up at Chez Panisse
Ordering rosé and answering cell phones.
Beggin' for a man who finds box symphony seats the bomb
And knows how to sweet talk my Mom.
He's gotta be sanctified Sunday after sinnin' Saturday night.
His desire must be awakened by African skin on a body that's tight.
He reads Toni Morrison and bets half his check on the Knicks,
Saves for our baby's trust fund and new pair of kicks.
Drives his cobalt Porsche into the ground.
Brings home white tulips on the first day of spring without me making a sound.
Whispers in French as we walk along the Seine
After letting me call across the Atlantic to talk shit with my best friend!

SBF 1: Tell it! But come on, that's one tall order, sis! I don't think we'll find that on here.

SBF 2: Let's just go ahead and see if these folks can find some kinda match for me. What did it find? Is HE there?

SBF 1: Look, ten matches. Okay, wow. Which one? Chuck full of Nuts? Pimpin' Paul? Brooklyn Bobby? Or Chocolate Dream? No, I tried him. He's a nightmare. Ah, a new post. What about this guy, Just-in-time? An eighty percent match! He wants a woman just like you and he's nearly everything you're looking for.

SBF 2: Smart, sexy and ed-u-ma-cated!

SBF 1: Let me enlarge his photo. Oh, my—isn't that your ex? That's—

SBF 2 & SBF 1: (*in unison*) Justin! Damn!

SBF 2: Just-in-time? Just in time to piss me off. I guess it's true, you can find just about anything online. Let's log out. I think that's enough humiliation for one afternoon.

SBF 1: No, wait. I think I've got something sweet here.

SBF 2: A professional, unmarried, and wants kids?

SBF 1: Send him a wink! Good luck, girl. I can't wait to see what the cyber world sends you.

Scene 6. The Date

SBF 2 standing in bedroom rifling through closets and dressers while SBF 1 sits on the bed thumbing through fashion magazines.

SBF 2: (*standing in bra and panties in front of her closet*) What the hell am I going to wear? Uh! I can't believe I'm going out with a guy I met online.

SBF 1: It will be fine. Wear what makes you feel comfortable, mysterious, sexy. (*Beat.*) That's the least of your worries. Do you know the part of a date I worry about most? After the drinks, appetizers, main course, then dessert . . . the big question looms in the air. Who will pay for dinner? Usually, I pay and assert my feminist ideals.

SBF 2: If he pays? What does he get besides salmon and baked new potatoes with a side of steamed greens and a starter of mussels? Most of the time waiters place the bill skillfully between our well-clad bodies. Why should I pay when I know he makes three times my salary?

SBF 1: That's right. He pays and you pay later.

SBF 2: Yeah, I pay and still have to wrestle with this mothafucka on my sofa.

SBF 1: Who really pays? Has anyone ever calculated the true cost for women to stay date material in the new millennium? (*sound of antique adding machine*)

SBF 2: Let's see, eyebrows, bikini line, and upper lip waxed? One hundred and ten dollars.

SBF 1: Gym membership for thigh control, one hundred and fifty dollars per month.

SBF 2: Teeth whitening process, three hundred dollars.

SBF 1: How about the particulars for tonight?

SBF 2: Spanx and Donna Karan sandal foot ultra-sheer nylons in jet black, two pairs at twenty-five dollars each.

SBF 1: Two pairs?

SBF 2: In case of a run!

SBF 1: Of course. Next?

SBF 2: Foundations.

SBF 1: What are we constructing here? An office building?

SBF 2: No, honey, we're building toward a dream.

SBF 1: Or a nightmare!

SBF 2: Wonder-ful bra and lace panties—courtesy of La Perla.

SBF 1: Of course. Price tag?

SBF 2: Some things are private.

SBF 1: Shoes?

SBF 2: A pair of Christian Louboutin three-inch high come-fuck-me pumps. Four hundred and twenty-five dollars.

SBF 1: Well spent! Don't forget the smell good—Issey Miyake Eau de Parfum Spray, eighty-two dollars.

SBF 2: Applied to all the pulse points. (*SBF 2 demonstrates the application of perfume.*) Behind the ears, each wrist, ankles and . . . (*motions toward crotch*)

SBF 1: Wait! No! Don't do that. It burns. Trust me. Makeup?

SBF 2: Lipstick by M·A·C—The black middle-class woman's form of crack. (*rifling through her purse*) Chintz, Media, Frenzy, XS, XTC, Film Noir, Diva, Photo, Fetish, Icon—

SBF 1: Wait. Are those your favorite colors or a commentary on American popular culture?

SBF 2: Same thing, different shade. Foundation by Prescriptives.

SBF 1: Custom blended for our skin color. Before M·A·C and Prescriptives, a colored girl couldn't get a break. Remember those shades our mothers had to wear? Frosty pink eye shadow? Devastating.

SBF 2: Yeah, no more beige coverage for brown skins or bright orange lipstick for full lips.

SBF 1: Mascara, eyeliner, shadow.

SBF 2: For that sultry look.

SBF 1: And blush.

SBF 2: For that demure look. Let's see, makeup, three hundred and eighty-five dollars. Oops! I can't forget the dress. A nice silk cream Calvin Klein number. One hundred and twenty-five.

SBF 1: One hundred and twenty-five dollars? Not bad.

SBF 2: Century 21, girl. Grand total?

SBF 1: Well over two thousand dollars in credit and cash payments.

SBF 2: How much did he spend to get ready for tonight?

SBF 1: Nothing. He took a shit, a shower, and a shave. I think you better make sure he's paying for dinner.

SBF 2: Damn right. He better give up some lovin' too, so I can get my money's worth. (*Doorbell rings. SBF 2 opens the door and greets her unseen suitor in the hallway.*) Good evening. I'm just about ready, sugar. Turn around and let me see that package. Tight. Nice. (*to SBF 1*) Good night, girl, text you later!

Scene 7. Sexual Suspect

SBF 2 arrives at the doctor's office.

SBF 2: I really hate going to the doctor's office. (*whispering*) No, not for the flu, but when I have to go to the . . . gynecologist. Women's health is a pain in the ass!

(*Lights up on SBF 1 putting on a white lab coat, glasses, and stethoscope.*)

There is something so sterile,

(*SBF 1 puts on latex gloves in a pronounced manner.*)

so impersonal about it. Just business as usual, especially while I was in college and all I could afford was St. Vincent's. No, I'm not trying to get an abortion. The date wasn't that good. I'm here so I don't need to go there. I just have a yeast infection, AGAIN! I hate women who tell me they never had one. I find that just as annoying as those sistas who have never experienced cramps. Well, this particular yeast infection has no respect for that over-the-counter Monistat. I need some nuclear bomb stuff for this one.

(*SBF 1 as white male doctor picks up a clipboard and begins reading the chart, then approaches SBF 2.*)

SBF 1: Okie dokie. So what was the first day of your last menstrual period?

SBF 2: Huh?

SBF 1: I'm sorry, how are we today? What's bothering you? (*starts to scribble notes furiously*)

SBF 2: My colleague referred me to Dr. Feel Good because he's supposed to be the best but, what can old boy be writing before I've even said anything? (*to him*) I have some discomfort (*whispers*) with intercourse. And some, uh, vaginal itching. And some (*whispers*) discharge.

SBF 1: (*loudly*) Describe the discharge.

SBF 2: (*to audience*) Discharge, why do I always think about the army and dishonor when I hear that word? (*to doctor*) Yes, it's a little . . . a little, it's kinda . . .

(*Two stirrups drop down from the ceiling for SBF 2 to put her feet in.*)

SBF 1: Okay, let's get a look down there. Undress from the earrings down, put on this thin gown that couldn't keep an ant warm that has its back open so that your ass is out to the world, sit on this cold table and wait for me while you look at our stack of out-of-date magazines. You may also study our informative signs about the reproductive system, the varieties of birth control pills, and scary posters about HIV testing. Freaked out? You may calm yourself by glancing at our fake Monet. (*Beat.*) But sister, don't even think about stealing gloves, KY Jelly, Rantex wipes, or those really big cotton swabs that you can't fit in your ears anyway!

SBF 2: So I'm sitting there waiting for him to come back, and this man I've known all of three minutes will look at the place my parents told me not to touch unless I was cleaning it—and then, don't look!

SBF 1: Put your feet in these ice-cold stirrups so that you can cock your legs wide open. Now, scoot down so that your buttocks are practically off the table. A little bit more. (*Pause.*) A bit more. One more. (*smothered sound*) Ahh, lady, that's too far! I can't breathe!

SBF 2: Then while this stranger has his latex fingers inside me, I start to imagine all kinds of crazy things. I'm an attorney, I know that it's inappropriate to say, but there are clients I really don't care for. If I'm honest, I know that they don't always get my best work. Is this guy going to give me the best health care if he doesn't like me? Then it hits me. I recall the disdain on his face when he first looked at me. Dear God, what if he's a racist? TUSKEGEE!

SBF 1: Well, looks a bit tender here. New partner?

SBF 2: I wanna say, "And what of it, asshole?" But instead I say, "Yes, but we're careful. We use protection every time."

SBF 1: I wanna tell her, "Slut, I reviewed your chart and every time you go to the doctor you have a new partner." But instead I say, "That's good, perhaps you'd better use more lubricant with your partner if he's, uh, excessively large."

SBF 2: Honey, don't believe the hype, not all brothas are hung like horses.

SBF 1: You'd better consider your fertility. Do you want to have children? Now that you're thirty-five, you are now considered a woman of advanced maternal age, so becoming pregnant can really become an issue.

SBF 2: Which I hear as—

SBF 1: You better have yourself some babies, you old maid! How did you make it this long without having children? Being single never stops the rest of you hot black mamas from droppin' some illegit shit!

SBF 2: I do want a child . . .

SBF 1: A baby . . .

SBF 2: A son . . .

SBF 1: A daughter . . .

SBF 2: But I also want a father for my children. Not a baby daddy. Call me a right-wing traditional anti-black matriarch. Can somebody help me with this? Husband, are you out there?

SBF 1: Well, good luck with that. Ha!

SBF 2: What is this ritual? The annual Pap smear sprinkled with occasional emergencies—a female problem. I wonder what slave women did when they suffered from bad cramps, or better yet, a yeast infection.

SBF 1: (*as slave wench number 9*) Massa, I sho' cain't get in them fields today. No suh, my feminine itchin' gots me real bad like.

SBF 2: Then, just about every six months—my favorite moment.

SBF 1: From your chart, it looks like you're about due for another HIV test—being that you're single and all . . .

SBF 2: (*rolling up her sleeve*) Yes. (*to audience*) This is even more of a blast!

SBF 1: I'll need to take some blood. Have Sandy set up an appointment for your results.

SBF 2: They never have trouble finding my vein. I just wish that the only pain was from the needle prick.

SBF 1: Now, that wasn't so bad, was it? Miss, you do have a little yeast infection. Not bad enough to take off work, but I'll write you a prescription. Now, you'll need some self-acceptance, a nice gentle lover, peace with your parents, satisfaction with work and, of course, exercise and a healthy diet.

SBF 2: Can you phone all that in to a pharmacy near my house?

SBF 1: No problem.

Scene 8. Holiday

(*Loud Christmas music blares from the apartments above and below. Lights up.*)

SBF 1: Damn! Christmas again. Hey, turn it down! (*bangs on floor*) Turn that crap off! The holidays make me scream. No, scream, then faint. These sentimental days force me to deal with my aunts, my mother's gang of four sisters from Texas— Aunt Leola, Auntie Price, Aunt Ernestine, and Aunt Mabel Dear. Otherwise known as the married Mafia! They'll all be asking those questions. You know the drill.

SBF 2: Baby, you look like you've gained—

SBF 1: Or lost—

SBF 2: Too much weight. Are you eating right? All that working you do, it's just a shame. Don't let them white people make you crazy, now.

SBF 1: They're also in rare form during that other American women's guilt orgy— Mother's Day.

SBF 2: I'm sure happy to see you, sugar. I guess I can't expect for you to visit since you've got that fancy job. Our little baby, a big-time college professor and all. You young folks have to live your lives, I guess.

SBF 1: Then that wonderful question we've all been waiting for.

SBF 2: (*using megaphone*) Sweetie, when are you gonna get MARRIED?

SBF 1: Yes, every Christmas, Valentine's Day, Easter, Thanksgiving, and Hallow-een! But especially during Christmas. Everybody wants you to be happy. I'm convinced that all the Yuletide festivities, from shopping to holiday parties, were designed to make me feel like a loser. Am I the only single person left in the world? At Aunt Mabel Dear's annual Christmas Eve gumbo get-together, those gray-haired gangsters always ask me that same question.

SBF 2: When you gonna get serious about somebody?

SBF 1: For years I just apologized. I'm sorry nobody wants me, but I did finish my Ph.D. last June.

SBF 2: Honey, Junes are for brides. That little degree is all fine and good, but it won't keep you warm at night, baby.

SBF 1: My family is crazy. I try to explain, "Oh, I'm not really into the traditional marriage thing—sexism and patriarchy make marriage an oppressive institu-tion for women." Wrong answer. Never give the feminist line to women who believe you'd better fix a man's plate at any human gathering.

SBF 2: Baby, he looks a little peaked. Maybe he needs a bite of something.

SBF 1: But Aunt Leola, we are at the Bronx Zoo. They only have stale peanuts.

SBF 2: Never let a man go hungry, sweetie.

SBF 1: When I visit Auntie Price, it's even harder. I have to answer questions like—

SBF 2: Have you considered practicing an alternative lifestyle?

SBF 1: Auntie Price has always been a bit—eccentric! Auntie, if I was practicing anything, I would have it right by now.

SBF 2: Now, as I figure it, being tri-sexual might better your odds. Seems to me that liking both men and women ought to make things easier. More love to choose from.

SBF 1: You would think so, Auntie Price.

SBF 2: Too bad that Clayton is a gay. He's such a nice, intelligent young man. And so well dressed, too.

SBF 1: Clayton and I are happy being friends. I'll meet somebody soon.

SBF 2: Well, one of my friends at the church tells me her daughter met and married some man she met on the superinformationhighway.www.com. Try that!

SBF 1: Okay, Auntie Price. (*turns to audience*) Usually, I'm battling the aunts with smart quips. My new reply can even silence the very best-meaning, rude-sounding black maternal figure over fifty years old. (*cautiously turns to another aunt*) Well, Aunt Ernestine, I'm just being a patient and obedient Christian. Whenever the Lord sees fit to bless me with a God-fearin' husband, I guess I'll plan my wedding day. Believe me, when that day comes, you'll be the first to know. Until then, I will do the work He has put before me.

SBF 2: Well, I just hopes your daddy will be alive to walk you down the aisle some summer afternoon in the distant future. Ain't none of us gonna be here forever.

SBF 1: It's not that I hate the holidays. I wouldn't say that. I just don't celebrate the questions that come along with these festive events. I wish I didn't have to eat the advice that my dear aunts put on the side of my plate next to that extra help-ing of banana pudding. But you know what? That pudding sure helps it slide down easier. For some strange reason, of all the holidays, I love the Fourth of July. Don't tell my friends, but something about this mid-summer holiday makes me mushy inside. Most people get bent out of shape on New Year's Eve because they don't have a date or Valentine's Day when they are absent a sweet-heart. But for me? I feel so unloved sitting on the beach or at the family BBQ with nobody to slather butter on my corn on the cob. Nobody to wipe the Texas sauce from the corner of my lips. Not a soul to feed me peach cobbler. Yes, the big joy of the summer is the fruit. Plums, nectarines, cherries. Oh, I love man-gos! And what self-respecting African American doesn't just fall on their knees for a juicy piece of watermelon? In private, of course. As far as I'm concerned, it's the epitome of solitude to pick my own melon and eat it. I'm tired of sifting through those bins. I'm tired of lugging home my prey and hoisting it up the two flights to my one-bedroom apartment. I'd like to ask my baby to come on down and help me lug it up the stairs. I want to share my piece of watermelon on a blanket underneath the warm summer night sky exploding with fireworks!

SBF 2: (*enters dressed in a summer dress and hands SBF 1 a large piece of watermelon, then sits down beside her*) Happy holidays!

(*Mariah Carey's "Fourth of July" plays softly. Lights slow fade.*)

Act 2. Secrets: How We Got This Way

Scene 1. Why I Will Never Marry

Nancy Wilson's "Never Will I Marry" plays as SBF 1 revises and reads from a list in her journal.

SBF 2: I've got it! I know how we got this way. I just returned from a Shapely retreat in the Adirondacks.

SBF 1: Shapely?

SBF 2: You remember, I tried to get you to attend, too. S.H.A.P.E.L.Y., Sisters Hop-ing and Praying Energetically for Love, Yea! It's a holistic retreat for black women trying to look within to discover how they can heal from family wounds and societal expectations and still find long-lasting monogamous attach-ments. I discovered exactly why you are still single.

SBF 1: This I've got to hear.

SBF 2: You hang out with gay men all the time, you read far too many articles in *Essence* magazine, and you watched way too many episodes of *Sex and the City*.

SBF 1: What? Well, Miss Shapely, you wouldn't recognize real love if it kissed you on the lips. The real reason you are single is that you jump too fast into bed with the wrong ones, and are too slow to warm to the marrying type.

SBF 2: Ow! You may have a point, but you—

SBF 1: Stop. It's fine. I don't need your explanations. It's not just about being cho-sen. I have my own reasons for never getting married.

SBF 2: Are you still working on that list? Okay, let's hear it.

SBF 1: I now have fifty reasons. Check out number forty-nine: I don't want to spend eternity saying—

SBF 2: What do you want to eat tonight?

SBF 1: I don't know, what do you want?

SBF 2: I don't care. I'll have whatever you want.

SBF 1: Let's get Chinese, then

SBF 2: Chinese again? I'm so tired of eating Chinese.

SBF 1: Then why did you say, whatever you want?

SBF 2: Don't start.

SBF 1: I'm not starting, you are.

SBF 2: Or, how about reason eight? Having to ask, "What's wrong?" and hear—

SBF 1: (*sighs*) Nothing. Yes, then there is reason number forty-seven. I refuse to listen to my partner's taste in music. You can't always fall in love with somebody with superior taste. Invariably you find out when it's much too late that they love Kenny G. That's not jazz.

SBF 2: How about reason number forty-five? I don't have to like anyone else's parents. That's self-explanatory.

SBF 1: And my favorite, number thirty-seven, retaining total and complete power over the remote control. Yes, I watch television: from SOAPnet to ESPN. I've been with my thirty-two-inch SONY longer than I've been with anyone. And my TIVO knows me better than I know myself!

SBF 2: Wait! What about reason twenty-four?

SBF 1: I get to sleep with a new person (or more than one person) whenever I want! Why do you want to get married?

SBF 2: The same reason every SBF wants to get married? You get to have a wedding! A wedding; a thirty-thousand-dollar party. A big public, yet sacred bash that's all about celebrating the man you get to fuck for forever—for the mortgage and health insurance, of course.

SBF 1: No, for love! You get to be husband and wife. How grand.

SBF 2: Well, I refuse any more weddings except my own. Moreover, I refuse to attend another commitment ceremony, whether it's held in City Hall or on Fire Island. They drag on forever and my gay friends get divorced just like straight folk. Alternative lifestyle, alternative result, right?

SBF 1: You think so? Come on, fuck the dumb shit! Are you expecting perfection from folks just because they're gay?

SBF 2: Honey, all I know is that I spent over four hundred dollars on Isaiah and Demante's nuptials, not including my own outfit, and they stayed together for six months. Six months! I have had a rash longer than that. I want the gift back! No! Damn it, I want it all! After waiting all these years I don't plan to settle now.

SBF 1: So, you honestly want to become a wife? Come on, the world has changed. Now women don't have to stay at home and take care of the kids. In this new progressive age, opportunity abounds. You get to have a fabulous career as a lawyer, architect, or doctor—then come home and take care of the house and kids. We've come a long way, baby. Shoot! I want a wife, too. Yeah, love and marriage.

(Soft spotlight shifts to SBF 2 while SBF 1 moves in the background with another soft light on her. Nancy Wilson's "Never Will I Marry" plays softly.)

Scene 2. Malcolm and My Other Xs

SBF 1 discovers a stack of photographs on the bookshelf and begins to go through them, laughing to herself and showing them to SBF 2 as evidence. During the scene they project photos of former lovers with a solid black bar covering parts of their faces.

SBF 1: Black love. The kind of love you had with Malcolm. Malcolm—

SBF 2: X. Malcolm X. Let's just leave the last names out of things to protect the guilty, the innocent, and the truly pathetic.

SBF 1: Right. (*to audience*) Don't worry, this isn't political. He wasn't the Nation of Islam brotha she dated. (*to SBF 2*) That's the only type of man you haven't— (*makes exaggerated air quotes*) dated.

SBF 2: Malcolm was the last man I truly loved.

SBF 1: (*to audience*) By any means necessary, she was going to keep that relationship going.

SBF 2: He was loving, supportive, sexy—

SBF 1: And jealous! He believed you were out there screwing anyone and everyone. (*as the boyfriend*) What's up with you and Darren?

SBF 2: What do you mean, what's up?

SBF 1: First of all, you are always at his shows every Friday and Saturday night. Second of all, you are always going shopping and shit.

SBF 2: That's true, but honey, you know that Darren is gay? He's not on the DL, he's a drag queen!

SBF 1: It doesn't matter. I know you're fuckin' him!

SBF 2: Ooh, yeah, he was nuts.

SBF 1: What about that Kelvin character?

SBF 2: Armani suits, Prada loafers, Thomas Pink shirts, and fragrance by Dolce and Gabbana.

SBF 1: Talk about my credit problems! Didn't he buy all that stuff with your Visa and MasterCard? Yep. You even co-signed for a Discover Card just so he could help you discover some more debt and discover himself some more clothes at Neiman Marcus.

SBF 2: Wait a minute. All the men I've loved aren't paranoid, crazy, cheap dogs.

SBF 1: Really? What about Simon? He was adopted and had a few abandonment issues.

SBF 2: Yeah, who doesn't?

SBF 1: What about Mr. Perfect, a.k.a. Mr. Julian Nathaniel Richards III?

SBF 2: A forty-one-year-old divorced father of none. Tall, muscular, and black black black. So black the man was blue, like the Atlantic Ocean at midnight. And bald, just like Michael Jordan. Um.

SBF 1: He spoke French, Italian, and Spanish.

SBF 2: Fluently.

SBF 1: Wasn't he also learning German so he could read Kant without the fumbling interpretation of a translator?

SBF 2: Julian.

SBF 1: You just knew he was—

SBF 2: Thee One.

SBF 1: I couldn't find you most weekends. You two spent Friday nights recuperating from the week by cooking recipes out of the vegetarian cookbook his mother sent you as a housewarming gift.

SBF 2: So we played house. Honey, there ain't nothin' like live-in dick. You no longer have to worry about a date for Saturday night. On Sunday mornings Julian and I lounged around our loft eating toast smothered with homemade strawberry jam and reading the *Times.*

SBF 1: Wrestling over the Arts & Leisure section. Love. Remember that rainy October night he cooked a five-course gourmet meal and for dessert put a two-carat promise on your finger?

SBF 2: Thee finger!

SBF 1: (*holding up the ring*) Exhibit A!

SBF 2: Julian told me the ring belonged to his grandmother and that it had belonged to her grandmother, who was a slave who stole it from her mistress. Took sixty lashes to have this slaveholder's heirloom. It was now on my hand.

SBF 1: It was black history and black pain redeemed by black love.

SBF 2: We danced and cried. Candles burned our silhouettes into the brick walls of our living room. The rain serenaded us as we drifted off to sleep. Magic.

SBF 1: The next day the phone rang at my office. I'll never forget. It was exactly 4:18 P.M. and I had a line of students outside my door waiting to complain about receiving an A minus.

SBF 2: Girl, you won't believe this! Julian's ex-wife called. She lives in Baltimore. She wants the ring back. It belonged to a slave, all right. Her Aunt Sandy, who was a maid in the suburbs of Virginia in 1979, stole it from her boss. Emancipation! She got fired and I just fired him.

SBF 1: For lying about the ring?

SBF 2: No, for lying about the divorce. They are only separated.

SBF 1: Oh, yeah. The review of this breakup was brought to you by Miller Genuine Draft. In recognition of this and every other breakup, Miller would like to contribute seventeen cents to the United Negro College Fund. A black woman's womb is a terrible thing to waste. Thank you. (*Beat.*) I don't know about you, but after every breakup I'm completely embarrassed. I hate to see my colleagues and friends. "So, how are you and so-and-so doing?"

SBF 2: That's because for some reason you can't keep your big mouth shut when you've found what appears to be new love.

SBF 1: I have to share my new joy with the world. (*phone rings; SBF 2 answers*)

SBF 2: Hello?

SBF 1: You won't believe it. I'm in love.

SBF 2: What! (*SBF 2 abruptly hangs up the phone.*)

SBF 1: After a few dates—

SBF 2: Or a few months—

SBF 1: Even after a few years I must reveal to the world that once again I am back in the land of the single people. (*Beat.*) We broke up—my favorite refrain.

SBF 2: He left you.

SBF 1: My mother's favorite refrain.

SBF 2: It just wasn't meant to be. What can you learn from this?

SBF 1: My therapist's favorite refrain.

SBF 2: Fuck him! He ain't shit.

SBF 1: My homegirl's favorite refrain.

SBF 2: Yeah, maybe it's me. Nobody is perfect. But I'm always more suspect if a guy doesn't have something major that needs changing. So, maybe it's me.

SBF 1: It certainly can't all be THEM.

SBF 2: Ahmad?

SBF 1: Too arrogant.

SBF 2: Elijah?

SBF 1: He was too smothering.

SBF 2: Phillip?

SBF 1: You did fuck that up.

SBF 2: Hey, wait! Isn't this the part when you act supportive?

SBF 1: Well, you were only eighteen, so that doesn't count.

SBF 2: Yeah, young love. Hey, what about your college sweetheart, Brian?

SBF 1: Too demanding. He wanted too much too soon. He wanted us to get married before I finished . . . before we finished school. Now, that was out of the question!

SBF 2: And didn't he catch you messing with his cousin?

SBF 1: (*under her breath*) That was actually his line brother.

SBF 2: Whoa! Not the one he went through the burning sands with. Damn!

SBF 1: Listen, I was freaked out. I certainly didn't understand commitment at that stage in my life. Will I ever live that down? Can we change the subject?

SBF 2: (*grabs another photo*) Hey, how about your girl phase? We can't forget about you and Miss Simone.

SBF 1: I was tired of being alone and being a lesbian in the late nineties seemed so cool, so Tracy Chapman. So k.d. lang . . . (*sings*) "constant craving, that's always been."

SBF 2: Girl, you talked about Simone all night and all day and all night again.

SBF 1: She had my attention. I found Simone—

SBF 2: Captivating?

SBF 1: We enjoyed ourselves.

(*Loud club music from the 1980s—like Janet Jackson's "Don't Know What You Got 'Til It's Gone"—begins to build.*)

SBF 2: Enjoyed? Every weekend you two held everybody at Brown Sugar hostage with your notorious enjoyment.

SBF 1: Simone, is that your ex? Is that Gina?

SBF 2: (*starts to dance seductively*) Yeah. So what. Are you going to move your body or what? I want to dance, baby.

SBF 1: Simone! What were you doing in the bathroom with her?

SBF 2: She had a little blow. Don't trip. Come on.

SBF 1: I don't want to dance, Simone. I want to know what's up, Simone. Don't put me through all this—

SBF 2: Drama! You two deserved the Tony, Emmy, and Oscar. Your exploits at every girl bar in the city are absolutely legendary.

SBF 1: I know. The shouting matches, the crying jags, and plenty of she said, she said.

SBF 2: Everybody needs a little drama to help tell all the days apart. But I don't get it. I had hopes for you and Miss Simone. Honestly, I always thought lesbian relationships would be different. You can double your wardrobe. Both of you understand your cycles. You can process every ounce of your relationship down to the last sigh! I thought all the bullshit was reserved for the war between the sexes.

SBF 1: Wake up! It isn't about sexuality, honey—it's called love. Man? Woman? Parakeet? We're all just trying to find love. Love . . . (*finds another photo*) Now, what about Charles? I really liked you guys together. Wasn't he some kind of scientist?

SBF 2: He called, sent flowers, and made measured slow sexual advances display-ing the correct amount of passion and respect. But, he was so . . . nice. And his style reminded me that most nerdy men wear the wrong clothes! It can be very, very distracting. He just got on my nerves.

SBF 1: Well, a couple of weeks ago I saw him pushing a Bugaboo stroller through Central Park with his wife. He was cute; she had him dressed impeccably in Banana Republic weekend wear. Happy. Nice. Like a family.

SBF 2: Maybe I never should have let him go. Wow, I feel like I'm watching the clock tick and this game of musical chairs has me standing in the corner while every-one else has a seat.

(*Beat.*) Oh, honey, I needs me a drink.

Scene 3. Sleepin' with the Enemy

SBF 1 and and SBF 2 mix martinis.

SBF 1: You're not going to win us any support if you insist on sharing this part. It's a delicate subject.

SBF 2: We've already covered yearly pap smears and online dating. I really don't think they are leaving. Besides, we can't discuss life for single black women over thirty without discussing the interracial thing.

SBF 1: Well . . . I'm not going start. I don't want to offend—

SBF 2: Whatever! White girls!

SBF 1: Tell your story.

SBF 2: So I'm visiting my homegirl in L.A. and we hit this funky club off the strip where everybody is skinny and slightly acerbic. Folks are posing with their cool hair, cool clothes, and cool cigars. The DJ is playing neo-soul, hip-hop house music and we are divas in Hollywood. I'm with two other fine sisters out to hear some slammin' beats overlaid with ghetto voice tracks. Know what I mean? We've just got paid and feel like wearing shoes that hurt and shirts that give titty lovely. We're eating calamari and drinking like we ain't got no sense.

SBF 1: (*takes another drink*) It sounds like a good night.

SBF 2: We aren't even thinking about sex.

SBF 1: Excuse me?

SBF 2: Okay, we're always thinking about sex and we get to talkin'.

SBF 1: You are never going to believe what happened in the department meeting last week.

SBF 2: And talkin'.

SBF 1: Where did you pick up those bad-ass shoes? Those are delicious!

SBF 2: At some point I notice that we are the only sistas in the entire joint.

SBF 1: I do hate partying in Hollywood.

SBF 2: But this is not Wyoming! It's Los Angeles—thee sprawling Negropolis of the West Coast. South Central, Baldwin Hills, Leimert Park, Nat Holden, Maxine Waters, Kobe!

SBF 1: True.

SBF 2: I know this not the chocolate city, but is it vanilla town?

SBF 1: What happened to the black people in Los Angeles?

SBF 2: Then my other girl, Miss Life is a Miracle, says—

SBF 1: Oh stop! There are plenty of black people. There. There and there.

SBF 2: Wait. Those ain't people, those are black men! The plot thickens. We decide to make some advances. This is war. I start dancing in front of the stage. I'm flirting with this dreadlocked brotha in the band playing the keyboard. We make eye contact, laugh, and dance together. He's on stage and our sweating bodies are mirroring each other. Hot.

SBF 1: Uh, oh. Did that blonde just step on her toe?

SBF 2: Kirstine! Heather! Tammy or whatever your name is, you tramp. You can't even dance.

SBF 1: Come on, girl. Let it go.

SBF 2: Let it go? She was so close I could smell her cheap perfume. Here I am trying to get at one of the few brothas in the club and I'm outdone by an ABC—an average blonde chick! When I shared my feelings, she says, "Like, I'm sorry, okay? What's the problem? I was just dancing. Why are you people so angry?" Angry?

SBF 1: Listen, sister. You're going to have to leave.

SBF 2: What? No, I'm, . . . I haven't finished my drink yet! She steps on my toe and you're throwing me out? Why are you picking on me?

SBF 1: Nobody is picking on you. You're just paranoid.

SBF 2: Paranoid? I'm being bounced by security and my black ass is paranoid? White women! White women! White women! You can't turn on the television without seeing some dead or missing white woman. Yet nobody cries for little black girls. You know, only sistas understand that O. J. Simpson murdered his wife as an act of aggression and an absolute rejection of African American women. With every slash of her throat O. J. said loud and clear—I would rather be with a white woman that I have to murder to keep than spend my life with some black bitch. Wait! Maybe I'm paranoid.

SBF 1: Just a little. Girl, you've taken this white girl thing a bit too far. Don't you realize that who you love is a personal decision? You're putting too many politics into the personal.

SBF 2: What about you? Are you going to tell me you haven't noticed this little trend in our postmodern, post-race world? Brothas get all the play and there isn't exactly a stampede of white men running down to the NAACP for a date. I guess sistas aren't much better at sampling all thirty-one flavors. You ever dated a white man?

SBF 1: I was always worried about what people would say. Call me a wimp.

SBF 2: Wimp. So let's hear it. If given the chance, what white man would you date?

SBF 1: Don't laugh.

SBF 2: Not another list! How many of those do you have?

SBF 1: (*reading from her journal*) Here is my list of white men that even a self-respecting nationalist sista might date. Let's see, Gregory Peck.

SBF 2: Yes, Atticus Finch. So stately and principled.

SBF 1: Marlon Brando—

SBF 2: Before he got so damn fat and drove his kids crazy.

SBF 1: Cary Grant, Luciano Pavarotti—

SBF 2: Somethin' about that tenor I think is sexy.

SBF 1: Paul Newman, Robert Mitchum—

SBF 2: Wait. Wait. Why are all those white men dead? There must be somebody who is still alive. What about Keanu Reeves?

SBF 1: I don't like him. I prefer my white boys a bit more quirky, like Johnny Depp.

SBF 2: Tom Cruise?

SBF 1: Mission impossible! Mr. Scientology? I don't think so! He's a white boy's white boy. Plus he's crazy. I wish he would jump up on my couch. I do love me some Brad Pitt, though. Hey Brad, if Angelina messes up, holla at a sista!

SBF 2: How about Sting?

SBF 1: I can see that. He's got that leftist Amnesty International thing going. (*Beat.*)

SBF 2: Then there's George Clooney. . . . (*Pause.*) Okay, I've got a confession. I almost dated a white guy in ninth grade. He had the worst acne and greasy hair. Myron was a sweet, quiet boy. He played the clarinet in the band. I liked him and he liked me.

SBF 1: You want to go to the dance this weekend? Or we could go to the museum. I mean, if you want.

SBF 2: Oh, Myron. Yes. I'd love to go. (*sitting on her front steps waiting*) A date. A real date. Mom said no dance, but we were going to the museum and McDonald's for lunch. She called Myron's mother and they discussed it and everything.

SBF 1: (*on phone*) Okay. Myron can walk over here. Yes. We'll be expecting him at—. Yes, well of course you'll want to discuss this with your husband. That's fine. No, I'm sure they'll be no problem. The kids. Yes. Well, fine.

(*hangs up the phone*)

SBF 2: I don't understand why Mom was so worried. I guess she didn't want me to act up and embarrass her. I put on my lavender cardigan with my gray skirt. I had to wear my knee-highs because Mom said—

SBF 2 & SBF 1: No daughter of mine is gonna dress fast!

SBF 2: I waited up in my room listening to my big sister's records. I played Smokey Robinson and the Miracles. I started with "Ooh, Baby, Baby" and ended with "Tears of a Clown." Myron never showed up. By the end of the afternoon it was raining. My mother made my favorite, red beans and rice with hot water cornbread, but I wasn't hungry. Later that night she and Daddy went to their room and shut the door so I could watch whatever I wanted on television. I watched *Get Christie Love*. She was one bad mamma jamma doing her super Mama thing. She kicked a bunch of white boy's asses that Saturday night just for me. Then I fell asleep.

(*Gladys Knight's "You're the Best Thing That Ever Happened" plays as SBF 2 falls asleep on the couch under the watchful eyes of SBF 1.*)

Scene 4. Mother Wit

SBF 2: Mom told me—

SBF 1: It's important to know how to set a table.

SBF 2: Grandmother said—

SBF 1: Always wear pretty underclothes. You never know.

SBF 2: Mom always reminded me that—

SBF 1: Too much makeup is worse than not enough. Simple is better, but too simple is just plain. Don't laugh too loud and be sure to cover your mouth whenever you cough, sneeze or—

SBF 2: Burp?

SBF 1: Girl, I better not catch you burping anytime, anywhere. You're never going to amount to nothing actin' like that. I'm raising you to be a fine colored lady.

SBF 2: Mom also said—

SBF 1: Keep your legs closed. Your mouth shut and your hand open. And never go anywhere with anyone with no way to get home.

SBF 2: But Grandmother told me, "With a smile like that you'll never have a hard time getting home or anywhere else!" Godmother told me—

SBF 1: Sugar, go on and get me some cigarettes at the corner store and take the change to buy yourself some of those jujubes and bring me some, too. On the

way home make sure you watch out for them bad-ass boys on the corner and
don't you get in Old Man Watson's van no matter what that crazy fool says!

SBF 2: My big sister made me promise—

SBF 1: To never let no man ever mess over you and always make sure you can take
care of your damn self!

SBF 2: I always did what I was told.

Scene 5. Pops

SBF 2: My father worked with his hands. My girls don't know this but I've always
had a weakness for a big, strong brotha who sweats at his job. I love the feel of
a calloused palm on my cheek. The truth is, I really don't have a problem with a
man who doesn't wear a tie to bring bread home.

(*SBF 1 puts on an oversized denim work shirt, boots, and hard hat.*)

SBF 2: Keep on walking and look straight ahead. That's what Pops said about walking by a construction site. Don't slow down or speed up, just walk on by. Shoot,
whenever I pass by a brotha in a hard hat I break Pops's rule and honk a hello
if I'm driving, or blow him a little kiss if I'm walking by. A hard working man
deserves a lift every once in a while. Especially if he's fine.

(*SBF 1 whistles in appreciation.*)

Yeah, I like my coffee strong. Why else would I drink it? To tell the truth, for
most of my life I didn't understand how my folks got together and fell in love.
Pops was a tough guy all his life. A bad-ass nigga.

(*SBF 1 lights a cigarette and pulls a fifth of brandy out of his back pocket.*)

Mom taught me about Puccini, Chagall, and Frank Lloyd Wright. She took me
to see Leontyne Price for the first time when I was all of seven years old.

(*SBF 1 sits on chair and flips through TV channels with the remote.*)

We're leaving now. Sure you don't want to go?

(*SBF 1 continues flipping through channels.*)

SBF 1: Yeah, I'm sure. Go on now, woman. (*pats SBF 2's behind*)

SBF 2: She was delicate and loved her garden. He fixed cars and ran with women.

SBF 1: Well? I'll be here when you get home.

SBF 2: On Friday nights Pops got home early from work. On most nights he stayed
out 'til way after I fell asleep and dinner got cold. But come Friday? Mom said
his paycheck burned a hole in his pocket. (*SBF 1 puts on man's blazer and hat*) My
uncle said he dressed like he was on his way to church and it was the wrong day
of the week for those clothes, but I never saw anyone dress like that at Third
Baptist Church. He was sharp—like a straight razor and smooth . . . like butter,
baby.

SBF 1: (*looking at himself in the mirror*) Um, um, um. Hot damn!

SBF 2: One November night I walked into the living room and saw Pops with Mom.

SBF 1: Come here, woman.

(*They slow dance to Dinah Washington's "This Bitter Earth."*)

SBF 2: When I watched my parents dance, I knew how they fell in love. The smell of his amber fruity cologne tickled my nose and made me giggle. Our whole house smelled like that, even after he was gone. Will I ever find that kind of love?

(*SBF 1 and SBF 2 freeze their dance.*)

Epilogue

SBF 1: That's a good question. Will we ever find love? What is love anyway?

SBF 2: We've been conditioned by this society to think that having it ALL means having a husband, a career, a home with a white picket fence, 2.5 kids, and a minivan. I took the bait. I'm trying to be super woman, but these men think I look funny in this cape and tights. I don't understand it. We did what we were supposed to do! We earned ourselves law degrees, Ph.D.s, IRAs, and 401ks. We bring all this to the table and Tiger Woods marries a nanny? I could have avoided all those student loans if that's all men want.

SBF 1: If 50 percent of all marriages fail, why are so many of us anxiously waiting our turn to play THAT game?

SBF 2: Is there another game? It's not all about marriage, but we all want somebody. I'm not ashamed to say I'm lonely. The other day I sat next to a darling older couple at Starbucks who told me they've been married for fifty-five years. Fifty-five years! Before they shuffled out the door the husband stopped at my table and whispered to me that he has been the luckiest man alive ever since the day she married him. That's the kind of sweetness I still believe in. I want to be with a man who still feels blessed half a century after our wedding day. How do I get something like that? All my life I've waited for someone to pick ME. Don't I deserve some soul to share this journey with?

SBF 1: Yes, you do. I hear you. From the looks of things I will not be wed anytime soon. This is not the life either of us expected to have as little girls, and that's what hurts. Yes, we are fierce and brilliant and stylish, but deep down? We are just little black girls who want to find someone to make us feel like chocolate magic sunshine.

SBF 2: That's cute! Yes, chocolate magic sunshine. I like that.

SBF 1: So, I guess we are making our own history.

SBF 2: And we ain't going nowhere. (*Beat.*) Let's go shopping!

LIGHTS FADE DOWN.

End of Play

LYNN NOTTAGE

A former national press officer for Amnesty International, Lynn Nottage has received many prizes and awards for her plays, including the 2009 Pulitzer Prize for *Ruined*, OBIE awards for *Ruined* and *Fabulation, or The Re-Education of Undine*, a National Black Theatre Festival August Wilson Playwriting Award, and two AUDELCO awards. She is also a 2007 recipient of the prestigious MacAuthur "Genius Grant" fellowship. Nottage earned a B.A. degree from Brown University and an M.F.A. in playwriting from Yale University. Her plays cover a range of issues, some serious and tragic, others very comical, but behind her prolific writing is the spirit of the activist. Nottage describes herself as a storyteller; she researches, collects, and then produces the stories of women whose voices need to be heard. Her plays include *Intimate Apparel*, *Crumbs from the Table of Joy*, *Las Meninas*, *Mud, River, Stone*, *Por' Knockers*, *Poof*, and *By the Way, Meet Vera Stark*. Nottage has also developed projects for HBO, Showtime, and Harpo Productions. In 2003 Nottage co-founded a production company, Market Road Films, with two-time Emmy Award–winning film director Tony Gerber. The company is committed to producing independent projects—fiction and nonfiction—from the international community of artists, writers, and others who have stories that might not otherwise be heard.

Fabulation, or The Re-Education of Undine received its world premiere and an extended run at Playwrights Horizons in New York, opening on June 13, 2004.

Director:	Kate Whoriskey
Undine:	Charlayne Woodard
Flow/Ensemble:	Daniel Breaker
Mother/Ensemble:	Saidah Arrika Ekulona
Accountant Richard/ Ensemble:	Stephen Kunken
Hervé/Guy/Ensemble:	Robert Montano
Stephie/Ensemble:	Melle Powers
Father/Ensemble:	Keith Randolph Smith
Grandma/Ensemble:	Myra Lucretia Taylor
Set:	Walt Spangler
Costumes:	Kay Voyce
Lighting:	David Weiner
Sound:	Ken Tavis
Stage Manager:	Gillian Duncan

FABULATION, OR THE RE-EDUCATION OF UNDINE

Act One
Scene 1

Undine, thirty-seven, a smartly dressed African American woman, sits behind a large teak desk sporting a sleek telephone headset.

UNDINE: Can I be honest with you? I admire your expectations, but they're unrealistic, love. Yes, I can deliver something within your range. But your ambition outpaces your budget. But, but, listen to me, it's going to be a total waste of our energy. I've been doing this for a very long time. People give more when they get more. They want a seat next to a celebrity and a five-pound gift bag. It's the truth. Five years ago you could get away with half glasses of chardonnay and a musical theatre star, but not today. Generosity doesn't come cheaply. You're competing with heifers and amputees, rare palms and tuberculosis. What about the cause? Love, people don't want to think about a cause. That's why they give. Yes, I want to hear your thoughts. I am listening. Listen, I'm at the outer limits of my time and so I'm going to ask you to speak more quickly. I will. Yes. We'll talk tomorrow about the new budget. Bye-bye.

(Undine hangs up and unfurls a pleased, self-satisfied smile. She buzzes her assistant.)

Stephie, if Altrice calls back tell her I've left for the day. *(Excited)* Oh and did Hervé call? Buzz me when he does. *(Undine climbs onto the edge of her desk.)* And sweet pea, where are we with tonight's event? Oh God, don't tell me that. You know the rule: if you can't get a celebrity, get me someone celebrity-like. Wait, wait. I don't understand what you're saying. Stop, stop, stop. Get in here *(To herself)* Okay, now how difficult is it to find me someone who can make an entrance?

(Stephie, a spacey twenty-something, enters in a very, very short light-blue-fur mini-skirt.)

Jesus, how difficult is it? They can send probes to Mars, and I'm just asking for someone slightly fabulous.

STEPHIE: Like?

UNDINE: Like the fuck blonde with the perky nipples. You know the one. She's what's-his-name's girlfriend. The comedian. You know. Her!

STEPHIE: She's an alcoholic, Undine.

UNDINE: So? The photographers adore her—

STEPHIE: She got sloppy drunk at the Wild Life benefit and puked on the buffet table.

UNDINE: I don't care if she's an alcoholic. As long as she can hold it together long enough for a photo-op. After that she can swim to Taiwan in booze for all I care.

STEPHIE: But—

UNDINE: Tell her it's an open bar. That way she'll get there on time.

STEPHIE: It . . . it doesn't feel right.

UNDINE: Oh, it doesn't feel right? Visualize a job behind a counter, okay? How does that feel? Yeah. I thought so.

STEPHIE: Why are you being such a harpy this morning? You're acting like, I don't know, a—

UNDINE: (Mimicking Stephie) An employer? Oh please, back to the list, my little hater!

STEPHIE: I've been through the list like four times. I've called absolutely everyone.

UNDINE: What about the contingency list?

STEPHIE: Done.

UNDINE: What about—

STEPHIE: She's doing something with—

UNDINE: Fuck her. She hasn't had a movie in two years. Two years and I'm offering her free publicity.

STEPHIE: Sorry. I spoke to her myself and she's like on some sort of spiritual—

UNDINE: Goddamnit! If I hear about one more celebrity on a spiritual journey, I will, I will . . . It's okay. She's closed that door. Let her go. Let her do her yoga thing, I don't care. So? How are we doing with our friends in the media?

STEPHIE: The perennial from WBAI and some intern from *Newsweek* confirmed, and everybody else is wait and see. Like, no one cares about Fallopian Blockage. It isn't exactly—

UNDINE: Hush! This is going to be fine. We're okay, we have plenty of time. Call George, tell him Undine is cashing in her favor. I need someone up and coming, young, hip. Hip-hop in fact. On the verge. Gangster-ish enough to cause a stir, but not enough to cause a problem. And don't let him weasel out. I don't want *New York Times* hag-fest photos. Fun, fun, fun. *Vibe*, *Vanity Fair*. The V's. Let's mix and match a little bit, shake it up. Mix and match. Goddamnit, if we can't find a celebrity, we'll create a new one. This is going to be great. What are you wearing? Goodbye!

STEPHIE: But—

UNDINE: Goodbye!

(*Stephie moves to leave, then remembers something.*)

STEPHIE: Oh, I forgot. Your accountant's waiting outside.

UNDINE: Oh God. What does he want? Give me a minute.

(Stephie leaves. Undine weeps uncontrollably. She stops abruptly, takes out a mirror, reapplies her lipstick, checks her teeth and wipes away the tears. Intercom.)

    Send the little pussy in.

(The Accountant, Richard, an elegantly clad man in his mid-thirties, enters, shaking his head ever so slightly. All charm.)

    Richard. Oh come on, it's a little early in the day for a visit. Put away your business-school face. I'm not signing anything.

RICHARD: Why didn't you tell me you and Hervé split?—

UNDINE: Why? Because I only just found out. Apparently I was the last to know.

RICHARD: Jesus, I'm sorry, Undine—

UNDINE: You?—*(A moment)* How do you think I felt when I woke up this morning and his closet was bare?

RICHARD: Yikes, how'd he manage that?

UNDINE: I don't know. He took clothing to the dry cleaners every day. I didn't question it. I just thought he had a compulsion to be clean. Little ferret. How was I to know that he was slowly sneaking out of my life, piece by piece.

RICHARD: Do you know where he is?

UNDINE: Uh . . . No, and frankly I don't care.

RICHARD: Well, I wish you did.

UNDINE: We had dinner last night. I mean, we talked about redoing the living room in Antique White. Stupid fucker. He was actually attentive and warm—

RICHARD: *(Blurts out)* And he was, well, he . . . Oooo . . . he was also slowly siphoning money out of your accounts. *(A moment)*

UNDINE: *(Intercom)* Stephie, would you come back in?

RICHARD: Undine, did you hear what I said?

(Stephie reenters.)

UNDINE: Sweet pea, will you have Jeremy run out and buy me some aspirin, a pregnancy test kit. I also need a pair of panty hose, and tell that idiot that I don't wear flesh tone or natural; I'm suntan or bronzed or cocoa. Oh yes, and I desperately need a triple café latté, no milk.

STEPHIE: You mean a *(Italian accent)* triple espresso.

UNDINE: I'm so pleased you learned something during your year in Italia. How much did that word cost your parents, five hundred dollars? But what I'm asking for is a triple café latté with no milk. Is that clear?

STEPHIE: *(Concerned)* Are you all right?

UNDINE: I'm waiting for my coffee. Pronto. That's Italian for do your job!

STEPHIE: Is there anything else?

UNDINE: Stephie.

STEPHIE: Yes?

UNDINE: I love you. Goodbye.

(Stephie leaves.)

RICHARD: Undine, did you hear—

UNDINE: You're not saying that Hervé?

RICHARD: Has disappeared with—

UNDINE: I don't believe it. He's a duplicitous conniving prick, but he's not a thief. Lighten up. He probably just took a cruise to Saint Martin's or moved the money into some mutual fund. He'll resurface when he gets bored. (*Richard laughs.*)

RICHARD: Saint Martin's? I see. Shall I break it down? When you made your husband a co-signatory on all of your accounts, you essentially gave him the power to do whatever he wanted with your money. Which is exactly what has been done.

UNDINE: I'm sorry, my mind just went totally blank for a moment. Come again?

RICHARD: Undine, do you understand what I'm saying? He's absconded with all of your money.

UNDINE: Absconded? That's a very British word, Richard. You make it sound as if he's not coming back. (*Undine begins to laugh. Stephie reenters.*)

RICHARD: I'm dead serious. (*Undine stops laughing.*)

UNDINE: (*To Stephie, curtly*) What?

STEPHIE: I have the caterer on line one.

UNDINE: And?

STEPHIE: Your credit card, like, didn't go through. Sorry.

UNDINE: (*Yelling*) Sweet pea, I can't deal with this right now! Make it work.

STEPHIE: But—

UNDINE: Richard, how much are we talking about?

RICHARD: A lot.

UNDINE: How much?

RICHARD: A lot.

UNDINE: What's left?

RICHARD: Um . . . (*Shuffles some papers*) $47.51.

STEPHIE: Uh, the caterer's on the phone, um, like, she really needs to speak to you. What should I tell her?

(*Richard lights a cigarette. Undine stands and paces.*)

UNDINE: (*To Richard*) Goddamnit, why didn't you do something?

RICHARD : He's your husband. I did what you asked. I didn't want to step—

UNDINE: But you're my accountant. I mean you've had dinner in my home. I bought a fucking five-thousand-dollar table to your wife's Blossom Buddy charity benefit. Good lord, I think we even got drunk once and made love in the men's room at Nell's.

(*Stephie lets out a little gasp. Undine and Richard look away from each other.*)

RICHARD: Um, I know the timing is awful but, Undine, we're going to have to consider bankruptcy. It's the only way to protect yourself. There isn't a stigma anymore.

UNDINE: No. No. No. I don't want to talk about bankruptcy. I've spent fourteen years building this company. And that implies that somehow I failed. Let me tell you something, Mr. Harvard M.B.A. My ancestors came shackled in wooden ships, crossed the Atlantic with nothing but memories! But I'll spare you my deprivation narrative. Let's just say their journey brought me here. Their pain, their struggle established me behind this fine, expensive teak desk. It is teak, a rare, strong and endangered wood. And now you want me to declare bankruptcy because that Argentine prick has run off with my money?

RICHARD: Well, yes.

UNDINE: I will do what it takes. I will beg and borrow, but damn it, I'm not giving up my business. That's what I have. This is what I am. I will meet this month's bills, and take it from there—

RICHARD: It's not that simple.

UNDINE: All right, Richard. Then make it simple.

RICHARD: You're broke, Undine. You're one month away from—

UNDINE: Goddamnit, don't say it.

(*A man dressed in a plain blue suit enters.*)

STEPHIE: Excuse me, but there's—

UNDINE: Why am I just finding this out now?

RICHARD: (*Snaps*) Because you don't return phone calls and you don't listen to your messages on your answering machine. The truth is you have not heard anything anyone else has said in years!

STEPHIE: Uh—

UNDINE: (*Annoyed beyond reason*) What? What? What?

STEPHIE: There's a man who's been waiting—

RICHARD: Um, there is one other thing.

UNDINE: More?

RICHARD: Undine.

UNDINE: (*To the man*) Who are you?

RICHARD: This is—

AGENT DUVA: Agent Duva from the Federal Bureau of Investigation.

RICHARD: He'd like, um—

AGENT DUVA: To ask you a few questions.

RICHARD: I'm sorry, but this is about a little more than a spring shopping spree.

AGENT DUVA: Undine Barnes Call-es?

UNDINE: (*Correcting*) Calles. Yes.

AGENT DUVA: (*Dramatically*) FRAUD!

UNDINE: Excuse me?

AGENT DUVA: Perhaps you're familiar with the term "identity fraud"? You may not be aware, but we've been investigating your husband's activities for quite some time. I know this isn't easy for you—it never is. We will find him, I promise.

But beg my pardon for saying, there is one thing that troubles us about this . . . matter. Mrs. Calles, we've thoroughly searched our files, but our investigation can find no record of your existence prior to fourteen years ago. Undine Barnes Call-es, you seem to have materialized from the ether. We are not quite sure who you are.

UNDINE: Give me a moment. Please. That means step outside.

RICHARD, AGENT DUVA, AND STEPHIE: Of course.

(Richard, Agent Duva, and Stephie slip out. Undine lights a cigarette. Her right hand begins to shake slightly.)

UNDINE: *(To audience)* Actually, this is where the story will begin. It is mid-thought, I know, but it is the beginning. In the next twenty seconds I will experience a pain in my chest so severe that I've given it a short, simple, ugly name—Edna. Forgive me, I *am* Undine Barnes Calles. Yes. I left home at thirteen. I was a bright child. I won a competitive scholarship through a "better chance" program to an elite boarding school in New England. I subsequently acquired a taste for things my provincial Brooklyn upbringing could no longer provide. I went to Dartmouth College, met and mingled with people in a constructive way, built a list of friends that would prove valuable years down the line. And my family . . . they tragically perished in a fire—at least that's what was reported in *Black Enterprise*. It was a misprint, but I nevertheless embraced it as the truth. Fourteen years ago, I opened my own very fierce boutique PR firm, catering to the vanity and confusion of the African American nouveau riche. And all seemed complete when I met my husband Hervé at a much too fabulous New Year's Eve party at a client's penthouse. Eleven months later we married.

(Hervé enters wearing a well-made suit and nursing a cocktail.)

Two years later he had a green card. Why? He permitted me to travel in circles I'd only read about in *Vanity Fair*.

HERVÉ: *(Thick Argentinean accent)* Corfu, Milano, Barcelona, Rio.

UNDINE: He gave me flair and caché. What can I tell you? Hervé was dashing, lifted from some black and white film retrospective. He was a romantic. But before I introduce you to Hervé, I will now introduce you to Edna.

(Undine grabs her chest, gasping for air. Her face contorts with pain and she collapses against her desk.)

Stephie! Stephie.

(Lights come up on a doctor's office)

Scene 2

Doctor Khdair flicks on the examining room light. Undine sits on the examining table. Dr. Khdair carefully inspects the chart.

UNDINE: So. Am I dying?

DR. KHDAIR: No.

UNDINE: *(Snaps)* What do you mean, no?

DR. KHDAIR: I thought you'd be relieved. I consider that good news.

UNDINE: Doctor Khdair, a heart attack at thirty-seven is never good news.

DR. KHDAIR: Well, you haven't had a heart attack.

UNDINE: Oh? *(Lighting a cigarette)* Then you won't mind if I have a little smoke.

DR. KHDAIR: Yes, actually I do. I wish you would stop.

UNDINE: Why? (*Dr. Khdair removes the cigarette from Undine's mouth.*) So I can live to a ripe old age like some demure grandmother and face dementia, incontinence and a sagging ass? No thank you. I decided years ago never to view myself as a victim. Doctor, I'm thirty-seven in the age of terror, an early death seems merciful.

DR KHDAIR: My God, that's tragic.

UNDINE: No, tragic is a crack-addicted woman breast-feeding her child. I'm far from tragic, thank you. Can I stand up?

DR. KHDAIR: No. Have you recently experienced any undue stress?

UNDINE: Like? Like if my husband left me suddenly, embezzling all of my money, leaving me on the brink of financial and social ruin?

(*Dr. Khdair laughs thinking that Undine is kidding.*)

DR KHDAIR: You're very funny. Oh no, no, no. I'm talking about pressure at the job, an upcoming deadline, an important speech.

UNDINE: Work is work.

DR KHDAIR: May I ask how much coffee you've had today?

UNDINE: Oh, I don't know, three, maybe four cups. I don't know. Is it important?

DR KHDAIR: Well, yes. I believe you've suffered a severe anxiety attack. It's not uncommon.

UNDINE: Anxiety? Me? Oh no, I don't think so.

DR KHDAIR: And why not?

UNDINE: Anxiety happens to weepy people on television news magazines.

DR KHDAIR: Well, all of your tests came back normal. But there's one other thing, Ms. Calles. I ran some routine tests and congratulations, you're pregnant. (*A moment*)

UNDINE: Pregnant? (*To audience*) I met Hervé at a dinner party three years ago. He was standing by the crudités dipping broccoli spears into the dip.

(*Hervé enters. He wears his well-made suit. He moves with the grace of a flamenco dancer. He holds a broccoli spear between his fingers.*)

He did it with such flair that I found myself hovering around the hors d'oeuvres table for most of the evening. I watched, dazzled, as he sucked the dill dip off the vegetable with his full lips.

(*He pops the broccoli spear into his mouth and wipes his lips with a napkin.*)

Up until then I'd been dating a rapper at the twilight of his career.

(*Rapper boyfriend enters.*)

He'd become addicted to pain killers and his paranoia was making the relationship tiresome. He'd drive around Bushwick, Brooklyn, in his SUV, tunes pumping, yearning for ghetto authenticity. His six-figure income had isolated him from the folks. But nevertheless, he was becoming more ghetto by the moment. Too ghetto for the ghetto.

(*Hervé gazes at Undine; their eyes lock.*)

Hervé looked over at me—I was five, I was twelve, I was seventeen, I was twenty-eight. I explored the full range of my sexual awakening in that moment. As he approached, I could not move my feet, and actually felt something I read a million times in romance novels: a tingle in my loins.

HERVÉ: (*With his thick Argentinean accent.*) Hello.

UNDINE: Hello. Did you enjoy the dip? (*To audience*) I could think of nothing cleverer to say and averted my gaze. Then I glanced at my boyfriend with the hostess and a Philly Blunt between his fingers. And I channeled all the charm in the universe.

(*Rapper boyfriend retreats into darkness.*)

(*To Hervé*) It is almost midnight and I see that you're alone.

HERVÉ: Yes, it appears so. (*A slow tango begins to play.*)

UNDINE: Have you seen the view from the balcony? It is spectacular.

HERVÉ: Yes . . . I have . . . seen . . . the view, and it is spectacular. Could I interest you in a dance? (*Hervé extends his hand. He pulls Undine in close.*)

UNDINE: (*Breathless*) What is this music?

HERVÉ: You have never heard of Andrés Segovia?

UNDINE: No. (*They begin to tango.*)

HERVÉ: *Por qué?* He is a master of classical guitar from España. The best, of course. He found a way to isolate emotion with his fingers.

(*Hervé leads Undine through a series of elaborate dance steps.*)

What he can do with a series of chords . . . is remarkable. I fell in love with his music in Madrid. I was curating an exhibition of important artists in España. I had the good fortune of dining in a café with the brilliant artist Ernesto Pérez. The music began. The guitar. A recording of Segovia's music. The place fell silent. We listened, intensely, for with a mere guitar he created an orchestra, indeed from those most basic chords he wove something so marvelously complicated that it made us ashamed of our own limitations. In that small café Segovia opened up possibility. *Querida,* I can't believe you don't know his music.

(*The music ends. Hervé kisses Undine's hand.*)

UNDINE: (*To audience*) And with a handful of words, I had fallen in love.

(*Hervé exits. Lights bring us back to Undine's office.*)

Scene 3

Allison, a well-turned-out African American woman, enters Undine's office with two glasses and a bottle of wine. She speaks with an affected continental accent and carries herself with great poise and self-importance. Actually, she struts.

ALLISON: Did you tell him? Does he know?

UNDINE: No.

(*Allison sits on Undine's teak desk.*)

ALLISON: What are you going to do?

UNDINE: Exercise my constitutional right.

ALLISON: He doesn't deserve to be a father—

UNDINE: Or a husband—

ALLISON: Bastard—

UNDINE: Oh God, why did I have to get pregnant?

ALLISON: Don't speak to me about fertility. Look at me—I'm on hormone cocktails, and it is hideous.

UNDINE: But you don't want a child, Allison.

ALLISON: Of course I don't, but everyone else is doing it and you know Daryl, he won't be left behind.

(*Allison unfolds the* Daily News *and holds it out to Undine.*)

Here. I brought you the *Daily News.* Page four. I thought you might—

UNDINE: I have it—

ALLISON: Did you see the photo that they used?

UNDINE: No kidding.

ALLISON: Terrible. You're not that heavy, darling.

UNDINE: Fraud! Can you believe that Argentine testicle was breaking the law on my nickel?

ALLISON: Don't talk to me about it. I've been there with Daryl and the whole broker-age house scandal. Page two, three days running. I don't want to relive those years. I had to scratch and claw my way back onto party lists and even now around Christmas the mailbox isn't nearly as full. There is nothing less forgiving than bourgie Negroes.

UNDINE: Who are you telling? My phone has stopped ringing—I even called the phone company to see whether it had been disconnected, that's how silent it's been. I've become some sort of social pariah—people act as if the mere presence of my voice on an answering service is enough to sully their reputation. I've called everyone: Diane Madison, Ken Brooks, Sylvia Foster-McKay.

ALLISON: Sylvia?

(*Movers enter. Throughout the rest of the scene they slowly disassemble Undine's office.*)

UNDINE: Yes. Most people never got back to me, and those that did seemed frightened by my predicament. Jesus Christ, you're the only friend who's bothered to visit.

ALLISON: (*Surprised*) Is that so?

UNDINE: No one seems troubled by the actual charges against me. No, the crime isn't being a criminal, it's being broke. It's apparently against the law to be a poor black woman in New York City.

ALLISON: (*Shocked*) You're broke, darling? You didn't tell me that. (*Truly disturbed by this revelation*)

UNDINE: Yes. (*Whispers*) They auctioned off my furniture; it was like a feeding frenzy, people I knew bidding on my possessions, waving little flags and purchasing bits and pieces of my life for a bargain.

ALLISON: Vultures.

UNDINE: At some point I thought they were actually going to put me up on the block and sell *me* to the highest bidder. And in a flash I thought, Thank God I got my teeth done last year. "Look at them teeth, she got a fine set of teeth y'all." How naïve, foolish of me, to assume that I was worthy of some comfort and good fortune, a better chance. They give you a taste, "How ya like it?" then promptly take it away. "Oh I'm sorry, we've reached our quota of Negroes in the privileged class, unfortunately we're bumping you down to working class." Working. I'm not even working. I think I'm officially part of the underclass. Penniless. I've returned to my original Negro state.

ALLISON: Enough! This talk is unsettling me. I need a glass of wine! (*Pours them each a glass of wine*)

UNDINE: I'm sorry, Allison. I didn't mean to burden you with all of this. I'm really glad you came. (*Taking in her empty office*) This is it, a lifetime of hard work. And here I am on the verge of becoming a statistic. I don't want to raise a child by myself. Not like this. Fuck him! I took vows. Two years, ten months and twelve days.

ALLISON: You could always marry that client of yours, the rapper, what's his name? Mo'Dough.

UNDINE: Yeah, and be a gangster bitch, a chicken head, no thank you. The money wouldn't last, and really, is there anything more pathetic than an aging broke b-boy who ain't got no rap left?

ALLISON: Then what you are you going to do?

UNDINE: I don't know! Don't ask me. Maybe I'll go to church or give alms. I'll climb a mountain or tend to some limbless African children in the middle of a malaria zone. (*They share a laugh at the notion.*) And by the way, when did you acquire that fabulous walk?

ALLISON: Do you like it?

UNDINE: Yes. I love it.

ALLISON: Good. I've been trying it out. I'm in my Eartha Kitt phase. I'm making bold social choices. You don't think it's too much?

UNDINE: Of course it is. But you do your thing, girl. (*To audience*) Allison, known in Harlem as Tameka Jo Greene, aspired to the Black bourgeoisie after a family trip to New Rochelle. She managed to transcend her modest childhood in the Langston Hughes public houses. Yes, a member of a Hundred Black Women, owns a house on Martha's Vineyard, an apartment on the Upper East Side (the low seventies). Then her husband appeared naked in a gay porn magazine, and the youthful indiscretion stripped her of her social status. But I admire her tenacity. It is an unrelenting struggle to regain social favor. And God bless her, she's on hormones and on the verge of a re-emergence.

ALLISON: I'm your best friend. Whatever you need, I'm here.

UNDINE: I have to move out of my apartment. May I stay with—

ALLISON: (*Dropping all affect*) Oh no Girl, we'd love to have you, but you know, we're in the process of renovating. (*Restoring the affect*) It's absolutely crazy. Listen, when we finish the new place on the Vineyard. You're welcome.

UNDINE: Thank you, but I've been told I can't leave New York, at least not until the investigation is complete. And Allison, I'm clinging to my last few dollars—
ALLISON: My goodness, look at the time.
UNDINE: You have to leave so soon?
ALLISON: I'm having lunch with . . . Sylvia.
UNDINE: Sylvia?
ALLISON: Yes, but we'll have dinner soon.
UNDINE: Soon.
ALLISON: Promise.
UNDINE: Promise.

(*Allison heads for the door. She stops herself. Dropping the affect.*)

ALLISON: Undine, you understand.

(*Allison exits. A Yoruba priest, dressed in white, enters carrying a candle and a Nigerian divination board. He speaks with a rich Nigerian accent.*)

YORUBA PRIEST: The spirits are speaking. The door to all roads is open.
UNDINE: (*To audience*) Richard, my accountant, recommended I see a Yoruba priest. It was his parting advice on coping with my predicament. They were roommates at Harvard Business School. So I thought, why not?

(*The Yoruba priest does a short chant and throws out a handful of cowrie shells on a divination board.*)

YORUBA PRIEST: It seems you've angered Elegba, the keeper of the gate. He opens the doors to the spiritual world. He's one of the trickiest and most cunning *orishas*.
UNDINE: Okay, so what does that mean?
YORUBA PRIEST: He's quite furious from what I see here.
UNDINE: Why on earth is Elegba angry at me? What have I ever done to the African spirits?

(*The Yoruba priest throws out another handful of cowrie shells on the divination board.*)

YORUBA PRIEST: (*Surprised and concerned*) Oh?
UNDINE: What? What do you see?
YORUBA PRIEST: It's what I thought. You have a bit of work to do in order to placate Elegba.
UNDINE: Work? Like what?
YORUBA PRIEST: He says it's been a long time since you've been home. And as such you must give him a thousand dollars and a bottle of Mount Gay premium rum.
UNDINE: What? You gotta be kidding. That's—(*Examines the cowries*)
YORUBA PRIEST: Oh no. He's one of the most unpredictable and demanding orishas. It's a symbolic offering, an appeasement. But—
UNDINE: Will he accept a heartfelt apology? I mean, really, what is Elegba going to do with a thousand dollars?
YORUBA PRIEST: I don't ask, I interpret. But I've experienced his wrath and believe me, if I were you, I'd pay the spirit.
UNDINE: Will he take a check?

(*The Yoruba priest throws out the cowrie shells, reads the configuration.*)

YORUBA PRIEST: No. Cash only. Kneel and repeat after me. Elegba, open this door—

(*Undine kneels next to the Yoruba priest. He passes Undine a cigar.*)

UNDINE: (*To audience*) I am taking no chances. *Ashé.* I lay my last thousand dollars at the altar of an angry African spirit, light a candle, smoke a Macanudo and on the advice of a spirit, I reluctantly return to my last known address in Brooklyn.

(*Lights cross-fade to a dining room.*)

Scene 4

The Walt Whitman projects. Undine's family. Mother, Father and Grandma are straight-forward no-nonsense people. Her brother, Flow, is a hipster with a tatty Afro and goatee. He has the habit of speaking a bit too loudly. They all wear security guard uniforms, except Grandma, who wears a brightly colored Conway housecoat. Grandma, regrettably, is confined to a wheelchair. The family sits around the kitchen table without speaking. Father places the Daily News *on the table and takes a long swig from a large can of malt liquor.*

UNDINE: So, can I stay here until I get back on my feet?

MOTHER: Let me get this straight—you want to stay here? Here?

UNDINE: Yes.

(*Mother looks to the others; they all look back at Undine.*)

MOTHER: But I thought you didn't do public housing.

UNDINE: Did I say that? I don't recall.

MOTHER: Well, the elevator don't work, there ain't been hot water since May and some fool's been flashing his ass at the ladies in the stairwell, but I suppose we got the room.

UNDINE: (*Forced*) Wonderful.

(*Uncomfortable silence*)

It's all right for us to speak.

(*A moment. Silence*)

FLOW: So.

UNDINE: Yes?

FLOW: You bugged out.

MOTHER: Shhh. Your sister's come home for a little rest and relaxation.

FLOW: What the fuck? Club Med was overbooked?

MOTHER: Shhh. Shhh.

FLOW: You ain't been here for years, and you just decided to stop in for a little R and R?—forgive my skepticism and tone of disbelief. I'm going to laugh real hard and long for a moment. (*Bursts into laughter*)

UNDINE: At least I left, Flow. Are you still working on the epic poem about Brer Rabbit?

FLOW: (*Suddenly serious, without a breath*) It is the exploration of the African American's journey. I'm exploring the role of the trickster in American mythology. I am using Brer Rabbit, classic trickster, as a means to express the dilemma faced by cultural stereotyping and the role it plays in the oppression on one hand and the liberation of the neo-Afric (to coin a phrase) individual, on the other. We at once reject and embrace—

UNDINE: (*To audience*) Flow was never the same after his tour of Desert Storm. I know it's a cliché, but something did happen to him in the desert. Military school, a year at West Point, the Green Berets and finally a security guard at Walgreen's. He couldn't ever reconcile his love of the uniform with his quest for personal freedom. Hence the poem.

FLOW: It is this very conundrum that intrigues and confounds. We love, but we despise him. We admire, yet rebuke. We embrace, yet we push away. This glorious duality enlivens and imprisons him. Because he ain't only hunting for "a way out of no way," as it's been said. And so you know, the poem is not about Brer Rabbit, he is merely a means to convey a truth—

FATHER: (*Urging Flow on*) Speak!

(*Grandma nods off at the dinner table. Mother loses herself in a book of word search puzzles.*)

FLOW: It is open-ended. A work in progress. A continuous journey. Oh shit, what time is it? They just got in the new Epilady and all the little motherfucking thieves'll be in tonight. I gotta roll in ten. (*Puts on his security utility belt*)

MOTHER: So, how long are you going to be with us? (*Looks up from her word search*)

UNDINE: Not long.

MOTHER: Well, I hope you don't mind sharing the bed with Grandma. I'll turn the mattress before you go to sleep.

UNDINE: That's okay, I'll manage.

FATHER: Shiiiiit.

UNDINE: Excuse me?

FATHER: You know Velvet Whitehead dead.

MOTHER: What?

UNDINE: Who's Velvet Whitehead?

FATHER: Snookie's cousin's brother's father. You know Velvet solved that mathematical problem yesterday. That equation they be talking about in the big paper. That problem all them scientists—

UNDINE: Mathematicians—

FATHER: Been 'rassling with.

UNDINE: Yeah, right.

FATHER: Fifty-thousand-dollar award for solving it.

FLOW: What?

MOTHER: Velvet Whitehead?

FATHER: Yesterday. We was sitting up in Cellar's Restaurant and he said, "Let me see that shit." Yes, he did. It took the brother all of ten minutes; he wrote the solution out on a napkin.

FLOW: Smart brother. Did two years at Stony Brook.

FATHER: Read the *New York Times* every mutherfucking day, subscribed to *The Economist*. *The Economist*—that's a magazine from England.

UNDINE: Yes, I'm familiar with England, I've actually (*Affecting a British accent*) been.

FATHER: You been to England?

FLOW: But you (*Affecting a British accent*) ain't been home.

FATHER: But our Velvet was an around-the-way brother. Real. You know, could talk some talk like he was a theoretician, and a minute later be bullshitting with some crazy-ass fool on the corner.

MOTHER: I bet Gloria is all torn up.

FATHER: Velvet saw the equation on the page, little printed x's and numbers—and bam—the solution revealed itself. It was a wonder to watch the brother work. His brain was like Coltrane on the sax, you know. (*Scats.*) 1, 2, 3, 7, 9, 6, 13. (*Scats like numbers are tumbling out of his mouth.*)

    He kept decades' worth of shit in his head—spreadsheets, numbers, birthdays, deaths—a statistical oasis. Yeah. He wrote out the solution like it was a phone number, drank down his beer, sucked the last bit of meat off his spare ribs, and talked about he was going to step outside for a smoke. I picked up the napkin, and I saw it, Jack. Little numbers and letters, written in perfect Catholic-school hand. We was laughing, 'cause we had already spent his fifty thousand dollars, when we heard the gunshot. BAM! By the time we ran outside Velvet was dead. A bullet to the right side of his head. Yeah, baby, they knocked his cerebellum clear out his skull, splattered onto the parking meter with ten minutes left. And I went back inside to call the ambulance and the waitress was wiping up the table with Velvet's solution. Easy come, easy go, baby.

UNDINE: I don't want to rain on your parade, but how do you know he really solved the problem?

FATHER: 'Cause he did. (*With intensity*) He looked at it, Jack. . . . And I saw it in his gaze, it was there for him. Absolute clarity. He talked about how white folks overcomplicate things by not seeing the basic formula and rhythm of life. I tell you, the solution was there as plain as the truth. It was the truth. And I believed him. They'll have us believe that the problem can't be solved, that it ain't even within our grasp. So a nigger don't even bother to reach. But there are brothers like Velvet all over this city.

FLOW: That's right!

FATHER: I met brothers in 'Nam that should have been generals, but left with an enlisted man's pension. That's what I'm talking about. Velvet solved that problem, baby.

UNDINE: You're a trusting friend. A folded *New York Times* and some scribbles on a napkin—with such faith you'd think there'd be no more problems in the world.

FLOW: What do you know with your bootleg ideas?

UNDINE: I know a fifty-thousand-dollar problem isn't solved on a napkin. I know something isn't so because you want it to be so. I mean, I'm sorry to hear about

Velvet, I am. But I didn't come all the way home to talk about him. (*A moment*) How are *you*, Daddy?

FATHER: I is and sometimes I ain't. (*Shrugs his shoulders*)

UNDINE: (*To audience*) My family. The fire victims. Mother and Father good hard-working people. They took the police exam six times back in the seventies, before they realized the city wasn't going to let them pass. They settled into a life as security guards at Long Island University, hence the uniforms. It is a safe home.

MOTHER: (*Circling a word in her word search*) "Relief." Look at that.

UNDINE: What are you working on, Mom?

MOTHER: Word search. Just finished my third book this week.

FLOW: So where's the baby daddy? What he gots to say about all this?

UNDINE: Isn't it time for your jackass pill?

MOTHER: Will you two please? Stop it! We're happy to have you home, Sharona. You stay as long as you want. There's plenty of room.

UNDINE: Mom, it's Undine.

MOTHER: I forgot, Undine, you gonna have to be patient.

FLOW: Well, I ain't calling her Undine. If it was Akua or Nzingha, a proud African queen, I'd be down with it. But you are the only sister I know that gots to change her beautiful African name to a European brand.

UNDINE: Correct me if I'm wrong, but you weren't exactly born with the name Flow. So shut up.

(*Grandma audibly exhales, and nods out.*)

What's wrong with Grandma?

MOTHER: She's just a little tired. Sometimes she nods off, the diabetes is taking its toll.

UNDINE: (*Loudly*) Are you all right, Grandma?

MOTHER: She's fine, just let her be.

(*A moment. Undine's breathing becomes labored. Anxiety.*)

UNDINE: (*To family*) Excuse me. I'm feeling a little nauseous.

MOTHER: If you're going to the bathroom, take Grandma with you.

(*The lights crossfade; we're now in Grandma's bedroom.*)

Scene 5

Grandma, all warmth and care, sits in her wheelchair crocheting a doily or something like that. Undine rests on the arm of the chair.

GRANDMA: You look good, Sharona.

UNDINE: I don't feel so.

GRANDMA: (*Taking Undine's arm*) You got that glow. A woman with child, ain't nothing more beautiful. (*Undine recoils*) Sweet pea, I been hoping you'd come home. I think about you a lot.

UNDINE: Nobody else seems particularly happy to have me back.

GRANDMA: Don't let them fool you, you prize heifer. And sweet pea, you don't know how these folks brag on you.

UNDINE: I hope you don't mind that I'm sharing your room.

GRANDMA: Bet it ain't as beautiful as your apartment, but it got a lovely view of the next building. I've counted the number of bricks, sixty-three thousand and ten . . . What happened, Sharona?

UNDINE: It went away.

GRANDMA: Things don't just go away. They get taken away, they get driven away, they get thrown away.

UNDINE: All of the above.

GRANDMA: June seventeenth. It was an unseasonably cold day. You walked out that door in a dark green linen suit, orange silk shirt, and never walked back through, until now.

UNDINE: I had to. And c'mon, you didn't expect me to come back?

GRANDMA: A visit, yes.

UNDINE: You have been getting my Christmas cards?

GRANDMA: Your Christmas cards are always lovely. If they didn't come every year I'd think you fell off the earth.

UNDINE: I've been very busy. If you knew—

GRANDMA: A year I can forgive, but it has been nearly fourteen.

UNDINE: Fourteen? My God. Fourteen years. I really wasn't aware that that much time had passed. Honestly. Time just passed. It did.

GRANDMA: Are you ashamed of us?

UNDINE: No.

GRANDMA: But, you ain't telling the truth. Sweet pea, why'd you come home?

UNDINE: I don't know what to say other than a month ago I sat in my doctor's office and she told me I wasn't dying and I was actually disappointed. Grandma, I wanted to—

(*Grandma tenderly grasps Undine, but her hands begin to shake ever so lightly.*)

What's wrong?

GRANDMA: Bad habit.

UNDINE: Are you all right, Grandma?

GRANDMA: Yes. No. Would you hand me that bag? I need my medicine.

(*Undine lifts up a paper bag. The contents tumble out into Grandma's lap: a baggie of white powder, a box of matches, a hypodermic needle, a spoon and a tourniquet.*)

UNDINE: What is this?

GRANDMA: What it look like?

UNDINE: Is this stuff Flow's? Oh no, don't tell me he's using heroin.

GRANDMA: Why would you think that? Flow is trouble, but he is a good man.

UNDINE: This belongs to somebody.

GRANDMA: I be that somebody.

UNDINE: You?

(*Grandma's hand shakes as she rolls up her sleeve. Bruises line her arm.*)

   (*Horrified*) Grandma, how long have you been shooting heroin?

GRANDMA: Since your grandfather died, baby girl.

UNDINE: Does Mommy know?

GRANDMA: If she do, she ain't said nothing. (*A hypodermic needle falls to the floor.*)

UNDINE: I don't believe it.

GRANDMA: Pass me my works.

UNDINE: (*Picks up the needle and Grandma snatches it from her hand*) This is crazy.

GRANDMA: Change be what it will. I'd say it were crazy if it wasn't so necessary.

(*She goes through the process of preparing heroin.*)

UNDINE: You nearly beat me down when you caught me smoking herb with Omar
   Padillo.

GRANDMA: Well, some things have happened since then. I got good and old for one.
   They think I'm diabetic. Your idiot brother even gives me the injections, my
   hands shake so bad these days.

UNDINE: I'm not going to watch you do this.

GRANDMA: I wish you wouldn't. (*Tightens the tourniquet*) Sweet pea, I thought that I'd
   get to this point and be filled with so much wisdom that I'd know just how to
   control the pain that's trailed me through life. The truth would be revealed, and
   some great doorway would open and God's light would encircle and lift me out
   of the ordinariness of my life. One would think you'd be closer to God at my
   age, but I find myself curiously further away.

UNDINE: How can you say that?

GRANDMA: (*Emphatic*) I'm old. I can't do it, Sharona. I ain't happy. What do I get to
   look forward to each morning? The view of that brick building across the way
   and a perpetually gray life. For a few dollars I get to leave this drab apartment.
   Who is hurt? At your age I already had five children. I did for others so long—
   well, now it's time to do for myself.

(*Grandma turns away from Undine and injects herself with the heroin. She slips into a heroin-induced languor, a junkie nod. She appears to be defying gravity as she leans forward in her chair. Just as she seems on the verge of falling out of the chair, she miraculously recovers. Undine watches, horrified, as her mother enters carrying a cup of hot chocolate.*)

MOTHER: I thought you might want some hot chocolate.

UNDINE: Do you know that Grandma is shooting heroin?

MOTHER: You always had an active imagination. (*Props Grandma up in the chair*)

UNDINE: (*To audience*) And this concludes the section entitled "Denial and Other
   Opiates."

MOTHER : She'll be all right, it's the sugar. (*Gives Grandma a kiss and exits*)

UNDINE: Grandma, Grandma.

GRANDMA: Yes, baby. Will you do me a favor?

UNDINE: Yes, of course.

GRANDMA: I need you to go out and get me some white lace.

UNDINE: What?

GRANDMA: My legs all swollen up, barely walk. But I'm gonna need another fix soon enough.

UNDINE: No, I'm not going to do it. I'm not. I refuse. No.

GRANDMA: You want me to die? That what you want? (*Shouts*) I don't need no moralizing. I need smack and I need it now.

UNDINE: I don't even know where to get it.

GRANDMA: On the corner of—

UNDINE: (*To audience*) One A.M. . . . Saturday night. My entire life has been engineered to avoid this very moment.

(*Undine sheepishly approaches a Drug Dealer lingering on the corner. She looks from side to side for some invisible jury.*)

Excuse me.

DEALER: What?

UNDINE: I'd like one hundred dollars of (*Whispers*) white trace, please.

DEALER: What?

UNDINE: White taste. White lace. Fuck. Heroin!

DEALER: Do I know you?

UNDINE: No, and that's how I'd like to keep it.

DEALER: Are you a cop?

UNDINE: No. Are you a dealer?

DEALER: You sure you ain't a cop?

UNDINE: Would you like me to fill out a questionnaire? Let's cut the bullshit—I'm not buying a condo. Just give me the goddamn drugs. (*Thrusts money in his direction.*)

DEALER: Bitch, put the money down. This ain't a fucking supermarket.

UNDINE: Listen, friend, this is humiliating enough without the insults. Can I give you a little business tip? If you treat your customers with respect, they'll give you a little respect in return.

DEALER: My customers are junkies. I ain't need they respect.

UNDINE: For the record, I'm not a junkie.

DEALER: Oh, you ain't a junkie, you just copping dope for a friend.

UNDINE: Yes, as a matter of fact.

DEALER: Bitch, give me the money. And get your tired junkie ass out my face.

UNDINE: You call me bitch one more time and I just might take my business elsewhere.

DEALER: Take it elsewhere. Bitch!

UNDINE: My man, there is no need to resort to some ghetto drug dealer cliché. It's late. I'm not going to wander through this neighborhood looking for drugs, that's not my ideal Saturday evening out. So let's just wrap up this little interaction.

DEALER: Show me the dollars, and get the fuck out of here!

(*Undine slips the Dealer the money; he gives her the drugs.*)

Ho! 5-o!

(*Police sirens blare; the Dealer tosses the heroin at Undine and runs. A flashlight hits Undine, who freezes like a deer caught in headlights. The Dealer has already disappeared.*)

UNDINE: (*To audience*) When you read the newspaper tomorrow and wonder, "How does it happen?" Now you know. One evening you're at a gala celebrating the opening of an expensive new museum wing, and the next you're standing on a street corner with a hundred dollars worth of heroin and a flashlight shining in your face.

OFFICER: Arms where I can see them.

UNDINE: Officer, I know this may sound ridiculous, but this is not my heroin. (*Drops the bag of heroin*) I bought it for my grandmother.

OFFICER: State your name.

UNDINE: Undine Barnes Calles.

OFFICER: Do you have anything that's gonna stick me?

UNDINE: No.

OFFICER: Miss Calles, you have the right to remain silent. Anything—

(*A photo is snapped. Camera flashes. Undine turns to the side. Camera flashes again. Undine is forcefully led to a prison cell occupied by two other women.*)

Scene 6

Undine stands apart from the other women in the prison cell. She steals a glance at Inmate #1, a hardened woman who speaks in a harsh, biting tone.

INMATE #1: Find what you looking for?

(*Undine self-consciously averts her gaze, and does not respond.*)

You ain't hear me? Yeah, you.

UNDINE: Excuse me, are you talking to me?

INMATE #1: Who else I be talking to?

UNDINE: (*Under her breath*) I don't know. Someone else, hopefully.

INMATE #1: What did you say?

UNDINE: Nothing.

INMATE #1: Don't make me have to come over there and teach you how to crawl. What, you think you special? There ain't no real Gucci here. This the mark-down rack, bitch.

(*Undine digs in her bag and puts on a pair of dark Gucci sunglasses and turns away.*)

Don't turn your head like I owe you money. Shit, you don't know me. (*Laughs with bravado.*)

UNDINE: No.

INMATE #1: No, what?

UNDINE: No. I don't know you. And if I was looking at you, I wasn't aware of it. I'm sorry.

INMATE #1: Oh, you sorry?

UNDINE: Yes, I'm sorry.

INMATE #1: That's right, you sorry.

(*Inmate #1 gets in Undine's face.*)

UNDINE: Yes, I'm sorry. I'm sorry that I looked at you. Okay? I'm sorry that you're so angry, I'm sorry that we're stuck here in the middle of the fucking night. I'm sorry for a whole series of things that are far too complicated to explain right now, and I'M SORRY THAT I'M SORRY. (*Unhinged*) So if you don't mind, I'm going to move to the other side of this . . . *cell*, and sit quietly until they call my name. If you want to hit me, hit me; otherwise back the fuck off.

(*Prison Guard enters.*)

GUARD: Hey, hey.

(*Undine, surprised by her own bravado, bursts into tears. The sudden display of emotion catches Inmate #1 off guard, and she backs off. The Prison Guard stares down Undine.*)

What's going on in here? Settle down.

(*Inmate #2, quiet up until this point, edges toward Undine. She's wearing only one high-heel shoe.*)

INMATE #2: Don't let her run over you, she born hard. She one of them prehistoric rocks been on the street too long.

(*The Prison Guard continues to stare at Undine.*)

Hey, sis, don't show him your tears. They get their strength from our pain. You cry the first time, you cry the second time, then the shit don't hurt so much after that. Suck it up.

(*The Guard leaves. Undine collects herself.*)

What's your name, sis?

UNDINE: Undine.

INMATE #2: That's a pretty name. For a minute you looked like this stuck-up bitch who used to live in my building, but that diva wouldn't be caught dead here.

(*Inmate #2 begins to laugh; Undine manages an ironic smile.*)

UNDINE: I'm not from—

INMATE #2: Your first time 'hoing?

UNDINE: NO! No. It was a misunderstanding. I don't really belong here—

INMATE #2: Guess what? I don't belong here; she don't belong here, but we here.

UNDINE: But you don't understand—

INMATE #2: Shit, all I was doing was buying formula for my cousin Leticia's baby over on Myrtle Avenue, right? And this dude was, you know, all up in my panties with his eyes, right? On my shit like he my man. "You don't know me, brother," I told him. But gonna get all pimp on me, like I's his bitch. Big fat Jay-Z-acting muthafucka. He think he all that 'cause he drivin' a Range Rover in my neighborhood. That don't impress me—show me a pay stub, brother. Show me a college diploma. But this dude is gonna step to my face. I told him, put your hands on me and see what happen.

UNDINE: And?

INMATE #2: Why you think I'm here? I showed the muthafucker the point of my heel and the ball of my fist. (*Demonstratively*) I told him, "I ain't yo' 'ho. I work from nine to five at Metrotech, my man, don't you look at me like a 'ho, don't you talk to me like a 'ho, don't you disrespect me like a video 'ho." Now, he gonna think twice 'fore he place a hand on another woman. Believe it! People think they know your history 'cause of what you wearing. Well guess what? I introduced him to the feminist movement with the back of my muthafuckin' hand.

INMATE #1: That's right. We don't got to take that shit!

UNDINE: They put you in here for that? It doesn't seem fair.

INMATE #2: Shit ain't fair! I mean, why are you here?

UNDINE: (*To audience*) There is the question. I imagine the blurb in my college alumni magazine. "Undine sends word from Rikers Island where she's enjoying creative writing and leading a prison prayer circle." (*Absorbs the horror of the question*) Why are we here?

INMATE #2: You know what you done, you ain't gotta tell me. We do what we gots to do, right?

(*Lights shift. The voice of Judge Henderson is heard.*)

JUDGE HENDERSON: Undine Barnes Calles. Please step forward. The court of King's County, having found you guilty of the criminal possession of a controlled substance—

UNDINE: Your Honor—

JUDGE HENDERSON: —in the seventh degree, hereby sentences you to six months compulsory drug counseling.

UNDINE: But, Your Honor!—

JUDGE HENDERSON: Failure to complete the program will result in a one-year jail sentence.

UNDINE: Oh my God!

(*Blackout*)

End of Act One

Act Two

Scene 1

Lights rise on a semi-circle of a diverse collection of recovering drug addicts who look to a sympathetic counselor for guidance. Undine, sipping a cup of coffee, is seated in the midst of the semi-circle.

ADDICT #1: I miss it. I miss the taste and the smell of cocaine, that indescribable surge of confidence that fills the lungs. The numbness at the tip of my tongue, that sour metallic taste of real good blow.

(*The Addicts savor the moment with an audible "Mmm."*)

It was perfect. I mean in the middle of the day I'd excuse myself and slip out of an important faculty meeting, go to the stairwell and suck in fifteen, twenty, thirty dollars worth of crack.

(*The Addicts savor the moment with an audible "Mmm."*)

I'd return a few minutes later full of energy, ideas, inspired, and then go teach a course on early American literature and not give a goddamn. In fact, the students admired my bold, gutsy devil-may-care attitude. Why? Because I'd lecture brilliantly and passionately on books . . . I hadn't read. Indeed, the university didn't know how high and mighty I was when they promoted me chair of the English department and gave me an office with a view of Jersey. It was fantastic—I could smoke crack all day, every day in my office, seated in my leather chair, at my solid oak desk. It was near perfect, it was as close to nirvana as a junkie can achieve. But my colleagues were always on my case. "Beep, Mr. Logan wants you to attend a panel on the symbolism of the tomahawk in *The Deerslayer*. Beep, Beep, Ms. Cortini is here for her thesis defense. What should I tell her?" Those thesis writing motherfuckers drove me crazy. And I wanted to kill them. But, you know what happened. I don't have to tell any of you junkies. "Beep, Sayer wants to see you in his office. Right this minute. Beep. He's getting impatient." Fuck you! But by that time I was on a four-day binge, my corduroy blazer stank like Chinatown. And I was paraded through the hallowed halls like some pathetic cocaine poster child. But, I don't remember when I became a criminal, it happened at some point after that. The descent was classic, it's not even worthy of detail. Bla, bla, bla.

(*A moment. Guy, a gentle man wearing a security guard uniform, speaks up.*)

GUY: But you're clean, son. You're clear.

ADDICT #1: One year. One year clean and I still walk around the city wondering how people cope. How do they survive without the aid of some substance? A boost? It makes me angry—no, envious. How come some people get to lead lives filled with meaning and happiness? And I become a drug-addled junkie scheming for my next fix.

ADDICT #2: Fuck them!

ADDICT #1: Excuse me, I didn't interrupt you. Thank you. And you know what I think? I think that they will never understand the joy and comfort of that very first moment you draw the smoke into your lungs, releasing years of stress, of not giving a damn whether you live or die. They won't know what it is to crave and love something so deeply that you're willing to lie, cheat and steal to possess it. They won't know that kind of passion. I accept that I may go to hell, but I've experienced a kind of surrender, a letting go of self that years of meditation and expensive yuppie yoga classes won't yield. And I hold on to that feeling, fiendishly. That feeling empowers me, because I know the Shaolin strength that it takes to resist it, to fight it, to defeat it.

(*A chorus of agreement rises up.*)

UNDINE: (*To audience*) The perversity of this moment is that in the midst of his loath-some confession, I'm actually finding myself strangely curious to smoke crack cocaine. I have now concluded that for every addict that the system cures, two new ones are created.

COUNSELOR: Undine, you've been sitting quietly. Is there anything you want to share?

UNDINE: Other than: "The only meaningful contact I have these days is with the first sips of coffee in the morning?" No. I'll just listen today.

COUNSELOR: You've been here five weeks. I think it might be helpful to open up.

ADDICTS: Open up, open up. (*They applaud in agreement.*)

UNDINE: (*To audience*) Oh, to share my addictions. To confess to the stack of fash-ion magazines that I keep in my bathroom like some treasured porn collec-tion, which I read and reread with utter salacious delight. No, I won't share that. Instead I manufacture some elaborate tale of addiction. I've decided to use Percodan as my gateway drug. And I concoct a tale so pathetically moving that I am touched by my own invention and regret not having experienced the emotions firsthand. But the tears are genuine. I am crying. And I weep and I'm applauded by the room of addicts and it is exhilarating. A rush. And I under-stand addiction.

(*Undine breaks down in tears. She is comforted by the Addicts.*)

COUNSELOR: Remember, this room is a safe haven. Whatever is spoken within this circle remains within the circle. And that trust is sacred as long as the circle is unbroken.

UNDINE: I'm pregnant and I don't know whether I want this child.

GUY: It is a blessing to be faced with such a dilemma.

UNDINE: What?

GUY: I said it's a blessing to be faced with such a dilemma.

UNDINE: Why?

GUY: A child, a possibility, a lesson.

UNDINE: (*To audience*) He is speaking in sentence fragments and I find him curiously intriguing. (*To Guy*) And?

GUY: 'Cause.

UNDINE: Yeah?

GUY: You know.

UNDINE: What?

GUY: A baby.

UNDINE: Yes.

GUY: Is a beautiful thing. (*Smiles*) Not all of us have so perfect a reason to stay straight.

UNDINE: Oh my. You're right.

GUY: How long have you been using?

UNDINE: Long enough.

GUY: I've been clean for two years. It's my anniversary tonight and I'm trying to figure out how to celebrate. Will you have dinner with me?

UNDINE: Are you asking me out on a date?

GUY: Yes.

UNDINE: (*To audience*) Dinner with a junkie? If I were a poet I would go home and compose a poem, threading the bits of irony through the improbability, but I'm not, so I say yes. BBQ on St. Marks and Second, a place I've shunned for a decade. He is reformed, he is magnificent and he is paying the bill.

(*They sit side by side in the restaurant.*)

GUY: I considered going into corrections, but a life of policing people behind bars seemed too, you know—

UNDINE: Depressing.

GUY: Yeah. It's like all my friends, they either in jail, they on they way to jail or they the brothers watching the brothers in jail. I don't want that. It ain't part of my schedule. I'm clean, my head's like in the right place. I've been working at the Cineplex as a security guard, and I'm gonna take the firemen's exam next month.

UNDINE: A fireman, that's wonderful.

GUY: I got good upper body strength—

UNDINE: I bet you do.

GUY: And I can withstand really high temperatures, since I was eleven. It's one of those things. I'm studying in the evenings. And this time next year I'll be a fireman.

UNDINE: Really, I believe you will.

GUY: Yeah? You think so?

UNDINE: You know, I had my own business, a public relations firm. It started in a restaurant over a glass of wine. I had an expression very much like yours. I went from employee to entrepreneur between dinner and dessert. Really.

GUY: (*Laughs*) I knew that about you. I knew that when you was sitting there quietly in counseling. I was right, wasn't I? You got it going on. I'd like to see you again.

UNDINE: Why?

GUY: 'Cause I dig you.

UNDINE: You dig me? I am dug. You are seeing me on a good day. You're seeing me way out of context.

GUY: Well, I'm liking what I see.

UNDINE: Oh, so you're going to get smooth? That's okay, bring it. But be warned, I am not an easy person.

GUY: That's cool, but can I see you again?

UNDINE: No, I don't think so. I don't think it's such a good idea.

GUY: Why not?

UNDINE: I can't be with a man in uniform.

GUY: (*Seductively*) What about a brother out of uniform?

UNDINE: In case you forgot, I'm pregnant.

GUY: So? I think you're brave to make a go of this alone. I got mad respect for you, battling dope, walking the straight and narrow.

UNDINE: It isn't an act of bravery, let me clear that up right now. I didn't plan for this to happen. It is a by-product of an unholy union.

GUY: And a blessing, no doubt.

UNDINE: You don't let up. You are going to give this a positive spin if it kills you.

GUY: I guess I'm that kinda brother. And I dig that you didn't laugh when I told you about, you know, what I want to do.

(*Undine stands up.*)

UNDINE: (*To audience*) His sincerity is sickening. He has none of Hervé's charm, which makes him all the more charming. Flash forward: a fireman, with a pension and a tacky three-bedroom in Syosset, Long Island. Flashback: Hervé.

(*Hervé, exquisitely attired, appears.*)

HERVÉ: Corfu, Milano, Barcelona, Rio.

UNDINE: (*To audience*) I am—

(*Guy and Hervé retreat into the darkness. Two women in their mid-thirties appear.*)

Scene 2

The courtyard of the Walt Whitman projects. Rosa pushes a stroller. She wears a Baby Björn baby carrier, which holds an infant. Devora is ghetto fabulous. Undine puts on her sunglasses, trying to avoid contact. She attempts to flee, but:

ROSA: (*Shouts*) SHARONA WATKINS, Sharona!

DEVORA: That can't—

ROSA: Yes, it is.

DEVORA: Oh no, no. (*Undine can't hide.*)

ROSA: Oh hell, somebody told me it was you. But I was, like, what?

UNDINE: Hey.

DEVORA: Hey?

ROSA: You don't remember us, do you?

UNDINE: I'm sorry.

ROSA: (*Sings*) Down, down baby . . .

ROSA AND DEVORA:

> Down by the roller coaster,
> Sweet, sweet baby,
> I'll never let you go.
> Shimmy shimmy coco pop, shimmy, shimmy pop,
> Kissed my boyfriend,

(*Undine, remembering, joins in.*)

ROSA, DEVORA AND UNDINE (*Sing*):

> Naughty, naughty
> Won't do the dishes.
> Lazy, Lazy,
> Stole a piece of candy.
> Greedy, greedy,
> Jumped off a building.
> Crazy, crazy . . .

(*The women laugh.*)

UNDINE: The Double Dutch twins.

DEVORA: Rosa Ojeda and Devora Williams.

UNDINE: Oh my God. How are you both?

ROSA: I got a little big, but that's what four children and a husband on disability will do.

DEVORA: (*To her sister*) Don't lie. (*To Undine*) She's big because—

ROSA: (*To her sister*) You don't want me to talk about you.

DEVORA: So, Mama. What's up?

UNDINE: I'm . . . I'm visiting with my parents, while—

DEVORA: For real? How's that fine brother of yours?

UNDINE: He's all right.

DEVORA: Tell him Devora from 2G said hello. He'll know what you're talking about. Hey!

UNDINE: (*To audience*) Rosa and Devora were the reigning Double Dutch champions in junior high school, but they were eventually beaten by six Japanese girls from Kyoto at Madison Square Garden. It was a crushing blow.

ROSA: I called out to you the other day, but you ain't see me.

UNDINE: I'm sorry. I'm like, you know, dealing with a lot. What are you up to?

ROSA: Not much. You know, the same old, same old. Finally living in building 10. Been on the list for seven years. I got me a dope view of Manhattan.

UNDINE: Building 10, no kidding. Congratulations. And Devora? Are you still living in 4?

DEVORA: Oh no. I just bought a brownstone in Fort Greene. I'm a senior financial planner at JP Morgan. I come around once in a while. You know, to see my girl Rosa. And you?

(*A moment*)

UNDINE: . . . I'm, um, pregnant and trying—

DEVORA: I bet it's tough, Sharona—

UNDINE: Actually, my name is—

ROSA: That's right, I hear you changed your name to Queen?

UNDINE: No, Undine.

DEVORA: Undine, funny, like that public relations exec, Undine Barnes Calles?

UNDINE: I—

(*Gregory, a stylish African American man, dressed for success, enters.*)

DEVORA: Pity what happened to her. I hate to see a sister get hurt. I hear she was quite a remarkable diva, but got a little lost. You probably don't even know who I'm talking about.

GREGORY: Honey!

DEVORA: Oh, there's my husband, Gregory. Anyway, it was great seeing you.

(*Gregory waves to the women. Devora starts to leave, but turns back.*)

Listen, I'm starting a financial planning program for underprivileged women. Rosa has joined us. I'd love for you to stop by. Here's my card.

UNDINE: (*To audience*) And as she thrusts the tri-color card into my hand, it gives me a slight paper cut, just enough to draw blood.

DEVORA: Call me.

UNDINE: (*To audience*) And she means it.

(*Devora and Gregory leave.*)

ROSA: She's doing it! And folks like us are just left to sit back and marvel.

UNDINE: But I—

ROSA: I know. Me too. So, when are you due, mama?

UNDINE: Oh, no, you don't understand, I'm not havin this baby. No. I just didn't realize it was so hard to find a reasonably priced clinic in this city, to you know—

ROSA: Girl, I got two words for you: social services. It's the Amen at the end of my day.

(*Lights rise on a Department of Social Services office. A line of exhausted people has formed.*)

UNDINE: (*To audience*) Social services. The poor man's penance. The most dreaded part of the system.

Scene 3

Department of Social Services. An impatient Caseworker with long air-brushed nails cradles a phone in her hand while doing her best to ignore the ever-growing group of people waiting in the endless line. Undine approaches the Caseworker and taps on her desk. An illegible sign hangs behind her head reading: Please ill out he orm.

CASEWORKER: You don't know how to fill out a form?

UNDINE: I didn't know there was even a form to be filled out.

CASEWORKER: What do the sign say?

UNDINE: Please ill out he orm.

CASEWORKER: So what do that tell you?

UNDINE: Nothing intelligible.

CASEWORKER: Fill this out and come back.

UNDINE: Do I have to wait in line, again?

CASEWORKER: Yeah. Next.

UNDINE: But I have already been waiting in line for two hours.

CASEWORKER: Yeah, and? I can't do nothing for you until the form's filled out.

UNDINE: Maybe it might be helpful if you let people know that they have to fill out the form before they get to you.

CASEWORKER: Maybe. Next.

UNDINE: Wait. Do I fill out both sides or just the front?

CASEWORKER: Listen, you can rap to me all day, but I ain't like all y'all. I got work to do. NEXT.

UNDINE: (*To audience*) So I meticulously fill out the form. Two hideous hours later.

(*The people move in a circular line, until they get back to Undine's turn again. Undine walks up to the Caseworker, who is on the phone.*)

There you go. I was wondering how quickly medical benefits will kick in—you see, I'm in a time-sensitive situation—

CASEWORKER: Well this ain't the right form.

UNDINE: This is the form you gave me.

CASEWORKER: You sure I gave it to you?

UNDINE: Yes.

CASEWORKER: Well, I can't do nothing for you unless you fill out the right form. Next.

UNDINE: Wait just one moment.

PERSON IN LINE: Come on!

UNDINE: What form do I need?

CASEWORKER: 7001.

UNDINE: Which form is this?

CASEWORKER: 7002.

UNDINE: Do you have form 7001?

CASEWORKER: (*Into the phone*) Hold on, girl.

(*Exasperated, she slams down the telephone, shouts.*)

Lance, you got any more of form 7001 back there?

LANCE: (*From offstage*) Yes!

CASEWORKER: Bring 'em!

UNDINE: This is crazy. I've been standing in this heat and I—

(*Lance enters. He hands the Caseworker a pile of forms.*)

CASEWORKER: You're gonna fill this out and get back in line when you're done.

(*Starts to hand Undine the form*)

UNDINE: (*Interrupting*): Excuse me? I'm not waiting another two hours in that line.

CASEWORKER: Then come back first thing tomorrow morning. Next.

WOMAN IN LINE: (*To Undine*) Don't get too upset. They always like this. I filled out four forms and spent three days here last month. And still ain't got no further than the front desk. In actuality, I don't think there is anything beyond this point. I think that they like to give you the illusion that they can help—keep us busy so we forget that they ain't doing nothing for us.

UNDINE: But don't you want to see what's in the next room?

WOMAN IN LINE: See what's in the next room? (*She and the other people in line laugh ironically.*) Good luck . . . Send word if you get to the promised land.

UNDINE: (*To Caseworker*) I demand to speak to your supervisor.

CASEWORKER: I am the supervisor. What you got to say?

(*A moment*)

UNDINE: Oh? You're the supervisor? Can I say, this whole thing is not being handled professionally. You're rude, and you treat people like cattle. You don't know what circumstances brought each of us here. We've waited all day to get to this point, we just want to sit in a room and talk to somebody, anybody. I mean, isn't there anyone in all this miserable bureaucracy who isn't merely concerned with what time to take lunch? We need help. We're entitled to this benefit. We've all humbled ourselves just by being here and you're behaving like some centurion guarding the gates to Rome. I mean, who gave you the right to condescend.

CASEWORKER: And you know what else? We just ran out of the form you need.

UNDINE: He just handed you a pile of forms.

CASEWORKER: So? You think you're entitled to some special treatment. Guess what? I ain't giving you shit. Step out of line until you can stand correct. Next!

WOMAN IN LINE: (*To Undine*) Oh no, baby, I wouldn't make her angry if I were you.

UNDINE: (*Unhinged*) GIVE ME THE MUTHAFUCKING FORM!

CASEWORKER: Miss, I'll have you medically removed from the building.

UNDINE: I'm not leaving without the form. (*Chanting*) Give us the form. We want the form.

(*Urges the others on, rallying the troops*)

Come on, people! Give us the form! Give us the form!

CROWD: (*Chanting*) We want the form! We want the form! We want the form!

UNDINE: We can come back tomorrow and start this whole damn process again. But who wins?

CROWD: Yeah!

CASEWORKER: NEXT!

UNDINE: (*To audience*) And I am medically removed from the building, which means the paramedics arrive, administer a mild sedative, strap me to a gurney and rush me to the nearest psychiatric facility. I spend a half hour speaking to a gentle intern who incidentally went to college with my assistant, Stephie, and I am subsequently released with a prescription for a powerful antipsychotic . . . which I can't use because I'm pregnant. And after all of that I still must go back to the office the next morning to fill out form 7001. And after weeks of agony and bureaucratic hell, I was finally able to see a doctor.

(*Lights rise on a waiting room in a public medical clinic.*)

Scene 4

We're in a waiting room. A very Young Pregnant Woman sits down next to Undine. The woman noisily sips on a can of grape soda. Undine tries hard to ignore her. Finally:

YOUNG PREGNANT WOMAN: Twins. A boy and girl. The jackpot first time around. What about you?

UNDINE: First.

YOUNG PREGNANT WOMAN: Your first? Really? But you're so old.

UNDINE: But you're so young. (*A moment. To audience*) Surely, I don't look that old, do I? (*To the woman*) I'm just thirty-seven.

YOUNG PREGNANT WOMAN: Wow. You're my mother's age.

UNDINE: Your mother is thirty-seven? (*To audience*) I say nothing, though I want to let her know that I don't belong here, that my life experience is rich and textured and not represented well in this low, coarse clinic lighting. As such, I show her a touch of condescension, perhaps even pity.

(*Displays a touch of condescension*)

(*To audience*) But I'm panicking. (*The Young Pregnant Woman looks at Undine.*) And I look at her and I realize, she's looking back at me with a touch of condescension. Pity, even. And we both look away. (*They both look away.*)

YOUNG PREGNANT WOMAN: My boyfriend is in Iraq.

UNDINE: (*To audience.*) I wish she hadn't told me. (*Opens a magazine*)

YOUNG PREGNANT WOMAN: I started—

UNDINE: (*To audience*) She wants to talk. I pretend not to hear her.

YOUNG PREGNANT WOMAN: We were planning to move out of the—

UNDINE: (*To herself*) Please, doctor, call me in. Call me in before Edna returns. I'm having trouble breathing.

YOUNG PREGNANT WOMAN: I hadn't planned on getting—

UNDINE: (*To herself*) Stop! I can't breathe.

YOUNG PREGNANT WOMAN: I'm scared.

(*A moment. Undine reaches out and, uncharacteristically, takes the YOUNG PREGNANT WOMAN'S hand.*)

UNDINE: I'm scared too.

(*Undine's breathing becomes labored. Anxiety. The lights shift and we're in the Doctor's office.*)

DOCTOR: Ms. Calles.

(*Undine stands.*)

UNDINE: Yes.

DOCTOR: (*Cold and indifferent*) Judging from the size of the fetus, I'd predict that you're a little further along than you say.

UNDINE: How much further?

DOCTOR: You're six and a half months.

UNDINE: No, no. I can't possibly be that far along.

DOCTOR: That's a conservative estimate.

(*The Doctor speaks slowly, adopting a patronizing, pedagogic tone.*)

I can't impress upon new mothers enough the importance of prenatal care to the health of the fetus. Do you understand what I'm saying?

UNDINE: Doctor, English is my first language, you don't have to speak to me like an idiot. Get to the point.

DOCTOR: Ms. Calles, you really should have come in sooner.

UNDINE: Listen, I tried to make an appointment with my regular doctor, but she wouldn't see me without health insurance. I attempted to make an appointment with another gynecologist but I needed a referral from the local clinic. I went to the local clinic but I didn't have the appropriate paperwork. Apparently when I became poor I was no longer worthy of good health care. Doctor, all I want is an—

DOCTOR: If you give this form to the nurse she'll set up your next ultrasound appointment.

UNDINE: No, no, no. You don't understand. I'm not having this baby. No, no, no. I'm not a mother-to-be. Okay. I am not a parent. What can be done?

DOCTOR: At this stage, nothing. You're too far along.

UNDINE: Yeah, but what can be done?

DOCTOR: Eat right and take good care of yourself. Here's a prescription for prenatal vitamins. I'll see you in a month.

(*The doctor passes Undine the prescription.*)

Oh, Ms. Calles, would you like to hear the baby's heartbeat before you leave?

UNDINE: (*Shocked*) What?

DOCTOR: Many women like—

UNDINE: No . . . yes. I'm not sure. (*A moment*) Doctor.

DOCTOR: Yes?

UNDINE: Do you think the baby knows what I'm feeling?

DOCTOR: I don't know. But I like to think so.

(*A moment. The Doctor exits. Undine sits, frozen. She looks at the prescription.*)

UNDINE: (*Contemplating, to audience*) Optimox prenatal tabs? I go to Duane Reade on the Upper West Side of Manhattan. It's like a vacation wandering the well-stocked aisles of the pharmacy tended by employees in pristine uniforms.

(*Lights shift, we're in Duane Reade. Pleasant music plays in the background.*)

Scene 5

Duane Reade. A young woman, dressed in a uniform, busies herself stocking items on a shelf.

UNDINE: Miss. I'm looking for calcium tablets and vitamins.

(*Stephie, startled, turns around in her pharmacy uniform.*)

Stephie?

STEPHIE: Undine.

(*They gawk at each other.*)

UNDINE: What are—

STEPHIE: This is only temporary. Actually I'm interviewing like crazy. I've come really close to several things. God, look at you.

UNDINE: Look at you.

STEPHIE: I tried to call you last month for a recommendation, but—

UNDINE: I've moved to Brooklyn.

STEPHIE: Great.

UNDINE: It's great.

STEPHIE: Great.

UNDINE: Great. (*A moment*)

STEPHIE: This is about paying a few bills. I'm told it's like important to have all kinds of experiences.

UNDINE: True.

STEPHIE: Man. How far along are you?

UNDINE: Seven months.

STEPHIE: You with a baby.

(*Stephie gives off a little laugh.*)

UNDINE: Why is that funny to you?

STEPHIE: I don't know. I'm sorry, but you always seemed like—

UNDINE: Like what?

STEPHIE: I don't know. Like. (*A moment*) Never mind.

UNDINE: The calcium pills are in which aisle?

STEPHIE: Seven, no, no. Four. I'm trying not to get used to this. I don't really want to know where things are, because once you do, you're sorta committed. Right? This is just temporary.

LOUDSPEAKER: Stephie, you're needed in aisle two, for stacking.

STEPHIE: Oh God, they're calling me. I'm like the stock guru. If I really wanted to, I could be Employee of the Month, every month. But there's nothing worse than bad blood between minimum wage workers. I'm not trying to go there.

LOUDSPEAKER: Stephie, you're needed in aisle two. Pronto!

STEPHIE: Coming! Like nothing changes. I gotta run.

UNDINE: Go.

(*Stephie turns to leave.*)

STEPHIE: Hey Undine. Undine! Are you happy?

(*Undine turns away.*)

UNDINE: (*To audience*) I want to turn back, but I don't. I do not answer. I slip the calcium tablets into my pocket, unpaid, and I keep walking. I walk all the way home fighting a tinge of envy, because Stephie, my former assistant, might actually be named Employee of the Month at the pharmacy.

(*Crossfade to the Walt Whitman projects*)

Scene 6

Kitchen. The table has chairs propped on top. Flow and Mother, as usual, are dressed in their security guard uniforms. Grandma is crocheting a doily. Mother, with a word search puzzle book tucked in her back pocket, sweeps the floor. Undine, ankles swollen, navigates the kitchen table, struggling to open a childproof bottle of pills.

FLOW: And I took the shoplifter to back of the store and gave him my Nelson Mandela speech. I said, "The African brother gave up twenty-eight years of freedom
for his ideals, for his principles, for the struggle to liberate Black Africans from
the grip-lock of apartheid." I said, "Little brother thief, liberating a box of lubri-
cated super-strong Trojans ain't a reason to go to jail. Don't let the system fuck
you because you're horny. If you're going to give up your damn freedom, make
sure it's for a just cause." And, Ma, I saw a little something in his eyes, a spark,
a touch of recognition, and I quickly unfastened his handcuffs. And then this
little fool is gonna ask, "Who Nelson Mandela?" I had to slap homeboy out of
his chair and call 911. Shit, there ain't no greater crime than abandoning your
history.

MOTHER: That's right.

(*Undine is breathing heavily, struggling with the pills.*)

UNDINE: Hello, could someone give me a hand?

MOTHER: Flow!

(*Flow helps Undine open the pills.*)

FLOW: Damn girl, you getting big.

UNDINE: What-ever.

FLOW: What's your problem?

UNDINE: (*Snapping*) I'm having a fucking baby!

(*Undine slaps the bottle of pills on the table.*)

FLOW: No shit, when'd you realize that? Sharona!

UNDINE: Ty-rell!

FLOW: Here's a little something for the baby daddy.

(*Flow does a series of elaborate tricks with his night stick. Undine grabs the club and tosses it on
the table.*)

MOTHER: You two are acting like teenagers. Stop it—Oh Undine, somebody called
for you while you were at the doctor's office.

UNDINE: Who?

FLOW: Did you tell them there ain't no Undine living here?

UNDINE: That's getting old. Okay?

FLOW: What's the matter with you?

UNDINE: My life is not exactly going as I planned. "Aw'right?" Mom, did the phone
call sound important?

MOTHER: I don't know. What does important sound like?

UNDINE: (*To audience*) A pardon. Absolution. My life back. Was it Hervé calling from
Barbados to say "Join me"? Would I? Oh, Would I.

MOTHER: I'm sure they'll call back.

(*Father, seemingly tired, enters wearing security uniform.*)

FLOW: Hey there. What's the word, Pop?

MOTHER: Hope you didn't forget the lotto tickets . . . Don't tell me you forgot.

FATHER: I forgot? (*Excited*) I ain't forget.

(*Father passes out the lotto tickets to the family. He gives Mother a kiss on the head.*)

The Lotto line ran around the block. Stood twenty-five minutes. Junie got heself one hundred tickets. He thinks this time he gonna be lucky 'cause Clarice momma had a dream about fish. (*They all gasp with excitement.*) But he doesn't want to share his luck with anybody, jack.

UNDINE: Excuse me, I don't mean to interrupt this precious moment, but Mom, was it a man that called?

MOTHER: Did she really dream about fish?

FLOW: When that woman dream fish, money fall out the sky?

UNDINE: Fish?

FLOW: Don't you know, girl?

GRANDMA: (*Suddenly*) It means good fortune coming your way, sweet pea.

MOTHER: (*To Undine, remembering*) Oh, that's right. It was a man that called, Grandma said—

UNDINE: You let him speak to Grandma?

MOTHER: I had a pot of gumbo about to burn on the stove.

FATHER: You made your gumbo?

UNDINE: (*Exasperated*) Grandma, was it my accountant? Was it . . . Hervé?

GRANDMA: Who's Hervé?

UNDINE: He's my husband. What did the man say? It's very important! (*Shouts*) I need to know!

FLOW : Don't you yell at her! She's an old woman! She's got diabetes, damn it.

UNDINE: Flow, she doesn't have diabetes. For God's sake, she's a junkie—a junkie! I've been taking her to the methadone clinic for a month. (*It's a ridiculous notion to all but Undine.*) Hello! People! (*Shouts*) Is anybody home?

MOTHER: Why are you so upset? It's just a phone call. If it's important the person will call back.

UNDINE: It isn't the phone call! It's . . . It's a phantom poem that won't ever be completed, it's thousands of dollars of lotto tickets that should have been invested in the stock market, it's a thrown-away solution and, Mom, when are you going to stop searching for words? It's the fact that Grandma is a—

GRANDMA: Oh lawd, she's carrying low. It makes some people crazy, in the third trimester.

UNDINE: Aren't you listening to what I'm saying? Are you blind and deaf? Or are we just going to sit around all day and talk about fish.

(*A moment. Flow suddenly jumps up.*)

FLOW: (*Furious passion*)

> This ain't the beginning you wuz expectin'
> It ain't a poem, but a reckonin'
> Be it sacred or profane,
> Or a divine word game.
> It all about a rabbit,

Or it ain't.

It ain't a holler or a song.
It ain't no geechie folk yawn.
It ain't a road that been tread,
With a stained rag around the head.
It all about a rabbit,
Or ain't.

It ain't a myth that so old,
That it been whole-saled and re-sold.
It ain't a bible lovers' tale
Or a preacher's parting wail.

Wait. Wait. Okay. Here we go.
It all about a rabbit,
Or it ain't.

'Cuz.

In that ghetto paradox,
When we rabbit and we fox.
And we basking in the blight
Though we really wanna fight.

It 'bout who we be today
And in our fabulating way
'Bout saying that we be
Without a-pology.
It's a circle that been run
That ain't no one ever won.
It that silly rabbit grin.
'Bout running from your skin,
'Cuz
It a . . . It a . . .

MOTHER: (*Coaxing Flow*) C'mon. C'mon.

FLOW: It a . . . It a . . . It a—

(*Flow stops mid-sentence as abruptly as he began, struggling to find the next verse in the poem. The family is as anxious to find it as he is.*)

FATHER: Don't stop, don't stop—

FLOW: It a . . .

MOTHER: C'mon.

FLOW: (*Frustrated*) It ain't finished. It ain't done till it's done. A fabulation takes time. It doesn't just happen.

UNDINE: A fabulation? Yeah, but how long, Flow?

FLOW: I don't know, fourteen years and nine months. What do you care? We died in a fire.

(*A moment*)

UNDINE: (*To audience*) It was an unforeseen tragedy, really. A misprint.

FLOW: What, you didn't think we saw the article?

MOTHER: *Black Enterprise*, page thirty-eight, article continued on ninety-one.

FATHER: You see, we ain't totally blind. We read.

MOTHER: It was a very good article, Undine. We were very proud of you, until the part where they said your family died in a fire. Baby, we didn't die in a fire.

UNDINE: Yes, I know that. I was apparently misquoted.

FLOW: A misquote?

MOTHER: That's what I told your father. You see, baby. I told him that. We're your family. I said, she's done many things, but she'd never do that.

FATHER: Is that true . . . Undine?

UNDINE: Surely, you can't believe everything you read.

FATHER: Is that true . . . Undine?

FLOW: WHY?

GRANDMA: 'Cause you know the Watkins family is there inside you. And we love it, even if . . . This *is* your home.

FATHER: Is it *true* . . . Undine?

FLOW: Why?

UNDINE: (*To audience*) Is this it? Is this the end of the story? A dramatic family confrontation. Catharsis. Is it that simple? A journey that began miraculously at the Walt Whitman projects and led me to Edith Wharton's *The Custom of the Country*, an intriguing parvenu discovered in an American Literature course at Dartmouth College. (*A moment*) No. No. I go to a street corner with a twenty-dollar bill balled up in my hand. I buy twenty dollars' worth of white lace. I take it to the stairwell. I really must have angered Elegba, I must have unsettled all of the powerful orishas. And I'm ready to surrender, I'm ready to concede. I'm so ready and just as I'm about . . . they unexpectedly find Hervé.

(*A prison waiting room*)

Scene 7

Hervé slowly emerges from the darkness, wearing a bright orange prison uniform; he moves with grace. Undine sits across from him at the visitor's table.

UNDINE: (*To audience*) They found him hiding out at the Ritz-Carlton, pretending to be a diplomat from Uruguay. Unfortunately for him, a diplomat from Uruguay was also a guest at the hotel attending a summit on global warming.

(*Hervé points to her bulging stomach.*)

HERVÉ: What happened to you?

UNDINE: What do you think happened to me?

HERVÉ: Who did this to you?

UNDINE: You did, you fucker!

HERVÉ: Me? . . .

UNDINE: Yes. (*A moment*)

HERVÉ: How?

UNDINE: How do you think?

HERVÉ: Yes, I see. (*A moment*)

UNDINE: Why?

HERVÉ: Why not?

UNDINE: All of it?

HERVÉ: It happened, *sí*. It is finished.

UNDINE: I could kill you. I cared for you, you little prick. And you didn't even have the decency to say goodbye.

HERVÉ: I am sorry.

UNDINE: You can take your sorry to federal prison.

HERVÉ: Let us talk.

UNDINE: I have nothing to say to you. My lawyer will speak for me. You took everything from me.

HERVÉ: Not everything. My father's name was Javier Dejesus Calles. He was a good man. I offer you his name, it is the name for my son, for my daughter.

UNDINE: Well, that won't do.

HERVÉ: But, I am the father of your child.

UNDINE: Oh please, you were fucking for a green card—that's enough to keep any Latin dick hard. (*A moment*) You are the father, but you won't be this child's father. You left our lives. You gave up your parental rights as far as I am concerned. I was generous to you. I was more than generous.

HERVÉ: I beg your pardon, *querida*, you were generous to nobody. I disappeared long before I left, but you just never noticed. Money? You'll make more money. Don't pretend it was about the money.

UNDINE: Oh please.

HERVÉ: I pity the child.

UNDINE: Why would you say that?

HERVÉ: I think you understand, Undine. (*Undine stares at Hervé.*) I was open, but you are a rotten oyster. We look at each other—now. It is the first time we stand face to face since we met, no? I am who I was, *querida*; you are who you were. We are ugly people. We give, we take, we are even.

UNDINE: (*To audience*) I've prided myself on not needing love, but it was different when I thought I was loved.

HERVÉ: Guard.

(*Hervé leaves.*)

UNDINE: (*Resigned*) Hervé! (*To audience*) And he is gone. But strangely, I dream of fish.

(*The sound of the ocean. Undine is surrounded by the group of Addicts.*)

Scene 8

The Addicts, including Guy, sit in a support circle. Undine enters.

ADDICT #2: Old friends, old friends. I shouldn't have rode in the car with my old friends. They were smoking herb and I thought, a little herb won't kill me.

COUNSELOR: Take a moment. We're not here to judge, this is a place of forgiveness. Take your time.

(Addict #2 begins to weep. Undine walks over to the coffee-and-tea cart. She lets out a loud involuntary gasp caused by a slight contraction.)

Are you okay, Undine?

UNDINE: Yes. I'm sorry.

(Guy breaks away from the circle and goes over to Undine. In a whisper, Guy and Undine carry on their own conversation. The group continues its work.)

GUY: Did you get my telephone message?

UNDINE:You? No.

GUY: No? Have you begun your birthing classes?

UNDINE: I haven't even thought that far ahead.

GUY: Don't you think maybe you better?

UNDINE: Yes. I suppose eventually I will have to give birth.

GUY: If you need someone to go with you to the classes, I'd be glad.

UNDINE: That's okay.

COUNSELOR: *(Rising)* Was there something you wish to share with the group, Undine?

UNDINE: Oh, no. I'm just getting a cup of tea.

ADDICT #2: *(Continues to speak in the background)* The radio was pumping, the feeling was familiar. Two hits, what's the harm? *(A collective groan)*

(Guy and Undine continue to whisper.)

GUY: Really, if you need a partner, someone to be in the delivery room with you. I know we don't know each other that well, but I'd be happy to be that person that, you know, who stands by you in the delivery room.

UNDINE: Really?

GUY: Yeah.

UNDINE: You'll hold my hand? Breathe in and out with me?

GUY: I'm serious.

UNDINE: Yes, I know that you're serious. And you're so sweet. But, would you really? Oh my God, this is going to happen.

GUY: You'll be fine. You ain't like the other addicts in this program. I mean you seem . . . stronger.

UNDINE: *(To audience)* But he doesn't know that Edna is pressing gently against my chest, slowly quickening my breath, squeezing. *(Touches her swollen belly)* Or that I feel the child kicking my side, and I hate that my body is not mine alone.

(Guy, smiling, gently places his hand on Undine's belly.)

GUY: Hey.

UNDINE: Why are you smiling?

GUY: You.

UNDINE: What?

GUY: You know.

UNDINE: Yes?

GUY: Look beautiful.

UNDINE: No. Don't say that.

GUY: Why? You make me happy. It has been a struggle, no doubt, but when I think about what's happened to me in the last few months, it's all good, for real. You. Two years ago I was living on the street. I'd see my moms, my boys and they'd pretend not to know me. I was starving, and they'd walk right by me. Ashamed. Yeah, I been that person. I been that brother you cross the street to avoid. I been wrong at times. I been to jail for six months. But that's over, never again. I let go of the bullshit. I hope you know that. Why do you look confused?

UNDINE: I've never heard anyone say they're happy and actually feel it. But when you say it, I'm looking at you, I believe you mean it. And I find that reassuring.

(*The Addicts slowly shift their attention to Undine and Guy who are still standing by the coffee-and-tea cart.*)

GUY: Why?

UNDINE: Because mostly I feel rage.

(*Undine realizes the Addicts are eavesdropping and finds herself including them in her confessional.*)

Anger, which I guess is a variation of rage and sometimes it gives way to panic, which in my case is also a variation of rage. I think it's safe to say that I have explored the full range of rage.

ADDICTS: Mmm.

UNDINE: And it has been with me for so long, that it's comforting. I'm trying to move beyond it. Sometimes I even think I have—but mostly I'm not a very good human being. Sometimes I'm less than human, I know this, but I can't control it. And now I'm more afraid than ever.

GUY: Why?

UNDINE: Because, what if I'm not a good enough person to be a parent?

GUY: Of course you are.

UNDINE: No! I'm not! I killed my family. (*A collective gasp.*) Yes, I killed all of them on the day of my college graduation. Dartmouth. My family drove two hundred and sixty-seven miles in a rented minivan, loaded with friends and relatives eager to witness my ceremony. They were incredibly proud, and why not? I was the first person in the family to graduate from college. They came en masse, dressed in their bargain-basement finest. Loud, overly eager, lugging picnic baskets filled with fragrant ghetto food . . . let's just say their enthusiasm over-whelmed me. But I didn't mind. No, I didn't mind until I overheard a group of my friends making crass, unkind comments about my family. They wondered aloud who belonged to *those* people. It was me. I should have said so. I should have said that my mother took an extra shift so I could have a new coat every year. My father sent me ten dollars every week, his lotto money. But instead, I locked myself in my dorm room and refused to come out to greet them. And I decided on that day, that I was Undine Barnes, who bore no relationship to those people. I told everyone my family died in a fire, and I came to accept it as true. It was true for years. Understand, Sharona had to die in a fire in order for Undine to live. At least that's what I thought. What I did was awful, and I'm so so sorry. And, Guy, you are such a good, decent man. And I wouldn't blame you if you walked away right now. But I don't want you to. I feel completely safe with you.

GUY: Then I won't.

UNDINE: I am not yet divorced, I'm being investigated by the FBI, I'm carrying the child of another man and I'm not really a junkie.

(*A collective gasp from the Addicts.*)

(*To Guy*) Are you still happy?

GUY: Yes, I think so.

UNDINE: And you're not medicated?

GUY: No.

UNDINE: Give us a moment.

(*A moment. The group turns away. Undine pulls Guy aside.*)

Is the notion of love frightening to you?

GUY: No.

UNDINE: Who are you? Why are you doing this to me? I'm sorry, I didn't mean to say that. I take it back. I mean, I like you a great deal—love is heavy, is deep and frightening and I apologize for floating it so carelessly. I really want to change, I do, but I'm afraid I can't. I'm not ready for this.

GUY: Stop. Stop speaking.

(*Guy leans in and plants a kiss on Undine's lips; she surrenders. A labor pain hits. The Addicts gasp and collectively back away. Lights slowly shift to the hospital room.*)

Scene 9

Guy and the Doctor help Undine onto an examining table. Bright, unforgiving light)

UNDINE: (*To audience*) A child? (*Panic*) My child—

(*Guy smiles. A pain strikes, interrupting Undine's words.*)

GUY: Breathe.

(*Undine lies down on the delivery table.*)

UNDINE: (*To audience*) Everyone wants me to breathe out, push, but I am trying desperately to hold my breath, hold it in. If I don't breathe then the baby will not come. (*Holds her breath*)

GUY: Breathe, Undine.

UNDINE: (*To audience*) I am holding my breath.

DOCTOR: Breathe.

UNDINE: (*To audience, holding her breath as she speaks*) I am holding on.

(*Undine refuses to breathe, Guy takes her hand.*)

GUY: Please, breathe.

UNDINE: (*To audience*) I won't. I won't a bring a child into this world.

(*Grandma, Mother, Father, Flow enter wearing their security guard uniforms.*)

FLOW: Breathe, girl!

MOTHER AND FATHER: Breathe, Undine!

(*Undine struggles to hold her breath. She's not going to give in.*)

GRANDMA: Breathe, sweet pea!

(*Undine looks at Guy and her family in their uniforms; she studies their concerned faces.*)

UNDINE: (*To audience*) And then I let go.

(*Undine wails, a tremendous release. Silence.*)

UNDINE: (*To audience*) I breathe.

(*A baby cries.*)

BLACKOUT

End of Play

CHRISTINA ANDERSON

Born and raised in Kansas City, Kansas, Christina Anderson has always been attracted to theater. She once said in an interview, "I love the fact that adults are willing to pretend for ninety minutes. I love the magic of it. The simplicity of it. It has the power to transform the viewer. It celebrates the dexterity of a good performer. It captures the brilliance of a great storyteller. It creates community. It sparks discussion. These things don't happen with every theater piece, but the possibility is always there." Her remarks are certainly true of her own plays. There is a simplicity to them even though the themes she tackles are often huge, for example, the complexities and dangers of living in the contained conditions of a housing project in *BlackTop Sky*; the tensions that develop between two sisters in *Inked Baby* when one agrees to be a surrogate for the other, whose infertility might be associated with a mysterious ecological condition; the dementia-laden memories of a dying grandmother and her grandson's inability to visit her in the hospital in *Drip*; and the warped and creepy philosophical musings that motivate the actions of a serial killer in *Man in Love*. Anderson received a bachelor's degree from Brown University, where she took playwriting workshops with Paula Vogel, and an M.F.A. from Yale University's playwriting program. A member of New Dramatists, Anderson, who resides in New York, is a prolific playwright. In addition to the aforementioned works, her plays include *Hollow Roots*, *Good Goods*, *Glo*, *Ashes Under the Gait City*, *Pen/Man/Ship* and several one-act and solo plays.

BlackTop Sky received its world premiere on January 26, 2013, at the Unicorn Theatre in Kansas City, Kansas.

Director:	Mykel Hill
Dramaturg:	Amanda Boyle
Ida Peters:	Chioman Anyanwu
Klass:	Tosin Morohunfola
Wynn:	Frank Oakley III
Scenic design:	Gary Mosby
Lighting design:	Alex Perry
Sound design:	Dan Warneke
Stage manager:	Tanya Brown
Costume design:	Georgianna Londré Buchanan

BLACKTOP SKY

PLAYERS:

Ida—18, Black American female
Klass—25, Black American male
Wynn—27, Black American male

TIME: The present

PLACE: An urban setting

AUTHOR'S NOTES

Given the context of the scene, the symbol =.= indicates an active moment of gesture or a moment of communion between characters that transcends language.

When the symbol "//" appears in a line of dialogue the following line should
begin:

IDA: You don't have to shout // about it.
WYNN: I'm not shouting.

Neighborhood sounds function as a constant hum throughout the play. The sounds
should explore the questions: What does "class" sound like? What does the "ghetto"
sound like?

The aural landscape should start out with familiar (some would say stereotypi-
cal) notions of the projects or the ghetto. But slowly other sounds could trickle into
the play. This shift could start when Ida and Klass look up at the sky for the first
time. By the end of the play, it'd be great if the sounds are a collage of "upper"-class
sounds or suburban sounds but are still considered a part of the projects. If this
doesn't make sense, feel free to ask the playwright for more details.

This play was inspired by the Greek myth Leda and the swan.

An aerial view. Four buildings face each other like this:

To form the David L. Hynn housing projects: in the center there's a blacktop courtyard. And in the center of that courtyard are two busted, broken-down, rusted-up benches. Streaks of sunlight make their way around the looming apartment buildings. We hear neighborhood sounds: children playing, men hollering, car horns, trucks, hip-hop music (with moments of reggae) playing from cheap radios or booming subwoofers. These sounds arrive in the courtyard as an echo, creating a world that is familiar yet distant.

The sun sets on the benches.

Night stands up. Streetlamps come on, casting a faint light across the courtyard.

The neighborhood sounds shift in mood to match the darkness of night, the arrival of artificial light.

Scene
Day.

Ida, perched on one of the benches, is in the middle of telling a story to a group of people unseen by the audience. She uses both benches as a stage, taking on the physical gestures of all the people who appear in her story. In another life, she would've been a great clown.

IDA: . . . mindin his own business.
He was standin up there on Park & Ives, mindin his own business.
He had this pocket radio that he kept close to his ear.
He was holdin it up like this (*cups her hand against her left ear*), like he's holdin on to a lil' bird.
And that bird is singin some kind of sweet song.
A song he's tryin to keep all to himself.
Antonio was straight up mindin his own business.
He's standin like this:

Ida takes on Antonio's position. She holds the radio up to her ear, bops her head to a silent beat, scopes out the area around her. (snaps out of it):

And you know how he always has his stuff situated on the ground?
He has his display laid out all nice.
First he sweeps the sidewalk,
then he takes that bright green sheet with the creamy white circles and folds it into a long rectangle.

Ida takes on a wide stance. She hitches her thumbs in the waist of her pants.

The other Thick Neck blocks him (*returns to her wide stance*),
blocks Antonio.
Then there's talking.
More talking.
Kneeling cop is picking at the necklaces, unzipping handbags.
Antonio's looking like that cop is diggin into him, tossing him around.

Then over the noise, over the people, all over everything
I hear Antonio yell:
"I DIDN'T DO NOTHIN!"
And the block stops.

      =.=
      =.=
      =.=

Freeze frame.
Red light.
Hold.

      =.=
      =.=

Kneeling cop is up on his feet.
Talking.
Talking.
Talking.
And then another police car pulls up.
Antonio's here (*maps it*).
Four Thick Necks are here, here, here and here (*maps it*).
Talking. Talking.
Another car.
Six Thick Necks: three here (*maps it*), three here (*maps it*).
A motorcycle.
Seven.
Talking. Talking. Talking.
Antonio is stone cold, his lips barely moving.
Then two of them Thick Necks just start shoving everything on the
sheet towards the center.
Roughing up all of Antonio's stuff.

Klass enters, carrying a plastic crate packed full of metal objects, plastic cups, etc. He's wearing a
winter coat with the hood up. It's lined with fake fur. He stands, listening to Ida's story.

IDA: Now you know Antonio don't handle his stuff like that.
           His shit is organized like a street hustle.
           He sees them treat his product like junk and he yells,
           "THAT'S MY PROPERTY! YOU CAN'T DO THAT TO MY STUFF!"
           Thick Necks get agitated.
           They move around him, acting like he's crazy, easily excited.
           Hands up like, "Hey now, come on, no need for yelling."
           That kind of attitude.
           A Thick Neck gathers the four corners of the sheet and scoops up
           everything.
           Antonio's way of making money, surviving is choked up in this cop's
           hands.

Then Antonio just flips out.

He jumps towards his stuff.

A Thick Neck one pulls out this yellow thing shaped like a gun, aims it at Antonio and then:

Ida makes a long zapping sound, her hands tremble.

IDA: Antonio snaps back like he got plugged into a socket.

Ida stands up on her toes, like someone or something has her by the back of the neck. She twists her face in pain. She yells.

Klass, startled, drops his crate. The crash seems to trigger Ida into the following series of movements: she folds her arms in front of her chest. Eyes roll back. She leans forward as if falling, but she catches herself. She leaps off the bench and stands on the ground. She snaps out of her trance.

IDA: But he ends up on the ground, rocking side to side.

Holding his chest.

Two Thick Necks manage to put him in handcuffs.

The back of my legs feel like they on fire.

I look down, makin sure I'm alright.

The cop who zapped Antonio slips it back in its holder.

=.=

=.= ·

I wanted to do something, but I just walked away.

Came back here. Home.

Ida looks over at Klass.

Klass looks at her.

He sits on one of the benches. He takes a can of grape soda from his pocket. He pops the top. Drinks.

Scene

Night. Hours later.

Klass sits in the same spot. Asleep.

His crate is tucked under his feet.

A streetlamp casts its artificial light across the blacktop.

A slim beam of light comes from offstage.

Wynn enters behind a small flashlight connected to his keychain. Ida follows. They stop at the edge.

IDA: (*hushed*) There. That was the last place I remember having 'em.

I was standing there telling everybody about Antonio.

Wynn aims the light at the shape of Klass. He clicks it off.

WYNN: (*hushed*) Uh-uh. I am not going over there.

IDA: (*hushed*) What? Why? You scared?

WYNN: You want me to rough up some homeless dude in the middle of the night?

IDA: Wynn, my mama is gonna kill me
           if she finds out I lost another set of keys.

WYNN: Shouldn'ta been over there anyway.

IDA: You promised to help me.

WYNN: And I did, Ida.

           We went all over, everywhere, retracing your steps.

           And I'm standing here now realizing two things:

           I'd do almost anything for you, but I'm not digging around that dude

           for your keys, and two, maybe if you kept your behind at home,

           you wouldn'ta lost 'em in the first place.

IDA: Why don't you cut the bullshit talk and just pull out the damn leash,
           Wynn?

WYNN: It's not bull—leash? Leash?

           Ida, so now you sayin I'm treating you like a dog?

IDA: Yeah, that's what I'm sayin, Wynn.

           But you know what? You won't have to worry about me bein out

           anywhere after my mama finds out cause she's gonna bust my ass up!

Klass shifts in his sleep.

Ida and Wynn fall into the shadows, hold their breath.

Klass settles into a comfortable position, continues his slumber.

IDA: =.= *(waiting)*

WYNN: =.= *(waiting)*

IDA: *(hushed, whiny)*   Wyyyyynn—

WYNN: Ida, no. He's crazy.

           Outta his damn mind.

           Wearing a winter coat in June.

           Lookin like a fat pigeon.

           I go over there talking bout, "My girl lost her keys."

           He'd talk some crazy and then we'd have to throw down.

           You want that?

IDA: I want my keys.

WYNN: Are you sure you lost 'em here?

           Let's keep going over your steps.

           If we still don't find 'em, we'll come back here.

           Maybe he'll be gone by then . . .

IDA: I have a picture of me and you attached to one of the rings.

           Somebody find my keys and know me. . . .

           they'd know where I live, break in the apartment

           and steal all my stuff, Wynn.

WYNN: As many sets of keys you lost folks would've robbed your house five

           times over. Everybody in the David L. Hynn towers knows Ida Peters

           loses things all the damn time.

IDA: Are you finished?

WYNN: Yes.

IDA:	Thank you. Now stop being a punk and look for my keys.
WYNN:	Who you callin a punk?
IDA:	The dude named Wynn, who's too scared to walk around a damn bench and look for my keys.
WYNN:	=.=
IDA:	=.=

Wynn clicks on his flashlight.
He crosses over to the benches. Black secret agent–style.
Klass sleeps.
Wynn shines the light all around the empty bench.
Nothing.
He inches closer to Klass.
Closer. Closer.
Shines the light around the occupied seat.
Nothing.
And then the light falls on Klass's wrist.
Ida's keys, the plastic frame holding a picture of Wynn and Ida, flash in the light.

> =.= (*a moment where the situation registers*)

Wynn calmly clicks off the light. He crosses over to Ida.

WYNN:	(*slight, but surprising, hysteria*)
	That crazy fuckin pigeon taped the keys to his damn wrist!
IDA:	What?
	Awwww, my mama's gonna break my neck!
	Lose my keys and then they end up with crazy pigeon man.
	Wynn, you gotta get 'em.
WYNN:	Fuck that!
IDA:	What am I supposed to do then?
WYNN:	Call the police.
IDA:	I'm not calling the police.
WYNN:	Why?
IDA:	Police come around here
	they'd zap him like they did Antonio.
	I don't wanna be responsible for that shit.
	He didn't steal 'em.
	He found 'em.
WYNN:	They have a better chance of getting 'em back
	than I would—
IDA:	No cops.
	=.=
	I gotta figure out a place to sleep tonight.
WYNN:	Come home with me.
IDA:	I'm not goin to your apartment with you.
WYNN:	Why not?

IDA:	Don't try and twist this into a tap session.
WYNN:	(*feigned shock*) Ida!
IDA:	Wynn, this is serious.
WYNN:	And I'm seriously and for real offerin my baby some shelter.
	Stay with me tonight. We'll come back over here after I get off work
	and talk to him before the sun goes down.
	Try to reason with him during the day. Alright?

Wynn grabs Ida. She resists at first but releases.
Wynn kisses her lightly on the lips. She kisses him.

WYNN:	Tell your mama you're staying at your friend's house.
IDA:	She don't like hearing things last minute.
	Pisses her off.
WYNN:	Ida you grown now. Eighteen. A high school graduate.
	Got the diploma two weeks ago as proof.
	You can stay over whoever's house you want to.
	And I'm inviting you to rest against me until the sun comes up.
	I can kiss you 'til you fall asleep; kiss those lips (*re: down south*) 'til you
	wake up.

A smile slides across Ida's face.

IDA:	Okay. Alright. Let's go.

She takes his hand. They cross in front of Klass on the bench. They exit.

Klass opens his eyes, raises his head, and looks in the direction they walked.
He was awake the entire time.

Scene
Sun rises.

Neighborhood sounds confront the sun.

Klass remains on the bench.
He's asleep for real this time.

Ida enters. She watches him, mustering up the courage to wake him.
Finally:

IDA:	(*scared*) Excuse me.

Nothing.

IDA:	Hey. Excuse me.

Nothing.

IDA:	Damn, are you dead? Excuse me.

Klass wakes up. He Looks at Ida.
Ida looks at Klass.

IDA: Hey, I didn't mean to wake you up.
                But, but you have my—

Klass screams.
Ida screams.
Klass jumps up on the bench screaming.
Ida runs away, screaming.

Scene
Afternoon.

Klass is perched on the bench just like Ida was at the top of the play. He uses a worn sheet of newspaper to polish a metal coffee pot.

Ida enters carrying a reconfigured wire hanger. She holds it out as a weapon for self defense. She announces herself.

IDA: Excuse me.

Klass looks up.

IDA: Hey!

Klass looks at Ida.

IDA: You got something that belongs to me.

Klass goes back to polishing his coffee pot.

IDA: Look, I don't wanna have to call the police.

Klass stops polishing.

IDA: Yeah, man, you heard Thick Necks fryin sane brothas
                so you know they'd blaze your crazy ass up.

Klass looks at Ida then returns to polishing his pot.

IDA: Those are my keys you got on your wrist.
                I want those back. You can act all types of stupid
                after you give me back what's mine.

Klass carefully places the pot on the ground.
Ida assumes he's going for her keys,
but instead he takes a drinking glass from the crate and wipes it clean.

IDA: You just gonna sit there
                like I'm not even talking to you?

Klass places the glass next to the coffee pot.
He takes out a spoon and wipes it.

IDA: My man gets off from work soon.
                I was trying to do you a favor and handle all this on my own without
                involving him. I told him you screamed at me.

You remember that from this morning?
Hollering at me like you a damn terrorist!
You remember that shit? He was not happy to hear
you flipped out on me. So, I would suggest you pull
your screws together long enough to do the right thing.

Klass stops polishing.
He sticks the spoon in the drinking glass.
He looks at Ida.

Ida looks at Klass.
She grips the wire hanger.

Klass gets off the bench.
He goes inside his coat, digs.

Ida panics, thinking he's got a gun.
She hits the floor, covering her head.

Klass pulls out a white feather.
He holds it out to Ida. Her keys dangle from his wrist.

Ida uncovers her head when no shots ring out.
She looks up, sees her keys.

IDA: Those are mine. See?
      You're wearing my keys.

She gets up,
stops when she sees the feather.
Klass looks at her,
a slight smirk on his face.
Ida looks at her keys . . . or the feather.
Klass holds the feather out for Ida to take it.
Ida looks at him, taking in his features for the first time.

IDA: How old are you?
      You look young.
      Might even be younger than Wynn.

Klass drops the feather, returns to the bench.
Ida catches the feather as it falls.
Klass picks up his pot, polishes it.
She watches him.

IDA: All the drug heads and street crazies around here are old men
      with gray hair and tight skin. That's not like you.

She holds up the feather.

IDA: Where'd you find this?
KLASS: =.=

IDA: I see crows sometimes.
           I look up and I see crows soaring.
           Wynn says I'm crazy.
           Didn't know we had birds like this (*re: the feather*).
                  =.=
           Can I have my keys?
           Please?
           My mama's gonna know something's up if I stay out two nights in a row.

Klass carefully places the coffee pot back in the crate.

IDA: I'm sorry I came at you with that hanger.
           I wasn't gonna use it.
           I don't do that.
           I don't hurt people.

Klass looks at Ida.

IDA: I don't wanna make this a thing.
           Don't want to call the police unless I have to.
           I need my keys back.

Klass picks up the drinking glass with the spoon in it.
He puts both things back in the crate.
He tucks the crate under the bench.
He sits down, folds his arms so that the wrist with the keys
attached are tucked under his other arm, pressed against his body.
Klass falls asleep.
Ida watches him.

IDA: (*to herself*) I don't believe this shit.
           No he just didn't sit up here and fall asleep . . .

Scene
Evening.
That same day.

No Klass, but his crate is still tucked under the bench.
Ida enters with Wynn.

IDA: Mr. Wheeler said he's been gone for a few hours.
WYNN: We should take his crate. He got your keys;
           we take his shit. Negotiate a swap.
IDA: I don't want that junk.
WYNN: It's leverage.
IDA: I don't need leverage. I need keys. I haveta go home tonight.
           Haveta tell my mama what the deal is so she can blow up
           about spending money to get the locks changed. Again.
WYNN: Maybe this is a sign, Ida.

IDA:	What?
WYNN:	Maybe all this came together
	to make us take things to the next level.
IDA:	"All this" . . . ? All of what?
WYNN:	Your crazy mama. Pigeon man. You losing your keys.
	All this disruption is bringing us closer together.
IDA:	It is?
WYNN:	It is. Or . . . it could. If we let it. All these signs are hooking up
	to tell us we should be living together.
IDA:	I didn't see any signs getting down like that.
WYNN:	Your mama's gonna tell you to walk right back out
	when you tell her why she had to unlock the door for you.
IDA:	(*hadn't considered this*) You think she'd kick me out?
WYNN:	She might. But if you decide to live with me,
	it won't matter what she says to you.
IDA:	She's not gonna kick me out.
WYNN:	She's got a temper.
IDA:	She needs my help.
WYNN:	That day nurse been handling most of the work.
IDA:	She wouldn't throw // me out. I'm her only child.
WYNN:	And you know who's gonna be there when she tosses you?
	=.= (*ta-da!!*)
IDA:	I haveta get those keys back.
WYNN:	You don't think it's a sign?
IDA:	Have you seen him (*re: Klass*) around here before?
WYNN:	Ida, I asked you a question.
IDA:	I asked you a question, Wynn.
WYNN:	=.=
IDA:	=.=
WYNN:	No. I haven't seen pigeon man before.
	// Now you gonna answer mine?
IDA:	Don't call him pigeon man.
WYNN:	Would you listen to me?
IDA:	He's your age.
WYNN:	Who?

He points at the crate.

IDA:	He is. I think y'all around the same age.
WYNN:	No way, man.
IDA:	I looked him in the face. He got that beard,
	but there's a baby face under it. He's young.
WYNN:	Wouldn't no dude my age *choose* to be like that.
IDA:	Who said it's a choice?
WYNN:	You comparing him to me?
IDA:	I'm not.

WYNN:	I hope not.
IDA:	Maybe the cops got him.
WYNN:	They would've taken his stuff.

=.=

=.=

Wynn takes out his wallet.
He pulls out a couple of bills and a business card.

WYNN:	Here.
IDA:	What's this for?
WYNN:	(*re: the business card*) I went to school with him. He's a locksmith now. Got his own business. Tell him you're with me, and he'll give you a discount. You pay him that much.
IDA:	Wynn, I don't wanna take—
WYNN:	Your mama can't bust you up if you already got a solution to the problem.

Ida takes in Wynn's gesture. She kisses him as a sign of gratitude.
He hugs her to seal the deal. While embracing an oblivious Wynn,
Ida looks to the crate.

Scene
Night.
Rain.

The bench is empty. The crate remains.
Suddenly, the slim beam of a flashlight appears.
Ida enters, carrying an umbrella and shining a flashlight.
She carries a black trash bag.
She crosses to the crate, puts down the umbrella,
pulls the crate from underneath the bench,
and attempts to wrap the trash bag around it.

Klass enters.

KLASS:	What are you doin with my stuff?

Ida jumps up, falls back.

IDA:	It's raining.
KLASS:	I know it's raining.
IDA:	Your stuff was getting wet.
KLASS:	You trying to steal my crate?
IDA:	No! No, I'm not. I wasn't, I'm not. I'm—
	I was wrapping that bag around it. Cuz, cuz, I know you take all that time polishing your pot and your glass.
KLASS:	How you know that? You watching me?

IDA:	I came here. I been here. I talked to you.
	Been talking to you. I'm the one you gave the feather to.
	You got my keys on your wrist.

Klass looks at his wrist. The keys dangle.
He looks at Ida. He sits.

| KLASS: | You keeping my stuff dry? |

Ida scrambles for her umbrella.

IDA:	Yeah.
KLASS:	Why?
IDA:	I figured you have important things in there.
KLASS:	=.=
IDA:	=.=
KLASS:	(*slow realization*) You taking care of my crate . . . ?
IDA:	Yeah, for real. No lie.

Klass studies Ida.
She watches him study her.
Klass stands and faces Ida.
He removes the keys from his wrist.
Holds them out for Ida to take.

She inches towards him.
She reaches out to take the keys from Klass.
There's the slightest pause for a shared breath.

Just as Ida clasps her hand around the keys, Klass grabs her.
Ida drops the umbrella. He holds her. . . . (is it a hug or squeeze?).
Ida is silenced as she struggles to break free.
Suddenly quiet noise pops from Ida.

Klass releases her as swiftly as he grabbed her.
She runs away, leaving the umbrella on the ground.
Klass watches her run. He crosses to his crate,
finishes wrapping the trash bag around it.
He takes the umbrella, sits.
He props it up to protect himself from the rain.
Klass sleeps.

Scene
Day.

The benches are empty. The crate is gone.
Ida enters, carrying plastic bags full of groceries.
The closer she gets to the benches, the faster she walks.
She avoids looking at them. She crosses the courtyard, exits.

Scene
Evening.

Wynn, perched on a bench, is in the middle of telling a story
to a group of people unseen by the audience.
Wynn isn't as good as Ida, but he enjoys the attention.

Ida keeps close to Wynn, almost unable to stand near the spot
where the earlier incident with Klass occurred.
She's distracted, avoids eye contact.

WYNN: . . . Antonio had a seizure in the holding cell. They had to take him to
the hospital. He's in a coma, but they still got him in shackles though,
got him handcuffed to the bed. He had a warrant. Missed a court date.
That's why they arrested him. This dude who works at the hospital brought his car into the shop this afternoon. Told me the whole
deal. The news don't even know about it, that's how recent it is. But I
don't think the news care one way or the other. They don't talk about
brothas minding they own business, getting shook down. They want
a big, loud, crazy muthafucka waving around a switchblade. Ida, you
heard anything on the news?

IDA: No.

WYNN: See? And Ida been sitting up in her apartment steady watching TV
like it's her job. Like she on some quest for that six-figure salary type
shit—

Ida smacks Wynn on the arm, hard.

WYNN: Yo, what the fuck?

IDA: Don't go around talking about how I spend my time.

WYNN: What you hit me for?

IDA: I didn't hear anything about Antonio, okay?
No need to tell people what I do.

WYNN: What's wrong with you?

IDA: I'm going back up.

Ida goes to exit. Wynn goes after her.

WYNN: (*grabbing her*) Wait a minute—

IDA: Don't touch me.

WYNN: What's wrong with you?

IDA: I don't feel like being outside.

WYNN: You bust me in my arm cause you hate being outside?

| IDA: | Fucking neighborhood stinks in the summer. All this heat. I don't like being out. | WYNN: | Why'd you hit me in front of everybody. |

IDA: Don't matter anyway. Everybody sees everything, but they don't
           care.
           Everybody is always out, in the streets. Day and night.
           People on stoops, leaning on cars, hanging out of windows.
           You can't get away from nobody.
           Building 1 (*Ida turns in the direction of the first building*), see?
           There's Mr. Wheeler smoking up, reading the paper.
           Building 3 (*turns in the direction of the third building*):
           Sasha is on the phone running her mouth.
           Building 4 (*turns*): Mrs. James is greasing her scalp.
           Building 2 (*turns*): my mama is sitting up there sleeping.
WYNN: Ida, what the hell are you // talking about?
IDA: Four buildings make up this project.
           And every building got seven floors.
           And every floor got eleven windows going across it.
           All those windows facing down to this courtyard, those benches.
           So Mr. Wheeler was smoking.
           So Sasha was talking bullshit.
           Mrs. James was sitting by the window, listening to the radio.
           But nobody said nothing to me. Nobody asked me anything.
           Am I crazy? I don't know if I'm crazy.
           Don't know if I'm making shit up.
WYNN: Ida—
IDA: Am I cracking out?
           Sitting up in my dingy-ass apartment, hiding out from what? From
           who?
           Something I made up? Must've. Had to have made it up cause nobody
           said nothing. It wasn't nothing. Nothing for me to sprint pass these
           benches every day. This is the only way out to the street, Wynn.
           When I leave my building I have to cross through here to get to the
           street.
           Every other exit is blocked by a fence with a thick chain and fat pad-
           lock keeping it shut. I can't even choose how I come and go.
WYNN: Ida, did something happen to you?
IDA: I'm glad I met you downtown at a movie theater.
           Nowhere near here, cause otherwise I'd only see all this (*re: the proj-
           ects*) when I look at you. But I don't. I don't, Wynn. And that's why I
           like you. That's why I need you.
                =.=
                =.=
           I'm going home. I'll talk to you later.

Ida exits, leaving Wynn speechless.

Scene
Day.

Neighborhood sounds bounce around the space.

The crate is back. Klass is back. He sits on the ground, fiddling with an upright vacuum cleaner on its side.

Wynn enters, carrying a small gift bag (a gift for Ida). He stops short when he sees Klass. On his cell phone:

WYNN: Yeah, I'm outside. Okay. Bye.

Wynn hangs up, watches Klass.

WYNN: Hey, man, how old are you?

KLASS: =.=

WYNN: My girl thinks you're my age. I don't think so though . . .
Good job giving back those keys. I woulda had to fuck you up
if she didn't get those keys back. Nothing personal.
I mean, I had other plans for me and her, but she wanted her keys
and I try to do what makes her happy.

KLASS: That's good.

WYNN: Yeah. It is.

KLASS: Nothing personal.

WYNN: Nothing personal.

                  =.=

                  =.=

                  Hey, what's wrong with you, man?
Why you out here, sitting under this hot-ass sun wearing a coat?

KLASS: =.=

WYNN: Alright. Cool. I understand. I need to mind my own. Cool.

                  =.=

                  You trying to fix that? What's wrong with it?

KLASS: I think something's wrong with the motor.

WYNN: I used to repair shit like that. I'd bust open a blender or a iron or a
fuckin vacuum and it'd just come to me. I could figure out what didn't
look right and then go in and fix it. I could see how it needed to be so it
would work. Then I went to automotive school. You been to school?

KLASS: No.

WYNN: I finished school. Been set ever since. I decided I had a skill,
and I figured out how to make money off of it. And I'm taking care of
myself, too. People need cars to get where they need to go.
And they need people like me to make sure those cars keep going.
I want one of those city jobs, working on the buses.
That's money. Me and Ida be set for life.

Klass stops working on the vacuum when he hears Ida's name.

He looks at Wynn. Wynn looks at Klass.
Klass returns to the vacuum.

WYNN: You can still probably get your shit together. You got time.
            If you good enough at fixing things, you could get a decent job.
            Be a super or something.

Klass stops working, looks at Wynn.

WYNN: You don't have the right tools if you trying to fix that, though.
            I'd let you borrow some of mine but my shit is too nice.
            Plus, I don't know you from that bench.
                    =.=
            What's your name?
KLASS: What's your name?
WYNN: =.=
                    =.=
            Wynn.
KLASS: =.=
                    =.=
            Klass.
WYNN: Class? Like in "classroom"?
KLASS: Yeah, but it starts with a "k."

Klass extends his arm to bump fists with Wynn.
Wynn hesitates but eventually leans over and bumps fists with Klass.

The men see each other in the other's eyes.
It's an awkward moment that shows Wynn's
uneasiness and Klass's stillness.
If we had any doubt about who's in control,
we assume from this gesture it's probably Klass.
Klass goes back to the vacuum.

WYNN: You do look young.
                    =.=
            I could be you. You could be me. You never know how these things end
            up. We both could be that brotha Antonio. You hear about that? That
            shit is crazy. But the cops probably harass you all the time. You used
            to that shit, ain't you?
KLASS: =.=
WYNN: You picked a good spot, hanging here.
            Those Thick Necks that patrol here are hired to contain, not prevent.
            Hey, did you see anything go down recently?
KLASS: =.=
WYNN: I think something happened to my girl, but she's not talking about it. I
            asked around. Nobody's claiming to see anything.
KLASS: (*working on the vacuum*) I can't remember.

WYNN:	You can't remember or you don't?
KLASS:	I can't. I'm not sure. I don't know. I don't. Remember.
WYNN:	=.=
KLASS:	=.=

Wynn studies Klass.

WYNN:	Well, if you hear anything or if you see anybody that's not right, let me know. I'm over here a lot with Ida.
KLASS:	If I see something that's not right, you'll be the first person I say something to.

Scene
Night.

Two crates of junk and a vacuum cleaner.
Klass plays the feather game.
He sits on a bench, holding out a white feather.
He aims for a glass that sits between his feet on the ground.
He lets go of the feather. It lands in the glass ... or it doesn't.
He picks the feather up, aims it, lets go.
In the glass ... or not. He picks the feather up,
aims it, lets go. . . .

Scene
Morning.

Klass has a small pocket radio up to his ear.
Quiet, muffled voices seep from its tiny speaker.
Maybe it's reggae or jazz.
Klass paces, circling the bench.

Ida enters, crosses the space trying to walk by unnoticed.
Just as she passes him Klass registers that it's her.

KLASS:	Excuse me . . .

Ida ignores him. She exits.

Scene
Evening.

Two crates full of junk, a vacuum, and a pile of brightly colored summer dresses.
Klass sits on the pile of dresses, polishing his coffee pot.
Ida crosses.

KLASS: (*a quiet melody*) Ida Ida Ida Ida Ida . . .

Ida ignores him, exits.

Scene
Afternoon.
Rain.

Klass has wrapped all of his things in trash bags.
He sits under Ida's umbrella, unfazed by mother nature's tears.

Scene
Night.

Klass has found a pen and a notebook with a picture of Destiny's Child on the cover.
On sheet after sheet he writes and draws and writes and draws and writes and draws. . . .
There's a carnivorous quality to his behavior,
as if filling the pages has the same satisfaction as ripping into or consuming flesh.
It looks weird because it is weird.

Scene
Day.

Two crates full of junk, a vacuum cleaner,
a pile of dresses, and an old floor lamp without the lampshade.
Klass sits on the ground, looks up at the sky, daydreaming.
He holds the notebook against his chest.
Beyoncé et al. smile out at the audience.

Ida enters.
Klass sees that it's Ida.
He jumps up on the bench and holds out the notebook.

KLASS: Excuse me.

Ida keeps walking.

KLASS: Excuse me, this is for you . . . Ida. I found this for you.

Klass leaps off the bench and into Ida's path.
She stops short with a slight gasp.
She looks around her. Is anyone noticing this?

KLASS: Someone threw it out. But I caught it. Saved it. For you.

Klass holds the notebook up to her.
He looks at her. She looks at him.
Sounds of the neighborhood pique.

KLASS: It's for you. I left parts of it blank. So you could fill it
with things about yourself. I wrote about me. I tell you about me.
You see that? (*points to the cover*) That's . . . (*as if saying a foreign word*)
Destiny's Child, but I got it because of the sky behind them. I like their
sky because it feels big. It looks like it can hold a lot. That sky.
When I sit here and I look up, our sky looks so empty. Saggy and limp.
Looks like it couldn't hold anything I try to put up there.
Too flimsy to hold any dream or idea or possibility.
But . . . Destiny's Child's sky is so full.
It could hold anything you need to keep.

Ida studies the cover of the notebook.
Then she looks up, studies the sky above them.
Then she looks at Klass. He's right.

Scene
Evening.

Klass sits on the ground, polishing a set of salt-and-pepper shakers.
The pocket radio rests next to him.
Jazz music squirms out of the tiny speaker.

Ida sits on the bench, reading through the notebook.
She comes across something that's shocking or disgusting.
She looks at Klass, who's concentrating on his shakers,
considers asking him about what she just read.
She decides against it, returns to reading.
She turns the page and reads.
She laughs out loud, covers her mouth,
looks at Klass slightly embarrassed. He doesn't notice.
She returns to reading.

Scene
Day.

Two crates full of junk, a vacuum cleaner, a pile of dresses,
an old floor lamp without the lamp shade, and a wooden footstool.
Klass sits on the footstool, stacking primary-colored saucers into the form of a pyramid.
Ida sits on the bench with a glass between her feet.
She plays the feather game while she talks.

The sounds of the neighborhood bump.

IDA: My mama says I need to start helping with the rent.
She wants me to pay for things now that I'm done with school.

	I told her I'm not done. Said I'm thinking about community college.
	She said I can think about that while I'm working at a job.
	But I don't know where I would work, though.
	Maybe I should just move in with Wynn.
	That could be fun. He'd probably pay for me to go to school, too.
	It helped him get where he is.
KLASS:	=.=
IDA:	I like sitting here with you. I like it because, because it's quiet.
	It feels quiet with you.
	=.=
	=.=
	I finished reading your part of the sky last night.
	I finished your pages. Is all that stuff you wrote for real?
	All that really happened to you?
KLASS:	=.=
	=.=
	Yes.

This lands heavy against Ida.
She looks at Klass, who doesn't look at her.
He keeps his gaze on the bright colors of the saucers.
Ida returns to the feather game.

IDA:	You used to live here. In building one.
KLASS:	=.=
IDA:	You got people that still live here?
KLASS:	I don't know.
IDA:	You should look for 'em. They probably don't recognize you.
	Practically live in that big-ass coat. They probably walk past you
	every day and don't realize you're a part of the family.
KLASS:	(*wanting to change the subject*) That dude died.
IDA:	What dude?
KLASS:	(*makes a zap sound*)
IDA:	Antonio? How'd you find that out?
KLASS:	I woke up last night, saw it in the sky. Walked around the neighbor-
	hood, heard it in the streets.

Ida looks up at the sky above them.

IDA:	What'd you see in the sky?
KLASS:	A crow.
IDA:	(*looks at Klass*) Flying?
KLASS:	Circling.
IDA:	At night?
KLASS:	Yeah. That's how I knew. And then I was getting these
	(*re: the saucers*) when I heard people talking about it.

IDA: Where'd you get all this shit from?

KLASS: I found it.

IDA: You stealing it?

KLASS: No. People throw away things they don't want.
           I catch it.

IDA: People already call you Pigeon, they see all this and gonna add "shit"
           to it.
           You want everybody calling you Pigeon Shit?

Klass smiles. He laughs. He thinks it's funny.

IDA: It's not funny, Klass. You want people talking about you like that?

Klass starts to coo like a pigeon.
He laughs,
makes shitting sounds with his mouth.
He laughs.

IDA: That's digusting!

But Ida starts laughing, too.
Klass coos again.
He walks like a pigeon scooting around the bench.
Ida laughs. She holds out the feather.
Klass takes it, perches on the bench next to her.
He places the feather in her hair. He coos.
Wynn enters.

WYNN: Ida!

IDA: Wynn!

Klass coos a hello.

WYNN: Ida, do I have to bust Klass in the face?

IDA: No!

Ida pushes Klass away.
He rolls off the bench, springs to his feet,
dusts himself off, then returns to the footstool.
He polishes his saucers.

WYNN: Why are you sitting out here? With him? Like this!
           You remember all that counting you did?
           Seven floors, eleven windows? Everybody can see.

IDA: We were just talking. Nobody's paying attention—

WYNN: What are you two talking about?

IDA: Antonio died.

WYNN: I know. He already told you that?

IDA: Yeah.

WYNN: I was coming to tell you that.

IDA: You still can.

WYNN: Don't act like I'm a kid, Ida.

IDA: Nobody's treating you // like a kid.

WYNN: (*re: the feather in her hair*) And what's that?

IDA: This?

WYNN: He pulled that from some bird and the only
birds around here are those nasty-ass pigeons.

IDA: It's white. White pigeons are doves.

WYNN: He told you that, too.

IDA: Yes.

WYNN: This is some cracked out shit.

IDA: What are you doing here, Wynn?
You're supposed to be at work.

WYNN: People telling me you been hanging out with pigeons.

IDA: I been talking with Klass.

WYNN: I'm taking you to lunch. I'm on my lunch break.
I'm coming to take you out for some food.

IDA: I'm not hungry.

WYNN: Well, then, come watch me eat.

IDA: I don't want to.

WYNN: I'm taking you to lunch.

IDA: I'm not going anywhere.

WYNN: Ida, come on!

Wynn grabs Ida's arm, but she escapes his grasp.
They look at each other.
Klass looks at them.

WYNN: You wanna sit up here with this fuck instead of spending time with
me?

IDA: I didn't say that.

WYNN: You actin like it.

IDA: Don't grab me like that.

WYNN: You want me to rub some dirty-ass feather all over you?
Is that it?

IDA: Don't grab me again.

WYNN: Don't *make* me grab you.

He steps toward her.
Ida dares him to come closer.
Wynn backs down.

WYNN: Whatever, Ida.
You find me when you get your shit together.

Wynn exits.

Ida watches him walk away, rubbing her arm.
Ida looks to Klass, who picks up a saucer and starts polishing it.

Scene
Night.

No Klass. Two crates full of junk, a vacuum cleaner, a pile of dresses,
an old floor lamp without the lampshade, and a footstool.
Ida's stretched out on the pile of dresses, looking up at the sky.
A pen pokes out of her mouth. Hip-hop music thumps in the distance,
but Ida rests as if she's in a serene meadow. The Destiny's Child
notebook is open, resting against Ida's hip. We see a block of text scribbled
across the top half of the page. Suddenly, Ida sits up, grabs the notebook,
and writes, writes, writes.

A man yells in the distance, sirens blare, a woman wails, dogs bark.

Scene
Evening.

Two crates full of junk, a vacuum cleaner, a pile of dresses,
an old floor lamp without the lampshade, a footstool,
and a bathroom sink. Klass is asleep on the bench.

Ida enters with a McDonald's bag. She places it next to him, exits.

Scene
Night.

Klass is asleep on top of the dresses.
He grips the sleeve of a dress, wrestling with demons in his sleep.
Grunts leap from his throat.
He wakes with a jump and scampers across the ground.

KLASS: Get away from me! Get away from me! Get back!

He scoots away from his invisible predator,
running to the bench as if it were a haven.
He climbs atop the bench, grabs a can opener,
holds it like a weapon. His words are wrapped in fear.
It should be clear that he can't follow through on any of the following threats.

KLASS: Don't touch me! Don't touch me! You touch me, you get your nuts
           snatched! Touch me and you get your face fucked with a razor, dick!
           Choke your throat with rusted nails, punk bitch! Make sure you shit
           needles, muthafucka!

Klass drops the can opener.

KLASS: (whimpers) Please . . .

He slumps into a ball.

KLASS: Please . . . Please . . . don't.

Buries his face. Heavy breath.

Scene
Morning.
Hot.
Real hot.

The floor lamp and vacuum cleaner are gone.
Klass has unzipped his coat. It's spread open to reveal his wiry frame
dressed in a white tank top and baggy khakis.
Ida shoots him with a water gun. He doesn't react to the hits.

IDA: This isn't even doin anything. Are you sure you getting cooler?

KLASS: =.=

IDA: Shit, it's too hot to play crazy with that coat.

She shoots him.

IDA: Don't you think you'll feel a little . . . lighter if you take that shit off?

She strolls gangsta style on Klass, shooting him
from different spots around the bench.

IDA: (*quoting Menace II Society*) What's up now, pot-nuh?!

Ida pulls the trigger several times.
Klass doesn't flinch.
Ida drops the water gun and transforms into the wailing mother
often seen in nineties gangsta flicks: exaggerated, loud, uncontrolled.

IDA: Oh gawd!! . . . Oh lawd!! Ricky!!

Ida fakes sobs, cradles Klass's head against her bosom.
Screaming to no one in particular:

IDA: You did this to him!!

This phrase triggers something in Klass.
Panic and worry slowly conquer his face.
It's as if he's slowly stepping into a painful memory.
Ida doesn't notice this but continues her performance.

IDA: You . . . did . . . this . . . to (*losing her breath*)
                MY BABY!!

KLASS: I'm sorry.

Ida is still wrapped in her performance.

IDA: Baby, I'm sorry too, baby!!!

Klass clings to Ida.

KLASS: I'm sorry. I'm sorry.

Klass buries his face in her bosom. He cries.

IDA: Are you cryin for real?

Klass's cry turns into a weep.

IDA: Klass, what's wrong?

*Klass climbs on the bench, perches on the seat,
never losing physical contact with Ida.*

IDA: I can't help if you don't tell me what's wrong—

*Klass wraps his arms around Ida. He squeezes Ida.
A weak sound escapes from her body due to the pressure.*

IDA: Klass, that's too tight.

He weeps, squeezes Ida tighter.

IDA: (*strained*) Klass . . .

KLASS: I'm sorry, mama. I'm sorry sorry sorry—
           I couldn't save you. I'm sorry . . .

Scene
Day.

*Two crates full of junk, a pile of dresses, a footstool,
a bathroom sink. And a yellow rug.
Several flyers are tacked to both benches.
Klass is asleep.*

*Ida enters wearing a T-shirt that reads "To Protect & Serve Who?" on the front.
A picture of a young black man (Antonio) is printed on the back.
The years 1982–2008 are printed under the picture.
Ida chants:*

IDA: Justice for our Streets !!
           Justice means Peace !!

*Klass wakes with a start.
He looks at Ida. Has she lost her mind?*

IDA: Justice for our Streets !!
           Justice means Peace !!
           Klass, oh my god, Klass, you shoulda seen it!
           People everywhere! Signs everywhere! Speeches!
           Chants! Shit, I should protest more often.
           I feel good!!

Idea!!

IDA: You should start one. You should make a sign, then
go down and call out those ignorant muthafucks sittin in those big
offices.
Shame those ignorant money whores who are only interested in helping
A people, not THE people, you know? They only interested in a certain kind of people who don't LOOK nothin like me or you. Who don't
LIVE like me or you. ESPECIALLY you. Go down there and bust some
knowledge in the face of those dudes who makin your life so hard. Got
you out here livin like this. We need to get you down there, Klass.

Wait a minute:

IDA: But, but you need a chant, though. We need to write a good one for you.
You gotta yell something in repetition. Make it have a rhythm to it.
Not too many words. Gotta be simple and to the point. So those cash
hoes know what you saying. They gotta know what you're willing to
do for your rights. For your justice. It's gotta be short cause the more
you say your chant, the more you believe it. You start yelling it. Getting loud!! And you feel it coming from your toes, your nose, your,
your lips, your eyeballs:

> Justice for our Streets !!
> Justice means Peace !!

This is how it's going down:

IDA: I'll make signs. One for me. One for you. And T-shirts.
We can make those together. We'll make T-shirts.
These (*re: the one she's wearing*) cost ten bucks or some shit.
We'll make some T-shirts. We'll go in the streets
and keep marching and chanting 'til they right the wrongs!

KLASS: But I don't wanna yell. I don't got nothin to yell about.

IDA: Yeah, you do. You got plenty of things to protest.
You wanna keep livin like this?

KLASS: What's wrong with it?

IDA: What's wrong with it? Are you serious?
You see anybody fightin to get a spot on this bench?

KLASS: You.

IDA: =.=

            =.=

I don't wanna live on a damn bench, okay?
Don't get all stinked with me. I'm talking about helping you.

KLASS: You woke me up.

IDA: Go back to sleep, then.

KLASS: You woke me up, talking some mess, and now I can't go back to sleep.

IDA: Some mess? A black man died, Klass. At the hands of some Thick
Necks.

	You should be upset about that.
KLASS:	Why?
IDA:	Hel-low! Black Man! That's you!
	They could snag you just like they did Antonio.
KLASS:	He was selling fake handbags. It's against the law.
IDA:	Folks sell fake everything on that block. All year round.
	The cops don't do anything about it until they have to meet a ticket
	quote.
KLASS:	Quota.
IDA:	What?
KLASS:	Ticket "quota."
IDA:	Are you correcting how I speak?
KLASS:	Maybe you should take notes at the next one. Get it right.
IDA:	Maybe you should watch how you talk to me.
KLASS:	=.=

Klass jumps up, Ida jumps back.
He rips the fliers from the bench.

KLASS:	And don't put this shit on my stuff.
IDA:	It's public property—
KLASS:	It's MY property. And I don't want pictures of a
	DEAD MAN hanging on MY property.
IDA:	I can hang whatever I want all over this damn bench.
	It belongs to the buildings and the people who live in those buildings.
	That's me. Not you. Me.
KLASS:	Oh, so, it's my property when you wanna sit up here
	and watch the sky? When you fightin with your boyfriend
	or mad at your mama? Post this shit where somebody gives a fuck.
	And find your own shit to protest, Ida. I don't need you protesting for
	me.

Klass angrily shifts his weight on the bench
to try and go back to sleep. Ida stands, speechless.

She quietly picks up the fliers that Klass ripped off.
She looks at him, anger swelling, but is unable to say anything.
She exits.

Scene
Night.

Klass holds the pocket radio up to his ear.
Quiet, muffled voices seep from its small speaker.
He circles the bench, head down.

Ida enters, stops just at the edge.
Wynn follows. He stands next to her.

He grabs her hand in defiance.
They cross in front of the bench.

Klass doesn't break his pattern around the bench. He doesn't look up.
Ida looks at Klass. Wynn tugs.
Ida and Wynn exit.

Scene
Night.
Rain.

Ida's umbrella is broken.
Klass sits on the footstool.
He removes his coat and wraps it around the notebook.

Scene
Evening.

Two crates full of junk, a pile of dresses, a footstool,
a bathroom sink, a yellow rug, and
a bicycle wheel with the u-lock still attached.
No Klass. Wynn and Ida are by the benches.

WYNN:	You talk to your mama yet?
IDA:	No. She's gonna say it's a bad idea.
WYNN:	Then she's wrong. It's a good idea. A great idea.
	Best thing I heard all week. All year. All my life.
IDA:	I've been thinking about it for a while.
WYNN:	Couldn't ignore the signs any longer?
IDA:	That's right.
WYNN:	I'm glad, Ida. I felt like I was the last thing on your mind.
	It's nice to hear you been thinking about it.
	It's hard to know when somebody's considering an idea.
	You haven't been treatin me like you been considering me.
IDA:	You haven't been treatin me like a consideration either.
WYNN:	=.=
	=.=
	I don't wanna put my hands on you.
IDA:	I know.
WYNN:	I shouldn't.
IDA:	You won't. Not again.
WYNN:	I won't. And you won't hang out with Pigeon.
IDA:	His name is Klass.
WYNN:	You won't.
IDA:	I shouldn't.

WYNN: Not again. No more.

IDA: I shouldn't.

WYNN: You thinkin they (*re: the building's tenants*) don't see.
         They see you.

IDA: There's a difference between seeing and recognizing.
         A difference between watching and looking.

WYNN: Don't p & q this talk, Ida.

IDA: Nobody cares, Wynn.

WYNN: Your mama knows you hanging out with him?

IDA: Yeah.

WYNN: What she saying?

IDA: She yells about it.

WYNN: Are you listening?

IDA: I hear it. Don't listen.

WYNN: You should be listenin.

IDA: Maybe I'll listen when she says I'm not ready to move in with you.

WYNN: No. Don't listen to that part. You might hear it, but don't listen to her.
         He's crazy. I'm not.

IDA: He's not crazy—

WYNN: If I have to grab you and take you away from him,
         I'll do that. I'll snatch you from this to save you.

IDA: From what?

WYNN: =.= (*how do I say this?*)
         You're not the kind of female who saves people.
         You can't fix him. You can't fix people.
         You settle into how they are. That's why I'm good for you,
         cause I got my shit together. And me having my shit together
         means you'll have yourself together, too.

IDA: It's hard for me to see the good in what you just said.

WYNN: It's in there. I want to help you. I want your dreams to come true.
         Shake you from playing pretend with Pigeon.
         You think he's gonna save you?
         You see what kind of situation he got his self in.
         What you want for yourself, Ida? I'll make sure you get it.

Ida thinks. She seriously considers her wants and needs.

IDA: I wanna go to school.

WYNN: Good. Yeah. Definitely. I think you'd do well.

IDA: I wanna get a job I like. And I think I have to learn more things
         before I can work at the places I wanna work.

WYNN: Absolutely.

IDA: I wanna be your equal.

WYNN: For sure.

IDA: Where you gonna take me?

WYNN: Where you wanna go?

IDA:	I want a nice place. Lots of windows. Lots of light.
	I want to see the sky. I want a view.
	Not just staring into the side of another building.
WYNN:	Okay.
IDA:	And I want a big refrigerator. With an icemaker.
WYNN:	Crushed, shredded, and cubed.
IDA:	And I don't want all this noise all the time. I want it to be quiet.
WYNN:	Done. Whatever you want, Ida.

=.=

	You'll tell your mama? You're coming to be with me?
IDA:	You wanna be there with me? When I tell her?
	I want you there. She won't act too crazy if you're there smiling at her.
WYNN:	Yeah. Okay. I will.

They kiss.

WYNN:	No more Pigeon.
IDA:	No more.

Scene
Day.

Two crates full of junk, a pile of dresses, a footstool,
a bathroom sink, a yellow rug, and a bicycle wheel
with the u-lock still attached surround Klass.
The notebook straddles the back of the bench.
The Destiny's Child cover hangs horizontally.
The trio of smiling faces gleam at the audience.

Klass stands next to the notebook.
His coat is on the ground among the other things.
He's wearing a brown T-shirt with unreadable markings on it.
Looks as if someone slashed it with a black sharpie.
On the other side of Klass is a pile of T-shirts in
an assortment of sizes and colors.

Klass has rearranged his possessions into the curved shape of a bustling crowd.
He addresses the objects around him
as if he's addressing an eager and devout congregation.

(Side note: Klass evokes a performance style similar to that of Robert Preston's "Trouble" from
Music Man, 1962. He also taps into a Baptist minister style à la Reverend B. W. Smith. If a middle
ground can be found between these two, that'd be so so cool.)

KLASS:	You may not be fully aware of the times we're livin in.
	The times that they don't print in our papers or splash
	across our screens or pump through our radios.
	I suggest you might not be aware because I see you.

I watch you. I see you holding on to what little sanity and security you have left, squeezing it so tight that the color is leaving your fingers, draining from your hands. The squeezing is causing your muscles to ache. Jaws to clench. And you think that pain is a sign of sanity? Security? It's not, my friends. It's not.

=.=

There's a wind blowin through you.

=.=

A violent gust of truth.

=.=

It starts out as a breeze somewhere in here: (*points at his heart*) and it wakes up all the noise inside of you.
Then that breeze gets in your blood. Travels through every vein. Head to toe. It gathers enough speed to the point where it won't let you sleep at night. That breeze becomes a gust and that gust won't let you be still. Won't keep your troubles quiet. You sit on stoops, lean against cars, stand under the moon—restless. You walk to one end of your neighborhood then back to the other end, go sit back on that same stoop, sit under the sun—restless. The gust is stirring your soul. It's pulling up memories from way down deep, from the cracks and crevices covered with scabs and scars. We swallow what we think is liquor, inhale what we think is weed, inject what we think is freedom. We alter our state of reality so we don't have to participate in it. So we can't be responsible, aware, dependable.
And what happens when we hear a scream? When we see someone who looks like us, cornered? Pleading? Hm?

Klass turns away as if he's ignoring a weeping soul.

We cross the street. We turn the music up a little louder.
We drink, smoke, squeeze . . . but we still hear it.
It never goes away. The wind, the noise, that somebody pleading . . . it's not going away. And then the next somebody is cornered.

Klass turns away.

And then the next one . . .

He turns away.

And then the next—until it's you. And then you want to know why no one's coming to save you, to take you to a safe place?

Throughout the rest of his speech Klass slowly sheds the "performance."
His genuine self floats to the surface.

I know it's scary. It's terrifying when you hear about
Thick Necks taking dudes out, and, and you hear about drug heads snatching bags, and you see people walkin the streets, talking crazy.
All you wanna do is turn away. But, but we shouldn't do that anymore.

Klass gestures to the pile of T-shirts next to him.

> I made these protest T-shirts. You can pick whatever you want.
> Take whichever you want. Each one of them says different things.
> I wrote different things on each one.

Klass grabs a T-shirt from the pile, holds it up.
The message is unreadable.

> This one says: Hi, my name is Klass. I live on a bench
> in the David L. Hynn projects. Say "good morning" when you pass by.
> I won't hurt you.

He tosses that shirt out into the crowd of objects.
He picks up another one from the pile
and displays it. The message is unreadable.

> And this one says: I used to sleep in a shelter in another city
> far, far from here.

He tosses it, grabs another one.

> And this one says: My daddy used to be the Super here.
> His name was Paul. He went to people's apartments and fixed things.
> He was very nice.

He tosses it and reads from another shirt.

> My daddy taught me how to change the chain on my bike.
> I don't know if I ever loved him. I just know he fixed things that
> were broken and then I could go play outside.

He tosses it, grabs another one.

> My moms wanted me to have siblings: a brother and a sister.
> My daddy wanted to name my baby brother Taylor and my baby sister
> Grace. My dad is the one who named me Klass with a "k."

He tosses it, grabs another one.

> My name isn't Pigeon.

He flips the T-shirt over to the back side.

> You think you can call me whatever you want
> but you can't. You don't know me.

He tosses it, picks up another shirt.

> I used to live with my family in building one.

Klass points in the direction of building one.

> I got pulled out when I was a kid.

He tosses the shirt, grabs another one.

> This is a fire. And this . . .
> (*he points to a spot on the shirt*)
> is my folks in the fire.

Klass turns the shirt over to the back side.

>These are the hands that pulled me out.

He drops the shirt on the ground,
letting it fall wherever it falls.
He's lost interest in the crowd.
He travels back into his memories.

He picks up another shirt, but doesn't bother displaying it.
From this point on he addresses the shirts
as if he's going through a photo album.

>This is the room they put me in at the hospital.
>I was a kid. I was eight.

He tosses it, grabs another one.

>A social worker told me what happened to my folks.
>She hugged me.
>I remember the side of my face pressed against her chest.
>That was the night the system got a hold of me and didn't let go
>'til I was eighteen.

He tosses it, grabs another one.

>This is the dude who started the fire.
>He lived in the apartment below ours.
>He was a few years older than me.
>He used to kick my ass every day.

He tosses it, grabs another one.

>This is the foster building I lived in for ten years.
>The day I got out I found that dude
>who started the fire and slammed him in the face with a brick.

He flips the shirt to the back side.

>Here's a picture of that brick.

Klass drops that shirt.
He looks down at the one he's wearing.

>And this one is me in the future
>fixing the chain on my daughter's bike.

He stretches to catch a glimpse of the back side.

>This is me and her mother
>watching our daughter ride around.

Klass waves at his future.

>All these shirts are free.
>Take however many you want.

He steps down from the bench,
sits. He looks at the notebook.

Justice for our streets.
Justice means peace.
Justice for our . . . streets.
Justice means . . .

Scene
Evening.

Klass is asleep. The notebook rests in his lap.
All of his things (two crates full of junk, a pile of dresses, etc.,)
are neatly packed under both benches.

Ida enters but stops at the edge. She looks at Klass.
She crosses to the other side, then exits.

Several moments pass.

Ida enters and goes over to Klass.
She looks at the notebook on his lap.
She ever so slowly reaches and grabs the notebook
then scurries away on tiptoe.

Scene
Night.
Hours later.

Klass wakes with a jump, reaches for the notebook.
It's gone. He looks around. Nothing.
Did he put it back under the coat? No.
Is he sitting on it? No.
Where is it?
He looks under the rug.
Pulls out one crate, digs through it, then the other.
Pulls out the dresses from the bathroom sink.
Shakes out each one. Nothing.

Wynn enters.
Klass spots him.

KLASS: Did you steal my stuff?
WYNN: What?
KLASS: Did you steal my stuff?
WYNN: Man, don't nobody want that junk.

Wynn keeps walking. Klass leaps into his path.
Wynn steps back, ready to defend himself.

KLASS: I had my notebook when I fell asleep and now it's gone.

WYNN:	That ain't got shit to do with me.
KLASS:	Did you take it?
WYNN:	Look, if you wanna throw down let's do it. None of this talkin shit.
KLASS:	Did you take it!
WYNN:	Oh, you wanna yell at a brotha? Crazy mutha—

Wynn shoves Klass.
Klass shoves Wynn back.
They look at each other, breathing hard.
The duel ensues. They lock horns, spin, then break away,
circling each other. Each time they come together they form a tight knot.
One of them wails or screams, then they break away.

The bout builds and builds until Klass pens Wynn behind the bench.
Klass grabs hold of his arm and bends it back until there's a popping sound.

WYNN:	Ahhhhhhh! Fuck!!!!!!!

Scene
The following morning.

Klass sleeps on the ground.
The dresses cover him like a blanket.
Ida enters and throws the notebook at him.
Klass snaps awake.

IDA:	I took it.
KLASS:	=.=
IDA:	I snatched it while you was sleepin.

Klass picks up the notebook, flips through it.

IDA:	I tore out my pages.
KLASS:	Why'd you steal it?
IDA:	Cause I don't want you carryin me in there anymore.
	I was on half those pages and I took my half back.
KLASS:	It's my notebook. You just can't go around stealing people's stuff.
IDA:	I gave it back, didn't I?
	Wynn is bringing his boys to come beat your ass.
	You broke his arm. He works with his hands.
	He's losing money cause of you.
	Is that shit (*re: the notebook*) that important to you?
	That shit worth taking away somebody's livelihood?
KLASS:	Your livelihood, too.
IDA:	What?
KLASS:	I break his arm; I break your ATM.
IDA:	Half the time I'm with you, you don't say shit.
	And when you do speak you end up tryin to talk shit about me?

KLASS: Don't matter if you rip those pages out. It don't matter.
           Doesn't matter, Ida Peters. Ida Peters.
           Ida Peters Ida Peters Ida . . .

Klass tosses the notebook to the side. He doesn't need it.
He recites her life as if it's an old Negro chant.

KLASS: Your name is Ida Peters. You're eighteen years old.
           It don't matter if you take those pages from me. . . .
           Born and raised in the David L. Hynn housing projects.
           No brothers. No sisters.
           Your mama's living on disability checks.

IDA: =.=

KLASS: Your father's been living on the other side of the city all your life.
           But you only talked to him three times. Saw him once.
           You have a picture of him from when he was eighteen.
           You only know what he looks like when he was your age.
           You wouldn't know him if you saw him today. Right now.
           You claim you would. But you know you wouldn't.
           You feel like my eyes hold you just like
           the eyes in your daddy's picture.

IDA: =.=

Klass looks at Ida.
She returns his stone-cold gaze.

KLASS: Ida Peters.
           I don't need those pages . . .
           don't matter if you take 'em from me—

IDA: Klass Washington. Twenty-five years old.
           No brothers. No sisters. No mother. No father.
           You're still too scared to fall asleep inside four walls,
           under a ceiling. Still too scared if sirens wake you up.
           Still need to have a can of grape soda every day
           because it's the last sweet thing your mama gave you.
           You don't consider yourself a real man because you never got the
           chance to leave home. Your home left you.

Klass gets on his knees.

IDA: Klass Washington. I don't need those pages either.

Ida looks at Klass.
He returns her stone-cold gaze.

KLASS: You want to work behind a desk.
           Answering phones for Young White Man Esquire.
           You want to wear pretty cotton skirts with the complementary
           blouses that make Young White Man Esquire smile. Readjust his
           junk. And maybe . . . the afternoon before you leave early for Christ-
           mas holiday, you'll let Esquire touch your cheek.

(Klass gestures a grip on Ida's ass)

	Squeeze your cheek.
	Bite. Hard.
IDA:	You still have the bite marks on your shoulders.

Ida falls to her knees.

	Two scars on the left. Three on the right.
	One of them was a biter. And if he couldn't bite you there because of the scabs, he'd chew on the back of you. He'd chew on your hair. You shaved it off, he'd bite your scalp. You stopped deciding what was worse: him topping you or the skin breaking on the back of your head. Him drinking your blood.
KLASS:	You hear your mama strugglin to open a drawer or pick up a cup, but you don't move. You let her struggle because she's getting what she deserves. Everything is her fault.
IDA:	You were the smallest in that foster home.
	And the smallest one gets busted by the bigger ones.
KLASS:	You want her to suffer. . . .
IDA:	The light-skinned one sits up first. . . .
KLASS:	Never no money for nothing.
	Only enough for her medication, for her nurse. . . .
	No cell phone for you, no new kicks, no new clothes.
IDA:	And then he wakes up the one with the crooked teeth. . . .
	Then the oldest one gets up. . . .
KLASS:	Sometimes you put stuff out of her reach
	cause you know she'll need it. She'll struggle to get it.
IDA:	They surround your bed. The oldest one flips you over.
	They know you're not asleep even though you try to act like it.
KLASS:	*(imitating Ida's mama)* "Ida! I-da! I know you hear me!
	Ida, I need help in the kitchen!!"
IDA:	*(imitating the boys from the foster home)* "That's right, man. Don't make a fuckin sound. Keep your mouth shut while we handle this shit right here."

They reach out with one hand and grab
each other by the neck at the same time.
They squeeze. They strain to breathe but hold on.
They look at each other.

The neighborhood bustles. Hip-hop bumps in the distance.

Klass lets go, falls back.
Ida lets go, falls on top of him.

They roll. He's on top of her.
She pushes him away, pulls him in.
They roll. She's on top of him. She gets up.

He grabs her, pulls her down.
She struggles. She surrenders. She pushes.
She pulls. He pulls. He licks. She bites. He scratches.
She grunts. She gasps. He whimpers. He inhales.
He releases. She pulls. She wails.
They hold. Tears. They hold. Gasp. They hold.
Klass rolls away from her.

Ida stares up at the sky, chasing breath.
Klass stares up at the sky, chasing breath.

Ida slowly rises to her feet.
Without a word or a glance, she walks away.
Klass watches the sky.

Scene
Day.

Two crates full of junk, a pile of dresses, a footstool, a bathroom sink,
a yellow rug, and a bicycle wheel with a u-lock still attached.
No Klass.

Scene
Evening.

Two crates full of junk, a pile of dresses, a footstool,
a bathroom sink, a yellow rug, a bicycle wheel with a u-lock
still attached, a pile of T-shirts, a microwave, and a box fan.
No Klass.

Scene
Night.

Three cans of soup sit on the bench.
The dresses are stuffed into the microwave.
The T-shirts are draped across the other bench.
No Klass.

Ida enters, carrying two plastic bags full of groceries. She crosses, exits.

Scene
Day.

The notebook is shredded; pieces of it blow in the wind.
The sink is gone.

The lamp is back, tipped over, leaning across a bench.
Empty soup cans lie about.
No Klass.

Scene
Evening.

One of the benches is destroyed. The slats are gone.
The rusted metal frame remains.
No Klass.

Wynn enters pulling a big suitcase. His arm is in a cast. He crosses, exits.
Ida enters carrying a box. She crosses, exits.
Wynn enters, crosses, exits.

Klass enters wearing his coat.
The hood is pulled up, casting a shadow across his face.
He carries a colander and a handful of straws.
He sits.

Ida enters. She sees Klass, keeps her head down.
Klass ignores her. Ida crosses, exits.
Klass polishes the colander.

Wynn enters pulling another large suitcase.
He redirects his path so that he walks in front of Klass.
He purposely and aggressively kicks Klass's things as he crosses.
Klass ignores him. He polishes his colander.

WYNN:　　　(*mumbles*) Dumb ass, punk.

Wynn exits.

Klass puts the colander down, fishes for the salt and pepper shakers.
He polishes them.

Ida enters carrying too much. She drops a few things.
Klass ignores her.
Ida puts everything down and reorganizes her load.
She picks it all up again, crosses, and exits.
Klass stops polishing, turns his head to watch her.
He pulls down his hood, reveals a bruised and swollen face.

Scene
Night.

Klass is asleep. He wakes up with a jump.
He bats at the back of his head, his neck.

KLASS: (*terrorized*) Get away from me!

             Get away from me....

He falls off the bench and scoots away from his invisible predator, throwing objects in its path.
Klass musters up the courage to stand up for himself.
He scrambles to his feet.

          Come on! Come on!

          Let's do this for real. Come on, muthafucka!

He wrestles with the air, falls to the ground.
He wiggles out of his coat and springs back to his feet.

          Ha! Yeah, you thought you had me!

          You ain't got shit!

Another razzle-dazzle move Muhammad Ali–style.
Klass goes in for the attack.

          Blam!

          Blam!

          Blam!

          Blam!

          Try and breathe after that, punk bitch!

Victorious, the winded Klass falls to the ground.
Without warning, a police light lands on him.
Klass, wild-eyed, shields his face from the light.

A voice comes from behind the light.

THICK NECK 1: Hello.

KLASS: =.= (*breathing*)

THICK NECK 1: How are you feelin tonight?

KLASS: =.=

THICK NECK 1: Everything alright?

KLASS: =.=

THICK NECK 1: We got a call about a disturbance.

              Makin sure everything is alright.

KLASS: =.=

THICK NECK 1: My name is Officer Ryan. What's your name?

KLASS: I don't wanna go to jail.

THICK NECK 1: What's that?

KLASS: =.=

THICK NECK 1: You have some ID I can take a look at?

KLASS: No.

THICK NECK 1: You got somewhere you can go tonight?

KLASS: No.

THICK NECK 1: People tell us you been stayin here on these benches for a while.

KLASS: =.=

THICK NECK 1: Where are you coming from?

KLASS: =.=

THICK NECK 1: What's your name?

KLASS: They call me Pigeon.

THICK NECK 1: Is that your real name?

KLASS: =.=

THICK NECK 1: Well, Pigeon, I'm afraid I can't let you stay here tonight.

A siren pulls up. The siren shuts off.
Another light shines on Klass.

THICK NECK 1: Tenants called in. We have to remove you.

KLASS: This is where I live.

THICK NECK 1: We can check around with a few shelters.
                  See if they have beds tonight.

KLASS: No. No shelters. No beds. I want to stay here.

THICK NECK 2: It's usually easier to get a bed in the summer months.

KLASS: What about my stuff? I have things that I need to keep with me.
                  I can't leave any of it. And the shelter won't protect it.
                  Somebody'll take it.

THICK NECK 1 & 2: Whoa . . . hey, calm down . . .

THICK NECK 1: We won't let anyone take your things.
                  We will need you to calm down.

THICK NECK 2: (*to Thick Neck 1*) What's his name?

THICK NECK 1: Says it's "Pigeon."

THICK NECK 2: Clever . . .
                  Pigeon, we won't let anyone steal your stuff, okay?
                  But you'll have to calm down. We're here to help you.

KLASS: I don't need any help.

THICK NECK 2: Well, we disagree.
                  And the residents in these apartments disagree.

KLASS: =.=

Another siren pulls up, shuts off.
Three lights are on Klass.

THICK NECK 2: We can take you to get your face fixed. Looks like somebody got you
                  good. Who did that to you?

KLASS: Nobody.

THICK NECK 1: Well, you should get that fixed up. Infections can happen before you
                  know it.

Another motorcycle pulls up, shuts off.
Four lights are on Klass.
Thick Necks talk among themselves.
Klass strains to see past the beams of light.

THICK NECK 1: Stinks to high hell.

THICK NECK 3: No track marks.

THICK NECK 1: Well, there's obviously something wrong with him.
THICK NECK 2: Think the ward'll take him?
THICK NECK 3: Maybe.
THICK NECK 1: Hey, Pigeon, let's take you somewhere safe, alright?

Klass's eyes grow big and wild as the lights get closer.
He screams. Flails. Starts swinging.

KLASS: I don't want to leave! I can't leave.
Don't take me anywhere!
I didn't do anything!
I didn't do anything!

Police lights go out. Sounds of a scuffle.
A zap.
Klass falls to the ground. He moans.

Scene
Day.

Neighborhood sounds.

No Klass.
All of his things are gone.
The two benches are gone.

Ida enters, upset. Wynn follows. The cast on his arm is gone.

WYNN: Ida, slow down.
IDA: Ugh, she gets on my last nerve, Wynn.
Where she comin from sayin all that shit to me?
To my face! And expect me to sit there and take it?
WYNN: She ain't right, Ida. You know that. I know that.
IDA: I don't care. She still my mama.
She need to act like she got some repect for me.
I'm a married woman. I'm in school. I know things.
Tellin me I don't know shit about life.
She ain't never really lived hers.
How she gonna judge what I do with mine?
WYNN: She's just sad. Sad you left. Sad you been gone.
IDA: Why are you stickin up for her?
WYNN: I'm not stickin up for her.
IDA: Yes, you are. Don't forget she was bustin on you, too.
Calling you weak. Said you foolish for putting up with me.
WYNN: She don't know what she's talkin bout.
She don't know what she's sayin.
IDA: She says it like she does.

WYNN: She don't. Your mama sits up in that apartment all day watching TV, drinking Diet Coke. She ain't aware of half the shit she say.

She just talk to be talking.

IDA: You can let it roll easy, because she's not your mother.

        =.=

        =.=

I don't wanna come back here again.

WYNN: You don't mean that.

IDA: I do.

WYNN: Ida, you don't.

IDA: This is the last time I wanna walk anywhere near here.

I don't wanna see her again. Don't wanna walk across this courtyard. Don't wanna hear all this bullshit noise ever again.

WYNN: You gonna miss it. Miss her.

IDA: No. No I won't.

And don't make it seem like I'm fickle.

WYNN: Take it easy, gurl. Don't flip out on me, too.

IDA: =.=

        =.=

I bring up one thing about seeing my father and she . . .

Wynn hugs her. Ida relaxes.

IDA: Thank you for coming with me.

WYNN: You're welcome, my baby.

IDA: Thank you for anchoring me.

WYNN: Because I love you, Ida.

IDA: Thank you for takin care of me.

WYNN: I love you, Ida.

IDA: You saved me.

WYNN: Because I love you.

IDA: I was kickin, screamin, wailing for help and you saved me.

Ida kisses Wynn.

IDA: Will you take me home?

WYNN: I'll take you

wherever you want to go.

They exit, holding hands.

Distorted hip-hop music bumps in the distance.

End of Play

LYDIA R. DIAMOND

Lydia Diamond made theater history as one of three African American women whose plays were produced on Broadway during the 2011–2012 season. The other two were Katori Hall and Suzan-Lori Parks. Born in Detroit, Michigan, and raised by her mother, Diamond grew up around educators who were also musicians. Her grandmother was a pianist; her grandfather played the violin, and her mother played flute and piano. As an only child who spent most of her time around adults, Diamond became an avid reader and although she took violin lessons, she did not inherit her family's talent for music. She gravitated instead to theater. In 1987 Diamond enrolled in Northwestern University to study acting. She was introduced to playwriting in her junior year and graduated with a degree in peformance studies in 1991. Like many African American actors who turn to playwriting, Diamond was discouraged by the limited number of roles for black women, so she started writing for herself. After graduating, Diamond decided to stay in Chicago, where she founded a theater company with a very long name: Another Small Black Theatre Company with Good Things to Say and a Lot of Nerve. She later co-founded Onyx Theatre Ensemble and eventually became a resident playwright at Chicago Dramatists, a company committed to new play development. Her career began to take off after Chuck Smith, an associate artistic director at Chicago's Goodman Theater, directed her play *The Gift Horse* in 2000. This led to a commission in 2006 from the Steppenwolf Theater Company to write *Voyeurs de Venus,* which was subsequently produced at Chicago Dramatists. *Voyeurs de Venus* and *Stick Fly* (premiered at Congo Square Theatre Ensemble) were both produced in the same season, and both received Joseph Jefferson Best Play nominations; *Voyeurs de Venus* won the honor. *Stick Fly* went on to Broadway in 2011. Other Steppenwolf commissions include two for Theater for Young Adults: an adaptation of Toni Morrison's novel *The Bluest Eye* (2005) and a play inspired by Harriet Jacobs's slave narrative *Incidents in the Life of a Slave Girl*, titled *Harriet Jacobs* (2008). Diamond has taught playwriting at numerous colleges and universities, including Boston University, where she was on faculty for eight years. She has been a resident playwright at Chicago Dramatists, a TCG/NEA playwright in residence at Steppenwolf Theater, and a 2013–14 Playwright in Residence at Arena Stage in Washington, D.C. She lists among her honors and awards an honorary Doctorate of Arts degree from Pine Manor College in Chestnut Hill, Massachusetts. Diamond's plays have received numerous productions around the country.

·   ·   ·

Voyeurs de Venus had its world premiere in 2006 at Chicago Dramatists.

Director:	Russ Tutterow
Sara Washington:	Tania Richard
James Bradford:	Christopher Cordon
Saartjie Baartman:	Penelope Walker
Alexander Dunlop:	Ron Quade
William Bullock:	Carl Richards, Ron Wells
James Booker:	Alfred C. Kemp
Georges Cuvier:	Michael Joseph Mitchell
Millicent Ducent:	Cameron Feogin
Becky:	Jamie Hayden
Dancers:	Maya-Camille Broussard, Camille T. Anderson, Jamie Hayden, Jessica Deahr
Set:	Simon Lashford
Costume:	Sharlet Webb
Lighting:	Jeff Pines
Props:	Linda Laake
Original music and sound:	Bary Bennett

VOYEURS DE VENUS

CHARACTER DESCRIPTIONS

Sara Washington: Early thirties, African American. Sara, a cultural anthropologist, has already garnered the professional respect of her peers. She is a tenured professor at a leading research institution and a very prolific writer. Sara is more confident in her professional life than she is in her personal life. Her intellectual bravado masks a social vulnerability.

James Bradsford: Early-to-mid forties. White. Strikingly attractive, very blond, tall. Sara's husband. Bradsford carries a palpable sadness and touching gentleness. He loves Sara with all his heart. Bradsford is not as professionally respected as Sara but holds a tenured position in the sociology department of her institution. He is a hard worker, though not terribly ambitious. He has learned to be content.

Saartjie Baartman (The Hottentot Venus): Early twenties. Saartjie is a brown-skinned, voluptuously proportioned African woman. She is an early nineteenth-century Khoisan woman. Her speech is rather unaffected, and she speaks French, Dutch, English, and a Khoisan dialect fluently. She has a self-possessed but nonconfrontational demeanor. Saartjie is extremely intelligent, though this intelligence is overlooked by her contemporaries. Also, wisely, she hides behind a rather sullen mask of apparent contentment.

Alexander Dunlop: Caucasian. English, in his fifties to sixties. Frumpy, terribly insecure. Dunlop is the ship's doctor who first brought Saartjie to England and displayed her. He is the first of several white "guardians".

William Bullock*: Caucasian. English, forties to fifties. Mr. Bullock is the distinguished director of a natural history museum in nineteenth-century Liverpool.

Carl Richards*: Mid-to-late thirties white. Contemporary. Publisher interested in Sara's book. He's a drip.

(*These characters should be portrayed by the same actor.)

James Booker: Mid-forties. African American. Editor-in-chief. Charismatic, elegant, brilliant. James comes from a humble background and has excelled through sheer force of will, ambition, and hard work. He has championed Sara's book. Sara and James must have an electric physical attraction for one another.

Georges Cuvier: French 1800s. Caucasian. Mid-thirties. Cuvier is extremely driven, relatively anti-social, inept with women. Cuvier definitely has a sadistic edge—a quality rather than a character trait. It is important that he not be cast as "the villain."

Millicent Ducent: French 1800s. Caucasian. Millicent is Cuvier's devoted assistant. She is admiring and loyal. Millicent appears plain but is actually quite attractive. She blossoms over the course of the play. Millicent could not be described as exceptionally intelligent, but is observant and well-spoken.

Becky: Appears in one of Sara's nightmares. A stereotype of a blonde, Caucasian suburbanite. (Should be played by one of the white dancers).

Two to Four African American women, all very attractive, all radically different in shape, size, and color. Two attractive white women. All should be excellent dancers.

Act I

Scene 1

Beautiful black women of different hues and body types, clad in exquisite white European finery of the early 1800s, wearing equally extravagant wigs. They stand on pillar-like platforms of varying heights. Out of the darkness a piercing spot flashes on one or another of them, alternately. Just long enough to establish their awe-inspiring beauty. Each strikes a Victorian pose.

A percussive beat turns into a funky groove and then into a pulsing go-go beat. The lights rise slowly on the women, who begin a highly choreographed, stylized go-go-inspired dance routine.

Three white women, topless, in banana skirts with braided hair, are raised on a podium center stage. They begin an expertly executed, authentic pan-African dance. The black women watch. A dance-off ensues. The black women go-go dance while the white women expertly execute more and more advanced African moves.

Stage goes to black.

Sara screams in the dark.

Lights.

Sara and Bradsford are in bed. Early morning. The present. Chicago.

Sara sits up, startled.

BRADSFORD: Again?

SARA: Yeah.

BRADSFORD: You aren't in it?

SARA: No. But I think I should be.

BRADSFORD: Is she there?

SARA: No, no that's the thing.

BRADSFORD: The thing?

SARA: I'm aware of her absence and it disturbs me. And it comforts me.

BRADSFORD: Is he there?

SARA: Cuvier? No.

BRADSFORD: You are so cute.

SARA: This is so not the time.

BRADSFORD: I'm just saying.

SARA: Save it. (*Beat.*) You know it's guilt.

BRADSFORD: Whose?

SARA: Mine.

BRADSFORD: Right. Right. You are solely responsible for the subjugation of your predecessors . . .

SARA: What is your day like?

BRADSFORD: It should begin with three more hours of sleep.

SARA: Do you love me at four in the morning?

BRADSFORD: No. But I tolerate you, because I love you so much at nine.

(*Bradsford turns out lamp. Sara turns it on.*)

SARA: Consider this for a minute, will you?

BRADSFORD: Why?

SARA: Last thing. I promise. (*Beat.*) We know that history is largely fabrication, right?

BRADSFORD: Not largely. (*Beat.*) Fine. If I agree, will you make your point?

SARA: Okay. If history is, arguably, a fabrication . . . at least to the extent that it can only be told through the socio-political-sexual-psychological lens of the person telling it, right, what then is fiction?

BRADSFORD: Good night.

SARA: Good night.

Scene 2

London, England, 1810.

Dunlop paces in front of a screen. Saartjie remains behind the screen throughout the scene. In silhouette we see her struggle into an elaborate, padded foundation garment. A brown dress hangs in front of the screen.

DUNLOP: No.

SAARTJIE: Come closer, and then?

DUNLOP: What did I tell you?

SAARTJIE: I'm sorry?

DUNLOP: Yes, you most certainly are. Only repeat what I have said.

SAARTJIE: I don't understand.

DUNLOP: Not important that you understand. Only that you do. I should be made a mockery of had I a witness. I don't know what the Dutch expected of you, but you are in Europe . . . and while it is true, we pride ourselves on a certain amount of gentility and restraint, you are testing me.

SAARTJIE: The petticoats are shorter than the ones you gave me on the ship.

DUNLOP: They are supposed to be. Now say it.

SAARTJIE: Come closer, I shall not bite. (*Beat.*) Will you pull the lacings please . . .

(*Dunlop stands in our view, reaching behind the screen. As he tightens the corset Saartjie turns sideways and we see that her bottom and bust are greatly exaggerated, even more so as her waist becomes smaller.*)

DUNLOP: Again . . .

SAARTJIE: That hurts. . . . This hurts.

DUNLOP: (*still pulling*) Please continue.

SAARTJIE: There. Stop.

DUNLOP: Fine. (*He ties the string.*)

(*Saartjie begins to struggle into a very tight-fitting knee-length dress.*)

DUNLOP: Now, again.

SAARTJIE: Come closer, I shall not bite. I am The Venus Hottentot. Just arrived from the most savage parts of the Dark Continent.

DUNLOP: Very nice.

SAARTJIE: Why should I bite?

DUNLOP: You shouldn't.

SAARTJIE: Why would I?

DUNLOP: You won't.

SAARTJIE: How is it?

(*Bullock reaches for her hand.*)

DUNLOP: Exquisite. You shall be the burnt toast of the town.

SAARTJIE: I don't think I understand . . .

DUNLOP: Ah, you're doing it again. Thinking. Stop that and let us have a look.

(*Blackout, before we see Saartjie.*)

Scene 3

Morning. The present. Chicago.

Sara stands in the middle of the room in pajamas.

She orates to Bradsford, who reclines in bed.

SARA: No, Mommy, . . . but I want to be the First Lady.

(*Beat. Sara waits for her laugh. It's not coming.*)

Maybe it's not funny. I should give them time to get acclimated, shouldn't I?

BRADSFORD: It was fine. It was funny.

SARA: No no no no no . . . anecdotes and jokes should come after I've run down my credentials. They aren't automatically invested . . .

BRADSFORD: Yes, but . . .

SARA: But I explained it . . .

BRADSFORD: You did? You did. Yes. . . . Coffee?

(*Bradsford gets out of bed while Sara continues.*)

SARA: But maybe if I start with credentials or a dissection of my pedagogy they lose the first four sentences re-orienting themselves. . . .

BRADSFORD: There's no reorienting, this is the twenty-first century. They're no longer shocked that black people can talk. (*Beat.*) Coffee?

SARA: Thank you . . . yes. And you know as well as I that isn't entirely true.

BRADSFORD: An articulate black person is not, in and of itself, a shocking thing.

SARA: Awight. Awight.

BRADSFORD: I only said they're not shocked, I didn't say they want to hear it. Look, they're bestowing the honor upon you, so it's a given that you're articulate. What they don't know is whether or not you're interesting and. . . .

SARA: Okay, okay.

(*Sara paces, takes a breath, rearranges papers, and ceremoniously resumes.*)

A while ago . . .

BRADSFORD: A while ago?

SARA: Recently?

BRADSFORD: Why when?

SARA: Why not?

BRADSFORD: I think "a while ago" undermines the urgency of . . .

SARA: You're picking.

BRADSFORD: Am I? Out of love, I'm sure.

SARA: You've seen me be brilliant. I thought you were getting coffee.

BRADSFORD: You're right. Keep on, I'm listening.

(*Bradsford exits toward kitchen.*)

SARA: Recently a story caught my attention.

BRADSFORD: (*O.S.*) I'm still listening . . .

SARA: (*Pulls a pen out of her hair and makes the edit. She resumes her former posture.*) A most interesting and somewhat startling bit of news caught my attention recently. (*Beat.*) Recently caught my attention. (*She makes the note.*) It was not hard news, but really neither was it soft.

BRADSFORD: (*O.S.*) Cute.

SARA: It seems the South African government had been in a protracted political struggle with France. The French Museum of Mankind, Le Musée de l'Homme, had been displaying a rather crude exhibit of an early nineteenth-century South African Khoisan woman. A wax mold of her body, then thought remarkable for its steatopygia,

BRADSFORD: (*re-entering holding two mugs*) Steatopygia?

SARA: Voluptuous ass. It's okay if they don't all know what it means. It's better if they don't know. I should tell them about Cuvier, shouldn't I?

BRADSFORD: Rhetorical?

SARA: Sure. In 1820 Georges Cuvier, known by many as the father of modern anatomy, made a wax mold of her body, then thought remarkable for its steatopygia, mounted her skeleton, and preserved pieces of her genitalia in a jar. It was all subsequently put on public display.

(*Bradsford hands Sara a cup. She takes a few gulps and hands the mug back, continuing.*)

Thank you. Okay. Baartman display, Baartman display . . . Okay. I was intrigued. It seemed to me the perfect intersection of history, anthropology, and popular cultures. Which has led me to Saartjie. Sara. Saartjie Baartman. Most often and insultingly referred to as the Hottentot Venus. Slide.

BRADSFORD: I thought you weren't showing her.

SARA: I'm not. I wouldn't. It's me.

(*A slide of a happy, somewhat nerdy eight-year-old appears on the scrim behind Sara. She's all teeth, hair, and horn-rimmed glasses.*)

SARA: So how does a toothy pre-adolescent grow into an obscure, if celebrated, social anthropologist? Circuitously.

(*Lights dim. Sara removes her pajamas, under which she sports a sharp suit. A white dancer in tribal costumes from the first dream sequence pushes on a lectern, another takes Sara's pajamas. They exit. Bradsford kisses Sara on the cheek and exits.*

A special rises on Sara. We are no longer in the bedroom. We are now the audience at an event.)

SARA: My desire to grow up and be the first lady disturbed my afro-wearing, feminist-minded hippie mother greatly. Slide, please.

(*Slide changes to a picture of the White House.*)

Like a mantra she imparted her desire to see me strive always for the most, the best, the highest pinnacle of whatever one should strive for. And she relentlessly drummed into my head the notion that I could, would, should obtain these goals. You can be a doctor, a lawyer, a Pulitzer Prize–winning novelist, a Nobel Prize–winning scientist. "No, mommy, I want to be the first lady." But you can be the president. "Yes, but I want to be the first lady." Slide, please.

(*As Sara speaks, photographs of first ladies alternating with previous image of Sara click in rapid succession.*)

I still wonder at the boldness of my earlier aspirations. I should think striving to be president a much more worthwhile and possibly attainable goal for a little black girl. It seems foolhardy at best to aspire to the ultimate white girl job when there wasn't even room for us on *Sex and the City* and *Friends*.

(*Pictures of female actors from both shows replace first ladies, Aisha Taylor last.*)

Okay. Mostly. Still, my point . . . I stand before you in these hallowed halls and unabashedly assert that I have a legitimate claim on popular culture. I am a cultural anthropologist. I write books and papers on the fluff that lives around the edges and sometimes threatens the meat of our existence. And I legitimize my observations by assigning a historical context. Slide, please.

Scene 4

London, England. 1810. Later that afternoon.

Alexander Dunlop paces in front of a tall crate, on top of which sits a smaller trunk. William Bullock, distinguished and well dressed, approaches.

DUNLOP: Mr. Bullock. Alexander Dunlop.

(He extends a hand, but is not reciprocated. Beat.)

> No doubt you received my communication. I suppose you would not have shown had you not. Received my communication.

BULLOCK: My time is valuable.

DUNLOP: Certainly. Certainly. I have not had the, shall we say, opportunity to visit your esteemed museum, yet I have heard that you stand at the forefront of modern science, technology and art.

BULLOCK: Please, sir.

DUNLOP: In Paris, as you know, the latest trend is in the exhibiting of live creatures.

BULLOCK: I am a museum director, not a zookeeper.

DUNLOP: Certainly. Certainly. But I have some artifacts that I should think would be of scientific interest to you and a curious and might I add, paying, Liverpudlian public. I've just returned from the Cape of Good Hope. May I show you?

BULLOCK: Africa?

DUNLOP: The southern most part of the Dark Continent. The things I have seen.

(Dunlop opens the trunk and removes a giraffe hide.)

> I supervised the skinning of this spectacular creature. All in one piece. I should think the mounting of it on a form a most worthwhile and lucrative endeavor.

(Bullock examines the skin. He is impressed but works to conceal his pleasure.)

BULLOCK: What else have you?

DUNLOP: Perhaps you are not in the market for living artifacts. I have an appointment at Piccadilly this afternoon.

BULLOCK: What is it?

DUNLOP: What is she?

BULLOCK: She?

DUNLOP: Yes. In perfect condition, and quite well-mannered, considering.

BULLOCK: Considering?

DUNLOP: Considering the savage nature of the species.

(Dunlop begins prying the back end of the crate open with a crow bar. He stops every so often to wipe his brow and talk.)

DUNLOP: It's a thrilling story, really, how she came to me.

BULLOCK: What species?

DUNLOP: We had not been on the continent but a fortnight when a young fellow, Dutch, volunteered to take us into the forest to view the natives.

BULLOCK: What species? Feline?

DUNLOP: Certainly, certainly not. But you can imagine, to see cannibals and heathens in their natural environment. I had read accounts of trips into the Dark Continent, but had not been prepared for the beauty and expanse of the land. And such foliage. Did you know there is a plant that digests meat? A carnivorous plant. Have you a cigarette?

(*Bullock lights a cigarette for Dunlop.*)

BULLOCK: You've brought me a man-eating plant?

DUNLOP: Don't be ridiculous. And after a harrowing chase and some very clever tracking, I managed to catch her without getting a scratch. Thrilling, really. Could I have a hand here? Right there, if you will just hold this while I pry. Almost. Almost. . . .

Scene 5

The present. Bright lights up on Sara. A split image of models and Congolese women in tribal gear fades from the scrim behind Sara. House lights rise slightly. Sara packs up and rolls the lectern offstage as she speaks to the audience.

SARA: (*to audience*) My audiences eat it up. They fancy themselves hard-core intellectuals, and I give them permission to indulge in the most delicious of guilty pleasures—popular culture.

(*Sara gestures for house lights to rise a bit more and makes herself comfortable at the lip of the stage.*)

Oh my . . . don't you all look beautiful this evening. Really you do. Don't be afraid. I won't throw something at you, or make you speak, or make fun of you. I just wouldn't do that. I just need to really look into your eyes, to (*beat*) get real, if I may. This notion that art is something apart, something to be viewed rather than participated in, is a Western convention. In other cultures art is a part of the fabric of the society, not merely something the privileged classes pay to see. It's okay if we all squirm a little. See, that makes it a dialogue. That makes this not television. Okay. So here we go. Many years ago I saw *Pretty Woman* seven times opening week. (*Project picture of* Pretty Woman *poster.*) Oh, don't judge. I'm sure a great many feminist-minded women whose politics are much more evolved than mine watched that movie . . . and got, how to say this delicately?—tingly—when Richard Gear went down on Julia on the piano. We all know the whole Pygmalion-meets-Hollywood-Ho-Cinderella fantasy is fucked. So I deconstructed the hell out it and made it my senior thesis. And in what can only be described as an academic anomaly, it was published in the leading anthropological journal, and then almost verbatim in the *New York Times*

Magazine. Which made me a bit of a rock star on campus and secured the trajectory of what has been a terribly fulfilling and sporadically successful career. Here's why they loved that paper.

(*Lights rise in Sara's bedroom... fading on previous as she walks into new area.*)

When I had finished pointing out the subtle and not so subtle race, class, and gender problems, with all the articulated brashness of a twenty-three-year-old who thinks she's smarter than God . . . I then, "bravely," said the reviewers, copped to having really liked the movie. They loved it. She's smart, she's young, she's black, and she has racial identity issues. Such was the social conundrum for me. No, Mommy, I don't want to be president, I want to be a white whore and marry Richard Gere when I grow up. (*Pause—phone rings.*) Hold on. (*Sara takes the phone out of her pocket and hits the ignore button.*) Let me be clear. I don't have racial identity issues, but I live in a culture that struggles with contradiction.

(*The phone rings. Sara holds it up to the audience.*)

I was summoned.

BOOKER: Sara, this is James Booker, editor-in-chief at . . .

SARA: The only thing better than being summoned by James Booker is receiving a big gold "O" in the upper right corner of a mainstream novel. But, since I neither write fiction nor am a suffering southern white woman speaking in the first person, Mr. Booker would be my man.

BOOKER: We would like to schedule a time for you to meet with Carl Richards, senior editor, and myself.

SARA: And myself.

BOOKER: We're intrigued.

SARA: We?

(*Sara puts the phone on speaker, holding it up for the audience to hear, and plays it again.*)

BOOKER: Sara, this is James Booker, (*Still holding the phone up, Sara presses a button*), James Booker (*Sara presses a button*), James Booker, Editor-in-Chief at Branham and Dunn. We would like to schedule a time for you to meet with Carl Richards, senior editor (*Sara presses a button*), to meet with Carl Richards, (*button*) to meet with Carl Richards . . . (*button*) We're intrigued. (*button*) We're intrigued.

BRADSFORD: (*entering*) They're intrigued. You're about to be a well-paid almost-famous public intellectual.

SARA: Which would make you?

BRADSFORD: The husband of a well-paid, almost-famous public intellectual.

SARA: No, my dear, it would make you the walking contradiction of a confused, moderately paid, well-dressed public intellectual.

BRADSFORD: A second, please, to enjoy the moment? (*Beat.*) Honey, the people who will hate you for me will hate you anyway. Come here.

(*Sara walks into a warm embrace.*)

BRADSFORD: And what are you going to do?

SARA: When?

BRADSFORD: When you meet with the publishing gods.

SARA: Kick some publishing ass?

BRADSFORD: That's my girl. (*They kiss.*)

Scene 6

London, England. 1810. Same afternoon. Dunlop, sleeves rolled up, disheveled from the effort, continues to pry open the crate.

DUNLOP: It seems to be stuck . . . very sorry. What you must understand is that in the southern tip of Africa, the natives and the Dutch have successfully reached a manageable state of cohabitation. Due in part, I think, to the rather low evolutionary state of the Dutchman himself. Hardly better than the heathens he fancies himself superior to. I have, with mine own eyes, witnessed evidence of interspecies copulation. Little hairless, brown-skinned monkeys rolling about in the dirt. It would turn the stomach of a lesser man.

BULLOCK: I hope you have not brought me a monkey.

DUNLOP: You insult me. What I have brought you is an investment.

(*Dunlop finishes prying off the side of the crate. Bullock moves in for a closer look.*)

BULLOCK: You've brought me a bloody Hottentot?! The abolitionists would have my balls for breakfast.

DUNLOP: Ah, then you have you seen one before?

BULLOCK: Not one this wild. But the abolitionists . . .

DUNLOP: It's not a slave. I have a legal contract. Watch this.

(*Dunlop barks orders into the crate.*)

Turn around, Saartjie. There, look at that arse.

BULLOCK: That's a rather impressive posterior. May I touch?

(*Bullock reaches into the crate.*)

Jesus! The filthy bitch bit me! I thought you said she was tamed.

DUNLOP: I said well-behaved considering her species. You came at her too fast. Approach her as you would a dog. No surprises. Let her sniff the back of your hand. There.

BULLOCK: I see no profit in this.

DUNLOP: Then you are short-sighted.

BULLOCK: What can she do?

DUNLOP: She can stand erect for long hours, and can lay on her back as sufficiently as anyone.

BULLOCK: Are you selling me an exhibit or a concubine?

DUNLOP: I certainly would never, never presume to tell you what to do with your property.

BULLOCK: Property?

DUNLOP: I would not presume to dictate the parameters of whatever agreement you might arrange with (*beat*) her.

Scene 7

The present, Chicago. Publishing offices of Branham and Dunn. Lights rise on Sara sitting with Booker and Carl.

SARA: He only purchased the giraffe, but for his trouble was a given a longer audience with her, right there in the box.

BOOKER: That's fascinating.

SARA: That's fiction.

CARL: That's well-written historical documentation. That's biography.

SARA: That's historical fiction.

BOOKER: You sell yourself short, Dr. Washington.

SARA: Please, Sara.

CARL: We saw your presentation at the University Club . . .

BOOKER: . . . and read your article in *The American Anthropologist*. It was very well documented. When do we see her?

CARL: Well, you know, *Jaws* . . .

SARA: The movie?

CARL: . . . is a classic because they waited for so long to reveal the . . .

SARA: The movie? Is he comparing . . . I know he's not comparing . . . your point?

CARL: Just that *Jaws* . . .

SARA: Isn't that reductive.

CARL: (*Beat.*) Reductive, (*He has no idea.*) right.

BOOKER: I think Mr. Richards is saying . . . (*Beat.*) Has anyone else written about her?

SARA: Of course, a wonderful play, a very famous poem, many, many academic writings.

BOOKER: Had you heard of the story, Carl?

CARL: Not before seeing Ms. Washington's Hottentot talk at the lecture series.

SARA: (*to Carl*) My Saartjie Baartman talk. Hottentot is derisive.

CARL: I wish you'd shown a slide of her.

SARA: *Hottentot* was the *nigger* of the nineteenth century. (*to audience*) I've gotten ahead of myself.

(*Sara crosses toward bedroom area, where Bradsford sits, editing pages of a manuscript.*)

SARA: (*to Bradsford*) I don't know. What's more important? Pretty or smart? I mean, I'm thinking they already know I'm smart, right? I could do professorial with a hint of ethnic, or the "I'm a player" tailored pants suit . . . or . . . maybe ethnic and "I'm a player."

BRADSFORD: Just be yourself.

SARA: But does this make my ass look big?

BRADSFORD: Is that bad?

SARA: Of course.

BRADSFORD: Then no . . . well, turn around. No. Your ass is perfect, you'll get the deal.

SARA: Don't make fun.

BRADSFORD: I'm enjoying you. This is why boys like girls. Just be yourself.

(*Sara walks back into the previous scene.*)

SARA: I was saying?

BOOKER: He only bought the giraffe.

SARA: This we know happened.

BOOKER: What drew you to this project?

SARA: Well, first let me say that I wasn't drawn to the project to write a mainstream novel. I was drawn to Saartjie. Her story is interesting, disturbing, entertaining. It resonates for black and white women alike. It's fascinating and . . .

CARL: I think we're all fascinated, don't you, Booker?

BOOKER: It's a story the world needs to know.

SARA: But as much as I'm a fan of popular culture, I'm not convinced that Saartjie's . . .

CARL: Saartjie?

SARA: The Venus, I'm not convinced that her story is ready to be consumed by the masses . . . or that the masses are ready for her story.

CARL: I don't understand.

SARA: It's our fascination with her that appeals to me. She was bigger than J Lo . . .

CARL: Wow, that's big.

SARA: Her persona, though yes, the Europeans hadn't previously encountered such a substantial posterior. (*Beat.*) So, Dunlop is stuck with her, and puts aside his medical profession to manage her career. Which means he displays her, freak-show style, until the delicate sensibilities of the British elite become offended. Charges of slavery are brought against Dunlop, they go to trial and. . . . well, the rest is history.

CARL: They go to trial and . . . ?

BOOKER: We'd like to move on this, Dr. Washington.

SARA: Really, Sara is fine.

CARL: Why didn't you include her picture in your presentation?

SARA: The camera had not been invented.

CARL: But drawings. I Googled her after your presentation, and there are images.

SARA: Interpretive images. The people illustrating her had a vested interest in. . . . Anyway, I don't show them because it seems unnecessary. Out of respect I've decided . . .

BOOKER: You know, we aren't a university press.

SARA: (*to Booker*) I'm sorry?

BOOKER: We aren't a university press.

CARL: We cater to an erudite public. Still, our cultivated audience is looking for entertainment as well as intellectual stimulation. Do you feel up to that, Ms. Washington?

SARA: Doctor . . . Sara. . . . Just call me . . . (*Beat.*) Certainly I'm up to it, but I'm not sure that I want to . . .

BOOKER: We like your voice, Sara. It's unique. You may just be the black female voice of the new millennium.

SARA: It's not so new.

BOOKER: Tru dat. Nineties, eighties, seventies, all rolled off the tongue so nicely. What to do with the two-thousands.

CARL: The Zero Zeros. (*Beat.*) I was just riffing.

SARA: So, you're offering me . . .

BOOKER: A book deal. A well-promoted, big, big book deal. Which I'm sure will be followed by a movie deal.

CARL: I have many connections in the film industry. You saw *The Bridges of Madison County*. Well, let's just say I was instrumental in the development of that project.

SARA: That's reassuring.

BOOKER: We need a decision.

SARA: I need time.

BOOKER: Sure. But remember, Ms. Baartman is public domain and we do have a stable of respected writers poised to . . .

SARA: You're threatening me?

BOOKER: Of course. I, we, want you.

Scene 8

Saartjie, a stocky, voluptuous Khoisan woman, stands behind the crate. We can see only her bare shoulders. Sara sits at a desk, piled high with papers, working on her laptop.

SAARTJIE: Entertaining?

SARA: Beg your pardon?

SAARTJIE: You said, about me, my story, interesting, entertaining, disturbing, and fascinating. Entertaining, really?

SARA: It was a pitch, a hard sell.

SAARTJIE: For a book you are not sure you will write?

SARA: You were telling me about your siblings?

SAARTJIE: Six. Four brothers, two sisters. I didn't know them as siblings. The Cezars only bought two of us. We were lined up from tallest to shortest. I was eight, my youngest brother, M'tabo, was seven. M'tabo was the only one of us that was half Dutch. I think they liked the way he looked with his dark skin and blue eyes. They only took me to keep him company. Really, nothing was expected of me until I was eleven. That's when I learned to service the brothers, in other ways.

SARA: They molested you?

SAARTJIE: Is that what you call it? It was a condition of my existence. Sometimes it was even tolerable, as I'd never been shown affection. It was attention. I have since learned that they were more thoughtful and gentle than they could have been. They were quite (*beat*) humane. And I stayed with them until they made arrangements with Monsieur Dunlop. The oldest brother was getting married. I think it was easier to be rid of me.

SARA: How do I write that?

SAARTJIE: And still "entertain?" (*Beat.*) It is grotesque. Embrace it.

SARA: Is that how you see yourself? Grotesque.

SAARTJIE: Stop it. You know I see myself as you see me.

SARA: How do you know so much?

SAARTJIE: I'm tired.

SARA: I've been studying you for months and every account gives a different version. You were twenty, you were twenty-three, you died of syphilis, you died of
smallpox, you drank yourself to death.

SAARTJIE: Either way . . .

SARA: I know.

SAARTJIE: I was . . .

SARA: I know.

SAARTJIE: You will have to work him in.

SARA: Cuvier?

SAARTJIE: Of course Cuvier. He's the father of modern anatomy.

SARA: I know.

BRADSFORD: (*enters*)You know what?

SARA: I wasn't talking to you.

BRADSFORD: There's a place they put public intellectuals who've gone over the edge.

SARA: It's not the same place they put anyone who's gone over the edge?

BRADSFORD: Sure, but we tell them it's a special place, just for the intellectually elite.

SARA: You surprised me.

BRADSFORD: Of course I did. I was stealthy.

SARA: Cute.

BRADSFORD: Was she here?

SARA: You worry about me?

BRADSFORD: No. Yes. Sometimes. Mostly I just think it's beneath you.

SAARTJIE: You should be insulted.

SARA: I'm hungry.

BRADSFORD: What are you afraid of?

SARA: I'm not.

SAARTJIE: He's right, you are.

SARA: Fine.

(*Saartjie exits.*)

SARA: Lunch? Please.

BRADSFORD: It's a good opportunity.

SARA: Yeah.

BRADSFORD: There's a problem?

SARA: Remember the problems I had with my paper. The soft history filtered
through these dead white men. And there's no way I can do this without alien-
ating someone.

BRADSFORD: And it's very important that everyone love you.

SARA: Her story is important . . . and she's finally gotten her funeral. Who am I to dredge it all up, and for what purpose? When I think of the black literati reading my book and calling me an exploitive sell-out, I can't breathe. When I picture white housewives reading it on the beach, and middle-American buffoons discussing it at steakhouses, it—really, it makes me ill.

BRADSFORD: Okay, what's your problem with middle America?

SARA: It's ugly.

BRADSFORD: You're classist.

SARA: Maybe.

BRADSFORD: It's your story as much as hers. Why shouldn't it be theirs?

SARA: Really, I'm hungry. Lunch? Now?

BRADSFORD: I can't. I have a journal deadline and a department meeting at 5:00.

SARA: How are the sociologists? Still think they're better than us?

BRADSFORD: Of course. They are.

SARA: So between now and 5:00 you won't be eating?

(*Bradsford exits. Sara picks up the phone and dials. Lights up on Booker with his cell phone.*)

SARA: Tru dat? Do you say that to all the authors you're courting?

BOOKER: Courting?

SARA: Professionally.

BOOKER: Of course. But I'm not courting you. You're writing the book.

SARA: I haven't said yes.

BOOKER: Are you afraid?

(*Pause.*)

SARA: So you remember saying "tru dat" when we met?

BOOKER: I always know what I'm saying. (*Beat.*) Have you had lunch?

SARA: Thanks. My husband's taking me out in a few minutes.

BOOKER: It's important that my new star writer keep herself nourished.

SARA: Tru dat. (*Beat.*) I'll talk to you when I have an answer. Meantime, peace out, my brotha.

Scene 9

1805. France.

Georges Cuvier stands center stage in a concentrated pool of light reflected from a massive mirrored chandelier. He is dissecting something obscured by white sheets on the hospital table in front of him. His gloved hands are covered in blood up to his elbows.

The walls behind him are overflowing with well-labeled manuscripts, volumes of leather-bound books, and jars and jars of unidentifiable organs floating in formaldehyde.

Millicent enters.

MILLICENT: Will that be all for you this evening, sir?

CUVIER: Oui. Merci beaucoup.

MILLICENT: Il n'y pas de quoi! Monsieur Cuvier, you haven't eaten today.

CUVIER: That will be all. Merci.

MILLICENT: A shipment from Bombay arrived this afternoon. It's in the foyer. Shall I have it brought up?

CUVIER: Living?

MILLICENT: I think not. It's a small, closed crate.

CUVIER: May I show you something?

MILLICENT: Sir?

CUVIER: Over here. It's this bitch.

MILLICENT: The mongrel delivered yesterday?

CUVIER: A West African jackal. Very rare.

MILLICENT: I thought it was alive.

CUVIER: It died.

MILLICENT: It died?

CUVIER: For science.

MILLICENT: How may I help you, sir?

CUVIER: Come. I want to show you.

(*Millicent gingerly approaches the table.*)

Bring that candle there. Yes. See this. These are the reproductive organs of the poor creature. Really. What do you suppose this is. (*Beat.*) I'm asking you to speak, Mademoiselle. What do you see?

MILLICENT: Honestly, sir, a disquieting amount of blood. And I did eat today. So if I might . . .

CUVIER: It is the principle of the correlation of parts. . . . Leading to the development of a principle of determination.

MILLICENT: I found the bones in the rocks more tolerable.

CUVIER: All part of the same. This is the beauty of these creatures. All creatures. Even we are creatures, are we not, Mademoiselle Ducent? (*Beat.*) I have asked you a question.

MILLICENT: Yes, Monsieur, we are creatures.

CUVIER: What I am trying to help science understand is that the entirety of an organic being forms a coordinated whole.

(*Cuvier hands Millicent a tong-like metal instrument.*)

Reach in there. There. You see, the intestines of this poor beast are organized in such a way as to digest only fresh meat?

MILLICENT: Yes. Only fresh meat?

CUVIER: Please, I'm talking. And so, if the creature must digest fresh meat, its jaws must be constructed to devour its prey; its claws, here, you see, constructed to seize and tear its prey apart, its teeth to cut and chew. And, come closer, please. This I find most exciting. Nature has placed in its brain . . .

(*Cuvier takes a chisel and mallet and hammers where the creature's head would be. Blood squirts across his and Millicent's white aprons.*)

Here, you see, the required instinct to know how to hide and set traps for its victims. It has the ability to . . .

MILLICENT: She had a brain? Thoughts?

CUVIER: Instinct. Please don't interrupt.

MILLICENT: I'm sorry.

CUVIER: I beg your pardon?

MILLICENT: For interrupting.

CUVIER: I was saying?

MILLICENT: Instinct.

CUVIER: Yes, we think in these lower forms it is all instinct. A brain, to mimic and act, but never to think. It is this and this alone that separates us from the beasts.

MILLICENT: Not opposable thumbs?

CUVIER: These conditions I have shown you form the kingdom of carnivores.

(Cuvier stands, as if in a trance, scalpel raised. There is a long moment of silence. He has forgotten about Millicent.)

MILLICENT: So. A sandwich, Monsieur?

CUVIER: Thank you. I'll take it here. And you may have the boys bring the crate up for cataloging.

MILLICENT: Will you be needing anything else, sir?

CUVIER: I will be all night. I am a good fifty species behind in my classification. In the book, I should like to classify the remains of at least two hundred mammals or oviparous quadrupeds. Sleep is for the weary.

MILLICENT: Will you be needing . . .

CUVIER: I heard you. I heard you. Yes. Additional tapers and a stenographer.

MILLICENT: Bonsoir.

(Cuvier is now fully engrossed in his subject. He does not notice Millicent's departure.)

CUVIER: Amazing! In order for the jaw to seize something, anything, it must have a certain coordination between the points of resistance, a certain volume in the temporal muscle, a certain convex shape in the zygomatic arch under which it passes. I should write this down. Fascinating. Millicent? Millicent!! Millicent!!!

MILLICENT: *(enters, looking alarmed)* Sir?

CUVIER: I wish you would not ask a question and leave. *(Beat.)* So yes. Tell them extra tapers and a stenographer, please.

Scene 10

Stage is in dream lighting. A rock version of "My Favorite Things" from The Sound of Music *plays loudly.*

The black women, in white ball gowns, all stained with a circle of blood at crotch level, line up Chorus Line style, from tallest to shortest. They wear huge afro wigs with remnants of the decorative notions that adorned the wigs in the opening dream sequence. Each carries a Venti Starbucks cup.

We see that they are singing, but can't make out the words because of the music. The music fades. And they are all singing, at the same time, loudly. Half bellow a Negro spiritual, the other half "Do, a Deer." Musically the two songs should fit together. At irregular intervals the singing stops and, in unison, each woman takes a sip from her coffee cup and pulls out a plug of hair.

The music and action crescendo until...

Sara screams.

BLACKOUT.

Scene 11

The present. Chicago. Early morning. Sara and Bradsford's bedroom.

Sara, in T-shirt and panties, paces. She dials the phone frantically. The women in bloody dresses from the previous dream sequence help Sara into her clothes.

SARA: I'd like to speak to Mr. Booker, please. (*Beat.*) Sara, Dr. Sara Washington, he's expecting my (*He's been patched through; it suprises her.*) ... Mr. Booker. Okay, sure, Booker. (*Beat.*) I'll do it. (*Beat.*) No, uh-uh. I wasn't being coy. I was hesitant before, yes. But she won't let me sleep.

(*Lights rise on Booker in his office. Sara continues talking as she dresses and moves into his area. The women exit.*)

SARA: Or at least I can't sleep. I knew it was a good story. Hell, when I wrote the paper I knew I'd found something. But I never considered its popular appeal. I wouldn't mind being Jill Nelson or Norman Mailer. I'd even be Studs Terkel. Is that wrong? Do I exploit her if I want that?

BOOKER: She's dead.

SARA: So you know what I mean.

BOOKER: I don't care what you mean. I only care that you deliver four hundred pages that keep turning.

SARA: Well, thank you for letting me vent.

BOOKER: No problem. (*Beat.*) Anything else?

SARA: There are those who will say we're using an overly exploited black woman's memory for personal gain.

BOOKER: No. They will say *you're* using an overly exploited black woman for personal gain. (*Beat.*) Are you?

(*Sara does not respond.*)

BOOKER: Again, she's dead. I'm not sure the dead can be exploited.

SARA: The question haunts me.

BOOKER: What does James think?

SARA: James? Oh, Bradsford, yes. He always thinks the most of me. (*to audience*) That's why I love him. (*lights change*) He looked at me and saw something unselfish and good, and noble, for whatever reasons he saw those things. That's a nice way to be seen. I suppose that was it. That, and his shoes.

(*Sara crosses down left, sitting on a tightly lit pew.*)

Faded, brown, custom-made on a small cobblestone street in London, I'll take care of you, I'm responsible, I'm stable, kind of shoes. We met at the bar mitzvah of an associate's son. Seriously. I had arrived early and was feeling very (*beat*) brown, wondering if a pew in a synagogue is a pew, or something . . . else. I bent over to adjust an ankle strap that was digging into the fleshy part of my foot just below my ankle when . . .

(*Sara bends down to adjust her strap. Bradsford enters.*)

. . . the classiest, most substantial pair of shoes I've ever seen appears, as if out of nowhere. And they are connected to a pair of beige corduroy legs that go up and up and up and past a dark orange, almost burgundy cashmere turtleneck to the most Nordic man I've ever seen in my life. He's Robert Redford and all of those little blonde kids from *The Sound of Music*, and maybe he's even related to Dick Cavett. Ordinarily I'd have found that level of white obscene. But on him it worked. (*Sara chuckles.*)

BRADSFORD: Are you waiting for someone?

SARA: No. (*gesturing to bench*) Please.

BRADSFORD: Friend or family?

SARA: Seriously?

BRADSFORD: Seriously.

SARA: (*Beat.*) Family. Yes. I'm Peter Hornstein's first cousin.

BRADSFORD: Okay.

SARA: I'm joking.

BRADSFORD: Okay.

(*Pause.*)

SARA: Sara. I work with Melissa.

BRADSFORD: James Bradsford.

SARA: Relation?

BRADSFORD: I doubt it. You look nothing like my siblings.

(*Bradsford sits. Long moment of silence. He reaches into his breast pocket and removes a tin of mints.*)

BRADSFORD: Mint?

SARA: Oh, do I need one?

BRADSFORD: Yes. Yes, you do.

SARA: (*taking mint*) That's funny.

(*Bradsford notices her necklace.*)

BRADSFORD: A diamond Tiffany Bean. Someone really loves you.

SARA: No. No. (*Beat.*) Someone has a lot of money and wants to sleep with me.
   (*Beat.*) It's suspect that you know what a Tiffany Bean is.

BRADSFORD: I recently broke up with a woman who thought I should love her that much.

SARA: Oh. (*Music begins; they stand. Whispered.*) You didn't.

BRADSFORD: I can't afford to love anyone that much.

(*Long pause; we hear the cantor.*)

SARA: Do I seem like the kind of woman who would put out for a Tiffany Bean?

BRADSFORD: No, not at all. But then, I'd have pegged you for Peter Hornstein's cousin.

Scene 12

London. Saartjie sits on a bale of hay in a tight square of light; shadows indicate bars. She is adorned with many strands of colorful glass beads.

Dunlop stands outside of the "cage."

SAARTJIE: So you're leaving me here without the funds?

DUNLOP: Funds—

SAARTJIE: You promised that there would be—

DUNLOP: Funds?

SAARTJIE: In the contract. Our agreement. You said—

DUNLOP: Then you did not read the—

SAARTJIE: You read it to me, you said . . . you told the inquisitors of the contract. I told them. You promised them more comfortable clothes and that I would collect my portion when our contract ends. You said more meat, warmer clothes, and a share of the profits. I would not have come all this way . . .

DUNLOP: Because things were so much better with the Cezars?

SAARTJIE: Because you promised me . . .

DUNLOP: But you signed it. It was contingent upon our making a reasonable profit. I fed and clothed you . . .

SAARTJIE: Clothed?

DUNLOP: The garments you complain of were made for you.

SAARTJIE: So burlap, if expertly made, is a luxury.

DUNLOP: Quiet now. Put your baubles in a sack and get in the damned box. This is why you must go, if you must know, this is where you, . . . you exhaust me. You talk back, you think you are more clever. You're a bloody Hottentot. No more, no less, and nothing ever else shall you be. Your cleverness was amusing when I first discovered it, who knew, a clever Hottentot, . . . but now I find myself weary of it. You look at me with those eyes and I think I am less than I know I am. Have I ever hit you?

(Beat, raises his hand as if to hit her.)

Answer me!

SAARTJIE: No.

DUNLOP: Have I ever caused you undue pain or stress . . .

(Dunlop raises his arm as if to backhand her if the answer is incorrect.)

SAARTJIE: No.

DUNLOP: We have shared . . . You ask for too much.

SAARTJIE: I have only asked for a warmer dress and more meat in my stew. I told them you were good to me. I told them we have a contract.

DUNLOP: You hate me.

SAARTJIE: I did not know you required my . . . affection.

DUNLOP: Then shut it and be grateful. He'll be here soon. Get in. The circus will suit you.

Scene 13

The present. Sara and Bradsford in the living room. Saartjie sits on couch as Sara works. She is barely acknowledged by Sara, not seen at all by Bradsford, who reads Sara's pages. Booker and Carl read in their "office" space.

A red sun appears on upstage scrim.

SAARTJIE & BRADSFORD: I was taken from my home on the Cape without my shoes. I do not think it was an intentional act of maliciousness.

BRADSFORD: Intentional act of maliciousness?

SARA: Keep reading.

SAARTJIE: It was time to leave and I think Dunlop was afraid that I would reconsider.

BRADSFORD: Reconsider?

SARA: Fine . . .

SAARTJIE: I think Dunlap was afraid that I would (*beat*)

SAARTJIE & SARA: Run away . . .

SAARTJIE: So he grabbed me by the wrist and dragged me to the boat. It was fast. He said we would leave in the morning, and before the great sun had even come up, he had taken me. I was not afraid because I knew I was going. But I was confused because I did not think it would be so, so rough. So abrupt. I did not get to say goodbye to my brother. I did not even get to take my shoes. And that stays with me because now I have learned that they think we do not wear shoes. We had the best shoes. We made good money selling our shoes to the white men. And because of it my feet were soft, and everything hurt. The earth, the rocks on the ground, the shells on the beach, and especially the soft, slimy splintered wood on the deck of the boat.

BOOKER: It's good.

CARL: It needs pictures.

SAARTJIE: It was still dark when we got to the boat, and the sailors were asleep. Dunlop rubbed lye on my body and poured seawater over me. He said they would make me leave the ship if they thought I might give them a disease. I did not understand, because we protected our skin with a special oil, and clay. It was red and had a sweet, earthy smell that I remember fondly. And then Dunlop shaved my head and rubbed my scalp with seaweed and lye and again the salt water, which leaves your skin rough and dry, and ashy. And after I was cleaned, I was given a skirt and blouse and he laughed because I did not know how to fasten it. And he laughed because the skirt hung too short in the back. And he laughed because I did not know what to do with a corset. So he showed me. And that was the first time he touched me.

BRADSFORD: I don't buy it.

SARA: Nothing to buy. It's documented. A contract was signed. She boarded a ship to Europe.

BRADSFORD: She's too articulate.

CARL: Would she be this articulate?

SARA: That's what they say about me. (*Beat.*) Why wouldn't she?

BRADSFORD: Why would she?

CARL & BOOKER: I don't buy it.

SARA: What's to buy? She was employed since girlhood by Dutch intellectuals, raised in a place where Dutch and French were the languages of the oppressors, brought up to serve the oppressors. Why wouldn't she . . .

BRADSFORD: You'll be criticized.

SARA: Then I'll be criticized. Whose side are you on? (*Beat.*) Fine! (*She types furiously.*)

SAARTJIE: Eeet was a beeeg sheep. The beeeggest I haf ever seen weeeth my own eyes. She bobbed up and down een the water like the great mother sun deeescending from the heavens at the end of another day.

BRADSFORD: The mother sun?

BOOKER: (*to Carl*) The mother sun?

CARL: Nice. The mother sun. The great orange mother sun.

(*The sun on the scrim becomes orange.*)

SAARTJIE: Like the great orange . . .

SARA: Golden . . .

(*The image of the sun becomes golden.*)

SAARTJIE: The great golden mother sun descending from the heavens at the end of day. I was afraid and in chains, but I deed not protest. I knew of slavery, and there is no, how do you say, no circumstance, under which it is a pleasant experience. But thees kind of slavery was unlike anything I had known. On the sheep I was washed with seawater and forced to give pleasure to Monsieur Dunlop. Later in the voyage men would pay him for my company. A line of filthy men from the captain's quarters to my little cabin. No more than a bed in a cupboard, really. It left me always empty and aching. This was not like I had known before. I did not understand. Never had I been treated so roughly, repeatedly, at the hands of so many strangers.

BOOKER: It's good.

SARA: You think?

BRADSFORD & CARL: It's good.

CARL: If you could just show a little more . . .

SARA: Ass?

CARL: Action. We need to experience it all with her. Right now I feel removed.

SARA: Well, it didn't happen to you, Carl.

Scene 14

Lights rise on Sara, working in her office.

Saartjie joins her.

SARA: Did you get more meat?

SAARTJIE: Does it matter?

SARA: I suppose not. And then you went to Cuvier?

SAARTJIE: No. Dunlop sold me to Monsieur Reaux, a carnival, you say circus, owner. I lived in cages with animals, slept on straw, barely fed. It could be said that Monsieur Cuvier rescued me.

SARA: You and Monsieur Reaux had an understanding?

SAARTJIE: Monsieur Reaux wasn't interested in women. Only in money. Monsieur Cuvier and I had an understanding, eventually.

SARA: Did you have a relationship with Cuvier?

SAARTJIE: Relationship? (*Beat.*) Relations?

SARA: They are different. A relationship implies . . . more.

SAARTJIE: Then no, I do not think so.

SARA: Did you find him attractive?

SAARTJIE: Perhaps once, for a moment? No. (*Beat.*) Do you not sometimes find powerful people attractive?

SARA: I find kindness, humor, compassion, and long legs attractive.

SAARTJIE: But not power?

SARA: I don't know.

(*long pause*)

SAARTJIE: I have never, as you say, "made love" to a man. I did, once, have to copulate with what they called a Pygmie for a private crowd in Piccadilly. We were both afraid and ashamed, and I did not speak his language. I think we were each angry with the other for being a witness to such degradation. When it was over they took him away, and then I was left alone with the men for the usual . . . (*Beat.*) And so, you were trying to convince me of something?

SARA: I think we are done for today.

SAARTJIE: You are tired?

(*Saartjie exits.*)

Scene 15

The present. Evening. Sara's study. Bradsford stands in a doorway, watching Sara write.

BRADSFORD: How goes it?

(*Sara does not respond.*)

BRADSFORD: I say, how goes it?

SARA: I'm bleeding all over the keyboard here, and still . . . it won't come out the way it needs to.

BRADSFORD: You're blocked?

SARA: I'm frozen.

BRADSFORD: Are you writing what's in your heart?

SARA: I know you're not presuming to tell me how to write?

BRADSFORD: Okay.

(*Bradsford turns to leave.*)

SARA: Was that mean?

BRADSFORD: What keeps you from writing what you know to be true?

SARA: Am I a narcissistic bitch?

BRADSFORD: Of course you aren't a bitch.

SARA: Booker wants me to . . .

BRADSFORD: Booker?

SARA: James . . . Booker, that's what I call . . .

BRADSFORD: You . . .

SARA: People call him Booker. Anyway, I think he wants it more graphic, and Carl says it's not romantic enough. Graphic I guess I could do, but romantic?

BRADSFORD: So a little courtship before the raping?

SARA: Something like that.

BRADSFORD: I've never had a book deal like this one. You know I write for eggheads. But in my limited experience it just seems that your story is heart-wrenching without any . . .

SARA: I know . . .

BRADSFORD: Histrionics. Just finish it.

SARA: Finish it and come to bed?

BRADSFORD: Or, just come to bed. I could put your mind on other things.

SARA: You could, could you? (*They kiss.*) Oh, you could.

(*They kiss again. The embrace becomes more heated. Clearly both are enjoying the moment of intimacy. Bradsford's hand caresses and then holds Sara's bottom. She recoils as if slapped.*)

SARA: I'm sorry. I need, I have to meet with Booker tomorrow, and I should . . . at least the rest of this chapter. . . .

BRADSFORD: Of course.

LIGHT FADES.

Scene 16

Dream lighting. Minstrel show music plays. Women in white dresses, men in black tuxes, all in white masks enter doing a rousing minstrel-inspired dance routine.

Sara enters in her pajamas. The dancing stops, and the white masks are removed to reveal black-face masks.

The dancers face forward and, to a Mozart minuet, perform ballet positions.

Sara begins a frantic soft shoe in the middle of it.

BLACKOUT

Scene 17

Sara stands center stage. Alone. Sara and Bradsford's past. Bradsford enters, leans over her, and whispers something in Sara's ear. She laughs.

SARA: (*to Bradsford*) That's quite a proposition from a man in such sensible shoes. (*to house*) I hadn't seen him since the bar mitzvah. Then the university put us on an interdepartmental search committee. He fought for a female Indian anthropologist, and a young brother who was clearly a cut above, but the search committee was hesitant. Bradsford broke it down. I liked his politics. I liked his haircut.

(*Bradsford whispers in her ear.*)

He whispered it in my ear in one of those sexually charged, completely professional moments.

BRADSFORD: (*to Sara*) There was nothing professional about it.

SARA: You can smell it.

BRADSFORD: And you know.

SARA: Even if you choose not to acknowledge it. I was distracted by the smell of him. I was riveted by the fine, almost white blond hairs above his knuckles . . . and I wanted to touch a freckle that resides above his upper lip and below his left nostril. I still like to touch that freckle. This is what he said . . .

BRADSFORD & SARA: If I could taste your neck I would finally be able to sleep.

SARA: I beg your pardon? (*to audience*) I heard him.

BRADSFORD: If I could taste your neck I would finally be able to sleep. There was a palpable sadness in you that matched my own. I asked you about it once. And I made the mistake of referring to it as "melancholy." To which you quickly explained . . .

SARA: I prefer to call it—

BRADSFORD & SARA: A perpetual state of ennui.

SARA: Melancholy makes it too much mine. This is an internalized response to a constant barrage of negative external forces. But life without my ennui would be like a day without earrings, or worse, a watch. Something's missing, something that defines you is not where it should be, but still you go on.

BRADSFORD: How could I not love her? (*Beat.*) I found it utterly delightful to spend time with a woman who wrapped herself in her—

SARA: Ennui . . .

BRADSFORD: Like a protective cloak.

SARA: The other day Bradsford asked me where my politics had gone. Where had I put the rage, where did the anger live? I tried desperately to explain that sometimes life happens to your politic, but I couldn't make it cogent. I still haven't. Possibly because it's not. My politic shifted to the peripheries to make room for him, or me, or us. Life. Or maybe my politic shifted because it was getting heavy. Carrying it had become exhausting. Exhausting not in a tired way, exhausting in an excruciatingly fucking painful way.

Sara steps down into a separate light. Bradsford's light fades.

Scene 18

France, 1811. Cuvier's bedroom.

Cuvier stands near his bed in dressing gown and ascot. Millicent enters.

CUVIER: Good evening, Mademoiselle.

MILLICENT: Monsieur, I am surprised. It seemed you would not be needing my assistance this evening.

CUVIER: The work went well.

MILLICENT: I am pleased for you.

(*Millicent begins turning down the bed covers.*)

Would you like a brandy?

CUVIER: No. I said the work went well.

MILLLICENT: I am pleased for you. Where should I stand?

CUVIER: By the candles, please.

(*Millicent turns toward a small table on which rests a stack of books, with prominent bookmarks.*)

CUVIER: Please, I have marked several passages. Just read one and then the other. I shall stand here.

(*Cuvier stands near bed.*)

MILLICENT: Shall I begin?

CUVIER: Please.

MILLICENT: William Ten Rhyne on the Hottentot, 1704. "The Women are distinguished from the men by their deformity, being generally round shouldered. They have a peculiarity. Out of their privities you see two labels hanging down, like part of a man's yard. . . . Of these they are so proud, that if a stranger happens to come into one of their huts they will show the stranger."

CUVIER: Please read more slowly. The next one.

(*Cuvier wipes his brow.*)

MILLICENT: *The Vouyage and Adventures of Francois Leguat*, 1707: "the vanity of these ugly witches is incredible. They fancy themselves the finest women in the world. 'Tis said, they are of a strange temper, and that at certain times have a madness come upon them, during which they emit a strong vapour from their bodies, as those of a Hind in Season."

CUVIER: Next, please.

MILLICENT: "They are a people very stupid and very brutal. In many respects they are more like beasts than men. Their complexion is dark, their noses flat, like those of a Dutch dog, their lips thick and big, their teeth exceedingly white, some sticking out of their mouths like boars' tusks. Their hair is black and curled like wool."

(*Cuvier becomes more excited. He sits on the bed, legs crossed, and puts a pillow in his lap.*)

CUVIER: Please, another.

MILLICENT: *An Account of the Vouyages Undertaken by the Order of His Present Majesty for Making Discoveries in the Southern Hemisphere*, 1773 . . .

CUVIER: Please, just the passages.

MILLICENT: "We were very desirous to determine the great question, whether the women of this country have or have not that fleshy flap or apron which has been called the Sinus pudoris, and what we have learnt I shall relate."

CUVIER: Slower, please.

(Cuvier closes his eyes and becomes very excited. Millicent is unflustered, seeming neither put upon nor aroused.)

MILLICENT: "Many of the Dutch who received favors from Hottentots, positively denied its existence. But a physician declared that he had never seen one—"

CUVIER: A Hottentot?

MILLICENT: "A Hottentot without two fleshy, or rather skinny appendages, proceeding from the upper part of the Labia, somewhat resembling the teats of a cow, but flat."

(Through the following Cuvier becomes very excited and climaxes quietly and violently. Toward the end of the passage, he wipes his brow and lies on his side, spent.)

MILLICENT: "They hung down, he said, before the Pudendum, and were in different subjects of different lengths, in some not more than half an inch, in others three or four inches."

CUVIER: One more, please, and we shall be done for the evening.

MILLICENT: Sparrman, *A Voyage to the Cape of Good Hope*, 1785. "Besides the pleasure the Hottentots enjoy in besmearing their bodies from head to foot, they likewise perfume them with a powder of herbs, with which they powder both their heads and bodies." Shall I retire, sir?

CUVIER: I'll just close my eyes. If you could read another, and leave quietly, I would . . . that would be most . . . thank you. . . .

MILLICENT: Abbé de la Caille's *Journal historique du voyage fait au Cap de Bonne-Esperance*, 1763. "The women adorn themselves with necklaces of shells: for even in this country, says the Abbé de la Caille, the sex have their charms. To this end, they not only grease all the naked parts of their body, to make them shine, but they braid or plait their hair as an additional elegance." *(Beat.)* Goodnight, sir.

(Millicent does not turn around, but blows out the candles on the table and exits with her own.)

CUVIER: Perhaps tomorrow we can continue with the mating habits of the southwestern antelope.

Lights fade.

Scene 19

Circus music plays. Dream lighting.

Booker, wearing exaggerated horn-rimmed glasses and a white lab coat, stands in front of a veiled cage with a pointer, in front of a slide.

BOOKER: Esteemed colleagues, ladies, and gentlemen, we stand at the brink of a new era. A most exciting time in history. Modern science makes new, bold leaps forward today. By discovering all we can about the other, we learn more about ourselves. But I'm preaching to the choir. I give you, yuppipus whitus femalinus. Commonly known as Becky. We've taken her from her natural environment and subjected her to a battery of emotional and physical tests. Becky has done well. Her people would be proud. We ask that you refrain from taking pictures. And please, keep your inevitable gasps of wonderment to a minimum.

(*The veil is removed, and beneath it stands a very composed white woman, clad in khaki peddle-pushers and a pink polo, with a ponytail sticking out from the back of a baseball cap.*)

BOOKER: We found Becky reading *The New Yorker* at a Starbucks in Chicago's Lincoln Park. Her mental acuity and emotional adaptability have impressed us. She is most responsive when enticed by a Venti Soy, half-decaff carmel-macchiato, and has a near sexual arousal when presented with Kate Spade handbags, Prada shoes, and sport utility vehicles.

BECKY: He wants me, Sara.

BOOKER: She uses her upper register and speaks through her nose with a well-articulated, if annoying vocal dexterity.

BECKY: They all want me, Sara.

BOOKER: Please remove your hat, Becky.

(*Becky removes hat and shakes out her blonde, waist-long ponytail.*)

BOOKER: Thank you.

BECKY: He wants me, Sara.

BOOKER: Her sexual organs . . . (*Becky begins to unfasten her belt.*) That won't be necessary, Becky . . . Please bring in exhibit number two.

(*Saartjie is wheeled in, clad in a skin-colored thong and bikini top. Her cage is placed next to Becky's and the two pose in unison.*)

BOOKER: You see, in comparison, Becky is oddly proportioned. An inadequate posterior is attributed to sitting in cold climates at an early age. Still, it gives me a hard-on. We have yet to determine the cause of the lack of pigmentation in the areola and lips. But I want to taste its cotton candy sweetness. There is a noticeable lack of fleshiness in the lips, that in some creatures we have found has been surgically altered to resemble the physical makeup of black women. Strangely, I wish to place my gargantuan lips over those delicate petals. No, really, that's not necessary. Put your shirt back on, Becky.

(*Sara mounts a third podium, falling in line with Saartjie and Becky's choreography.*)

SARA: Usually, if I fall asleep in the middle of a nightmare, it will go away. Sometimes I can jump off of something high. But it's easier when I'm the voyeur. As soon as I become a participant I'm less aware that I am dreaming.

BOOKER: Sara, will you remove your clothes, please?

Sara removes her clothes as she speaks.

Booker soundlessly continues his lecture as he points to parts of Sara's, then Saartjie's, and finally Becky's anatomy.

Sara joins Saartjie and Becky's choreographed movements.

SARA: In my dreams I am completely uninhibited, yet full of shame. I am not ashamed because I am naked. I am ashamed because I disrobed voluntarily. Let me say again, it is not the act of being naked. It is the act of getting that way. Sometimes if I can turn the images around—

(*All three women turn their backs to the audience.*)

If I can alter the reality—

(*Cuvier and Bradsford enter, backs to audience. Each takes a place beneath a woman, Booker in the center, in front of Becky, Cuvier in front of Sara, Bradsford in front of Saartjie. They begin to masturbate.*)

SARA: I think of faraway places. I think of glossy coffee table books with my name on them. I picture myself being interviewed by Katie Couric. I'm poised. I'm smart. I'm beautiful. I'm fully clothed. Please stop that.

BOOKER AND BRADSFORD: We're almost . . . just a second . . . we're almost . . . one second . . .

SARA: Please, don't do that.

BOOKER: Can't help it.

SARA: Could you at least look at me when you do that?

BOOKER: I'm thinking about you, baby. It's all about you, baby.

BOOKER, CUVIER, AND BRADSFORD: It's all about you, baby. It's all about you. It's all about you. It's all about you.

Synthesized disco music begins to play. Sara, Saartjie, and Becky begin a suggestive strip-club dance routine. The lights become brighter, the music crescendos.

BLACKOUT.

Scene 20

The present. Sara's office. Sara paces. Picks up the phone. Puts it down. Picks it up. Dials. Hangs up. And again.

Lights up on Booker on the phone in his office. Sara's phone rings. She jumps out of her skin.

SARA: Hello.

BOOKER: What are you doing?

SARA: You scared the shit out of me. (*Beat.*) Star 69?

BOOKER: Caller I.D. Welcome to the twenty-first century. (*Beat.*) You called.

SARA: Terrible dreams.

BOOKER: Okay.

SARA: I need to see you.

BOOKER: At my office?

SARA: I think I need to see more of you than that.

BOOKER: I'm listening.

SARA: I think I need your help.

BOOKER: Now?

SARA: Yesterday. The day before.

BOOKER: Where?

Light fades.

Scene 21

(Sara sits in bed, wrapped in blankets. Bradsford works at his desk, in low light.)

SARA: I dreamt about a brown man who smelled of earth and had muscles that resembled the roots of a red oak. And he would love me and make me safe. His locks grow into my hair as we make love on a bed of moss and myrrh. There are no consequences, only the sweet acrid smell of love and sweat.

(We see that Booker is beneath the blankets.)

But he has a short natural with a slight fade and the bed is hard and right next to a fan that blows tepid air too loudly, in a beige and green medium-range business commuter hotel. It hurt and it hurt and it hurt and the pain somehow erased mine, or perhaps it woke up a part of me that was hidden. Yes, it pierced through the pain and made a not-so-slight impression, or a bruise, on my soul. More than anything, I had wanted him to want me. It was harmless. I didn't want him, I only wanted him to want me. She wanted him. I just wanted to give her what she . . . But I guess that's a kind of wanting. *(to Booker)*

SARA & BRADSFORD: If I could taste your neck I'd finally be able to sleep.

BOOKER: Is what she said to me.

(Bradsford's light fades.)

SARA: If I could taste your neck I'd finally be able to sleep.

(Sara lowers her head toward Booker's neck. He stops her.)

BOOKER: You don't want this.

SARA: Of course I know what I want.

BOOKER: I'm telling you . . .

SARA: The audacity . . . that you should presume to know what I want. That any man should presume to know what I . . .

(They begin to make love. Sara speaks to the audience while Booker begins to undress her.)

SARA: And first it was exactly where I was supposed to be. A safe harbor. It was safe for her, we were safe. And loved and . . . brown on brown. It was the culmination of five months of psychological and sexual foreplay that left us both helpless. No. . . .

(Sara breaks away. To audience)

There was no helpless about it. What sickens me is that I had my wits about me. I was not seduced. He did not seduce me. I'm not even sure that his interest in me was much more than circumstantial. There was no seduction. I made a choice. And the choice had been made when I said yes, I will give you your book, and my soul, and my husband's loyalty. I will hand it to you on a platter with my soul,

SAARTJIE AND SARA: If you will make love to us.

Saartjie walks into the embrace that Sara has just left. Saartjie and Booker begin to make love.

SARA: And it was all I could give her. It was all I knew to stop this sickening growing ache. This is how it felt. And this is how it felt. And this is how it felt. And then it was a shattering, splintering, exquisite pain, and . . .

Lights go out abruptly.

Lou Reed's "Take a Walk on the Wild Side" plays in the darkness. House lights begin to rise as "the colored girls sing . . ."

End of Act 1.

Act 2
Scene 1

Dream music.

Lights have a bright, greenish, fluorescent quality.

Sir Mix-a-Lot's "I Like Big Butts" plays loudly.

Saartjie stands between two white women. All are on Stairmasters. All work out to the music.

The white women stop, look at Saartjie's bottom in unison, and then at their own. Saartjie stops, noticing that her anatomy is being examined. The white women begin working out furiously.

Lights out. All no more than forty seconds.

Scene 2

Sara on a Stairmaster in the bedroom. Bradsford reads the paper in bed.

SARA: It is quite possible that I am more full of shit than we even thought.
BRADSFORD: Is that how little we thought of you?
SARA: All anthropologists are full of shit.
BRADSFORD: I've been telling you that for years. (*Beat, putting paper down.*) So really, you didn't say anything?
SARA: No, it was like a big joke, and I laughed, and excused myself and went to the bar.
BRADSFORD: Was James there?
SARA: James?
BRADSFORD: Booker.
SARA: I don't think he heard. I'm sure he didn't. He would have said something.

Booker emerges from under the covers. We're seeing two conversations, two different times, imposed on this moment.

BOOKER: I heard.
SARA: You couldn't have.

BOOKER: Sure I could have.

BRADSFORD: I think you're giving him too much credit.

BRADSFORD & BOOKER: Sometimes there's nothing to say.

BOOKER: What would you want me to say?

SARA: (*to Bradsford*) He would have said something like . . . I don't know, like . . .

BRADSFORD: That's outrageous and insulting . . .

SARA: And unconscionable.

BOOKER: Unconscionable, to the president of the board? Really?

BRADSFORD: You laughed?

SARA: He was the president of the board. Look. This cracker stares me in the face and says, "I would have paid to see that ass." And I'm standing there, and I thought, no, no, no, surely I didn't just hear that, but then they're all laughing. The guys, their over-Botoxed wives . . . they're all laughing . . . It's my press party.

BOOKER: And so who better to put him in line?

SARA: But he's with your company. You should have . . .

BOOKER: You think I'm editor-in-chief for fighting every little battle. Honey, I fight the big ones . . . the ones I think I can win.

SARA: That's disgusting.

BOOKER: That's how you got a book deal. (*Beat.*) Are we gonna do this?

SARA: I'm tired.

BRADSFORD: I'm sorry I couldn't be there. Come here, I'll make you feel better.

BOOKER: I have an appointment at 3:00. If this isn't happening . . .

SARA: Do you think less of me?

BOOKER: Of course not.   **BRADSFORD:** No.

BOOKER: I'll think a little more of you if you bring that ass over here and give me some.

BRADSFORD: You hold yourself to a higher standard. Sometimes, honey, there just aren't words.

Bradsford kisses Sara on the forehead and exits. Sara goes to Booker.

Lights fade as they embrace.

Scene 3

Paris. Millicent spreads white sheets over Cuvier's work table. The table is fitted with crude-look-ing stirrups and leather for fastening down arms and legs.

A tall gas floor lamp with a magnifying glass stands at the end of the table. Cuvier stands in the doorway, unnoticed.

MILLICENT: Sir. You startled me.

CUVIER: That was not my intention. Thank you for . . .

MILLICENT: This is what you requested?

CUVIER: Oui. Did you send the invitations?

MILLICENT: I sent a messenger to Monsieur St. Hilaire and Monsieur de Blain-ville. I have heard only from Monsieur de Blainville. He thanks you for the opportunity and is looking forward to joining you and Monsieur St. Hilaire. (*Beat.*) Shall I prepare a lunch for the occasion?

CUVIER: A light supper after the examination.

MILLICENT: Will you be needing my assistance?

CUVIER: That shouldn't be necessary, merci.

(*Millicent has finished preparing the examination table. She walks toward the door, standing awkwardly in front of Cuvier.*)

MILLICENT: If that will be all, then . . .

CUVIER: Oui, merci.

MILLICENT: Shall you be needing anything more?

CUVIER: Non.

MILLICENT: Perhaps later I could . . .

CUVIER: Non.

(*Pause.*)

MILLICENT: Good night then, sir. (*Beat.*) I shall be in my quarters should you need . . .

(*Cuvier doesn't reply. He is now engrossed in studying the instruments on a tray by the examination table. Millicent waits for a reply and then exits.*)

Scene 4

BOOKER: (*enters*) I need more pages.

SARA: I'm working on it.

BOOKER: The deadlines are hard.

SARA: It's coming. I promise.

BOOKER: You're distracted.

SARA: I am. (*Beat.*) Do you think Saartjie made compromises?

BOOKER: Compromises?

SARA: Yes, or do you think one must enjoy a certain amount of privilege for compromise to be an option.

BOOKER: Example?

SARA: All right. Complacency. Compromise. Complicity in gentrification.

BOOKER: We're talking about gentrification?

SARA: Complacency, Compromise, Complicity.

BOOKER: The alliteration leads to a point?

SARA: Yes. A point, about how life encroaches upon our best intentions and before we know it, we are more than complacent.

BOOKER: We are complicit.

SARA: Example? Okay. Take my neighborhood. In the early eighteen hundreds the landed aristocracy landed and built big brick mansions. Not as ostentatious as the southern ones because they would not have had the free labor . . . still, quite lovely. Fast forward a hundred years. Some Poles move in and there goes the neighborhood. So the aristocrats move to the suburbs. Maybe they had to shove a few Indians aside, but no no no no no, not so much, that had been done.

The Indians were gotten rid of long before my story begins. So, another hundred years, the Irish move in and there goes the neighborhood.

BOOKER: You're serious?

SARA: Hear me out. The Irish build some truly amazing Catholic churches and community buildings and then the Puerto Ricans and the Mexicans move in and there goes the neighborhood. They introduce better food, more impressive landscaping, and all is well, until some poor white artist hippies move in. The hippies feed the unofficial economy of the neighborhood because they need dope enough to keep everyone in microwaves and satellite dishes. And then the *pseudo*-hippie artists moved in.

BOOKER: That's you?

SARA: Not yet. Anyway, the *pseudos* have trust funds and renovate buildings that become hot, hot, hot. They demand better schools and libraries and police protection and outdoor cafés, and they have even more money for drugs. And soon you don't have to be an artist, as long as you're white and have a big dog and an SUV. Suddenly J. Crew, Starbucks, and Pottery Barn appear and you know what happens to the Puerto Ricans and the Mexicans, but a few hold on. Finally, aspiring upper-middle-class, scholarly types decide it's worth the high rents, so you have some blacks and some Asians, and a few lesbians, Puerto Ricans, Mexicans, and wealthy whites. And we can all say, "I love my neighborhood, it's unfortunate that it's changing, but still it's very diverse." Bradsford and I say it to one another daily. And I just don't tell anyone that I hang out at Starbucks. But I do, because I can plug in my laptop for free.

BOOKER: Guilt is so wasted on our people.

SARA: You're confusing my amusing story of gentrification and selling out for guilt. It's an acknowledgement of complicity.

BOOKER: If it smells like guilt . . .

SARA: I wasn't crying. We haven't moved.

BOOKER: My point exactly. What, you're absolved as long as you can articulate it?

SARA: I suppose so. It takes a certain amount of depth to be aware of your contradictions. Yes, I am absolved.

BOOKER: And so, you are guilty. Absolution, forgiveness, right? (*Beat.*) Follows guilt. I'm right, you're wrong, dinner's on you.

SARA: Why did you push for this project?

BOOKER: I saw you online and thought you were cute.

SARA: That's disgusting.

BOOKER: That's a joke. It made my pinky itch. Really. It's a great topic.

SARA: It is?

BOOKER: It's a sellable topic.

SARA: Why?

BOOKER: You, queen-of-popular-culture-meets-obscure-intellectualism, don't know why?

SARA: But why?

BOOKER: White folks love stories about suffering blacks. Black folks love stories about suffering black folks. We put some fuchsia letters and cut out figures on the front, fifteen pages of glossy illustrations in the middle, and we've got a legitimized mainstream hit. You'll be sitting right there next to Stephen L. Carter and Alice Walker, just raking it in, my dear.

SARA: I'm Washington, I'll be after Walker.

BOOKER: Have you found any photos of the jars?

SARA: No photographs. It's not a fucking freak show.

BOOKER: I know this nice little Middle Eastern/French fusion restaurant in Bucktown.

SARA: I should call Bradsford.

BOOKER: Does he like Middle Eastern/French fusion?

SARA: Do you have a soul?

BOOKER: It's not required. But sure. I haven't sold it, if that's what you're asking. But here's what I do know, you care too much what they think.

SARA: They?

BOOKER: Look, it's so simple. They don't like us. That's it. It ain't deep. You can turn yourself inside out and upside down tryin' to make them hear you, tryin' to make them like you, and they won't because they don't. Oh sure, they'll let a couple of us in at a time, but do not delude yourself. It's because you serve their purpose. Whether it's to assuage their guilt, or keep them on the moral high ground, or make them some money, it's what you can do for them. And let me tell you, if you can hand up all three you've hit the jackpot. Never think someone's gonna give you a little piece so you can work out your shit.

SARA: So where do you stand?

BOOKER: You haven't figured it out, genius? I'm gonna stand where I need to to get as much of what's mine as I can. I'll know that the power is temporary, and I'll bank as much as I can so my kids are poised when it's their turn for a little piece.

SARA: And never mind the message.

BOOKER: Honey, the message is what we're here for. You need to suck it up and do what you need to do. Honest, there's no time for guilt, and you don't have enough power to indulge in that fantasy. Guilt is for the children of the people with the power. I wouldn't waste your time worrying about where you live or who you live with, for that matter. Just do what you gotta do.

SARA: No photographs. No drawings of Saartjie.

BOOKER: Just get me the pages.

Scene 5

1813. France. Saartjie and Cuvier sit in his study.

SAARTJIE: Monsieur Cuvier.

CUVIER: Saartjie.

SAARTJIE: Mademoiselle Baartman, Monsieur.

CUVIER: May we use French, Saartjie?

SAARTJIE: Oui.

CUVIER: You were informed of our present goals?

SAARTJIE: That you were to study. Investigate. Explore me?

CUVIER: You are an oddity.

SAARTJIE: At home I am only a little better than average.

(*Saartjie gestures toward the decanter of brandy conspicuously placed on the desk in front of her.*)

CUVIER: When we have completed our interview and examination.

SAARTJIE: You will test me?

CUVIER: We will examine you.

SAARTJIE: We?

CUVIER: Monsieur St. Hilaire, Monsieur Henri de Blainville, and myself. It was not explained?

SAARTJIE: Monsieur Reaux said for three francs or two pounds and not beneath my gown.

(*Cuvier pours Saartjie a cup of brandy. She downs it.*)

CUVIER: Where were you born?

SAARTJIE: Caffraria. Two miles outside of the Cape of Good Hope.

CUVIER: Siblings?

SAARTJIE: Six.

CUVIER: And your parents?

SAARTJIE: Died by the time I was two. I was raised by and worked as a servant for the Cezars.

CUVIER: The Cezars?

SAARTJIE: Dutch farmers. Hendrik and Peter.

CUVIER: So you were born into slavery?

SAARTJIE: I was born into servitude. It is different from your understanding of the . . .

CUVIER: And how do you find yourself here?

SAARTJIE: Very well, thank you.

(*Holds out glass for more brandy.*)

CUVIER: Not yet. How is that you have come to us?

SAARTJIE: On a boat.

CUVIER: By what agreement have you come to us?

SAARTJIE: By the agreement that I would board a boat and sail to England.

(*Holds glass out for more brandy. Cuvier pours.*)

Mijnheer Alexander Dunlop of Middlesex. We agreed that I would travel to Europe in his company, and would there be employed as a performer for a period not to exceed two years, after which I would be repatriated. It was agreed that I would share in the proceeds over boarding and clothes.

CUVIER: (*amused*) Whatever would you do with the money?

SAARTJIE: Whatever one does with money.

CUVIER: And that would be?

SAARTJIE: I imagine I would buy clothes, friends, and respect.

CUVIER: But I have read that you wear only mud in your country.

SAARTJIE: I am now in your country.

CUVIER: You are impudent.

SAARTJIE: Monsieur Reaux said for three francs or two pounds.

CUVIER: More?

(*Cuvier offers her yet another glass of brandy. Saartjie holds out her glass, but does not drink.*)

SAARTJIE: Thank you.

CUVIER: I have some pretty things I should like you to see.

(*Cuvier pulls handfuls of colorful glass and crystal beads from a small chest on his desk.*)

Do you find these impressive?

SAARTJIE: They are very pretty.

CUVIER: Would you like some?

SAARTJIE: Are they precious, or paste?

CUVIER: Precious is in the eye of the beholder, then. Is it not?

SAARTJIE: Monsieur Reaux said two francs or three pounds.

CUVIER: These are worth more.

SAARTJIE: They are very pretty.

CUVIER: Would you allow us to examine you for the price of your favorite ones?

(*Saartjie downs her untouched glass of brandy.*)

SAARTJIE: I should like to speak with Monsieur Reaux.

CUVIER: He has left you in my care. Please try on this one. It flatters your complexion so.

Scene 6

The present. Sara's office.

SARA: The more Saartjie makes herself known to me, the less I have to say on her behalf.

BRADSFORD: At a certain point you just have to write.

SARA: Thanks. Thanks—that's very helpful.

BRADSFORD: You're just sitting there.

SARA: And there you stand. It's a process. Don't you have something to do? Don't you have a deadline?

BRADSFORD: How's it going?

SARA: I used to be so full of conviction. So full of what I was at least trying to say. Now I feel sick and numb and I keep hoping maybe it's the metal fillings in my mouth affecting my brain.

BRADSFORD: It's your immune system.

SARA: What?

BRADSFORD: The mercury in metal fillings attacks your immune system.

SARA: Again. Thank you. (*Beat.*) And now I can feel the effects of all the television I watched when I should have been reading, reading anything. Some sort of mass-media, uberconsumeristic, insomnia-induced apathy.

BRADSFORD: You're blocked.

SARA: I'm frozen. And Saartjie was obscured by billions of pounds of rubble, and now the rubble is gone and still she eludes me.

(*The phone rings.*)

BOOKER: (*on phone*) Hey, Sara.

SARA: Hey. (*to Bradsford*) It's Booker.

BOOKER: How's it going?

SARA: Great. Yeah. Great.

BOOKER: Terrific. Can't talk now, huh.

SARA: No, no. I'm working. I'm writing.

BRADSFORD: Should I leave?

SARA: No. Of course not.

BOOKER: Okay.

SARA: No, I was talking to Bradsford. (*Beat. To Bradsford.*) Booker says hi.

BOOKER: So, how's it going?

SARA: Good. I'm feeling really good about it.

BOOKER: Great. Lunch tomorrow?

SARA: I really should write.

BOOKER: Okay. Then I'll catch you later.

SARA: Great. Thanks for calling.

BOOKER: Bye.

SARA: Bye.

BOOKER: Bye.

SARA: Hanging up.

BOOKER: Okay, talk later.

SARA: Okay. Bye.

(*Sara hangs up.*)

BRADSFORD: That was weird.

SARA: Not so much.

BRADSFORD: Okay. (*Beat.*) I'll let you work. You were right, I have a deadline. Oh, and in case you've forgotten. I'm on your side.

Scene 7

Paris. 1813. Millicent enters. Saartjie crouches in a corner of the laboratory, barely covered by a sheet.

MILLICENT: Hallo? Hallo? Oh, there you are. (*Beat.*) Monsieur Cuvier thought you might be more comfortable in this. I will just leave it on the table for you.

(*Millicent sets a bundle of clothes on the table and begins to exit. Saartjie does not move.*)

I'll go then. (*Beat.*) Is there something I may assist you with?

SAARTJIE: I am fine.

MILLICENT: Are you hungry?

(*Saartjie does not respond.*)

All right, then. I'll leave you.

(*Millicent walks to the door.*)

What did they do?

(*Pause. Saartjie does not respond.*)

What have they done to you?

SAARTJIE: Are you curious or concerned?

MILLICENT: I suppose that I am curious.

SAARTJIE: What do you think they have done?

MILLICENT: I imagine they have examined you, as Monsieur examines all of his live specimens.

SAARTJIE: I am not *his* specimen. I am Monsieur Dunlop's . . . specimen. Is that what you think I am?

MILLICENT: I was told to treat you as such.

SAARTJIE: How is that?

MILLICENT: Cautiously.

SAARTJIE: Because of something I might do?

MILLICENT: Because we do not know what you might do.

SAARTJIE: Experience has taught me that it is I who should be cautious.

MILLICENT: I will bring you some soup and yesterday's bread.

SAARTJIE: Are you Monsieur Cuvier's wife?

MILLICENT: Of course not.

SAARTJIE: Still, you cook for him?

MILLICENT: Yes.

SAARTJIE: You provide . . . comfort . . . for Monsieur Cuvier.

MILLICENT: I assist Monsieur Cuvier in domestic matters.

SAARTJIE: Are you a slave?

MILLICENT: Of course not.

SAARTJIE: Still, you cook for him. And . . . do other things.

MILLICENT: Yes. Monsieur Cuvier pays me for my domestic services.

SAARTJIE: Oh, so you are a prostitute?

MILLICENT: I am a domestic and a companion.

SAARTJIE: I think I understand.

MILLICENT: I should go. Monsieur Cuvier may need my assistance.

SAARTJIE: Please wait.

(*Saartjie approaches the table cautiously and grabs the clothes. She begins to dress behind a low bookcase. We see only her head and shoulders.*)

MILLICENT: I really ought to . . .

SAARTJIE: Could you help me please?

MILLICENT: I should . . .

SAARTJIE: With this garment. I have not mastered these um, fasteners, in the back. If you could just . . .

(*Saartjie moves from behind the bookcase. She wears a plain black dress of Millicent's.*)

MILLICENT: Oh . . . that's mine. It fits you well.

SAARTJIE: Thank you.

MILLICENT: I was instructed not to get too close. Perhaps Monsieur Cuvier could be of assistance.

SAARTJIE: Monsieur Cuvier has assisted me enough, thank you.

MILLICENT: You're not what I'd expected. You seem very civilized.

SAARTJIE: I would say thank you, but I am not sure that's a compliment. (*Beat.*) My work dress fastens in the front.

(*Millicent begins fastening Saartjie's dress.*)

Merci beaucoup. (*Beat.*) You seem very . . . civilized as well.

MILLICENT: I have read that you couple with whoever is nearest.

SAARTJIE: You read this? About me?

MILLICENT: Your people.

SAARTJIE: Coupling does require that two people be near one another. How do your people couple?

MILLICENT: We are supposed to marry and couple with that person only.

SAARTJIE: You are not married, and so you do not couple?

MILLICENT: That is what we are taught.

SAARTJIE: And so with whom do the prostitutes couple?

MILLICENT: It's complicated.

SAARTJIE: It certainly is.

MILLICENT: Society must have order.

SAARTJIE: And so, it is right if you are married, and wrong if you are not. It is wrong if you are paid, but it is fine for no money, but again, only if you are married.

MILLICENT: With some exceptions. But those are the rules we pretend to follow.

SAARTJIE: Where I am from there is less pretending. Still there are ways that we do things, rules, but they are not tied to pretense. Great value is placed on saying what you mean and doing what you say you will do.

MILLICENT: What did they do to you?

SAARTJIE: I think I am ready to eat now.

Scene 8

Sara and Booker are in bed.

BOOKER: How 'bout you never quote that to the press.

SARA: It's cute.

BOOKER: It's disturbing.

SARA: I got over it by junior high school. My budding feminist sensibility finally helped me understand that there was something intrinsically wrong with aspiring to be first lady.

BOOKER: Still, we'll keep that to ourselves. So then what?

SARA: I went to Andover. I did okay. In college I decided that I would be a psychologist, and then fell in love with a professor in the sociology department. She was a glamorous Asian woman who studied the sociology of modern West African political movements. You like that, don't you?

BOOKER: Political movements?

SARA: That she was a she.

BOOKER: If you have to ask.

SARA: She had this spectacular house with all this great African art. It was fine except I wasn't a lesbian, which was maybe okay, except the power dynamic was fucked. She had all the power, I ate all the . . .

BOOKER: See, you always take it a little too far.

SARA: It ended civilly. I got an A in Intro to Sociology and switched my major to anthropology. The next professor I slept with was a Nigerian anthropologist who studied Native American cultures. His house was also gorgeous, because his wife had great taste. That lasted about five minutes. I dropped the course and kept my major. I stopped sleeping with professors, and made it a hard, fast rule only to sleep with professional equals and strangers. Actually, after that I didn't sleep with anyone.

BOOKER: And so you never believed in monogamy?

SARA: Why do you say that?

BOOKER: You were painting this picture of Miss free love . . . and . . .

SARA: That's my point. The love was never free. And so, until James I was the model of Victorian prurience.

BOOKER: And again I say, you never believed in monogamy?

SARA: I've never been unfaithful to James. I've never been unfaithful to anyone . . .

BOOKER: Do you hear yourself?

SARA: Before . . .

BOOKER: Before . . .

SARA: You.

BOOKER: Aah.

SARA: Could we, um . . .

BOOKER: What?

SARA: Not. Please. I can't, if we're going to talk about him. I have to keep it separate.

Scene 9

Paris. Cuvier's bedroom. Saartjie sits at his desk drinking brandy. Cuvier is in bed.

SAARTJIE: This is not the same as yesterday's.

CUVIER: You're being ridiculous.

SAARTJIE: It is different.

CUVIER: Brandy is brandy. Perhaps we've spoiled you.

SAARTJIE: If we are finished I should like to go back to my . . .

CUVIER: Your?

SAARTJIE: The room you have so generously provided.

(*Long pause.*)

CUVIER: I should teach you to read.

SAARTJIE: Why?

CUVIER: To test my skill.

SAARTJIE: Are we finished, then?

CUVIER: Yes.

SAARTJIE: The brandy is bitter. But perhaps the bitterness is favorable to this . . . existence.

Saartjie begins to leave. As she approaches the door she reconsiders and returns to the desk for the brandy. Cuvier catches her by the wrist.

CUVIER: Why did you come?

SAARTJIE: You sent for me.

CUVIER: Why did you come here?

SAARTJIE: You ask as though I had a choice.

CUVIER: One more question and you may take the whole thing. (*Beat.*) Do you enjoy the time we spend together?

SAARTJIE: Of course.

Saartjie takes decanter and exits.

Scene 10

A lilting waltz plays. A tight spot shines brightly on a bare stage. A white couple dressed in seventeenth-century evening wear waltzes through it. Saartjie, also in evening wear, and Cuvier waltz into the light. The light expands, and they continue to waltz.

Millicent, in her maid uniform, waltzes in with Bradsford, in contemporary clothes. The three couples begin to waltz in unison. The couples continue waltzing, at the same pace, even as the music changes. "Ain't Gonna Bump No More (With No Big Fat Woman)" begins to play. Podium rises, Booker in a top hat and tails, and Sara in the "tribal" outfit Saartjie will wear later, do the bump.

Music changes to "Brick House." Waltzing couples and Sara and Bookman all begin to do the hustle.

Dance routine ends with "Shake Your Booty."

LIGHTS OUT.

Scene 11

Booker and Sara are in bed. They're laughing.

BOOKER: And you?

SARA: We were lower-middle-class with delusions of grandeur.

BOOKER: All middle-class black families have delusions of grandeur.

SARA: We thought we were a little classier, a little savvier than the all the white people we worked for.

BOOKER: And you probably were. It's part of who you are. Embrace it.

SARA: I don't want my children to be arrogant.

BOOKER: You're not arrogant.

SARA: I'm narcissistic and sometimes arrogant, yes.

BOOKER: You're the opposite of narcissistic. If you think of yourself too much it's only because you can't find yourself. And if you really think you're arrogant, well then, stop it.

SARA: Thank you, Dr. Phil. (*Pause.*) This is nice.

BOOKER: Careful, don't mistake me for a relationship. Remember, we fuck, we don't love.

Saartjie enters, sits on the edge of the bed.

SAARTJIE: Fuck?

SARA: (*to audience*) Such were the ground rules. It wasn't supposed to happen again, until it happened again. And then, that would be the last time, until the next time.

SAARTJIE: Please, what is fuck?

SARA: I'm told your vocabulary is already too large.

BOOKER: Sara?

SARA: It's fine. I'm fine. We're smarter than this. It's an affair. People've had them since the beginning of time. We'll let it run its course and end it amicably.

SAARTJIE: Amicably, amiably? . . . friendly, kindly . . .

SARA: I love my husband, and you love . . . (*to Saartjie*) Please go away. (*to Booker*) Not you. As long as what we have stays physical, I think we should be able to keep it . . . clean.

BOOKER & SAARTJIE: Right.

SARA: May I have some tea? Please?

(*Booker exits.*)

SARA: Look. I know. I know you're a part of my process, or whatever. But it's time for you to go. Somewhere, anywhere. I can't do this. Why don't you tell me what to write so I can put you to rest, huh?

SAARTJIE: It isn't all about you, baby.

(*Saartjie exits.*)

Scene 12

Paris. 1814. Cuvier's study. Millicent holds a tray piled high with dirty dishes. Cuvier writes furiously. Distracted. Agitated.

MILLICENT: Will that be all then, Monsieur?

CUVIER: Yes. Where did I put the . . .

(*Cuvier searches through papers, looking for something he has misplaced.*)

It was just, I had it moments ago. Bugger it.

(*Millicent continues to stand.*)

MILLICENT: There really is nothing else I can help you with?

CUVIER: You're still here.

MILLICENT: You have seemed very agitated. Perhaps you are worried about Saartjie?

CUVIER: Surely you see I am working.

MILLICENT: I thought that since Saartjie was—incapacitated—you might need . . .

(*Pause.*)

(*Millicent has gotten Cuvier's attention. He works to conceal his amusement.*)

CUVIER: I'm listening.

MILLICENT: Saartjie did not finish her soup this evening. She seems to forget where she is.

CUVIER: You were asking if I might need . . . ?

MILLICENT: I thought you might require some . . . assistance with your . . . studies. Perhaps later.

CUVIER: Assistance?

MILLICENT: That I might help you in some way.

CUVIER: You may unburden yourself?

MILLICENT: I am not sure what I am expected to say.

CUVIER: The tray.

MILLICENT: Oh, yes. Of course.

(*Millicent sets the tray down. Long pause.*)

CUVIER: May I tell you what I am working on?

MILLICENT: Your book, sir?

CUVIER: Yes. It is almost done. Hundreds of species of animals classified, genus and species specified. Groundbreaking really.

MILLICENT: And so you are almost finished?

CUVIER: I am making an addition. I have determined that Saartjie represents an evolutionary link between man and animal. I have told you that we are all mammals, but Saartjie is living proof that we evolve. Her brain vacillates between primarily instinct and a modicum of intellect.

MILLICENT: She thinks?

CUVIER: In a way. Would you like to read her passage?

(*Cuvier hands her a stack of papers.*)

MILLICENT: Shall I turn around?

CUVIER: That shouldn't be necessary.

(*Millicent begins ruffling through papers.*)

CUVIER: Come closer, let me see. Yes, right here—Hottentot, between Hippopotamus and Hyena.

MILLICENT: Natural History of Mammals, Georges Cuvier, 1814. "Her movements had something of a brusqueness and capriciousness, much like a monkey. She had a habit of protruding her lips quite like I have observed in the Orang-Outang. Her character was gay, her memory good, and she recognized, after several weeks, a person whom she had seen only once. She spoke Dutch, which she had learned at the Cape, knew English, and had begun to speak French. Necklaces, belts of glass beads, and other savage finery pleased her very much; but what flattered her taste more than anything else was brandy. I might even ascribe her death . . ."

(*Millicent looks at Cuvier.*)

MILLICENT: Death?

CUVIER: I am working a bit ahead of myself. Continue.

MILLICENT: "I might even ascribe her death to an excess of drink, to which she gave herself up during her illness."

CUVIER: Thank you.

MILLICENT: And so you are almost finished.

CUVIER: Soon.

(*Cuvier reaches for the papers. As Millicent hands them to him, he grabs her wrist and pulls her into an embrace. They kiss. Cuvier stands, continuing the embrace. As lights fade, he bends her over the desk and begins to raise her skirts.*)

Scene 13

The present. Sara's study.

SARA: (*to audience*) I was driving south on Lake Shore Drive the day I understood. It became so clear. And may I take a second just to say that I am awed, no, overcome by the inspiring beauty of my city. On this particular morning the sky was so blue, and the lake reflected it back green, and then God put just a few clouds, in just the right places, just to let us know she could. And there's a strange something that happens driving toward the city on Lake Shore Drive. You look and the city is on the horizon. And it's glorious and hazy gleaming. And the next time you look up, it's right on top of you. There's the Drake and then you're rounding the bend. And I've tried to catch the in-between time, and I've decided there isn't one. It's in the horizon, and then it's on you. It's the same moment that I miss when I'm waiting for a wound to heal. First you notice a part of your body that you had so taken for granted. Oh, my, with this wound I can't cut lemons. It hurts. When I take a shower, it hurts. It hurts in the sun, or the cold. And then one cold, sunny day, you find that you are cutting a lemon in the shower and you didn't notice it. It's healed and you've missed it.

(*Bradsford enters, unnoticed.*)

This is how Saartjie let me know what I must do. What I had to do. The way it was and the way it must be.

BRADSFORD: A breakthrough?

SARA: Of sorts. She's tired.

BRADSFORD: You're beautiful.

(*Sara takes a moment and really studies Bradsford.*)

SARA: I'm so sorry.

BRADSFORD: Don't tell me why.

SARA: I'm sorry that I haven't lately taken the time to see you. It's been hard to see you, I think.

BRADSFORD: You think.

SARA: All the time. You know that. (*Pause.*) But soon it will all be done and we'll be normal again.

BRADSFORD: All better.

SARA: Sure. (*Beat.*) What is your mind on these days?

BRADSFORD: Same as always. State of the Nation. Classes, deadlines, publishing, tenure committees, hiring committees, committees, committees, committees. But I won't bother you with it until you are done. Soon. Soon?

SARA: Very.

BRADSFORD: There's something I want to say. It has something to do with love and patience.

SARA: So we're talking?

BRADSFORD: Just something about where patience and love become complacency.

SARA: I don't know what you're saying.

BRADSFORD: Of course not, I don't. But I'd warn you that complacency can start to feel like disregard, which is very close to hate. I'm trying to tell you something. I'm trying to say something . . . about love and sacrifice and feeling like a chump. If sometimes it feels that you've given up a part of yourself, know that I've given up things as well. And that it's been worth it. Just a warning, not a threat, just a warning that you may not want to wait for me to figure it out.

Scene 14

Paris. Saartjie sits on the edge of her bed. She wears a European designer's exaggerated rendition of an African costume. With its beads and feathers and headdress, it most closely resembles that of a Vegas showgirl.

Saartjie is very sick and somewhat inebriated. It is a struggle for her to hold up the headpiece.

Millicent stands near her, wearing an elegant evening gown. This is the first time we've seen Millicent out of uniform. She is prettier than we might have imagined.

SAARTJIE: So you are wearing a costume tonight too?

MILLICENT: You have seen evening clothes.

SAARTJIE: I do not think I can do this one.

MILLICENT: This is the party of Madame Du LeVeir . . . really the most important party of the year. It is an honor that we have been invited. You must not embarrass Georges.

SAARTJIE: Georges?

MILLICENT: Monsieur Cuvier.

SAARTJIE: Of course. Perhaps if I could just lie down for a moment.

MILLICENT: You bring it on yourself. You do not eat and you drink too much.

SAARTJIE: Have I done something to anger you?

MILLICENT: You think you are quite special, don't you? You think this attention is flattering. They mock you.

SAARTJIE: Mock?

MILLICENT: They laugh in your face and you think that because you laugh too, they are not laughing at you. You are the court jester. And I tell you only because I have grown used to you.

SAARTJIE: Perhaps I could give you the costume and you could go in my stead. It hurts and I am so tired. Just please let me sleep. Perhaps I will sleep until I have seen my family. I think sleep is favorable to this. You have been kind, mostly, and I thank you.

MILLICENT: I will tell Monsieur Cuvier that you are too sick. Is there something I can do to make you more comfortable?

SAARTJIE: I am sorry if I compromised your position. I have learned to do what I am told, and that is all.

MILLICENT: You should stop talking. I will stop in when we have returned.

Scene 15

Dream music. Frenzied, classical—Paganini perhaps, and lighting.

Cuvier and Millicent stand in front of the examination table. Lights are bright white and light bounces off of their very white, blood-splattered aprons and hats.

Cuvier wears a doctor's lamp on his head. They both use exaggeratedly large surgical tools.

They cut and dig; blood splatters. The sight is maniacal.

The cadaver sits up and we see that they have been dissecting Saartjie. She screams and then begins to laugh hysterically. Music turns into twisted circus music.

Cuvier hits Saartjie over the head with a large mallet.

Saartjie's laughter stops. She lies down.

Sara rises between Cuvier and Millicent.

She wears pajamas, a white tank top and flannel bottoms. She digs in. All three are up to their elbows in blood. Occasionally one pulls out an entrail.

Saartjie screams.

BLACKOUT

Scene 16

The present. Sara sits at the edge of the bed, deep in thought. Booker is still under the covers. It is day. Sara removes gloves from the previous scene. She still wears the blood-stained clothes.

BOOKER: Smile.

SARA: Why?

(*Long pause.*)

BOOKER: Penny for your thoughts.

SARA: Surely they're worth more than that.

(*Long pause.*)

BOOKER: You're fun.

SARA: Yes.

BOOKER: Hungry?

SARA: Sure.

BOOKER: What do you have taste for?

SARA: Whatever.

BOOKER: Sushi?

SARA: Whatever.

BOOKER: Middle Eastern?

SARA: Sure.

BOOKER: McDonalds?

SARA: I'll get my coat.

(*Sara exits. She enters again, dragging the coat behind her.*)

SARA: They call that motherfucker the Father of Modern Anatomy.

BOOKER: What?

SARA: Cuvier. The motherfuckin' Father of Modern Anatomy. You know the Kingdom, Phylum, Class, Order, Family, Genus, Species stuff? That was him. He, not God, named the animals. And you know what he did? He killed her. He might as well have. And he's celebrated. He and his friends examined her. He spread her legs and had an artist draw her labia. He let her die. They all killed her, but he let her die, and he cut out her vagina, and put it in pickle juice and labeled it and put it on a shelf. Then the freak makes a wax mold of her body, cuts out her entrails, drains her like a cow, like a pig, boils the flesh off of her bones, and mounts the skeleton. He did that to her. And then, just for posterity, he publishes a picture and description of her in his comprehensive book of mammals. She is, according to him, this woman who spoke at least four languages, the link between man and animal.

BOOKER: That's why it needs to be written. You empower her. You give her story to the people.

SARA: You know that's bullshit. (*deadly calm*) I don't empower her. I let it happen again in front of witnesses. I celebrate it. And you know as well as I that they'll line up to read it, and call it empathy, and enjoy it for the freak fuckin' show that it is. And it will have been because of me. And I won't. I can't. We can't.

(*Sara takes the manuscript out of her briefcase.*)

BOOKER: *Mein Kampf* is still one of the best sellers in America. It's not because every American is an anti-Semite. It's because we need to know. It's because we have to be reminded.

SARA: That's bullshit. They know, Booker. We know. It's the same story over and over again. I'm sorry that I didn't understand why this was so difficult. I'm sorry that I couldn't articulate it sufficiently, but you have to look inside and know that we contribute nothing. Like you said. They don't like us. They don't really care. Just as long as we stay victims, it's a great story to consume. It's so much easier to confront us in a historical context.

She only just got a proper burial three months ago. The museum just gave her back to South Africa . . . after hundreds of years of degradation. For hundreds of years people from all over the world came and looked at her body, her skeleton, her genitals, and then went out for lunch and a stroll down the Champs Elysées. Could we please let her rest? Please can she rest. She has to rest now.

(*Sara savagely rips the manuscript to shreds.*)

BOOKER: You stupid theatrical bitch. I have the PDF. You signed a contract. So, I'll tell you what. Why don't you take your confused, miscegenated ass back home to your white husband. You want to get crazy on me? Fine. I work with writers, I've seen every kind of crazy there is. So save it. Ask Mr. Bradsford what he thinks you should do. He'll tell you. Work it out on your own time.

(*Booker has finished putting on his coat.*)

I'll have Fran send you the galleys. You take care of yourself, Okay? And get some help.

(*Booker exits.*)

Scene 17

African music plays softly. It's beautiful. The black women enter in authentic African garb. Colorful, festive, hair natural, feet bare.

They begin a soothing dance that becomes increasingly acrobatic and rhythmic.

They exit dancing.

Sara enters, dressed in an "ethnic" evening gown. She holds an award. The house lights come up.

She steps forward.

SARA: Well, I'm speechless. Let me first begin by saying, Thank you, God. Thank you, Mom and Dad, and especially Brad for seeing me through what has been a challenging and glorious ride. And finally, I must thank James Booker for having had the courage and wisdom to give voice to such a tragic and compelling story. That we might all be better for it. That we might all remember . . . that we all might look within ourselves for a better tomorrow. And thank you, Ms. Baartman, your story is more than history . . .

(*African music plays loudly over Sara's words. Saartjie stands in silhouette behind a screen. Sara continues speaking. We cannot hear her, then:*)

Your story is our story, the world's story, and we must challenge ourselves . . .

(*more African music*)

History is elusive, mercurial, evasive. Try as we might to understand . . .

(*more African music*)

The Venus Hottentot . . .

(*Sara holds up the book. We see bold geometric designs on the cover. Show slide of book—bold geometric cut-out of a black woman in silhouette—reds and yellows vital.*)

. . . blends a tangible anthropological perspective with a comprehensively researched, painstakingly documented . . .

(*African music becomes louder.*)

We celebrate Ms. Baartman and thank her for pointing us to the best and the worst in ourselves. I'd like to show you a model of Ms. Baartman that was displayed . . . Slide, please.

(*We never see the slide.*)

(*Music rises. Lights fade.*)

End of Play

J. NICOLE BROOKS

An artistic associate at the nationally acclaimed Lookingglass Theatre Company in Chicago, J. Nicole Brooks was trained as an actor and attributes everything she knows about playwriting to her experiences as an actor. When she decided to try her hand at playwrighting, she didn't take classes or attend workshops—she just started writing on an old laptop that a friend gave her. She graduated from Northern Illinois University in 1998 and after returning to Chicago from Dekalb, Illinois, she began taking Saturday morning acting classes at Lookingglass. She later was invited to work on a few projects for Lookingglass and never said no, even to unpaid work at the company. Brooks attended ensemble meetings, participated in company retreats, and most important, she read scripts. She did so because she liked the company and its aesthetic and the people. What she didn't realize at the time was that she was giving herself a valuable education in theater—in acting, directing, and producing, an important part of theater in which actors rarely receive training. Her willingness to work and her spirit of collaboration led to a series of larger projects and to her being cast in some of the company's plays. In 2004 she was asked to join the company. As an associate she now had an artistic home and the support she needed to develop her plays. In 2007 Lookingglass produced Brooks's play *Black Diamond: The Years the Locusts Have Eaten*, which she co-directed. In 2012 she directed the company's production of *Mr. Rickey Calls a Meeting*. She described directing the all-male cast as one of the greatest experiences of her career.

AUTHOR'S NOTE

This play is written in a language and style that reflect agility and imperfection.... It's in the realm of the experimental, I suppose. The characters often topple over one another speaking. They stammer, are bilingual, have unexpected moments of silence, or know when to speak with sharp precision—much like we do in real life. The play draws on mythology and ideas from many cultures. From its Greek tragedy origin to the French interpretation of Racine, this retelling is influenced by mythological gods like Erzulie and Oshun. It incorporates ancient cultures of Persia and Iran, the Americas, Antilles, and even cinema. Malcolm X believed that the black man would never be truly respected unless Africa became a world power. He paid close attention to the revolutions that were occurring throughout Africa and Asia. Considering that Haiti is one of the poorest countries in the Western hemisphere, I wanted to imagine it as a superpower. I wanted to free my self as an artist from colonial oppression and what we see in the media. Perhaps one day, in this lifetime, Haiti as a superpower will not be mythology.

• • •

Fedra premiered at Lookingglass Theatre Company on September 30, 2009.

Director:	Laura Eason
Fedra:	J. Nicole Brooks
Hippolytus:	Anthony Fleming III
Panope:	Lauren Hirte
Aricia:	Sharina Martin
Theseus:	Morocco Omari
Afrodite/Ismene:	Tamberla Perry
Theramenes:	Michael Salinas
Enone:	Lisa Tejero
Set:	Meghan Raham
Costumes:	Alison Siple
Lighting:	Christine Binder
Properties:	Chelsea Meyers
Sound:	Joshua Horvath
Composition:	Kevin O'Donnell
Fight choreography:	Matthew Hawkins
Director of production:	Alexandra Blunt
Stage manager:	Jonathan Templeton

FEDRA

... and besides, there are no men without tragedies,
there is only what you believe.
Everything is costume.
Everything seems the way you see it on the street,
unconcerned, ambling along the pedestrian crossing of appearance.
Everything smells of rules, and keeps its secret.

    —Louis Aragon, *Henri Matisse*

PALAIS DE ANTILLES:
THE ROYAL FAMILY

Fedra Philomene Narcisse	Queen of the Greater and Lesser Antilles
Enone Françoise Batiste	A nurse and confidant to the queen
Panope Morisseau	A servant woman
Theseus Narcisse	King of the Greater and Lesser Antilles
Hippolytus Hes am Narcisse	Prince of the Greater and Lesser Antilles
Theramenes Gamboa	Confidant to Prince Hippolytus
Aricia Pallas-Toussaint	A princess of royal blood in captivity
Ismene del Negro*	Confidant to the princess
Afrodite*	A goddess

*The same actor portraying Ismene should play Afrodite.

Act 1

Scene 1

Bird Poop = Good Luck

Early morning. Palais de Antilles. Monday.

3 A.M. The dimly lit queen's boudoir. Lavish curtains, portraits, architectural pieces, rich fabrics, exotic fruit, chaise lounge, etc. If possible, there is a pool or other water source into which actors can submerge themselves. FEDRA NARCISSE, Queen of Haiti and the Antilles, stands center stage in a bedazzled hospital gown and robe. Her wrists are bandaged. Her hair is unkempt and her skin lackluster. She has been up all night. She is morose and post-suicidal. She listens to radio reports and flips stations via remote. She smokes a cigarette almost to its filter. The news montage underscores the scene with various reports and pundits weighing in about the royal jet going off radar during inclement weather. As the lights brighten in the space we see AFRODITE, a goddess oozing all things love and sex, standing nearby. Even when unseen by mortals, her presence and power are felt. She controls mortals with a single gesture. She watches Fedra's every move.

V.O. REPORTS: In our top story, the wreckage of King Theseus' jet, which crashed two days ago in Tropical Depression Persephone, has not still been found.

(Fedra slowly peels the bandage from one of her wrist wounds. Mesmerized, she stares at the healing scar.)

V.O. REPORTS CONT.: . . . coast guard has suspended its search and recovery efforts for the day, due to *(channel changes)* . . . royal jet, which was piloted by the King, had several top officials aboard. *(channel changes)* The aircraft lost contact with control towers . . . *(channel changes)* As the search continues, there is much speculation about who will be heir to the throne if the king is not found alive . . . *(channel changes)* but where is the queen? The people want to hear from her. People are afraid . . . Prince Hippolytus gave a statement to the press corps on behalf of the royal . . .

(A sound bite of Prince Hippoltyus speaking about the crash causes Fedra to double over with emotion. She's having a manic fit. She extinguishes her cigarette into her arm. Afrodite makes a gesture and Hippolytus' voice loops in the soundscape. Tears stream down Fedra's face. Afrodite walks over to Fedra and lifts her chin. She smiles a wicked smile at Fedra.)

AFRODITE: The scene is set. Lights.

(Lights transition)

(Enter ENONE BATISTE and PANOPE MORRISEAU. Enone, the queen's nurse and confidant, moves with precision but is serpentine in behavior. Panope is a fragile beauty and does her best to stay in favor. They open doors and windows to reveal the sky. The marine layer is thick. They bow to the queen.)

ENONE: Good morning.

PANOPE: Bonjour, your majesty.

(Panope busies herself with activity.)

ENONE: Ça va? Did you rest? Why are you on the floor?

(Enone takes the remote and switches it to music. Panope presents a tray of breakfast food.)

ENONE: The chef has created the most wonderful thing. Soy boiled eggs. Especially for you. They taste just like the real thing.

FEDRA: Maker's Mark four fingers, neat.

ENONE: You don't eat, you don't drink. Besides, drinking is bad for your complexion.

(*Fedra reluctantly takes an egg and munches. A nervous Panope continues her duties. Fedra eyeballs her.*)

FEDRA: . . . and look at this one. Hey, Odd Job. Hey! You know you won't look like that forever. There's a prettier bitch born every minute. You ought not invest in that. (*She catches a reflection of herself in a mirror.*) Standards of beauty have destroyed our society. My mother once declared her daughters to be the most beautiful—you should never tell little girls they're pretty. Tell them they're smart or cool, or . . . or . . . (*She cries softly.*)

PANOPE: Oui, madame.

ENONE: (*interjects*) Your majesty, we have important matters to discuss. The king's council has been behind locked doors making decisions that directly affect the lives of you and your two sons. We must have faith in the gods for your husband's return, but we must also act now.

FEDRA: Did you hear the last bird on earth just died? The gods have taken our birds. They've taken everything from me. Fuck the gods.

(*The family portrait shifts abruptly. Panope and Enone take notice.*)

PANOPE: Please, your majesty. The gods hear unholy prayers.

ENONE: Leave us, Panope.

FEDRA: Stay, little girl. Stay right where you are. (*hurls eggs at Panope*) Let's have some more of these "soy eggs," they are delicious.

(*Enone gives Panope a gesture to leave. Panope exits. Enone approaches.*)

ENONE: You should be grateful that the gods saved you from yourself. To try and take your own life . . .

FEDRA: Which was a complete fucking failure.

ENONE: Madame, I know this is difficult, but we must face the facts. Your husband is missing in action, presumed dead. The Privy Council will decide the heir to the throne. Your eldest is too young and you must rule in his place. They won't appoint you, if you are in this condition.

(*Melina Mecouri music plays in the BG. Fedra hums along. Afrodite draws near.*)

The king is gone and people are frightened.

FEDRA: He'll come back . . . . The king will . . . (*overcome with emotion*)

ENONE: There are uprisings led by those rebels as we speak. They want Aricia Toussaint's release. And what about your husband's son? The purest blood of Haiti must rule, not the king's half-bred bastard. The crown could go to your stepson, Prince Hippolytus.

AFRODITE: Don't worry, your secret is safe with me . . .

(*Fedra freaks.*)

ENONE: What is it?

FEDRA: Get out! I told you not to mention his name! I don't want to talk about this anymore.

ENONE: Your majesty, I must insist that we discuss—
FEDRA: If you don't get out of my ear . . .
ENONE: As you wish.

(*Enone exits.*)

Scene 2

Insert Toto, Foreigner, and Elton John Love Songs Here

Wednesday. A set transition to a hallway near the queen's boudoir.

Enone stands and recovers. She pops a cigarette into her mouth and frantically searches for a lighter. THERAMENES GAMBOA glides into the space. He's a magnetic young executive loyal to Prince Hippolytus. He smiles brightly at Enone.

THERAMENES: Mademoiselle Batiste. Ooh. Looks like somebody got a new mini-mizer. You're looking less butch—
ENONE: You wish.
THERAMENES: All work and no play makes Enone a dull boy. You look awful.
ENONE: I need a light.
THERAMENES: Smoking's bad for your teeth.

(*He playfully waves a piece of Nicorette chewing gum in her face.*)

Here you go, sweetheart. A little nicotine for you. Let's see you work those jowls.

(*She snatches the pack from him and shoves a piece into her mouth. She has a tiny moment of ecstasy.*)

You didn't summon me over to watch you chomp like a cow. What do you want?
ENONE: Your cooperation.
THERAMENES: Sorry?
ENONE: Don't be coy with me, little one. I've known you for years, and I can see when your mind is at play. What do you know?
THERAMENES: What—
ENONE: Is the council in favor of the queen? Will she rule in place of her sons? You can trust me. Any and all information will be held in the strictest confidence.
THERAMENES: Right here in the hallway near the queen's quarters, no less. You expect me to . . . nice try.
ENONE: I will offer you a seat in the new council if she is named ruler. But you have to play nice.
THERAMENES: Call me when you've read another chapter of *The Prince*. I don't think you're quite ready for your takeover.

(*PRINCE HIPPOLYTUS enters the hallway unseen by them. Hip is a thick-skinned young man fully dressed in royal garb and sword. He listens quietly.*)

ENONE: Oh, goddamn you. Don't be such a spineless twerp. I'm offering an alliance here.

THERAMENES: This conversation is both unnerving and unlawful. I don't gossip about affairs that do not concern me. Neither should you. Shouldn't you be removing her bed pan or feeding her cough medicine right now?

ENONE: Your insults won't distract me.

THERAMENES: She doesn't care about the affairs of state—

ENONE: And you think your precious prince frosty does? He—

HIP: Can speak for himself.

(*He enters the space. Enone is caught off guard and doesn't bow.*)

THERAMENES: Surely mademoiselle has not forgotten propriety in manners and conduct in her sleep-deprived state?

(*Enone bows.*)

HIP: Rise. What grief disturbs you?

ENONE: All is well, Prince Hippolytus.

HIP: And your mistress?

ENONE: All is well.

HIP: I've come to visit with Queen Fedra. Announce my arrival.

ENONE: Her majesty is resting at the moment.

(*Hip stares at her.*)

I'm happy to deliver any message you may have for her—

HIP: You know, every time I come see her, I only find you, telling me how tired she is.

(*Enone casts her eyes downward.*)

This is a crucial time for our nation. The people of Greater and Lesser Antilles need to see their queen healthy and strong, so if she needs to go back to rehab again—

ENONE: I can give her all of the care she needs, right here—

HIP: Is she cutting again?

ENONE: We have removed any objects that may be a hazard—

HIP: You think the council will ignore this? I have no intentions of jeopardizing the lives of millions for the sake of one. They will be made aware of her transgressions—

ENONE: With all due respect, your highness, I think our citizens would prefer an ill queen to a foreign prince. (*Beat.*)

HIP: Open your ear: I will not allow you or anyone to usurp the crown. Send a message to your queen that she and I have important matters to discuss. And if she is bedridden, confined, crippled, or debilitated—then I will take this matter to the council. She has twenty-four hours—correction: she has until the end of day.

(*Enone bows and exits. Theramenes and Hip turn and enter the prince's corridor.*)

Who the hell does Enone think she is?

THERAMENES: She wanted to recruit me to her army of one, to secure the throne for Fedra. Make no doubt about it, a plot brews.

HIP: I hate this place.

THERAMENES: Be swift, my friend. Grasp the reins of power and do so without delay.

HIP: My father's not dead. He's missing in action. He is still ruler of this land.

THERAMENES: And the rules state that, should our king go missing or become incapacitated, a successor will be named in his place until his return.

HIP: I don't want to be his successor, but I'll be damned if Enone slithers her way into a position of power.

THERAMENES: Fedra wants the crown.

HIP: I know. My sense of duty is fueled only by her lack of competence. When Theseus returns, the first thing I'm going to do is pick up and go.

THERAMENES: Pick up and—where to?

HIP: Reykjavik.

THERAMENES: Iceland?

HIP: I'd give it all up for a simple life. Enjoy the hot springs, ice caps, glaciers, spouting geysers. . . . Did you know the last bevy of birds on earth was there?

THERAMENES: Iceland?

HIP: Okay, maybe not. But . . . I could go back to Iran.

THERAMENES: You haven't been to Tehran since you were a small boy. The war there is over, but it's still too dangerous. Time to sober up, brother. You may not want the crown, but you are the best person for the job. Plus you have the main qualification: Theseus' DNA.

HIP: I'm only half Haitian. Wifey bore him two full-blooded Haitian sons who stand in line. And what about Aricia Toussaint?

(*Afrodite enters and observes.*)

THERAMENES: You're not seriously worried about Princess Anarchy getting the crown, are you? She's a political prisoner! The only support she has is from a group of democracy-loving rebels.

HIP: Yes, but she's pretty. Eh . . . pretty smart, I mean. She's smart. She's the daughter of a deposed king, and she could get the sympathy vote from the council. We should not underestimate her.

THERAMENES: The council holds you in favor. Trust me on that.

HIP: (*broods*) Oh gods . . . am I really considering this? Theseus acquired this kingdom in a bloody takeover. I don't want to uphold that political legacy.

THERAMENES: You don't have to follow your father's footsteps.

(*Afrodite lingers.*)

HIP: I don't know, maybe Aricia would be a better choice.

THERAMENES: Look, Fedra is incompetent and Aricia is a prisoner. *You're* the choice.

(*The wheels are turning for Theramenes. Hip broods.*)

Why do you do that?

HIP: What?

THERAMENES: Hip, every time Aricia's name is mentioned, you blink. And your face twitches.

HIP: No, I don't.

THERAMENES: I beg to differ. Aricia.

HIP: So what, I blink.

THERAMENES: And twitch. Aricia. Methinks you have a crush on her. Has Afrodite finally stomped her way into your proud heart?

HIP: No! Go get some papers for me to sign.

THERAMENES: You're all flushed. Admit it. I'm not here to judge, only to listen. Say it. Release. Spill the beans. C'mon, tell me . . .

HIP: I think of Aricia . . . and I feel changed. It makes no sense. I've pledged my chastity. She's my family's sworn enemy. If she knew how I felt, she'd be disgusted.

THERAMENES: Well, if you become king, you can grant her freedom, profess your love, and alter your fates. Star-crossed lovers, I think not. See? Life is so simple.

(*Phone rings. Theramenes takes it.*)

Theramenes Gamboa—(*Spanish*) yes . . . yes . . . have they been notified? Right . . . okay . . . I will. Thank you. (*Sí . . . sí . . . hay señales de sobrevivientes? Se han notificado? Bueno. Okay. Yo sí lo haré . . .*)

(*Theramenes hangs up.*)

Your father's plane has been found. Off the coast of Maiquetia, Venezuela.

HIP: Survivors?

THERAMENES: No bodies have been found. With any luck from the radar, we may be able to figure out the flight path and search in another place. However, it's unlikely anyone survived that crash.

(*a moment of silence*)

THERAMENES: I'm so sorry.

HIP: What the hell happened?

THERAMENES: . . . Hopefully we will find the black box. The investigation can take months.

HIP: We don't have months. We have to get to the council and urge them not to do anything, make any decisions.

THERAMENES: I think we should prepare the family's official statement and arrange the press conference. Make plans for the memorial service—

HIP: My father is not dead! Unless the council has substantial evidence, I will not let them make any decisions until we have irrevocable proof. Marshal some forces. Your best men. They'll be entering enemy territory, but you tell them they cannot return until they bring my father back. Dead or alive. I'm going to council.

(*Hip exits. Theramenes hops on his cell phone and exits.*)

Scene 3

Marquis de Sade v. Marquis de Sade

Later. The queen's boudoir.

Fedra enters with a fashionable dress. Enone follows.

FEDRA: Stop it. Get off me. Why are you making me dress?

ENONE: The prince demands to see you right now.

FEDRA: No. I cannot. I'm too tired.

ENONE: Would you like some almonds for energy?

FEDRA: No! No damned nuts gonna give me any energy. You're dragging me out of here in this thing. I look like an idiot. He'll laugh at me. I look awful.

ENONE: You look beautiful.

FEDRA: You think clumsy trinkets and fucking dead bird feathers will take away my pain?!

(tosses accessories from her body and hair at Enone)

I won't have any of it. I will not allow you or anyone else to make a fool of me.

ENONE: I merely suggested that you get dressed so that you could meet the prince. It was you who demanded that we adorn you! We styled your hair, dressed you in a couture gown. Manicure. Pedicure. Ass wax. Lady, whatever you wanted, we did it!

FEDRA: *(laughs heartily)* Well played. I can always count on you for the truth. I did make you give me an ass wax.

ENONE: I've missed the sound of your laughter. Oh, sister, I am so worried about you.

FEDRA: As long as the sun is in the sky, I am protected.

(Afrodite draws near.)

Aykaash Meetoonestam Khorsheed ro behesh hedieh bedam. (I wish I could gift him the sun.)

ENONE: Madame? Were you speaking Farsi?

FEDRA: Leave me.

(Fedra crosses to the cabinet for pills. Enone snatches them away.)

ENONE: They are going to take everything you have. Hippolytus is building a case against you. He intends to prove that you are unfit. You must stop this, or they will—

FEDRA: Let them! *(She cracks.)* I see how they all look at me. How you look at me. Like I'm some crazed junkie bitch who can't keep it together. *Eh bien, c'est peut-être vrai.* (Well, maybe it's true.) My children may be better off without me. They don't need me. No one needs me. I don't have a reason to live. I don't have anything left. . . .

ENONE: Sister. You have me. Haven't I always been there for you? To listen without judgment?

FEDRA: No.

ENONE: I know that I am abrasive, but I am loyal to you. Has my counsel ever led you astray?

FEDRA: No. But I am tired.

ENONE: I know. But you must fight for your children. Your sons are too young to rule, but you can rule in their place until they are of age. But if Hippolytus gets the crown, your sons will be slaves. We'll all be slaves to that Middle Eastern foreigner. Before you know it, we'll be running around in hijabs and chadors, bombs strapped to our bodies, three steps behind the men—

FEDRA: Oh, would you shut up!

ENONE: Retribution is at hand, lady. You punished the prince endlessly as a child; don't think he won't do the same to your sons.

FEDRA: If Theseus were here, I would be fine. He would protect his queen. Who will save me now?

ENONE: Your majesty, I can protect you.

FEDRA: You cannot protect me.

ENONE: Of course I can. Whatever you need, I will provide.

FEDRA: She has destroyed the women of my family.

ENONE: Your majesty, I don't follow?

FEDRA: You cannot protect me from the kinslayer, Afrodite.

ENONE: Afrodite?

FEDRA: What wild things she sent upon my mother. And now I am her victim. (*a moment*)

ENONE: *Oh! Mon Dieu.* What curse afflicts you? Have you . . . have you taken a lover?

FEDRA: No.

ENONE: But you love?

FEDRA: Yes . . . truly, madly, deeply. All of its fever.

ENONE: Look at me. You need to tell me everything.

FEDRA: But you already know everything, Enone.

ENONE: Stop talking in circles.

FEDRA: You know his face . . .

ENONE: Whose face?

FEDRA: I die to save myself a full confession. Leave at once.

ENONE: Not until you confess.

FEDRA: You disobey your queen?

ENONE: If it saves her life? YES! Tell me his name!

FEDRA: HIPPOLYTUS!

(*Sounds of birds flash through the space. Fedra and Enone stand for a few moments.*)

FEDRE: Please, say something.

ENONE: Well, this most certainly will be another long night. Shots?

(*She crosses to the bar and quickly fills the glasses with a boozy concoction.*)

FEDRA: I love him, and there isn't anything I can do to stop it.

ENONE: No, this cannot be. You hate Hippolytus—this cannot be true love.

FEDRA: If a god gives you a feeling, curse or no, doesn't that make it real? If the gods are all-powerful . . . omnipotent . . . then how are we guilty? My mother was cursed to fall in love with a bull. Was she guilty? (*Enone looks away.*) It doesn't matter. I fear my sins. I hate my life.

ENONE: This is why you tried to kill yourself. Does the prince—

FEDRA: No. He can never know.

ENONE: I am here for you. Together we will sort this all out . . .

(*Panope comes in. She's in a tizzy.*)

PANOPE: Madame, forgive me for interrupting. I hate to be the bearer of bad news, but all of our fears have come to pass.

ENONE: Make it plain, girl.

PANOPE: The wreckage has been found. King Theseus has been pronounced dead, and the council has issued his death certificate. Hippolytus was there to stop them, because no bodies have been recovered, but his efforts were too late. A successor to the throne will be named by the Privy Council. Some councilmen would have Hippolytus as our ruler because he is the king's first-born son. Others agree that the queen should rule, until her sons are of age. And some argued the crown rightfully belongs to our prisoner, Aricia Toussaint.

ENONE: Traitors!

PANOPE: But the council's favor seems to be leaning towards Prince Hippolytus. It is believed that he will be appointed king.

ENONE: Thank you, Panope. The queen has heard your message.

(*Panope bows and exits. Fedra drops to the floor with emotion. She crawls toward the pool.*)

ENONE: Did you hear that? Hippolytus will become king.

FEDRA: . . .

(*Enone pulls Fedra together.*)

ENONE: Your husband is gone now. Listen to me . . . you are safe, and I will let no man hurt you. There is no shame in your passion, your feelings are yours, own them . . . but Hippolytus will not welcome your love. That boy clutches to his chastity and arrogance like a bow and arrow. Let it go. Release it. Tell yourself it's a falsehood. Lay to rest your feelings for him. Poise your self, girl. Time is a thief. We have work to do. Go to Hippolytus. Appeal to him for clemency. You have always had the power to attract whatever you wanted, and now you must use that power for what you need: freedom for your sons. Throw yourself on his mercy.

FEDRA: No . . . I don't like any of this.

ENONE: There is no other recourse. You must go to him.

FEDRA: I'll fall apart, I know it.

ENONE: Not with me by your side.

FEDRA: Please don't make me. Let's wait for the king's council to advise. Surely they will be on my side.

ENONE: Are you going to trust your life to a group of old men who don't respect you or womanhood? Or are you going to trust me? Don't you trust me? It's me!

FEDRA: Tell me what to do.

ENONE: Warm his cold heart. Blast away his haughtiness by simply saying you're sorry. If you don't, your sons face imminent doom. Now you must stand. Fight! Go to the prince. Fear not, I will be by your side. But you must follow my counsel and my counsel only. You are the queen of a mighty nation! You are not a lovesick puppy.

(*Enone takes some of the water and splashes it in Fedra's face, in a revival sort of way. Fedra breathes and coughs, and fights to get on her feet.*)

ENONE: Give consent. Give consent. Give consent!

FEDRA: I consent!

ENONE: For the sake of your sons.

FEDRA: For the sake of my sons, I consent!

ENONE: And for the sake of Haiti.

FEDRA: For the sake of Haiti, I consent.

ENONE: For my own sake.

FEDRA: For my own sake.

ENONE: My queen, of this great nation, I bow to you.

LIGHTS

Scene 4
A Hero Ain't Nothin but a Sandwich

Lights up on the palace prison cell. Meet ARICIA TOUSSAINT, a young woman in denial of her beauty. Her arm is in a cast and she absentmindedly picks at it. She has a wickedly dry sense of humor and sardonic wit. She watches an old recognizable 1970s or 1980s American TV show on her ancient laptop computer. The sound blares. Enter ISMENE DEL NEGRO, her lovable motor-mouthed friend and servant. Ismene speaks into Aricia's ear. Aricia mutes the sound.

ARICIA: Holy shit. Theseus is dead? I've been waiting my whole life to hear those words. Finally, the house of Narcisse will crumble. And what about queenie?

ISMENE: Crazy as a mad hatter! More on that later. We have to get you ready.

(*Ismene springs into action, tidying the cell, putting away any anti-government materials.*)

ARICIA: Ready for what?

ISMENE: Prince Hippolytus has sent word. He's coming to visit you here.

ARICIA: Visit me? The fuck?

ISMENE: I don't know why, baby girl, but he'll be here soon. And please stop saying fuck so much.

ARICIA: Unless they're letting me out of this shit hole, they can all fuck off.

ISMENE: Look, I don't know why he's coming, but you have got to be on your best behavior. And don't be a Poindexter, okay? Sometimes you talk about No Mao

Zey Dong or . . . or precolonial Songhai empires, and don't nobody know about that. Please, no endless prattle about Assata, Nightzee—

ARICIA: Nietzsche.

ISMENE: Or the other dude who turned into a bug. And nothing about these ancient movies you're always watching. No bio-diesel talk, fracking, over fishing sharks, agrarian physics, or saving Middle Earth. God, you look like a raccoon! Your hair. Here, maybe we can do a little sexy librarian, geek chic . . . Oh, what's the use.

ARICIA: Awfully sexist of you, to think I need to be attractive to him. This is a jail—

(*A sound and lighting cue indicating the arrival of a royal.*)

ISMENE: Don't curse, slouch, or turn your back to him. Be mindful of eye contact and you must must must bow deeply—

ARICIA: Or what? He'll arrest me?

(*Theramenes steps into the doorway. Hip enters. He blinks and all that. Ismene bows. Aricia bows. Theramenes and Ismene take their place upstage.*)

HIP: Good afternoon, ladies. Princess Aricia. Thank you for meeting with me.

ARICIA: Okay, but really I didn't have a choice. And it's not a meeting. You came to my jail cell.

HIP: Pardon the expression.

(*She folds her arms and stares, doesn't make eye contact with him.*)

HIP: I don't know if you've heard by now. My father has been lost in a plane crash.

ARICIA: I heard.

HIP: Right. And, well, things are a bit precarious at the moment. This was all very sudden and is difficult for the family.

ARICIA: My ass weeps for you.

(*Ismene, horrified, tries to run interference.*)

ISMENE: Would anyone like any iced tea? How's about lemonade? I can make a pretty good Arnold Palmer. Or how about some frappé? Sherbert frappé—

HIP: No, thank you. (*to Theramenes*) This is going really well.

(*Hip struggles for his cool. Aricia remains sour and picks at her cast. He looks around and comes across her sketch book.*)

This is incredible. You drew this?

ARICIA: Yeah.

(*He looks her over.*)

HIP: What's wrong with your arm?

ARICIA: What's wrong with your eye?

(*re: his nervous eye twitch*)

HIP: Uh, . . . allergies. Nice work here. These birds are beautiful. What do we have here? Queen Fedra as a praying mantis standing over a bloody headless man. King Theseus—wait. . . . No. What is . . . Is this one supposed to be me? Is this you?

ARICIA: Whatever, yeah.

ISMENE: That's her as Princess Leia. And your highness, you are Jabba the Hutt.

HIP: Jabba the Hutt?

ISMEME: Ooh, you've never seen—

ARICIA: Never mind. Just an old old myth.

ISMENE: Oh, I'll tell you. See, they had some Star Wars and she was his love slave, Jabba, in the movie, but then she killed him—

ARICIA: Please stop talking.

ISMENE: Oh, it's not like, anti-royals kinda stuff. Show the prince the one with him as Han and you as Leia.

ARICIA: Go shave some ice, will you?

ISMENE: I'm just saying . . . parallels.

ARICIA: This meeting could go a lot faster if you allow the prince to say what he's gotta say.

(*Ismene sucks her teeth at Aricia, but bows sweetly to Hip. Hip nods for Theramenes to leave. They both exit.*)

ARICIA: Are you done inspecting my cell, warden? What is it that you want from me?

HIP: I want to apologize. On behalf of the Narcisse family for any suffering you have endured.

ARICIA: Oh man, you gotta work on your delivery. What suffering? Go on, tell me about my suffering. I want to hear you say it all.

HIP: Your punishment has been cruel and unjust—

ARICIA: Flowery words.

HIP: I inherited a socio-political—

ARICIA: I've been stuck in this fucking prison since I was eight years old. Looking at the same ocean, that I could never swim in. The same guards, the same everything! Nothing changes for me. I speak four languages, but really with no one here to talk to. I don't even know how to fucking talk to people, I'm socially gorked. I've done everything to escape this place. I've broken bones, banged my head against this very wall . . . there isn't a revenge fantasy I haven't had . . . the taste of blood is always on my lips. My greatest fantasy was to watch Theseus suffer and die. Just like I had to watch my own father. . . . Theseus is dead. And you know what? His death won't bring my family back. Neither will your apology.

HIP: I know that an apology is not adequate restitution, but your imprisonment has always, in my eyes, been unjust. Nearly every day that I've lived in this castle I've wished that I could help you. It appears that Haiti may rule in my favor. And when I govern, my first priority will be granting your freedom.

ARICIA: What a rousing campaign speech. Would you like a slow clap with that?

(*does a slow clap, à la 1980s cinema*)

HIP: Your freedom is my priority. I want you to be free. I give you my word. You're young and beautiful . . . prison is the last place you should be.

ARICIA: Young and beautiful spirits are incarcerated all the time. You gonna free them too?

HIP: I know you hate me and I don't blame you. I'm not a politician. I'm just trying to . . . I might be a little out of touch with the people of this land, but I'm trying to correct—change that. I didn't put you here and I don't believe you should be here. If it's the last thing I do, I'll see that you get your freedom. Please, let me do that for you. I'll do anything . . .

(*Aricia is filled with emotion.*)

I won't take much more of your time. I just wanted to see you . . . I mean tell you face-to-face. We don't have much in this lifetime, except honest moments like this. I'm sorry for my father. I'm sorry for the pain I've caused you, Aricia. Please forgive me . . .

(*She finally turns to face him. They have a moment of vulnerability and chemistry. He goes to touch her, she nervously recoils.*)

ARICIA: What are you doing?

HIP: I didn't mean to. Forgive me. (*He goes to exit.*)

ARICIA: Wait.

(*Hip stops.*)

Just give me a minute, alright.

(*Aricia plants her face into a small pillow. She lets out a primal scream.*)

Fuuuuuuuuuuuuuccck!

(*She fills with emotion again. She cries.*)

Are you fucking with me?

HIP: No, your highness.

Aricia cries harder. Ismene, all smiles, enters the cell carrying a small tray with a pitcher of beverage and copper cups. She sees Aricia crying and looks to Hip who is trying not to freak out. Ismene motions for him to pour her a drink and be chivalrous. He is timid at first. Ismene motions to him as if to say "buck up!" Hip nervously pours a drink and offers Aricia a hankerchief from his pocket. She takes the cup from him, and ignores the hankerchief. Instead she grabs a sash of his royal garb and wipes her tears from her face. After a while, she speaks.)

ARICIA: I'm told I say "fuck" a lot. Sorry if that offended you.

HIP: Please don't apologize—

ARICIA: Okay, so here it is. I'm glad your father's dead. No wait, not like that. I mean . . . you can't be worse than Theseus. God, I'm trying to say something nice, but it's not coming out right.

HIP: You don't have to say anything.

ARICIA: It's just . . . I've been in here so long I don't know how to talk to people. God, I'm such a freak.

HIP: I don't think you're a freak. It's easy to feel isolated here, even when you're not a prisoner. I don't always know how to talk to people either.

ARICIA: Guess we have more in common than I thought. We both lost parents to bloody politics and now we're both socially inept. Think there's a support group for that?

HIP: I wish.

ARICIA: I didn't know you were so short.

HIP: Well, we haven't stood next to each other since we were kids.

ARICIA: What are you talking about?

HIP: After the war Mother died, and when my father brought me to live here, I didn't have any friends. No one to play with. But after a few months, I spotted a little girl in the garden. It was you. You were wearing a yellow dress. And your hair was pulled into two little afro puffs.

ARICIA: Excuse me, I never wore afro puffs.

HIP: Okay, well then this other little girl and I were new arrivals to the palace. I was alone and scared, but seeing her made me feel a little better. I don't even think we spoke the same language. But somehow, I asked her to play with me. She did play with me.

ARICIA: *Baazi.* That's what you said. I remember.

HIP: You do?

ARICIA: You said *Salaam.* Then you motioned toward the maze and off we went. We chased each other through the maze, until our adventures were cut short by one of your father's guards. But I remember that day.

HIP: Well . . . who needs a maze when we can make our own path?

(*Hip boldy touches her wounded arm. Aricia doesn't protest. Hip gently runs his finger along her arm brace.*)

ARICIA: (*softly*) Ouch.

(*They lock eyes. Hip goes in to kiss her. Theramenes, accompanied by Ismene, interrupts the moment.*)

THERAMENES: My apologies. Sire. A word.

ARICIA: (*to Theramenes*) Man, come on—you have the worst timing.

HIP: Sorry, please—just a moment. (*to Theramenes*) What?

THER: The queen has requested you.

HIP: Tell the queen that I am "resting." Go.

THER: Sire, I don't mean to argue—

HIP: Go.

ARICIA: Sorry to interrupt, but this is all getting weird. Yeah, this is my jail cell— not some royal office. Go deal with your queen. Thank you for the visit Prince Hippol—

HIP: No . . . please call me Hip.

ARICIA: Hip. You should probably go before the wicked witch sends some flying monkeys here. Here's your sash.

HIP: Keep it. I'll get it back when I return. Again, I'm sorry for the interrupti—

THERAMENES: Sir, we've got to—

HIP: Timing, you gotta work on your timing. Peace, your highness.

(*Hip turns back to Aricia. He bows and kisses her hand. Aricia finally cracks a smile.*

He goes to exit. She softly says goodbye in Farsi.)

ARICIA: *Khoda hafiz.*

(*Pleasantly surprised, he turns back.*)

HIP: Khoda hafiz.

(*He and Theramenes exit.*)

ISMENE: *Khoda hafiz?* What was that?! He's got you speaking in tongues already? Like father, like son. Did I ever tell you about the king and I? And I don't mean the musical . . .

ARICIA: No, hot lips, he was speaking Farsi. He promised me my freedom.

(*Meanwhile Hip and Theramenes head toward the great hall.*)

THERAMENES: I think somebody just found their prom date.

HIP: Oh, my god, she was so beautiful, and she's really smart. Do you know who Jabba the Hutt is?

THERAMENES: Never mind that. The queen expects you momentarily in the Great Hall. The council is deadlocked on their decision . . . but I think it's in your favor. Stay cool and only speak when spoken to.

Theramenes and Hip arrive in the Great Hall. Fedra and Enone enter moments later. They regard one another from opposite sides of the room. Fedra is dressed in stunning couture and is shockingly sober. She clings to Enone.

Scene 5
3:10 to Yuma

FEDRA: There he is. My blood freezes. I don't know what to say. I don't know what to say—

ENONE: You stick to what I've told you, and you will be fine.

THERAMENES: We've got her right where we want her.

HIP: If the council is on my side, why should I speak with her now?

FEDRA: He's going to hate me, I know it. *Non. Je ne peux pas l'approcher.* (No. I cannot approach him.)

ENONE: No no no. You must do this. For your sons.

THERAMENES: Remember, she is still a queen and is higher in stature. Until it's official we must follow protocol. Now focus.

ENONE: Focus.

ENONE/THERAMENES: I'll be close by.

(*Theramenes takes his place upstage. Enone takes her place upstage. Fedra composes herself. She goes to take her place on the throne. They all bow to her.*)

HIP: Your majesty—

FEDRA: Have your boy wait outside.

HIP: Beg your pardon? My boy?

THERAMENES: Yes, madame.

(*Hip and Theramenes exchange glances. Theramenes exits. Fedra crosses to the prince. Hip is aloof with her.*)

FEDRA: Well, young sir. It certainly has been quite a while since we last met.

HIP: I have made many attempts to see you. You have refused every visit.

FEDRA: Yes . . . well, does it matter? We're here now. It seems that Haiti may rule in your favor and I plead my fears for my son. My eldest. He is faced with a thousand foes and only you can defend him. Remember, he is your half-brother.

HIP: I carry no malice against your sons. They are only children. I'm not that kind of person.

FEDRA: Unlike me, right? It's all right, I know I tore my drawers with you a long time ago. Even my children have treated you poorly.

HIP: It's not uncommon. A mother who is jealous for her own children will seldom love the child of a mother who came before her.

FEDRA: You think I am jealous of that Amazon?

(*He shows great restraint.*)

HIP: Queen Antiope died fighting for the rights of women throughout Africa and the Middle East.

FEDRA: I—

HIP: Do not call her that Amazon. Carpet pilot. A-rab bomb builder. Camel jockey. Or any other hateful name that you have said in my presence. It ends now.

FEDRA: Of course. All respect to the fallen Queen Antiope. You poor boy. No one to love you. No mother, no father . . .

HIP: We don't know for a fact that your husband is dead. His guardian god may grant him safe return.

FEDRA: Yes, Theseus has always pulled a rabbit out the hat. Or a lion.

(*The joke goes over poorly. She presses on.*)

I don't like both of us standing. Makes me nervous.

HIP: Your majesty—

FEDRA: Please don't speak . . . let me just . . . I was so young when I saw Theseus for the first time—he was so proud, charming, so beautiful. His skin was bronzed to perfection. It was as if the sun had licked him entirely. You look just like him, you know. You have the same skin. You even have the same sad eyes as he did . . . you smell like him.

(*Fedra oozes onto him; Afrodite looks on.*)

He was such a mighty warrior with big arms. My warrior had a big sword. I bet you have a big sword, too.

HIP: (*grabbing hold of her*) Have you forgotten yourself? You are Theseus' wife!

FEDRA: (*coming to her senses*) Why should you think I've forgotten it! Un-ass me!

(*He releases her arm and goes to exit.*)

You have not been dismissed from audience with the queen!

HIP: Audience with the queen? I'm not one of your subjects—

FEDRA: I am still the queen of Haiti. I own you, boy. You don't leave unless I say so.

(*Hip, once again showing great restraint, crosses back into the room. Fedra circulates and regains herself.*)

Now, please . . . we're getting off to a rough start. Well, don't look at me like that, I'm not going to eat you. I just want to take this opportunity to tell you how sorry I am for having treated you so poorly, and that . . . there's no reason that we can't be friends. United. For Haiti. So that's that.

HIP: That's that.

FEDRA: Yes, Hippolytus. Your father commanded you to love me. And for me to love you. And I do, Hippolytus.

HIP: I think . . . I don't quite understand.

FEDRA: No! You understand me far too well. Does Theseus' widow dare to love her stepson? YES, she does! I see you and I hear the songs of the beautiful birds that have long since left us.

HIP: I think you should be taken back to your chambers.

FEDRA: Or I could come to yours. Look at me.

(*She pulls on the fabric of her garments as if to undress.*)

He's gone now, and there would be no treachery between us.

(*Hip, incredulously, stares at her.*)

HIP: I will not stand here while you disrespect my father. He was your husband and he gave you the world!

FEDRA: And now he's dead.

HIP: You disgusting piece of filth. I only wish my father saw you for the monster that you truly are—

(*She draws his sword from his holster. She aims the weapon at him.*)

ENONE: Don't!

(*a standoff*)

HIP: I dare you.

FEDRA: Oh, look, Enone. The boy has balls. And he's been shining them for this very moment.

ENONE: Your majesty, please—

(*Fedra turns the blade toward herself.*)

FEDRA: Come. Prove yourself worthy of your valiant father.

ENONE: Gods in heaven!

HIP: Drop my sword. Drop it right this instant!

FEDRA: Don't bitch up on me now.

ENONE: Your majesty!

FEDRA: Theseus killed many monsters. Be like him! Strike deep!

(They struggle. Hip shoves her to the ground and raises the sword. Fedra lifts her chest to receive the blow. He relinquishes the sword. Enone gathers Fedra from the ground and picks up Hip's sword. Theramenes enters.)

ENONE: What have you done! Go quickly!

THERAMENES: What in hell just happened?

(Fedra and Enone exit.)

HIP: She's out of her mind!

THERAMENES: Where is your sword?

HIP: Summon a guard. I want them both locked up.

THERAMENES: We cannot. Haiti has cast her vote. The council has spoken. In favor of Fedra.

HIP: How!

THERAMENES: I'm sorry. You are not king. Your brother has been appointed. Fedra will rule in his place until he is of age.

HIP: Un-fucking-believable!

THERAMENES: But listen to me! There are reports that Theseus is among the living. My men believe that he's being held in a prison camp near the coral islands north of Venezuela.

HIP: We must find my father. Gods give me guidance. Give me strength—Save us.

BLACKOUT

Act 2

Scene 6

Oxycontin Blues

Palais de Antilles. Two weeks later. Afternoon. A radio voiceover plays while Fedra and Enone enter the queen's boudoir. Fedra is sober, but somber. Enone is walking on cloud nine. They are dressed smartly in fashion-forward business attire.

V.O.: An era has begun. Queen Fedra Narcisse has been named the absolute monarch of the Greater and Lesser Antilles. The queen was inducted into office with formal ceremonies. In attendance were leaders from across the globe including King William of England, President Mariama Sesay of Liberia, Queen Raina of Jordan, Prince Alexandre of Monaco, and Prime Minister Jolie.

ENONE: What a lovely coronation. You were terrific, my girl! I've forgotten how much fun these orations and pageants can be! This is a glorious day indeed! . . . What is it? We are the leaders of the most powerful nation in the world and here you are walking around with a rock in your shoe.

FEDRA: Did you see how he looked at me? Cold as marble, that boy. When his sword was pointed at my breast, he didn't even blink.

ENONE: What do you expect, that's how they treat women.

FEDRA: What would you know about how a man treats a woman?

(*Enone switches gears and goes back to work.*)

ENONE: These are the new Surinamese land acquisitions for you to review. Time-sensitive. Also I thought you might like to see this. Intelligence reports concerning the Toussaint Rebel Party activity—

FEDRA: BOOOOO. Stop talking. I don't want to hear a god-damned thing about rebels, inquisitions, time shares, or anything else.

ENONE: Things are stable for the moment, but you will always run the risk of being deposed. Don't make this new life any harder than it needs to be. Sign here, please.

FEDRA: (*signing a document*) I hold the rod of empire. Fedra Philomene Narcisse. Queen of the Antilles. . . . I don't want any of this. I want my old life back.

ENONE: It's because this place is filled with memories. Everywhere you turn, there are reminders of what was. . . . Hey, we could build a new palace. How would you like that? A new home for you and me. Just you and me against the world.

FEDRA: No. I cannot be away from him.

(*Enone, frustrated, busies herself with activity.*)

FEDRA: Against my will, hope crept into my heart. And like a fool, I opened up to him. I've never suffered such humiliation. I told you I would fall apart! I was doing just fine handling things on my own, and then you came whispering in my ear to go to him! This is all your fault, I want you to know that.

ENONE: What could I have done to save you? You were prostrate at his feet, begging for a place in his bed instead of securing a future for your children. Now, I am sorry that your feelings were hurt. Sign here.

FEDRA: If love cannot find a way into his heart, then we must touch him where he has more feeling.

ENONE: You can take me out of that "we." Sign here.

FEDRA: All men thirst for power. They like a sword in one hand, and a gavel in the other. You . . . Go to him. Dazzle his eyes with the prospect of power; that he may have the crown.

ENONE: I don't follow.

FEDRA: We must appeal to his better instincts. Legally, if he is my husband, then he can rule. Offer a proposal of marriage. And if he gets fussy, remind him of his obligation to this nation. Who knows what kind of peril the Haitian people face with a queen who has no control of her senses.

ENONE: Absolutely not.

FEDRA: I want no argument from you. It has been sanctioned. With time his heart will soften and eventually he will see me. They always do. Carry out my offer.

(*She whips around to Enone.*)

None of your tricks, old woman. Do as I say. (*Enone exits.*) Mighty Afrodite. . . . Are you done having your way with me? Where are you, you bloodthirsty demon! Maybe she doesn't exist. Gods can only exist if you give them power . . .

well, I don't give you any power, praise, or glory! No one reigns over me! Hear me, wicked spirit? I am the queen of Haiti!

(*Enone and Panope enter.*)

FEDRA: Well, that was fast.

ENONE: I think you should sit—

FEDRA: Did you tell him that he can have anything he wants?

ENONE: Listen to me! The king will soon appear before your eyes.

FEDRA: Hippolytus accepted my offer!

ENONE: The rumors were true. Theseus lives. Apparently junior marshaled forces to rescue him from captivity. He has just entered the grounds. He will, no doubt, expect to greet his queen. Come.

(*Enone heads to the wardrobe. Panope touches up Fedra's makeup and places her wedding ring back on her finger. Afrodite watches with glee.*)

FEDRA: He's going to know. . . .

ENONE: You had better catch a case of amnesia, girl, and I mean right quick.

FEDRA: He's going to know what I've done.

ENONE: Keep your mouth shut!

APHRODITE: Pop goes the weasel!

ENONE: For once in your life, STAND. Be bold! Do not crumble like the other women of your tribe. Handle this.

FEDRA: How?

(*Poker-faced Enone takes control.*)

ENONE: Strike first. Accuse Hippolytus. Say he wanted to lay with the queen. Of course you refused. So he assaulted you. There's proof. We have his sword. I saw him raise it against you. Accuse him.

(*Enone holds the sword. Fedra takes it and gently runs her finger along the blade. Blood trickles. Fedra looks at her hand in a trance.*)

ENONE: This is what we will tell your husband. Theseus will defend your honor and Hippolytus will have hell to pay.

FEDRA: What an extravagant accusation. What if there is bloodshed?

ENONE: When your reputation is at stake, you must sacrifice your conscience. I am here.

FEDRA: Forever?

ENONE: Forever.

FEDRA: My fate is yours, Enone. Do what you must. I give consent.

Scene 7

Vim Corpus Tulit

King Theseus' chamber. All players are present (sans Aricia and Ismene). Theseus is a well-built man, handsome yet ragged from his journey from hell. Freshly showered and dressed. He greets his son with an embrace.

THERAMENES: Your majesty.

THESEUS: Bless the gods!

HIP: Welcome home, father. We are ever so grateful for your safe return. May the gods keep you, King Theseus.

(*All bow deeply. Fedra and Theseus remain standing. The king reaches out to his queen.*)

THESEUS: My Queen. My little bird. The gods have blessed me. My greatest fear was never to feel you again.

FEDRA: I cannot. You have been wronged. I cannot!

(*She bolts from the room. Enone covers.*)

ENONE: Your majesty, please excuse her.

(*Enone quickly exits. Panope follows. The three men remain.*)

THESEUS: What was that?

HIP: Ask your wife.

THESEUS: Did you have a fight with your mother?

HIP: That woman is not my mother.

THESEUS: You're mighty puffed up.

HIP: No, sir. Listen, father, I need to talk to you. It's an important matter.

THESEUS: Well, it will have to wait—

HIP: I'm leaving Haiti.

THESEUS: You're leaving Haiti?

HIP: I realize I have my own path to walk. A life in the monarchy isn't for me. Before I leave, I have only one request, father. I'd like you to free one of our political prisoners. Aricia Toussaint. She is innocent and poses no threat.

(*Theseus approaches Hip. Theramenes steers clear of the action and moves upstage. The prince does his best to maintain.*)

THESEUS: What the hell kind of homecoming is this? Fedra says I was wronged. You're making a hasty exit from Haiti. You want me to free a political prisoner— a Toussaint.

HIP: Yes, sir. If we free her, it would show great compassion to our citizens.

THESEUS: I have shown her great compassion by allowing her to live.

HIP: She was a child. A little girl who witnessed the murder of her entire family.

THESEUS: Pallas Toussaint was a king who almost sank our economy with his movement toward democracy. He was bankrupting our country. If I hadn't interceded, Haiti would be an impoverished landfill. I alone saved this nation from an insolvent existence. Where is your loyalty?

HIP: I have always been loyal to you, to this family. Even when I suffer discrimination with no protection from my own father, the king, I remain loyal. I remained loyal when you left me to babysit your unhinged wife whom I despise— (*He clams up.*)

THESEUS: Go on. Finish. Know what I find funny? I've just returned from hell and now I have to listen to this bullshit. I sat defenseless and unarmed in a prison painted with the blood of men; I was chained, beaten, tortured. They siphoned all of my strength, hope . . . but the gods had pity and I escaped the eyes that guarded me. I crawled my way from hell because I knew I had to fight for my family. But my family seems broken. What is happening in my house? SPEAK. Theramenes, send for the queen, I want to get to the bottom of things.

(*Enone enters. Hippolytus is knocked off his square. Enone proceeds to the king.*)

ENONE: (*bowing*) Peace and blessings, your majesty. Gentlemen, my apologies for interrupting. Sire, may I speak with you, alone?

HIP: Father, I need to talk to you—

THESEUS: No, we're done talking.

HIP: Father—

THESEUS: Strike yourself.

(*As Hip exits, Enone regards him with a deep bow. Hip exits, followed by Theramenes. Theseus downs his drink.*)

THESEUS: Speak.

ENONE: I ask for your grace and compassion, for I bring alarming news.

THESEUS: Go on.

ENONE: Your loving wife, she has suffered a mighty blow. My mistress loves Hippolytus as a son. But he has taken advantage of her love. Hippolytus assaulted the queen.

THESEUS: Assault?

ENONE: Yes.

THESEUS: *He . . . violated my wife?* He wouldn't do that. Not my son. He wouldn't do that to his father.

ENONE: Yes, my lord. But—he did. . . . I have proof. This is Hippolytus' sword.

(*Enone presents the sword. Theseus snatches it.*)

THESEUS: Is why he wants to leave Haiti? This is why Fedra cannot face me? My own son?

(*He has a tantrum, bargaining between his fury and his pain.*)

Not this kind of treachery. Not in my house.

ENONE: I saw Hippolytus raise this sword over her frail body as she lay on the ground begging for mercy.

(*He grabs Enone by the throat. Her tiny feet dangle. She gasps for air.*)

THESEUS: And you did nothing to protect your queen? How dare you stand by idly while he violated her.

ENONE: My lord, to me alone you owe it that she lives.

THESEUS: (*releases her*) Pour.

(*He takes a seat. Enone quickly crosses to pour him a drink. She serves it to him. He drinks it. He speaks quietly.*)

THESEUS: Send Hippolytus back in here. Now.

ENONE: Right away.

(*Enone goes to leave. He halts her with a gesture.*)

THESEUS: Anything else?

ENONE: I have told you everything I know.

THESEUS: Are you sure?

ENONE: Yes, your majesty.

(*He dismisses her with a gesture. She sprints out of the room. Theseus fumes. Enter Hip. Mid-bow. Theseus cocks his son.*)

THESEUS: Was she good? Did you like it! You assaulted my wife! You have destroyed her! You filthy fucking criminal.

HIP: Father—

THESEUS: I am no longer your father! I am your lord and master. (*Theseus produces the sword planted by Enone. He encroaches on Hip.*) And if you don't talk fast, I will be your executioner.

HIP: Papa, listen to me. I have not done anything to harm your wife.

THESEUS: This is your sword. I know what you did! Enone told me everything.

HIP: She is a liar! Do not be bewitched by her tears.

THESEUS: You perverted monster. You have made my entire life filthy!

(*They struggle. Finally, Theseus overpowers Hip and holds the sword, or a sharp object, to his throat.*)

HIP: Don't do this.

THESEUS: (*in his ear*) This is my kingdom. I own everything and everyone in it. You pretty fucker. I ought to scalp all this hair off your head. Did you lose yourself and think that you were me?

(*He presses the blade into his skin. Blood trickles.*)

Admit your guilt. Confess! CONFESS! CONFESS!

HIP: I am guilty!

(*Theseus releases Hip. The king doubles over in pain. Hip carefully approaches.*)

HIP: Papa. Look at me. On my mother's life, I swear I am innocent of Fedra's accusation. But I am guilty of love. A woman, a real woman, who sees me for who I am. It is she who holds my heart. Princess Aricia Toussaint.

THESEUS: You expect me to believe this?

HIP: She has my heart.

THESEUS: LIAR.

HIP: Liar. Pervert. Monster. This is how you describe your son? Who never stopped believing that you were alive? I sent the fleet that came to your rescue. Why would I commit a crime so heinous, and then come to your aid? You know that I am not capable of this kind of betrayal.

THESEUS: You are a vile monster. Of all the monsters I've come up against, you by far are the worst. You . . . You're nothing to me. But don't worry, boy, you're not worthy to die by my hand. But you will die. You'll die soon. Gods! Take this wretched little man, vile worm of the earth, and destroy him! His arrogance has broken my household! Liquidate! Smash! Destroy this criminal!

(*A moment. The curse has been called.*)

HIP: Papa. Call back your fatal prayer.

THESEUS: I'm all prayed up.

HIP: *Baba, khaahesh meekonam.* Papa, please.

THESEUS: I'm all prayed up.

HIP: *Ay khodaa.* Oh, gods.

(*Theseus sips. Hip, defeated, bows deeply to his father.*)

Remember in this moment, I have professed the TRUTH to you. May the gods protect you and hold you, King Theseus.

THESEUS: Oh, don't worry about that. I'll be just fine. Now. Strike yourself.

(*Hip exits. Theseus looks upon Hip's dagger. The winds pick up. Theseus, frenzied and low-spirited, heads for the queen's boudoir.*)

Scene 8
Ward & June Cleaver. Parents of the Year!

Fedra sits in her boudoir listening to radio reports. Theseus stands in her doorway.

V.O.: There have been more guerrilla attacks for the rebels in the capital . . . eight casualties have been reported. Hurricane Quincy has been upgraded to a category four storm. It is expected to reach land by morning. Citizens are urged to exercise extreme caution . . . evacuations . . .

(*Theseus enters Fedra's boudoir. He approaches her. She covers her face in shame.*)

THESEUS: My queen. Feel no shame. You don't have to hide from me. Allow your man to nurse you back to health. Give over. Give over. . . .

(*She gives in. Relieved, they hold one another. He curls into her. Pillow talk.*)

FEDRA: Look at all these gray hairs.

THESEUS: I've missed you too, freckles.

FEDRA: I want very much to start a new life. Let us move away from this all. I can't stand to live here another moment.

THESEUS: I am sorry that I was not here to protect you from Hippolytus. You will be avenged.

FEDRA: Spare Hippolytus. Forgive him so that we can move on with our lives.

THESEUS: You defend the man who has assaulted you?

FEDRA: Please . . . Save me the last horror of having torn a father from his son. Forgive him. Forgive him. Forgive me.

(*She kisses him passionately. Theseus peels from her. Fedra freezes.*)

THESEUS: Forgive him? Look at what he's done to you.

FEDRA: There is something you should know. . . .

THESEUS: He may have escaped my wrath, but the hand of an Immortal holds his doom.

FEDRA: You cursed him?

THESEUS: Yes. You will be avenged.

FEDRA: Theseus, I must tell you—

THESEUS: You don't know all of his villainy. Your words, he says, are full of deceit. And his treachery doesn't stop there. That boy had the gall to stand there and profess his love—his "heart and soul"! Claiming to love only her—

FEDRA: What are you talking about?

THESEUS: Aricia. He loves Aricia!

FEDRA: Aricia?

(*Panope enters and curtsies.*)

PANOPE: Pardon.

THESEUS: What is it?

PANOPE: My lord, there has been a breach of security. The commanding officer reports that our prisoner Aricia Toussaint has escaped her cell.

THESEUS: Where is Hippolytus?

PANOPE: The guards are searching for him on the grounds . . .

THESEUS: Son of a bitch. He's run off with her. I know it. I'm putting an end to this. Have that C.O. meet me in my study immediately. Summon General Morricette to my study. (*Panope exits.*) Spare him? Hippolytus' days are numbered.

(*Fedra, shell-shocked, stares.*)

You will be whole again, I promise. You will be whole.

(*Theseus exits. Afrodite appears.*)

FEDRA: Hippolytus can feel, but not for Fedra! He can feel, but not for me! I almost confessed. I stood before my husband choked with fear and shame. Aricia stole his heart.

AFRODITE: What a deliciously tangled web.

FEDRA: You. You demon! Have you come to finish me?

AFRODITE: God, you make the ugliest face when you cry.

(*Fedra has a violent outburst.*)

Oh, well now, how shall I face an attack so violent? Watch your step, little girl.

FEDRA: Why? Why did you make him love her?

AFRODITE: Oh no, ma chèrie. Their love is pure.

FEDRA: I thought his heart could not be touched!

AFRODITE: Not by you.

FEDRA: Why have you cursed the women of my family?

AFRODITE: 'Cause I can. Love doesn't always have rhyme and reason.

FEDRA: How can I find favor with you?

AFRODITE: Oh, look, the daughter of the bull fucker has finally been humbled. But sorry, ma chèrie, it's too late. Your mother proclaimed her daughters more beautiful than me and I've been after your tribe ever since.

FEDRA: Please, I'm begging you to release me.

AFRODITE: Why don't you release yourself?

FEDRA: Why is it her and not me?

Not me.

FEDRA: Her	AFRODITE: Her

(*Afrodite disappears.*)

FEDRA: Not me . . . not me.

(*Afrodite exits. Enter Enone.*)

ENONE: You seem to be having a spirited conversation.

FEDRA: Oh, dear nurse! I've got a joke to tell. Knock knock? Who's there? Hippolytus and—Aricia.

ENONE: What?

FEDRA: Who would have thought it, nurse! All this time I had a rival. The chastity belt has been loosened! While I couldn't tame him, Aricia did. Oh, yeah, pick up your jaw, nurse. This whole time that I have suffered ecstasies of passion, the horrors of remorse—she had his heart. I was out of my skull for him and the whole time those two were fucking!

(*Enone, defeated, lights a cigarette and sits. She's exhausted by this game.*)

How? How could this be? When? When did it begin? You never told me about their stolen hours. Have they been seen together? Of course they have. Oh, gods. What do you think they do together? I bet he plays his stupid guitar to her on the beach. Do they sip milkshakes from the same glass? Ride bikes in tandem? Play Yahtzee? Is that it, nurse? You seem to have had answers for everything else! Oh, now you're quiet? Ain't this a bitch?

ENONE: Their love is forbidden, it won't last.

FEDRA: Their love will stay and it will last forever. Haven't you read the books or seen the movies? They may not be able to wed, but they will take a thousand oaths to bind them until eternity.

(*Fedra snatches off her earrings.*)

Bring her to me. Find that girl and bring her to me. I'm going to kill her.

ENONE: The ball of yarn is no more, kitty. Game over. You have a husband, two growing sons, and a beautiful home. Take some pills, put on an apron, and smile.

(*Fedra stares at Enone.*)

You are a mortal who was drawn by a fatal charm; it's in your blood but you survived it. Move on with your life.

FEDRA: Your counsel comes a little late, NURSE. You have destroyed me.

ENONE: Why! Because I saved you?

FEDRA: No more from your wicked lips—

ENONE: I interceded on your behalf—

FEDRA: It was YOU who slandered that boy's name. You made the accusation, not me. You have doomed poor Hippolytus. His father's unholy prayer clings to him as we speak. You have destroyed our home.

ENONE: You half-cocked spoiled bitch! What is it that I've not done to serve you? I have given you my life! I delivered your children! I nursed you when you were ill. I laid at your side when your husband was out fucking every other woman he saw. My only crime is loving you.

FEDRA: You are banished. I hope the gods repay you properly.

ENONE: Fedra, please—

FEDRA: DRIFT.

ENONE: Fedra—

FEDRA: DRIFT!

(*Fedra exits. A broken Enone stands alone.*)

V.O.: Widespread showers and thunderstorms over the Isle of Haiti are associated with a surface trough interacting with a mid-to-upper-level low. Upper-level winds are expected to remain unfavorable for the development of this system as it remains nearly stationary. Locally heavy rainfall is expected to cause flash floods. Again, citizens are urged to take precautions. Protect yourselves from this storm. Storm shelters . . .

(*The palace hallway lights remain. Theseus is on his walkie talkie shouting out orders to General Moricette. Panope runs up to the king.*)

THESEUS: Have the Alpha company secure the left flank. . . .

PANOPE: Your majesty! Your majesty, please don't go after your son.

THESEUS: What is the ETA of the Javid drones? Deploy each of them—

PANOPE: The prince is innocent! It was all a lie. A plot was set in motion by the queen and Enone against Prince Hippolytus.

THESEUS: Hold the line, General. (*to Panope*) Talk fast.

PANOPE: I witnessed their treachery. The queen submitted to Enone's every command. Your son is not guilty of the crime of which he is accused.

(*A message is patched through on the walkie-talkie from General Moricette. He reports that they are closing in on finding Hip. Theseus listens.*)

THESEUS: Are you telling me the truth?

PANOPE: Yes, my lord, I swear on my life! Everything Enone told you is a lie.

THESEUS: Go and fetch me Enone. General Moricette . . . upon capture . . . do not kill. I repeat. Capture but do not kill.

(*Theseus exits. Lights transition to Enone perched on a ledge of the palace facing the water. She is filled with emotion. Sounds of light and high winds from the storm. She stands stretching her arms outward. The sound of birds flapping their wings. She clutches her heart, then smiles victoriously.*)

Finally. I'm free. (*She leaps from the window into the sea.*)

LIGHTS

Scene 9

The Stranger Prince and Fugitive Princess Give the Cranky King and Crazy Queen of Haiti the Middle Finger

Later that day. Sound of rainfall, wind. Voiceover is heard in snippets.

V.O.: The Toussaint rebels have been engaged in combat with the Royal Army for the last six hours. There are reports of many fatalities on both sides.

(The storm is raging in the background. Howling winds and all that, rolling thunder. Hip is pensive. Aricia is concerned about him. Ismene nervously busies herself.)

THERAMENES: I've tried to pull every favor, but I can't find a pilot to fly in this storm. We'll have to stay here, until the weather breaks.

HIP: But Theseus' army is right on our heels.

THERAMENES: Nothing we can do. We can't defeat his army, but his army can't defeat a storm. So. We all wait it out. *(He looks out.)*

ISMENE: It's just like in the Star Wars. The sandstorm came and it was scary, but they all banded together and survived. So we'll survive this too. Right? Right. Long as nobody has to pee, cuz— we all have to stay in here right? Right. Revolutions are worth the scare, right? I can do this, sleep here through the storm. Okay everyone, I snore when I'm nervous sleeping. I talk in my sleep sometimes, but you know . . . I might not sleep. How you doin' sis? Are you guys scared?

ARICIA: Please stop talking.

THERAMENES: There are two soldiers posted just outside. Ismene and I will be with them. Avoid the windows and stay low if you can. Call if you need anything. *Bonne nuit.*

(Theramenes grabs Ismene and they exit. Aricia tends to Hip's bruises from the fight with Theseus. He grabs her hand. He kisses the inside of her palm. He takes her by the face, they kiss and stuff. A roll of thunder. Aricia jumps.)

ARICIA: Wherever we go, let's make sure there are no rainy seasons or hurricanes.

HIP: I hear Reykjavik's nice.

(Hip turns away from her.)

ARICIA: What's . . . hey, can you look at me? What is it?

HIP: *(turns to her)* I'm not going with you.

ARICIA: How can you say that?

HIP: My father's curse is coming for me and there isn't anything I can do to stop it. I want you to move far away and forget about all of this. Forget prison, forget the pain, and forget me.

ARICIA: Stop it. I'm not leaving your side. Theseus murdered my seven brothers, my parents, and I'm not going to let him take you.

HIP: Aricia . . . you have to leave Haiti. You have a chance at freedom. Don't throw that away.

ARICIA: Nope. *(She clings to him.)*

HIP: I'm cursed. Don't you understand? If I'm cursed, you will always be in danger.

ARICIA: Yes, I understand! And I don't care if we have five minutes or five years left. I'm going to have my happily ever after, and I'm going to have that with you. Hippolytus, any chance we have at peace will be away from here. I will not leave without you.

HIP: I promised you your freedom.

ARICIA: We can both be free. All we have to do is leave this place.

HIP: So . . . this is it?

ARICIA: Yep. We on the lam.

HIP: Are you sure? You deserve so much more.

ARICIA: What are you talking about? This is more than I thought I'd ever have.

HIP: Then let's fly.

ARICIA: We don't have anything to lose.

HIP: I love you.

ARICIA: I know.

(*She kisses him and they are interrupted. Ismene and Theramenes enter.*)

THERAMENES: Hip! The king's army has been spotted close by. We have to leave immediately.

HIP: We can't travel in this storm!

ISMENE: We don't have a choice. There's a convoy assembling for us now. Let's go.

Scene 10
The Empire Strikes Back

An hour or so later. The palace restores. Theseus paces. Panope runs in. She is visibly upset. She approaches the king. During this transition the king communicates orders into the walkie talkie.

THESEUS: (*ad libs*) Negative. No one can return until they are found. No response from the naval unit?

PANOPE: Your majesty.

THESEUS: I told you to bring me Enone. Where is she?

PANOPE: We just found her body . . . it washed up on shore. She committed suicide.

(*He stops in his tracks. It's all starting to add up for Theseus.*)

THESEUS: Shit.

(*She gives him a torn piece of paper.*)

PANOPE: The queen has barricaded herself in the room, and now I'm afraid for her life. She's taken too many pills. She keeps going on about her children being better off without her. She wrote you this letter, but at the last moment tore it to pieces.

(*Theseus reads the torn piece of the letter. A moment.*)

It's proof of what I told you.

THESEUS: Oh, gods! Oh, gods! You bring Fedra to me. NOW.

(*Panope exits. Theseus gets on the walkie talkie. The feed is quite choppy and audio transmission is difficult.*)

THESEUS: General Moricette . . . General . . . can you hear me? Come in. Report back to me immediately!

(*He hurls the device. He crosses to the fountain, splashes his face with water. He fights to catch his breath.*)

THESEUS: Oh, gods! I call back my prayer. Please bring my firstborn . . . home to me, unharmed. Safe. In the name of all things holy, bring him back safe. Bring him back—

(*Theramenes walks in wet and bloody. He is zeroed in on the king. He carries in his hand Hip's royal jacket. Heartbroken, Theramenes lays the royal jacket at Theseus' feet.*)

THESEUS: You tell Hippolytus to get in here, right now . . . his father demands to see him. What is that? Come on, man, talk to me.

THERAMENES: King Theseus—

THESEUS: I thought . . . they told me . . . he . . .

THERAMENES: Since when is an accusation a conviction? You know your son's heart.

THESEUS: Bring him in. We can sort this all out. Tell him I'm ready to listen. Please . . . please. I know he is with you. Where is he? Where IS HE?

THERAMENES: While crossing the Henri Christophe bridge a wave . . . a wall of water so violent, so brutal, that it only could have been sent by the gods—the wave crashed into our convoy.

THESEUS: Please no.

THERAMENES: Our driver lost control. We slammed into the rail, tumbled down the embankment and into the water. Ismene and I were able to free ourselves from the wreckage . . . but we couldn't get to them in time.

THESEUS: No . . . no . . .

THERAMENES: The water . . . it . . . the goddess of the waters swallowed them both.

THESEUS: What have I done? I did this. How could I have hastened his doom?

THERAMENES: Why don't you ask her?

(*Fedra appears with Panope.*)

THESEUS: (*holding Hip's jacket*) Accept your victim. My son is dead!

FEDRA: Oh, gods. . . . Husband.

THESEUS: DON'T!

(*Theseus melts. He goes to the pool. Fedra goes to him.*)

FEDRA: Theseus, I must tell you . . . Theseus, *je veux te confesser.* (I want to confess to you.)

THESEUS: Don't say a word. Please, baby, don't. . . . *Ne dis rien, s'il te plaît, pas un mot.* (Don't say anything, not a word.) Don't you say it. Because I believed you—I trusted you. You accused him.

(*Fedra takes his face into her hands and stares.*)

FEDRA: A god placed a baleful fire in me.

THESEUS: Wasn't my love sufficient? (*She clings to him. Torn and confused, he hugs and passionately kisses his wife.*)

FEDRA: Our children need you. Show them how to love. How to be honorable men. And when they ask about their mother, tell them to look for me in the sun—

(*Theseus plunges a dagger into her body. Fedra gives one spasm, but doesn't let out a cry.*)

FEDRA: I knew it would be you to save me.

(*Theramenes and Panope watch in shock. Fedra takes a few steps away from the pool and collapses. Moments. She dies.*)

THESEUS: Pick up your mistress. You! Pick up your queen. Pick her up.

Panope doesn't move. Theramenes doesn't move. Theseus goes to Fedra. He awkwardly lifts her heavy body and drags her to the throne. He props her on the throne. He sits on his throne. He reaches for his rocks glass. He pours. He sits and sits.

LIGHTS.

Fin

Photo by Dominic Taylor

KELI GARRETT

Keli Garrett began writing in her youth. Born and raised in Chicago, she attended Fannie R. Roberson Academy, later Park Vernon Academy, on the city's southside. The school had an enrollment of about one hundred students, allowing for small class sizes and individual attention from a cadre of dedicated teachers. For Garrett, Roberson Academy was an affirming experience, a place where her talents for writing and public speaking were encouraged. Later, as a student at Lindblom Technical High School, Garrett was an active member of the school choir, but it was when she enrolled at Columbia College that she decided to pursue theater, with a serious focus on acting. After completing her undergraduate degree, Garrett worked professionally as an actor in Chicago for several years before going to Brown University. There she earned an M.F.A. in creative writing, with a focus on playwriting. A 2011 recipient of a McKnight Artist Fellowship, Garrett resides in Minneapolis and is a Core Member alumni of the Playwrights' Center. A highly experimental playwright, she is strongly influenced by abstract visual art forms, the French New Wave, bebop jazz, and rap music. Garrett's other plays include *Zebra(s)*, *TOBAS*, *Space*, *Faith and the Good Thing* (adapted from the novel by Charles Johnson), and an adaptation of *The Purple Flower*, Marita Bonner's 1928 one-act play.

UPPA CREEK

A Modern Anachronistic Parody
in the Minstrel Tradition

CAST OF CHARACTERS

Mammy	Ol' Negress
Hepthesput	Young Negress
John	Massa
Young John	li'l Massa, the son and heir, nine years old
Ms. Anne	the Mistress, wife of Massa
The Good Doctor	Massa's friend
Thomas	a young Black buck
Li'l Annie	the daughter of Massa and Ms. Anne, seven years old

A Play in Eight Parts

TIME

A day sometime in early summer

PLACE

Somewhere South

SETTING

A plantation house and its surrounding environs, for example, the forest and hills.

The Friendly Confines is a southern plantation within the antebellum of our nightmares. There is a creek by the plantation that divides this play's world from another, which is our present reality.

. . .

Uppa Creek was inspired by the complete narrative of Kara Walker's silhouette etching *The Means to an End ... A Shadow Drama in Five Acts*.

NOTE

Between scene changes where music is indicated, anything stylistically in the way of vaudevillian, ragtime, Joplinesque music is appropriate.

AUTHOR'S NOTE

America's amnesia regarding four hundred years of institutional slavery continues to mystify. In this play, I span and therefore suspend time as we know it, in order to take a closer look at our antecedents and ourselves. I draw parallels between a peculiar past and an oblivious present. What we did and what we were have everything to do with what we have become. I mean "we" collectively, by the way. Why, as a nation, can we not face and interrogate our collective histories and confront every indignity and indecency the same way we embrace every triumphant achievement?

Part 1: A change in hams—I mean hands!

OL' NEGRESS: If the Massa should say jump—

MASSA: Jump!

OL' NEGRESS: You say—

YOUNG NEGRESS: (*jumping*) How high?

MASSA: Oh, I should say that the four inches or so you have covered will be fine . . . for now.

(*Enter Li'l Massa.*)

LI'L MASSA: Mammy? I say, Mammy? What you say about giving over them goods, huh? What ya say 'bout satisfyin' this awful canakerin' I got down in my tummy? What ya say you hand me over one of dem teets of yourn? Teets.

OL' NEGRESS: (*to Young Negress*) I 'spect you heard of the old sayin' "pass the buck." Li'l Massa, how would you like a fresh piece—uh, I mean a new mammy to gnaw on?

LI'L MASSA: Funny you should mention it, Mammy. I was just 'markin' to my mother—salt-of- the-earth, ivory-towered Ms. Anne with the patience of Ruth, always too busy at plottin' to catch house niggas in the act of stealin' biscuits to worry about the plight of her own flesh and blood, frigid cold, nonsexed, stuck on her pedestal, but a better woman than you will ever be—

OL' NEGRESS: Uh huh.

LI'L MASSA: Just 'markin to her the other day that now that I'm gettin' older on it won't do for the Massa's son to be botherin' with some ol' Negress with deflated bosom and thin milk.

OL' NEGRESS: Tha's right.

LI'L MASSA: My father has fresh meat, why can't I?

OL' NEGRESS: Good question.

LI'L MASSA: So, mammy, who'd you have in mind?

(*Ol' Negress presents Young Negress. Falling to his knees, Li'l Massa embraces Young Negress's breasts.*)

Speak not another word, woman, for you are happily replaced!

LIGHTS. MUSIC.

Part 2: Bitch's Brew

YOUNG NEGRESS: (*mixing over a boiling cup*) The potion is almos' right. A pinch a calamine with a dash of salt peter and we be all right. Gotta have this ready for the next—hmph—feedin'. Gots to make sure all's in perfect disray fo' I stray the hell on outta here. (*laughs*) My ship—well my taxi's— comin' in soon. Tou-Tou, my revolutionary comrade and lover in arms, I'm spectin' yo' fax later in dis day. Short and cryptic, he say. Better be. Last time he got through, faxed me a damn manifesto. I fax 'em back, "Baby, short and cryptic is da direc' opposite of long and specific! Stick wit da plan! A time and day in short code." (*places mixture in microwave and punches "start"*) Course it be simpler to feed it to him directly but I 'spect I got the constitution to handle my own brew. And while they're bawling over their dead boy, I'll be burrowing away to freedom! Thank you, Jesus!

LI'L MASSA: (*calling offstage and entering on his knees à la Al Jolson*) Mammy!

(*Young Negress ignores him and continues to add to her potion.*)

LI'L MASSA: (*arms outstretched*) Mammy! Feed me, Mammy!

YOUNG NEGRESS: Be wicha in a moment, Li'l Massa. Just gotta take my nourishment. Cain't milk the cow unless the teet is full.

LI'L MASSA: I'll milk ya, Mammy!

YOUNG NEGRESS: I know you will, you little degeneratin', lip smackin'. . . .

MS. ANNE: (*voice off*) Girl! I say, girl!

(*Enter Ms. Anne with Li'l Annie. Li'l Annie mimics her mother in every gesture and move.*)

YOUNG NEGRESS: Ma'am?

MS. ANNE: What time is it? I say, what time is it, girl?

YOUNG NEGRESS: (*playing the dumb role*) Why missus, judgin' by the set of the sun which is hotter than hell, by the way, and the (*she licks the tip of her forefinger and holds it up to the wind*) speed of the wind travellin' at . . . oh, I say 'bout zero point one felosophy, it must be around noon.

MS. ANNE: You stupid girl! It is one on the o'clock. What does that tell you, hmm?

YOUNG NEGRESS: Besides that it's one o'clock?

MS. ANNE: It should tell you that it's tea time, you duplicitous imp. Where is my tea—

YOUNG NEGRESS: Well, missus . . . I—

MS. ANNE: How many times do we need to go over this, you incompetent chit. You are nothing like ol' Mammy, that is for sure. You lack her obsequiousness, her lily spine, and her strong back for work. Work! Work! Work! No questions. No comments. When I say I want tea on the verandah at one, girl, I don't mean one fifteen, one oh five, or even one oh one. I mean one sharp. Sharp! Sharp! Sharp! You got that! You striplinged dunce?

YOUNG NEGRESS: Yes'm.

MS. ANNE: So where is it?

(The microwave DINGS!)

YOUNG NEGRESS: (a moment's hesitation) Right cheer.

MS. ANNE: Well, it best be enough for two. Young Missy Anne is joinin' her mother this afternoon like a real high-on-the-horse, shit-don't-stink southern belle, prettier and better than you will ever be. Once she is safely wedded and bedded to a future member of our fine southern stock, she will gladly be a progenitor for the race by bearing her husband at least two fine blond, blue-eyed, blue-blooded 'cause-we-say-so brats who will grow up to continue the oppression of your little nappy-headed comquats! You got that?

YOUNG NEGRESS: Yes'm, I do. (pouring potion into tea pot) So sorry I'm runnin' behind this afternoon. I declare, I've made enough tea for two if not three. Nothin' finer, Ol' Massa say, than acts of true gentility bred into the South's finest.

(in Massa's voice)

"Why, if women of the South drink tea out of the finest porcelain on the finest plantation porches, why, so too should our men folk—once in a while. For nothin' is a better sight to see than southern white men and women confabulating in genteel manner and regal posture as to set an example to slovenly white trash and nigger alike that they can only aspire and never achieve our cherished status as God's chosen people doomed to reign over them always."

MS. ANNE: Master really said that, you mimicking mince?

YOUNG NEGRESS: Yes'm, he did. I oughta know. Why, it was just after supper last night in my quarters, just after I had snatched off his boots and shuck his pants—

MS. ANNE: That's enough, you Jezebelled wench! It does sound perfectly sound to me. The first part, I mean. You say you have enough tea for three, huh? Well, three it shall be. Come along, little John. Today you shall forego your afternoon feeding and sit on the goddamned verandah and drink liquid out of a cup for a change.

LI'L MASSA: Oh, Mammy, don't let her take me and deprive me of your sweet nectar. Oh, mother, mother, mother. Cain't you see I'm still too young yet to sit with you and young Missy high-and- mighty, holy-terror-at-seven Annie whom I hate and revere as if she were my own flesh and blood—

MS. ANNE: She is your flesh and blood, you little cocker smite, and it's high time that you were weaned. I must say I have been mighty uncomfortable going on nine years now with your ravenous desire to constantly nurse from these black milk sows. Save some of that for when you own the place and I'm long dead and buried, you lascivious cherub. For now you will drink with your own kind. (boxes his ears) In public. Out of a cup! Girl! Tea is to be served on the verandah now!

Move with alacrity, you yodling yip. I expect you to be following me directly, tray in hand! Come along, you!

(*She drags out Li'l Massa by the ear with Li'l Annie following.*)

LI'L MASSA: (*arms outstretched à la Al Jolson*) Oh, Mammy!

YOUNG NEGRESS: Oh, yes'm. I'll be there directly with fresh pastry, milk, sugar, and poison—I mean potion—oops. No'm I mean . . . Aw, to blazes with it. You'll find out soon enough, you ol' shrew. When you and yo precious little ones are dead as door nails from indigestion or when you go as crazy as hens in a coop. Shit, I don't know which. All that yellin' make me lose my concentration. I cain't figure out which brew I was makin' first. One for death or one for madness. Let's see . . . if the cat o' nine goes in before the strychnine—Oh, never mind. One way or the other y'all won't be white—I mean right—again! (*She gives a mad laugh as she departs for the verandah with "tea" for three.*)

LIGHTS. MUSIC.

Part 3: When It Hits the Fan

(*Enter Young Negress.*)

YOUNG NEGRESS: Ooooh, I do declare, Hepthesput. You done done it now! Shouldn't be too long now. They gobblin' up that gobbly guck tea and cakes like there's no tomorrow. Ha! And there won't be one for them. At least I don't think so, or at least I hope not. Rest assured, come hell or high water, they gon' be burnin' or drownin'.

(*Enter Massa in a panic, dragging in tow Li'l Massa.*)

MASSA: Young Negress! Call the doctor, sound the bells! Crazy women runnin' thru the woods out yonder.

YOUNG NEGRESS: You say crazy women, suh?

MASSA: That's what I said, gal. What, are you daf?

YOUNG NEGRESS: No suh, but "crazy women" such a generality. Who you mean, exactly?

MASSA: It pains me to say it. It's my own wife, Ms. Anne and my daughter, li'l Annie. I need you to sound them bells, gal, and I'll have ol' Thomas round up the wagon and fetch the Doctor (*Young Negress rushes to sound the bells*) so's we can gather up my precious jewels before they are seen by anyone who can have a hand in ruinin' my reputation. Oh, this is a blight on my household sure 'nough! Meantime, (*thrusts Li'l Massa toward her*) feed the boy.

YOUNG NEGRESS: Yes suh, Massa, but—

MASSA: Don't sass me, gal. I've got no time to swing back and forth on this one. (*He gives her a lascivious glare.*) I'll see you tonight. (*He exits.*)

(*A moment*)

YOUNG NEGRESS: Well, well, well, young Massa John. S'pose you tell me what happened back there on the verandah?

LI'L MASSA: Not much. Mindless female chatter. The usual gabbady do about corsets, pearl laced petticoats, slave lashings, and the like. Mother thinks you're trying to poison us—

YOUNG NEGRESS: What you say, boy—

LI'L MASSA: Nothing, nothing! Just repeating what I heard, Mammy. Mother gabbled a lot. Then she started getting wild around the eyes. I don't know what was in that tea of yours but whatever it was—

YOUNG NEGRESS: There was nuttin' in that tea and speakin' of it, why in God's great heaven didn't you drink any?

LI'L MASSA: Oh, I had a little. But a sip or two is all I could stand. Never did care for tea. Awful stuff—

YOUNG NEGRESS: Aw, damnation!

LI'L MASSA: Oh, Mammy! Haven't we wasted enough time with all this talk? I've got a hole in my belly the size of Gettysburg. Remember my father's instruction: "Feed the boy." Well, I am the boy and I demand a feeding!

YOUNG NEGRESS: Oh, I'll satiate you soon enough, young Massa. But in the meantime, crazy or not, Ms. Anne wouldn't like it if I let the whole house go to waste. I've got to clear that verandah first.

LI'L MASSA: Oh, if it will speed my needs I'd be happy to stoop to house boy and fetch the tea tray for ya. Don't protest, Mammy. I shall be as quick as an Alabama rattler. (*He exits off.*)

YOUNG NEGRESS: Mind you, be careful on the walk back. Missy don't hold with no chipped china! Great father above! I gots to move quick! If the Massa ever found out what's in that tea, my goose ain't just cooked, it's burnt!

OL' NEGRESS: Not if I cook it first.

YOUNG NEGRESS: Ol' Mammy, what you doin' creepin' behind doors listenin' to folkses inner ramblins?

OL' NEGRESS: Came to see what all the fuss is about. But lucky I walks soft and piques my ears. And I done heard enough to know you dumber than I thought. If you try to take off it won't take long for Massa—stupid as he is—to figure you got some hand in dis.

YOUNG NEGRESS: Oh, they wadn't ever s'pose to drink it. I was gon' drink it myself and feed it to Li'l Massa and hopefully finish him good. But I lost my temper. And that little . . . why, he didn't even drink any. Claim he hates tea.

OL' NEGRESS: I coulda told you that. There's only one thing that boy likes and you gon' have to face light, 'cept that, and dish it out. You dumb as a post for sho. What make you think the potion won't hurt you?

YOUNG NEGRESS: Oh, I can handle my own, it's the brews of other women I cain't stomach.

OL' NEGRESS: Oh. I'll 'member that.

YOUNG NEGRESS: But what else can I do? The child be back any moment.

OL' NEGRESS: You best drop to your knees and pray da Lawd to help you come up wit a lie that Massa will take as truth.

YOUNG NEGRESS: Lie? Oh, how do I do that?

OL' NEGRESS: The same way you bold-faced handed over that "tea" to Missy Anne. Without a second's draw or a minute's thought. I best see what keepin' that boy. The sooner we get rid of that tea of yourn the better.

(*Ol' Negress exits. Young Negress falls to her knees.*)

YOUNG NEGRESS: Lawd Jesus, please open your heart and hear these cries from me, your humble servant. A miserable sinner I am who ought to have knowed better than to give over the power of my own hands to a callow cow like Ms. High-on-Her-Horse, Anne. But I swear, dear sweet Jesus, God as my witness, I only meant to free myself from the constant suckling of that despicable little monster, young Massa John. Howsumever, escape is the desired outcome. If I miss that freedom train I'll be beaten down sho nuf. I know the other side ain't pretty but it's s'pose be better than this. But do Lawd, if it is not your will, then I swear I will bear enslavement and the mad greed of that gluttonous chile. Just please! Please Lawd, spare me the Massa's whip, and Ms. Anne's vengeful wrath. 'Course, it's unlikely she and li'l Annie will remember anything, considering I musta brewed the brew to knock them outta their minds and at this very moment theresoomever, they probably don't know they butts from holes in the ground. Lawd! I wish I could see that!

(*Enter quickly the Li'l Massa and Ol' Negress. Li'l Massa flings himself dramatically into the Young Negress's arms.*)

LI'L MASSA: Good guggly muggly. Thanks be to heaven, ol' Mammy saved me! She saved me from a terrible plight!

YOUNG NEGRESS: What's wrong now?

OL' NEGRESS: Ms. Anne, that's what. Crazy as she is, she done got it into her head that all li'l nigga children should be rounded up and tossed into the creek down yonder! Claim they minions of the devil sent here to drive her mad.

LI'L MASSA: Yes, 'tis true. By the time ol' Mammy had her in sight she had already thrown several li'l pickaninnies in the creek. Lucky we could swim—

YOUNG NEGRESS: What chu mean "we"?

LI'L MASSA: Well, I was on my way to the verandah to get the tea tray as I said I would. Yet already, mother had beaten me to the punch, for she had the teapot turned up and was suckling the last few drops from the spout in a most unladylike fashion. In mid-suckle, she saw me out the corner of her eye. Shame. She didn't recognize me, Mammy! Her own son! She grabbed me by the scruff of the neck and shouted: "Here's another pickie for the pickin'!" and hauled me man-fashion to the creek, where she tossed me in wid all the rest of the children.

OL' NEGRESS: They all decided to stay in. Figured treadin' water for a few minutes was easier than gettin' throwed back in. All the folks was up in arms when I got there. I figured the only way I could retrieve Li'l Massa was to create a er, uh, dy-version of sorts.

LI'L MASSA: "Look, Ms. Anne!" Mammy shouted, pointing toward the grove. "There's a few niggas trying to escape you with they pickies."

OL' NEGRESS: And she took off, too. Tearin' for them trees like a hound after a fox. And to our further surprise, guess what should come bouncin' round the bend of dem trees?

YOUNG NEGRESS: Wha'?

OL' NEGRESS AND LI'L MASSA: Li'l Miss Annie ridin' a fox!

(*A moment*)

OL' NEGRESS AND LI'L MASSA: Backward!

YOUNG NEGRESS: (*falling to her knees again*) Oh, Lawd Jesus!

OL' NEGRESS: Don't despair now. We got work to do. Gotta haul them babies out the creek cause the rest of da folks too scared to do it themselves. Come on now! Keep it together.

YOUNG NEGRESS: We's ruined, I tell you. Ruined! But first I wanna see these white women shenanigans with my own eyes to believe it.

OL' NEGRESS: That's the spirit.

LI'L MASSA: Yes. And now that we are all in jollier spirits, what say we have a little celebratory libation?

YOUNG NEGRESS: Look here, little man, can you at least give me one moment's peace without hankerin' after me?

LI'L MASSA: I'll make it two if you promise that within the hour you givin' me a feedin' no matter—

YOUNG NEGRESS: Fine! Fine! You got a deal.

OL' NEGRESS: Now let's commence to the creek and save the children fo' Massa comes back and is up in arms 'bout his niggas runnin' and drownin' everywhere.

(*Exit all. Enter Massa and the Doctor. Massa carries a butterfly net.*)

MASSA: I tell you, Jimmy, I cain't imagine the ramifications of this situation reaching nothing but imponderable heights beyond the depth and reach of my quote unquote "fine reputation."

DOCTOR: Well, big John, if all you say is true, you have much to fear indeed. But first things first. Send ol' Thomas to spy the whereabouts of your errant lady so's you and I can have ourselves a drink and discuss Ms. Anne's pending fate. It's hotter than Beelzabub's lair out there. I'd kill for a mint julip or a bottle of rye.

MASSA: Rest yourself, then, Doctor! Gal! I say, gal! Hepthesput! Thomas!

(*Enter Thomas.*)

THOMAS: Yes, Massa?

MASSA: (*hands Thomas the butterfly net*) Run out yonder and find my crazy wife and spy to see if you can locate where my house niggas are. Threaten them with the fury of Zeus if they don't jump back here pronto, on the double. Then you return to me. I'll expect a full report.

THOMAS: A full report, yes suh. You want me to drag da rest back wid me along with that bawd, Ms. Anne?

MASSA: You sepia-toned savage! That's what I just said. And don't you touch my wife. But if you do see Hepthesput, by all means lay your hands everywhere you can and bring her back here too. The good doctor here is likely to faint from thirst.

THOMAS: Yes, suh. Hands everywhere, but don't touch the daughter of joy—

MASSA: The who?

THOMAS: Nothin' suh. Just feeling awful wistful 'bout poor Ms. Anne's plight. I 'spect now that the good doctor's here, he can fix her good.

MASSA: Yes, indeed. The good doctor will do her good.

DOCTOR: The good doctor can't even focus without a pick-me-up.

MASSA: Coax her like a sweet fly into the net, hear, boy? Don't just stand there, Thomas. Move, man. Move!

THOMAS: Yes suh! I will suh. Nah, let me get this straight. You want me to coax Ms. Anne into this here hair net like she were some waifsome fly?

MASSA: That's right. Coax, but don't touch, boy. For propriety's sake, you may not mar her milk white flesh with your coal black hands. Speak to her gentle, as if you were wheedling a dove.

THOMAS: A dove?

MASSA: Yes, Thomas.

THOMAS: Ms. Anne?

MASSA: Yes, Thomas.

THOMAS: All right, got it. Cajole that henpecker Ms. Anne like she were a dove of peace. Extend my metaphorical olive branch as a lure to meet her halfway. And bank on her being the lewd fishwife she is to chomp on the bait.

MASSA: Whichever way you can mean it, boy. Oh, and Thomas?

THOMAS: Yes suh?

MASSA: What's a bawd?

DOCTOR: Why, it's the same thing as a daughter of joy, John. You know that.

MASSA: Oh, that's right, I do. Carry on, Thomas.

THOMAS: Yes, suh.

(*Thomas exits. The Good Doctor pours a drink.*)

DOCTOR: Forced to serve myself. Yo' help is too slow in the comin'.

MASSA: Well, Jimmy. All is looking up, I can feel it. (*Silence. Crickets.*) I will happily disregard the eerie quiet as a portentous omen and focus instead on happier times of my own mind's making. Pass the bottle, will you, Jimmy?

DOCTOR: Certainly.

MASSA: My wife Anne has proved less her weight in gold for her constant demand. I tell you, I'm all tethered out—what with having to fetch you and scout out that lazy fox, Thomas—

DOCTOR: I know what you mean, niggas aren't what they used to be.

MASSA: You can harp that again.

DOCTOR: I know what you mean, niggas aren't what they used to be.

MASSA: Jimmy, you are certain it is the best thing?

DOCTOR: You are entitled to be happy, are you not?

MASSA: Why, yes, of course. But to remove her from the plantation? It is her home, for all that she has done so much to bring it crumbling down about me. It is true, her suspicions and paranoiac ramblings have driven me to drink . . . even more. She is constantly after the slaves, especially the negresses. Why, it has placed a severe strain on my er, uh—

DOCTOR: Carnal entitlements. The negresses are your property. You may do with them whatever you like. Which sounds damn appealing, I tell you.

MASSA: Yes, let's hope Thomas drags them back soon. I have one for you to see. She is quite a—

DOCTOR: Well, you can forget about her being much of anything so long as you have a wife who strains your natural desires.

MASSA: I've never seen her this riled up. I thought things were going very well. I tried everything you suggested—but suddenly, just like that—gone. Nuts. Kapooey.

DOCTOR: You tried the tonics?

MASSA: Yes, and she took them quite happily—

DOCTOR: Tighter corsets? Less oxygen you let to a female's brain the better off she is—

MASSA: Yes, yes . . . though that took some doing. She's got the mark of my boot on her back to prove it.

DOCTOR: Well, John, what else is there?

MASSA: Jimmy, you're the physician!

DOCTOR: Right, right, so I am. And as such, you need to heed my advice. Anne is hopeless. Your only hope now is to save the child from this delirium. It's in the blood, you know.

MASSA: Yes, yes.

DOCTOR: Now, let's see here (*rifles through his medical bag and pulls out a small handgun*) Give the girl a shot of this—

MASSA: No! no! The fox, you mean.

DOCTOR: There's a mad fox, too?

MASSA: It's rabid, Jimmy! And that (*pointing to the gun*) is a glockenspiel, not a syringe!

DOCTOR: Oh, right. Well, well. John, how would I practice healing without you? Well this, ha! (*laughs*) This is for the mad fox, of course. Why, I would never shoot li'l Annie. No, for her, I had something else in mind. (*pulls out a hypodermic*) A nice shot of lithium. Put her right out.

MASSA: Fine, fine. Long as you don't shoot her for real, but meantime I got to exorcise all options on the fate of one Ms. Anne, who has been none other than a pain in my gloots from jump.

DOCTOR: Aw, quit yo' crowing', Jethro. You got her to breed two children, one of each, run your household, and she looks good in public. What more did you want?

MASSA: Marital . . . rapture?

DOCTOR: (*breaks into laughter*) Shoulda married one of ya nigga women.

MASSA: It's illegal.

DOCTOR: Awww! What happened to the man I knew who could terrorize every whore in a brothel, drink a gallon of whiskey before the night was through, and still make it to church on time come Sunday morning? Where is the man who'd not hesitate to use his power and influence to squelch an enemy? I tell you, this Anne is a dark shadow of that sweet sixteen you plucked oh those many years ago.

MASSA: It's only been ten years, Jimmy.

DOCTOR: Are you kidding? For white women you gotta count the time in dog years. And now that she is no longer a nubile, pinkly beauty, what use is she now? Trespassing through the countryside. A member of your household! Out there doing God knows what, saying God knows what. Don't allow yourself to be whipped by this female or any other. Including that Negress of yours. You hear, John? Think of it, besides bearing children, what can they do better than the menfolk? Not a gosh-darned thing. There!

(*A moment. Massa moves to the phone. He picks it up, dials.*)

MASSA: Gov'nor George? I got a little er, uh, situation over here at my place. Yes, suh! That right? I'd love to poke a few holes with ya. Next Wednesday it is, then, one on the o'clock. (*gives a hearty laugh*) Oh, you know that's right. But seriously, George. It's my wife. Well . . . she's mad. Been attacking my property. Well, I'm gon' try to handle it my way, but I wanted to apprise you 'cause the moment may arise when I may in fact require some "martial" support. Yes, suh. In times of need, as you count on me, I know I can in turn count on you.

DOCTOR: Protect the ways of the aristocracy. Tactical rape, pillage, and larceny must continue as the codes by which we decimate lesser men. But the white man—

MASSA: (*lackluster*) Yes, yes, the white man.

(*Some drum major tempo song à la "The Battle Hymn of the Republic" softly underscores the Doctor's speech.*)

DOCTOR: The white man is burdened with the task of keeping intact the fallacies of a precarious history. It is the white man who amasses the task of keeping feudalism in continuum. For we owe it to our forefathers who lived in years of stone, castle, and moat. We conquered the seas, at least on paper because we conquered the people who created paper, but don't you tell nobody. (*he chuckles*) Us who have misconstrued, covertly squelched, miscegenated, misappropriated, Watergated, Cointelproed, falsified, "not recalled," forgotten, and eradicated any and every parcel of legitimate truth of our antiquity and modernity to continue the dominant progress of the race—

MASSA: Sure, Jimbo! What's done is done. (*pouring*) Have another and another and another . . .

DOCTOR: Cain't let some woman . . . that even though she be one of us, is still off her holy blonde rocker! Let her muck all that we have worked so tirelessly to hoard? Hell no! She is a blight on the path of the white—I mean right way.

MASSA: That's right! For the good of the Christian way, which is the only way of life. For the good of the South!

DOCTOR: For the good of all. Once she is disappear-ed you will breed your offspring as you were bred.

(*A moment*)

To conform to this way of living or risk excommunication, disinheritance, possibly even death—

MASSA: Don't you shoot li'l Annie, Jimmy.

DOCTOR: Now I told you I'm not gon' harm a hair on her head. Yet, conformity to your divine purpose must take place. It must be allowed to fester and grow. Make the necessary sacrifice of the mother of your children for the betterment of your good name, relations with a Negress concubine, puppeteering your offspring, and most importantly, yourself!

MASSA: All right. All right.

DOCTOR: Therefore, regarding the plight of your dear and undefiled virgin bride, we say—

MASSA: To the asylum with the baggage!

DOCTOR: (*toasting his glass*) The asylum it is!

BLACKOUT. MUSIC.

Part 4: All We Owe We Owe Her, A.K.A. "Splendor in the Grass"

(*The forest. Enter Ms. Anne, writhing in a suppressed fashion.*)

MS. ANNE: Now see? This ground here is the only place a body can speak without interruption or fear of rejoinder. I have picked and pitched in all 'bout sixteen pickannines into the creek cross-way over

(*She flails her arms wildly, like a bending windmill, pointing in all directions.*)

out yonder down by the creek way past the riverside right by yo' daddy's house. I have tossed every chocolate rodent I could spy into the gator creek in order that the edification of their souls take place in vermoned water. You picking up what I am laying down? Good. Serves 'em right, little snot-nosed bastards. God!

(*She gasps, clutching her torso.*)

I feel my lungs moving behind my vertebrae. It's these ridiculous garments and this barbarous iron clasp that they so lovingly refer to as a corset. I need to breathe. Off! Off! Off!

(*She pulls endlessly at her clothes, managing to pull or tear enough to make them give a bit, but the corset stays in place. She falls to the ground in tears; after a while she seems calm.*)

It's all right. Why, Anne Beauregard Eleanor McClamperty O'Tara! Have you forgotten who you are? Come, come. Think now. Think! What do you want most of all, 'sides laying hand on another black biscuit and settin' it bobbin' with the gators? You want out of this damned iron curtain. Now, now think. On nights like this when the sun is settin' deep noon and you're feelin' addle-pated from all that you are not doing, what do you do to pass the time?

(*Enter Thomas, the buck.*)

Great Cabin in the Sky! I got a feelin' it's somethin' serviceable. Somethin' in the interest of things cavorted and cuckolded!

THOMAS: Ms. Anne. Proselytizing in your favorite spot again, I see. (*brandishing the butterfly net*) Come on, now. Unfortunate for you, I have orders not to so much as stroke you.

MS. ANNE: Oh, phooey! Your orders be damned, heathen. Get on over here and unlace me.

(*A moment. She runs to Thomas on her knees, sobbing.*)

Oh, Thomas, Thomas! You can't mean you won't touch me ever. You can't mean you won't be the one to free me.

THOMAS: You heifer, I'm the slave.

MS. ANNE: Yet, I am shackled. You can't mean that you won't undo me! Please! Please. Please. Pleeeeeaaaaase! Undo me, Thomas. Undo me wee wee and I'll give you a tee tee. T-o-o-o-m-m-m-m-me-m-em-e-e!

THOMAS: Lower your voice, woman. You talking my undoing if you keep that chatter up. Poplar's my favorite tree, but I ain't no monkey, so there's only one way I'll swing from it. 'Tain't gon' be over you. You the one 'saultin me. (*He holds out the net.*) Come on, nah, and jump in here, Ms. Anne.

MS. ANNE: Undo me first and I'll be askin' how high. I hate my husband.

THOMAS: He does, too. Now, Ms. Anne, (*tries to disengage himself from her grasp*) what say we try to come to some 'rangement?

MS. ANNE: (*sobering*) Must we go through this again? Thomas, how long have you known me?

THOMAS: Too long.

MS. ANNE: How long, Thomas?

THOMAS: Long as I know myself.

MS. ANNE: Yes. Now, have you ever known me to consider arbitration? Have you, Thomas?

THOMAS: No'm.

MS. ANNE: Well, then, therefore do as I tell you. Break the veil that is over me. Tear it off. Rip this lace to . . . to tatters. You hear me, Thomas?

THOMAS: Listen, Ms. Anne. In the spirit of colonization, I have given over much of my body for your lye-sinchous appeasement. But I tell you, shit's gone hit your face if you don't get in dis net right cheer! Massa John ain't playin' wit you. He aimin' to get you by peace or in pieces, it don't matter to him which. He ain't let them dogs go yet. Come on now, Ms. Anne. I like ya least enough to rather see you dies in my own fashion or not at all. Come on, Massa John wants to make you better.

MS. ANNE: (*jumping up and down*) Oh, "Massa John! Massa John!" Let 'em go prod some heifer. I hate my husband, but I love this spot. (*She runs through the area wildly.*) And I will not allow my blessed husband to muck it up. (*She raises her fist à la any solidarity fighter.*) Freedom! (*Thomas covers her mouth with his hand.*)

THOMAS: (*Ms. Anne pulls Thomas's hand away, licks his palm.*) A pure hussy is what you is, Ms. Anne. Cut that out! (*Ms. Anne wrestles Thomas's clothes off.*)

MS. ANNE: Untie me, you bestial bombshell. Cluck! Cluck! I'm gon' be the chicken to make your rooster crow—

THOMAS: Ho!

MS. ANNE: (*pins him to the ground*) Hey! Ho! Wooo! Now . . . we can either do this the rough way or the tough way—for you, that is. Thomas, if you don't, I will tell your master that you did and that you made me, too. That you forced me to in so many dirty and disgusting ways. We know what would happen then, don't we? And monkey or not, you will swing. Okay? Now for the last time, untie me. (*He does. Ms. Anne crows.*)

LIGHTS

(*The forest. Enter Young Negress, Ol' Negress, and Li'l Massa.*)

OL' NEGRESS: Now massa li'l John, 'member what you been raised for and 'member nothin' else.

YOUNG NEGRESS: Yep. 'Specially yo' momma commencing with Thomas, her legs spread as wide as a pair of pliers.

OL' NEGRESS: Hush. Cain't you see the boy's got catonia?

LI'L MASSA: Oooh!

YOUNG NEGRESS: What is it? Is it the tea? Why, you munchkin head, you musta drank some after all!

LI'L MASSA: Naw, it ain't tea. Awww! I got's the most awfullest cramp. Got a crater in my gut the size of the gulf.

OL' NEGRESS: (*to Young Negress*) You 'bout the daftest thing I seen on this side of the dye-ass-pourer. Didn't we go through this earlier?

YOUNG NEGRESS: Go through what? Look, dis boy's hankerin's is unnatural. Don't no big chile like he is still s'pose to be wet nursin'. Why, before I know it, I'm gon' have a man in my lap.

LI'L MASSA: I grew an inch last week.

YOUNG NEGRESS: See what I mean? He's growin'!

OL' NEGRESS: Hush, girl. I'm sick of yo' bellyachin'. No pun intended, li'l Massa.

LI'L MASSA: None taken, Mammy. Just hurry with her set to so's she can throw me a little taste.

OL' NEGRESS: Yes, suh, Massa John. I will do that. (*pulling Young Negress aside*) Now see here, li'l Miss "I cain't perform my conjugal duties and otherwise 'cause I'm too busy mixin a brew to kill the rulin' aristocracy!" You might's well face it, Miss uppity moriney too cute. You's a member of the feudal class. And if you know what's good for you, you'll find a way to make this situation work out for the best. Girl, Massa lick the ground you walk on and so do his boy. Dere's power behind that!

YOUNG NEGRESS: What is you? An interloper? A spook crouching by the do' without thought to revolution and advancement of the cause? You got no regard for the plight of yo' fellow sistern and brethren?

LI'L MASSA: Ah, I can't see. I'm fadin'.

OL' NEGRESS: Plight, schmight! You best save all that rabble robble for the aboritionists and boogoisee Negroes up in da norf. Gal, you makin' me so mad I'm loosin' my edumication, cain't talk right. Listen here! You got's to feed that boy!

YOUNG NEGRESS: Who gon' make me?

OL' NEGRESS: I'm is.

YOUNG NEGRESS: Aw! Come on, ol' Mammy. I respects ya, but if I got to I'll beat you down, old or not, I will. I'll chalk it up as a necessary evil. (*She puts up her dukes.*)

OL' NEGRESS: Ol' Thomas, then.

LI'L MASSA: Fading fast. I smell . . . bread.

YOUNG NEGRESS: (*laughing*) Ol' Thomas? Hah. Missie Anne got her legs wrapped around him so tight that the man gon' have permanent curvature of the spine. He won't be able to run after she done with him. Or maybe he can bowl me over. Get it? (*imitating Thomas with a bent back*) Bowl me over?

OL' NEGRESS: Well, well, well. We feelin' mighty full wid ourselves, ain't we?

YOUNG NEGRESS: I'm is. Though I don't know bout li'l Massa John.

LI'L MASSA: (*in a dying whisper*) Getting difficult to breathe.

OL' NEGRESS: Somebody's got to feed him.

YOUNG NEGRESS: I'm happy to feed that brat with spoon, fork, and plate, but beyond that I will not abate. He's an umbilicaled parasite—

LI'L MASSA: Must have nourishment, Mammy. It's gettin' very difficult to . . . to keep up this . . . act.

YOUNG NEGRESS: There. You see? He is nothin' but all connivin'.

OL' NEGRESS: Looka here, Missus. Save the articafakin for when you's learn-ed and you can put yo' manifesto in wri—tin'. I'se all the way apolitical on this un. Dat boy dere, barring your personal reluctances, is fine-bred blue blood—cause they say so—stock. Dat boy been on a liquid diet for all his moons. You's the first Negress to protest his suckling. Don't make me turn darkie and bust yo' game—

YOUNG NEGRESS: (stubbornly) Nope. I'm a be one indentured wet nurse makin' a stand for many.

OL' NEGRESS: Uh huh. Well, stand this. Yo' hottentot ass got a lesson comin'.

YOUNG NEGRESS: I'm learnin' enough as I get by.

OL' NEGRESS: See here, Hepthesput. Dat's right, I'm callin' you by yo' heathen name. If you don't suckle that boy, I ain't left with no other choice but to sling you to da gallows.

YOUNG NEGRESS: You's a traitor—to the cause!

OL' NEGRESS: What cause? You da only one in yo' mono a mono army. All's I see is you. You ain't got da masses layin down dey black asses to back you in da rear. I'ma stay on the winnin' side. I cannot lie idly by and watch you rabble rouse my retirement years. Dis ol' mammy deserve peace at last and I'm willin' to sacrifice your youth to get it. You got till da count of ten to start undoin' that blouse—

YOUNG NEGRESS: Or what?

OL' NEGRESS: Or I'se gon' call ol' Thomas with all the heart my rich, deep contralto can muster. He gon' snatch you and catch you, and you know the rest.

YOUNG NEGRESS: Et tu, ol' Mammy? Et tu? Very well, I will feed that gluttonous monster, but I shan't like it. I ain't gon' forget this, ol' woman.

OL' NEGRESS: Go on nurse, get wet. Praise da lord, li'l Massa. Satisfaction's on da way.

LI'L MASSA: Sweet nectar of this black goddess, anoint my tongue—

YOUNG NEGRESS: You can can the Jacobean dribble, boy. I's only doing this 'cause the ol' lady got my bountiful booty in a bind.

(*Enter Thomas.*)

THOMAS: Praise God. I done found you at last! Come on along here, gal. Massa wont you.

YOUNG NEGRESS: Wont me for what? Ol' Thomas, I ain't done nothin', I swear. I don't know nothin' 'bout Ms. Anne drownin' no pickies!

THOMAS: Ms. Anne ain't nary yo' concern, gal. Massa requires yo' consummate attentions at da big house in da big boudoir while the Missus is "off"—so to speak.

YOUNG NEGRESS: Whatcha say? Dis behest be conjugal?

THOMAS: You catchin' on, Charlie. You gots a meetin' with da man, yes indeedy.

YOUNG NEGRESS: Praise Jesus! ol' Mammy, I cain't suckle the boy and Massa all in one. Well . . . I guess I could, but dat . . . There is one that I must serve first, and he is my Massa. (*She drops l'il John.*) Oh, well, it's been swell, kid, but da rules of the privileged still apply. Yo' daddy gets first dibs. Go on, Thomas. I'm on your tail.

LI'L MASSA: Bu . . . bu . . . but I am the fruit of my father's loins. His sole heir. Mammy! This cain't be happenin'. Don't . . . Don't! Thomas!

THOMAS: Sorry, li'l Massa, but this my own hide we talkin' about. (*They exit.*)

LI'L MASSA: Hogwash! I demand . . . that you . . . you. Oh! This an outrage (*They are out of sight now.*) NOOOOOO!

OL' NEGRESS: Come on, li'l Massa, dis ain't no way for a future autocrat to behave, now is it?

LI'L MASSA: No, indeed it is not. Ol' Mammy, the severity of my hunger forces me to swallow some rough decisions. Disrobe, ol' woman.

OL' NEGRESS: Now Massa, we had a deal.

LI'L MASSA: Deal's off, ol' gal. Just the top, please. Milk thin or not, it'll have to do 'til I win back my new Mammy. In the meantime, pass the duggy.

OL' NEGRESS: Oh, Lawd!

LI'L MASSA: Li'l Massa will do, but thanks for the reverence anyhow. Come on, ol' woman.

OL' NEGRESS: But Massa. Surely you can hold out. (*digs in her bosom*) See? Got somethin' for you. A fish cake, 'member how you like dose?

LI'L MASSA: Yes, of course. (*He gobbles up the cake.*) Now to wash it down . . .

OL' NEGRESS: Please, Massa . . .

LI'L MASSA: Enough, ol' Mammy! This will not do! We been conversatin' too much these days. I speak, you reply—in kind. Cut the mono a mono, the tête a tête, and let's make it teet to teet. Like the song go—"SET IT OUT!"

LIGHTS DOWN. MUSIC.

Part 5: Into the Woods

(*The forest. Enter Thomas and Young Negress.*)

THOMAS: Man's got a job to do. Man tell me to bring back his Negress and I do—not another word, Heppy, you hear? Though, wait nah. Was it bring the Negress and implore the Missus to return with me or was it implore the Negress to return with me and put Ms. Anne in this here net? (*He looks at the empty net.*) It was the Missie in the net! Damn!

YOUNG NEGRESS: Wha? You want me to jump in the net fo' we get to the house to give Massa the full effect?

THOMAS: Naw, I want you to shut yo' mouth so's I can think. I loss the Missus.

YOUNG NEGRESS: You sure about that? We spied you all a few yards back and it looked-ed to me like you found each other right mightily.

THOMAS: What chu talkin' bout, Heppy?

YOUNG NEGRESS: I talkin' bout yo' inability to know what we know and have been knowin' for some time. How Missie like to play you as her boy toy. Let me ax' you, Thomas, do Massa John know too?

THOMAS: Let me ax you, do Missie Anne know 'bout you and Massa John?

YOUNG NEGRESS: 'Course she do, why you think she constantly findin' an excuse to flog me so often?

THOMAS: 'Cause it get her off?

YOUNG NEGRESS: Thomas! There are some lines we dare not cross, even in parody!

THOMAS: I don't know, I've experienced that woman's dark side firsthand. Aw! My ass is grass if I don't find a way to coax her into dis here net.

YOUNG NEGRESS: Please! Dat dere net couldn't catch a fly. Whatcha need is to lure her in without givin' up da bait first. Lure her within the Massa's plain sight and make him do the rest. Shit, it's his wife. Don't you got enough scars on your back?

THOMAS: Right, I do, and damned if she didn't open up fresh ones. For once, Ms. Anne can be seen in her true cullurs. We gon' chase her back to da house and then Massa—

YOUNG NEGRESS: Whatchu mean, we?

THOMAS: I mean we. Slave work is team work. E'erbody know dat.

YOUNG NEGRESS: Don't believe what day tell ya. E'erbody black ain't in bondage.

THOMAS: Well, e'erbody I know that's black is. I ain't got time for no debate on da suzerhooty of white folks, Heppy. I need yo' muscle, woman, not your mouth, so's I can catch me a shrew.

YOUNG NEGRESS: Count me out. Come hell or high water, I'm fleein' dis coop. What's one mo' missin' Negress? Thomas, don't ya see?

THOMAS: Naw.

YOUNG NEGRESS: Now's as good a time as any to jet. (*Thomas doesn't move.*) To flee!

THOMAS: (*checking himself frantically*) What chu mean, flea?

YOUNG NEGRESS: I mean get the hell outta Dodge, or in this case Tara. It's da perfect time. Ms. Anne is gon' have Bellevue in da head 'til at least sunrise, you can bet on dat. And as long as we don't let her get a peak at yo' fine black buckness, we'll be halfway up da river by sup time. You know Massa and dat ol' Doctor already five sheets to the wind, so's they liable to drink demselves into a daze. Dey ain't gon' miss us, I tell you! Massa don't hanker for me when he drunk. Trust me, ol' Glory hardly reach half mast even when he sober as a nun.

(*There's a shot in the distance. Young Negress jumps on the back of Thomas, skirts and legs flailing.*)

YOUNG NEGRESS: Lawd Jesus today! Tell me dat wadn't no shot comin this way.

THOMAS: That wadn't no shot comin this way. (*Another shot is heard.*) And dat wadn't no shot ringin' closer either. But let's hide just in case.

(*They duck and hide. Li'l Annie runs onstage astride her fox in a backwards pose. She rears in, steps off, and faces the audience. She's changed. Gone are the glad rags of the southern belle. They've been replaced by the gear of a grunge/hip-hop/hardcore something—slacked jeans, moussed hair, shell top Adidas. Maybe even a Newport cigarette behind her ear.*)

LI'L ANNIE: Down with the JC! The just cause backed by the GF / Which equals the good fight / In direc' retaliation to white flight / Reserved as the right / Not of those of you's who'd / Ride out freely / Choosing willfully / As if they're in with you there is / A choice. Here this! Our mouths are moist / With the blood of our brethren—hunh! (*she spits*) and sistren—hsss! (*she spits again*) Who would mirage us / Beguile us / Under a guise of frailty / While extracting their fealty / In their quest for superiority / Over us / You and Me / In order that we / You and Me / Will fall in line / On the dime / Oblivious to time / Running out!

(*Pause. She rears up her fox and points in the direction of the gunshots.*)

Death to the rifled tyrants! Gettyup! It's Foxy's revenge! (*She exits, beating the beast's behind.*)

THOMAS: What da hell? What in the name of Yahweh are they on?

YOUNG NEGRESS: Their own madness. Come on. Let's run!

(*Another shot is fired. They hide again. Enter Massa John and the Doctor.*)

DOCTOR: (*flailing his pistol wildly*) Whicha way did they go?

MASSA: Jimmy, you never could shoot worth a damn. You suppose to shoot that rabid fox, fool, not my li'l angel. Gimme that pistol!

DOCTOR: Yo' little angel is hell on a pair of two mad legs. That damn fox is a health risk. What if he bites her?

MASSA: Not likely wid her ridin' it half ass backward.

DOCTOR: Well, let's hope it don't chase its tail.

MASSA: Where da hell is that nigga with my wacked and wayward wife? She s'pose to be in my plain sight right now. When I find ol' Thomas I'm gonna shoot his booty full a' buck shot.

(*Thomas lets out a squeak from his hiding place. The Massa discovers him and the Young Negress.*)

THOMAS: Howdy do, Massa John. I don' found your wayward Negress.

MASSA: So you have, you sly wool head. My Negress is in my possession at last, but where oh where is my son and heir? In your sweet bosom perhaps? Lewd gal! (*Massa fondles her.*)

YOUNG NEGRESS: Naw suh. I don't know where li'l Massa den got a hold to.

THOMAS: Suh, I spied him and ol' Mammy just back down da road a pace. The boy was lookin' mighty greedy by the look in his eye.

MASSA: That so? Well, as long as the boy's hunger is abated, I guess it won't matter to him whether it's thin milk or not.

(*He takes Young Negress by the arm and turns to the Doctor.*)

What cha say there, Jimmy? She's a beaut, ain't she? Plum, juicy pink lips. All the better to kiss you with, huh?

DOCTOR: (dozing off) John . . . you is one fornicatin' middle-aged fiend. Dat gal'll wear you out.

MASSA: Look at her. If she ain't the perfect and feral image of what is primally female. Look at this. Turn around, gal! I ain't gon' bite ya in front of company. Rotund buttocks! No flat plains hard packed and skimpy. No! We're talkin' hills, man. Hills!

(*He shakes his head, letting his jaws flop, emitting a sound like a horse braying.*)

Burrrrr! Aren't ya glad ya laid eyes on her, you old scoundrel? (*notices the sleeping Doctor*) What! He don' gon' and died on me, you good for nothin'—

THOMAS: He not dead, Massa, just pixilated.

MASSA: Huh?

THOMAS: Drunk.

MASSA: That so? Best return 'em to the house, then. But dangit all! I need to get that woman into an institution. I needed him to help me do it. (*He kicks at the Doctor's feet.*)

THOMAS: I'll carry him directly.

DOCTOR: (*singing*)

> Oh, whiskey you're the devil
> And I'll drink you all night and day.
> You're easier than a wanton
> At satisfyin' my hungerin'

Whiskey you spill me
The way mother's milk useta fill me
And I know that come the 'morrow
I'll regret dispensin' my laurels . . .

(*repeat*)

MASSA: Oh, Jimmy! Jimmy! Remove him, boy.

THOMAS: Yes, suh.

(*Enter Ms. Anne screaming, followed by Li'l Annie and her fox.*)

MASSA: What the blazes!

LI'L ANNIE: You remember your last fox hunt, don't you mother?

MS. ANNE: You little minx! I shoulda dropped you when I had the chance.

L'IL ANNIE: Foxy's revenge! Attack! Attack! (*They exit off.*)

MASSA: Gawdoggit! Thomas, you take the good doctor to the house. (*He grabs the Negress.*) You're coming with me.

(*Enter Li'l Massa.*)

LI'L MASSA: No, father. She is coming with me. After all, she is my Mammy, is she not? And we will both go with you.

YOUNG NEGRESS: (*aside*) Please, Lawd, concave this here ground. Send plague, beast or famine, but deliver me!

LI'L MASSA: (*arms outstretched*) Oh, Mammy!

MASSA: Oh, very well. Share and share alike. (*to Negress*) You are needed beyond the call of my leering looks and surreptitious fondlings. Yours is always a higher calling, to feed the boy.

YOUNG NEGRESS: (*simultaneously*) To feed the boy.

MASSA: Right. I've got to track her! That woman's headed for escape. (*cocks his pistol*) This could get ugly. I gotta blast the brains out that li'l fox of Annie's before she runs Ms. Anne onto the estates of any of our irreproachable neighbors. Guard my son as you would your own.

YOUNG NEGRESS: Sure thing.

LI'L MASSA: I'm nimble on your nipple pappy—uh, I mean I'm right behind ya. Let's track mother!

MASSA: Good. Let's see, judgin from their plight of direction, they will indeed hit our neighbors. If that happens, all of antebellum will break loose. We'll stop them by the creek. Oh, and boy?

LI'L MASSA: Yes, father?

MASSA: I'm not going to lie to you. You've always been my favorite because, well, you are a boy and you take after me in some ways—

YOUNG NEGRESS: (*snorts*) Oops, 'cuse me Massa. Caught a hairball.

MASSA: Today could very well be the day you become a man. I want you to know I will try my best not to blow your mother's and sister's brains out, but just in case, remember the bright side. If that happened, you would be rid of that paranoid dominatrix and her diminutive twin forever and stand to inherit everything.

LI'L MASSA: Sho, father, sho. I'll listen to any excuse you dredge up to satisfy your lust for gratuitous violence. Oh, and I swear that today will be the day I become a man.

MASSA: My son! Your emotional detachment is humbling to me. I'll remember this day. To the hills we go, then! To track woman and beast. Come along, son. Don't forget your wet nurse. To the hills!

LI'L MASSA: (*lackluster*) To the hills. But let me make a phone call first. I'll meet you there.

MASSA: Nonsense, son. (*flashes the Negress a lascivious look*) We should all perverse— I mean traverse together. We'll wait for ya. Take your time. And we will take ours.

(*He exits off with Li'l Massa dragging Young Negress behind him.*)

LIGHTS.

Part 6: Modern Necessities

The Friendly Confines big house. There's an incoming message from the fax machine on the bureau. Li'l Massa is pacing the room speaking on the telephone.

LI'L MASSA: Hey! My father bought your election. Listen, I speak for my father. How many times do we need to go over this? Yes, yes it is the only way. Wait! (*to offstage*) Fax!

(*Massa and Young Negress enter. Both are ill-dressed, though the Negress looks the worse for wear.*)

MASSA: (*checks his watch*) Has an hour gone by that quickly? No time! My broker know I don't do no tradin' after lunch. Mogulhood's got its limits!

LI'L MASSA: It could be important, father. Perhaps it's new news of the soon to be displaced and erased caricature of womanhood I've come now to know only as a pedestaled illusion: My mother, Ms. Anne! (*back to the phone*) That's right, we'll need a S.W.A.T. team on the premises right away. Two fugitives on the run. Yes . . . blond hair, blue eyes. One is five two, the other, about four two. Yes . . . I know. Man, we are talking Danger Will Robinson! Danger! (*hangs up*)

YOUNG NEGRESS: Oh, boy! All yo' scatological nonsense. (*She looks over the fax.*) Oh, this ain't nothin but a wrong number, Massa.

LI'L MASSA: How do you know? You ain't supposed to know how to read? 'Sides, it looks to be in code.

YOUNG NEGRESS: You wanna get fed or not?

LI'L MASSA: Yes.

MASSA: What was that, son?

LI'L MASSA: Nothing.

YOUNG NEGRESS: Dat's what I thought. (*huddles up to Massa provocatively*) Massa, e'erbody who you know know you well enough to know dat you don't trade in the pig's belly afta one on the o'clock.

MASSA: Know indeed, they should know, my velvet wench. I like another kinda trade in the noontime, heh?

YOUNG NEGRESS: (*with a giggle*) I know you do.

LI'L MASSA: Father!

MASSA: Cool your jets, boy. Just warming my hands, is all.

LI'L MASSA: Then your circulation is very poor indeed! Whatdaya got, le grippe? It's one hundred and eight in the shade if it's a degree—

MASSA: (*rubbing Young Negress's bottom*) Gettin' hotter in here though, huh?

YOUNG NEGRESS: You know dat's right!

MASSA: For a wrong number, that looks like a pretty long message, honeysuckle—

YOUNG NEGRESS: (*grabbing a lot of crotch*) Ain't as long as some things I know!

LI'L MASSA: Doh!

MASSA: Oooooh!

YOUNG NEGRESS: Hold on, daddy! Your pint-sized image is gaping like a monkey in a labo'try. Compose yourself nah!

MASSA: Damned yo' Jezebel-ed hide. Woman, you got the gloots to make a pompouused-ass man bawl.

(*She hurries to the fax, scans it quickly, and stuffs it in her ample bosom.*)

MASSA: What was it, honeybunch?

YOUNG NEGRESS: Why, da wrong number, baby, just like ya said.

MASSA: Did I now?

YOUNG NEGRESS: Why, course ya did, daddy. When you been known to be wrong?

MASSA: Sheet, never. Battin' an even thousand—

YOUNG NEGRESS AND MASSA: With the biggest bat in da whole damn galaxy!

LI'L MASSA: Father! I demand you listen. We got a wayward white woman to catch. The sun's sinkin' and the moon's winkin'. We losin' time with all yo' salacious shenanigans. You best remember dat, boy!

MASSA: Why, yes, suh, Massa John—Hey, now wait a minute. Who's da big boss 'round here, kid? Me or you?

LI'L MASSA: Why, you are, of course, big daddy—I mean, father. I was just trying to show you how's I been trying to be more in your image.

MASSA: Well, keep tryin, kid. I ain't dead yet.

LI'L MASSA: No, not yet. Off to the hills, though.

YOUNG NEGRESS: Oh, thank you Jesus! To the hills!

MASSA: To the hills! (*They exit, dragging the Negress behind them.*)

LIGHTS. MUSIC.

Part 7: Gots to Get over the Hump

(*Another part of the forest. Enter Li'l Annie riding her fox.*)

LI'L ANNIE: Go, Mommy! Go, Mommy! Go! Put the needle to the record! Put the needle to the record. (*repeat as necessary, exit*)

(*Enter Ms. Anne running, brandishing the butterfly net.*)

MS. ANNE: Soft of flesh and flight of feet, the woebegone, misbegotten, alabastered goddess/woman who runs with wolves stands livid and foaming, having been bitten by a riotously mad fox. (*clutches her wounded arm*) I've been hit! Somebody . . . somebody (*falls to the ground*) I smell bread. (*pops up*) And speaking of it, let us break bread together over the backs of our gun toting masters. All ye pioneers and frontiersmen beware, for I have a net—Ha! A butterfly net. (*laughs uproariously*) Where's my glock, huh? No need. My AK? Pshaw! Hey! (*addresses the audience*) Hey! You talking to me? You talking to me?

(*She hears something and runs about the stage flinging the net at any sudden movements.*)

I am sooooo sick of the constant chase, of the demands placed upon my body and mind. Woo! I fear I may have misplaced the latter. But this! (*grabs her boobs*) This here is mine, see? You bastards! I know you're after me, huh? You want some of this? You want a piece of me?! (*holds her head, reeling*) God in heaven. Merciful father! I am ill—

(*Enter the Young Negress.*)

YOUNG NEGRESS: (*pointing at her mistress*) Banish-ed! Banish-ed! Get out of my spot fo' I tell! White woman, you's a rotten apple hanging from Massa's tree of knowledge. You know too much! You done said too much! You's plucked!

MS. ANNE: Vermin! Puta! Dark feline! Thorn in my twenty-two-inched side. You—you—

YOUNG NEGRESS: Oh, watch it now, my cornsilked, all-blanched-out Afro-Diety! I got the whistle now, hear? All's I got to do is give the clarion call and Massa, the government, and that milk- crusted pre-teen son of yourn gone come runnin'. For blood.

MS. ANNE: (*hissing*) You wouldn't!

YOUNG NEGRESS: The hell I wouldn't. They looking for you, missus, and they lookin' good. I gave ' em the slip, said I had to answer a loud call of nature. They think with all the stress I'm runnin, but they ain't figured yet I'm runnin' more ways than one. I need this spot here. So's if you don't want me to blow your hide away—you'd better skedaddle.

MS. ANNE: How dare you presume to be the boss of me! You dark menace. I built this land. My people were slaughtering and quartering buffalo and native alike while your kin were still reveling in ritualistic hoodoo. You are a runaway. A bad girl! You're going in the creek! You—

YOUNG NEGRESS: EEEK! She's over here! I done found her, Massa! She's over here!

(*Shots are fired. Voices are shouting. Enter Li'l Annie and fox.*)

LI'L ANNIE: The revolution will be televised!

(*Li'l Annie exits off. There's a loud shot, a yelp, then a big thump. Young Negress takes cover in a bush.*)

MASSA: (*offstage*) Dammit! I said shoot to heel, not kill!

MS. ANNE: (*aside*) And suddenly the young mistress was filled with a newfound maternal instinct which heretofore had remained dormant, encased deep within the mistress's physiognomy, floating rootless and dead, much like all of her internal organs. It finally breathed life and rose to a fever pitch to scream: "MY BABY!!!!!!!!!!!!!!!!!!!!!!!!!!!!!!!!!"

(*Ms. Anne runs off the stage. Shots are fired again, and she runs the other way with the carcass of the dead fox slung over her shoulder. Offstage again, she shrieks, throwing the fox onto the stage. She enters and runs to the other side, emerging again, this time with Li'l Annie's corpse over her shoulder. There are gunmen behind her now, and she is running for her life. A cellular phone rings.*)

YOUNG NEGRESS: (*Hitching up her skirt, she removes the cellular phone strapped to her thigh.*) Tou-Tou! Baby, I told you never to call me at this number unless it is an emergency. This spot is hot. There's five-O everywhere. Naw, naw. Believe it or not, they huntin' white women this time.

(*Helicopters are overhead now. Searchlights move through the area.*)

MASSA: (*offstage*) Hold your fire!

VOICE FROM THE HELICOPTER: (*offstage*) Ma'am, drop the corpse and step away from the butterfly net!

YOUNG NEGRESS: Nothin', nothin'. I'm glad you got the new school ready, baby. 'Cause I'm gon' be plyin the chillun wit some serious Freedom Curriculum. We got to get to every mind we can for the cause. You got the reading list I sent you, right? But I was careful, sugar dumplin'.

(*Pause.*)

You know, I'm not gon' even say nothing about this fax I'm holding. Nigga, it's a damn dissertation! My game was almost up. All right, all right. I love you, too. Listen, I gotta take cover, lover. I'll meet you on the otha side of the creek, down ways a bit where this insanity ends and our pre-determinate future will—yelp!

(*Ms. Anne has the butterfly net against the Young Negress's throat.*)

I'll call you back.

MS. ANNE: You shan't take me alive! If I go, she goes with me! Worthless, whoring baggage!

VOICE FROM THE HELICOPTER: Step away from the nigga, ma'am. We don't want to shoot!

(*Enter running, Li'l Massa, Massa, Ol' Negress, and Thomas.*)

OL' NEGRESS: Lawd Jesus.

THOMAS: Don't shoot!

LI'L MASSA: Unhand my mammy!

MASSA: Leggo my ho'.

OL' NEGRESS: My poor Miss Annie! Let her go or you gon' get iced.

MS. ANNE: If they don't land that contraption, her neck gon' be spliced.

YOUNG NEGRESS: (*to the helicopter*) Hey!

VOICE: Yes?

YOUNG NEGRESS: Y'all got on dem infrareds?

VOICE: Yes.

YOUNG NEGRESS: And you sure I ain't yo' bullseye?

VOICE: Affirmative.

YOUNG NEGRESS: Okay, but just to be on the safe side . . .

(*She delivers a sharp elbow to Ms. Anne's solar plexus and ducks out of the way.*)

ALL: (*except Young Negress*) NOOOOOOOOOO!!!!!!!!

(*Ms. Anne is shot to bits—repeatedly.*)

(*The Young Negress is high upon a hill. Behind her a light springs from the setting sun.*)

YOUNG NEGRESS: Freedom! (*runs off*)

LIGHTS.

Part 8: Start Making Sense

(*La grande finale. Music.*)

COMPANY:	
	Over the hill
	Through the gale
	Our girl nig
	Ascends from hell.
	The
	bowels
	bowels
	bowels
	Of this nation's
	Worst ill.
	But chill!
	Nevermore
	We cry
	Nevermore
	For if you
	turn your back on us
	We'll gladly eat your dust
	Like a Phoenix
	Our little minx
	She cries for
	Freedom's way!
	But she'll soon learn
	The joke's on her
	Cause there's more
	Where we come from.

OL' NEGRESS:	The lilly-livered mammy.
LI'L MASSA:	The milk fixated chappy.
THOMAS:	The obtuse Mandingo.
MS. ANNE:	And poor dead Missy ho!
COMPANY:	And we don't mean garden tool!
LI'L ANNIE:	And even little Annie riding her red rabid fox
COMPANY:	Could never match the vengeance of the Big Massa's . . . Schlock! Ooops! Its size is all in his head!

So we say a pox
on you Freedom Lovers
A pox
on all you plebeian
Crusaders
fighting for Justice
And the Ameri-cain Way

'Cause we're not
Going anywhere
We're right here
Somewhere

Just when you think you've
left us
400 years of our misalignment
Will rise to the surface

And you will cry (so naïvely)
Freedom!

Ha!

A pox
on Liberty.

We blindfolded her
And we're coming
after you!

Never fear
We will knight you
For dim sight and the like
For we prefer you
With all hindsight askew

We'll stay in the
Dark

And just when you think
You see light
We'll strike
Strike!
Strike!

You
You and you!

And on that note
we say
Goodbye
Until we meet
again
So long!
Farewell!
Auf Wiedersehen!
Adieu!

End of Play

Copyright/Agent Information

SANDRA ADELL is a literature professor in the Department of Afro-American Studies at the University of Wisconsin–Madison. She is the author of *Double-Consciousness/Double Bind: Theoretical Issues in Twentieth-Century Black Literature*.

The University of Illinois Press
is a founding member of the
Association of American University Presses.

Designed by Jennifer S. Holzner
Composed in 10.5/13 Marat Pro
with Trade Gothic LT Std display
by Kirsten Dennison
at the University of Illinois Press
Manufactured by Sheridan Books, Inc.

University of Illinois Press
1325 South Oak Street
Champaign, IL 61820-6903
www.press.uillinois.edu